THE
SADDEST
WORDS

REBEL WORKS IN FR

i. N. Barnard.

THE
SADDEST
WORDS

WILLIAM FAULKNER'S CIVIL WAR

MICHAEL GORRA

LIVERIGHT PUBLISHING CORPORATION
A DIVISION OF W. W. NORTON & COMPANY
INDEPENDENT PUBLISHERS SINCE 1923
NEW YORK | LONDON

Frontispiece: *Rebel Works in Front of Atlanta, GA. No. 5* by George N. Barnard, ca. 1864–66.
DeGolyer Library, Southern Methodist University, Civil War: Photographs,
Manuscripts, and Imprints.

For information about permission to reproduce selections from this book, write to
Permissions, Liveright Publishing Corporation, a division of
W. W. Norton & Company, Inc., 500 Fifth Avenue, New York, NY 10110

For information about special discounts for bulk purchases, please contact
W. W. Norton Special Sales at specialsales@wwnorton.com or 800-233-4830

Manufacturing by Lake Book Manufacturing
Book design by Fearn de Vicq
Production manager: Julia Druskin

Library of Congress Cataloging-in-Publication Data

Names: Gorra, Michael Edward, author.
Title: The saddest words : William Faulkner's Civil War / Michael Gorra.
Description: First edition. | New York : Liveright Publishing Corporation, 2020. |
Includes bibliographical references and index.
Identifiers: LCCN 2020014188 |
ISBN 9781631491702 (hardcover) | ISBN 9781631491719 (epub)
Subjects: LCSH: Faulkner, William, 1897–1962—Criticism and interpretation. |
Faulkner, William, 1897–1962—Characters—African Americans. |
African Americans in literature. | Race relations in literature. |
Southern States—In literature. | United States—History—Civil War, 1861–1865—
Literature and the war. | Yoknapatawpha County (Imaginary place)
Classification: LCC PS3511.A86 Z7838 2020 | DDC 813/.52—dc23
LC record available at https://lccn.loc.gov/2020014188

Liveright Publishing Corporation, 500 Fifth Avenue, New York, N.Y. 10110
www.wwnorton.com

W. W. Norton & Company Ltd., 15 Carlisle Street, London W1D 3BS

1 2 3 4 5 6 7 8 9 0

For
BB and Miriam

Contents

THE
SADDEST
WORDS

———•◆•———

A Park Bench in Paris

What can the work of William Faulkner tell us about the Civil War, that central quarrel of our nation's history? And what do that war's dark hours tell us about the 1949 Nobel laureate, the most important American novelist of the twentieth century? How might we use them to think about each other? The war is everywhere in the Mississippi-born Faulkner, both an inescapable point of reference in his characters' speech and lives, and a determining factor in the very form of his fiction. He can no more get away from it than we can ourselves, from a conflict whose causes and consequences remain inscribed today on our every electoral map. But the war is also nowhere, in that he rarely makes it an explicit subject. At times it seems an ellipsis in his work, a lacuna; the eye of a hurricane, the still center of destruction. He doesn't do big battle scenes or follow the course of a campaign. The great generals are for him but names, not characters, and so too are Gettysburg and Shiloh; or they stand, rather, as offstage events whose reverberations can be felt forever. This book defines both the war's actual presence in Faulkner's work—those moments set during the struggle itself—and his account of its undiminished echo in the decades that follow. It uses the Civil War to help us understand the whole body of Faulkner's fiction, and it uses that fiction, in which the same characters and incidents recur in work after work, to help us understand that war, from secession through Reconstruction and on into our continual revision and rewriting of its history. Yet this book is also about the civil war within Faulkner himself, his own struggling attempt to come to terms with the war's meaning; which is to say, with slavery. His attempt—and ours.

William Faulkner was born in 1897 in New Albany, Mississippi, a whistle-stop forty miles south of the Tennessee border. He moved as a child to nearby Oxford, the home of the state's university and the seat of Lafayette County. And there he stayed. In his twenties Faulkner lived briefly in New York and New Orleans; he later spent a few years writing for the movies in Hollywood. Oxford nevertheless remained his home, his source, and he set almost all his work in and around what he called his "little postage stamp of native soil." That work drew on the history of his native region from the days of the first contact between white settlers and the indigenous Chickasaw people, through the establishment of a town he called Jefferson and the growth of a plantation economy based upon cotton and slaves; through the Civil War and its aftermath and on into the world of the New South and the automobiles and bootleggers of his own day. He was a superb historian and a better mythmaker. He called his imaginary place Yoknapatawpha County, after an actual local river, and the world he made of it is as vividly detailed as that of any fictional landscape, a setting matched only by the fever dream of Dickens's London. His work contains the richest gallery of characters in all of American literature, and in his handling of time and consciousness Faulkner stands as one of his century's most restless experimenters, in any language, with the form of the novel itself.

He was an uncompromising modernist, a difficult American counterpart to James Joyce and Virginia Woolf. Yet he also offered a distinctive regional voice: a hypnotic stylist who shaped the half-century of Southern writers that followed him, some walking in his path and others struggling to get as far away as possible. For many twentieth-century readers those strengths were enough. Forty years ago I was a new college graduate, teaching at a summer school where one of the novels on the syllabus assigned to me was his 1930 *As I Lay Dying*. I didn't much like it, not at first. I felt disoriented by the speed with which Faulkner switched from one first-person narrator to another—fifteen of them in all—and frustrated by my inability to tell just when the book was set; it began in a preindustrial farmhouse and ended in the glare of Jefferson's electric lights. But some things stuck. One of the book's narrators told me that "words dont ever fit even what they are trying to say at," and another announced that "My mother is a fish." I'd never read anything like it, and knew after my first class that I wanted to read more. And imme-diately. I wrestled with *The Sound and the Fury*, in which both memory and chronology appeared to splinter, and then I seemed to fall down a great well, drowning in the Jazz Age despair of *Sanctuary* and the Civil War stories of *The Unvanquished*. I read the ghoulish "A Rose for Emily" and both strug-gled and failed to understand the family history embedded in "The Bear," where incest and slavery stood as one. *Flags in the Dust* taught me about the corporate life of what Faulkner called his "apocryphal" town, and at the end of that summer I felt my jaw go slack at the hall-of-mirrors named *Absalom, Absalom!* as though the novelist had taken a bolt gun to my brain.

I have been reading and teaching Faulkner ever since, but the novelist I read today isn't the one I read then, even if the words are exactly the same. In his lifetime and for some years after, the usual way to make sense of him was to stress the contrast between the different groups of his white charac-ters. On the one hand were the representatives of the Old South, the descen-dants of slave owners and planters, like the Compson family of *The Sound and the Fury* and the Sartorises from *Flags in the Dust*. On the other were the up-from-nothing Snopes clan, erstwhile sharecroppers who in the capitalist, post–Civil War world of the New South had replaced the old order. That was the view of the left-wing editor Malcolm Cowley in *The Portable Faulk-ner*, the 1946 anthology that first suggested the scale and coherence of the writer's achievement. To Cowley, Yoknapatawpha's old families embodied a sense of honor and tradition, and though they rarely lived up to it they were at least conscious that they'd slipped. The Snopeses, in contrast, stood as a moral infestation, "gnawing like rats at the standards by which the South had lived," and Cowley's argument found its counterpart on the right in a band of writers who had emerged in the 1920s at Vanderbilt University in Nashville.

They called themselves the Agrarians, and the set included the poets John Crowe Ransom and Allen Tate, along with a young Kentuckian named Rob-ert Penn Warren, who would find his own greatness with a 1946 novel about a corrupt Southern politician, the Pulitzer Prize–winning *All the King's Men*. The group remains best known for a book called *I'll Take My Stand* (1930), a collection of essays by "Twelve Southerners" that set the image of an idealized agricultural order against the industrial world of modernity itself. The Agrarians saw the nation as divided still, not into slave states or free, but between a firmly rooted rural subsistence on the one hand, and the dislocating forces of the urban market on the other. Yet the regional distinction remained as before, a distinction they prized and celebrated. Virtue lay below the Mason-Dixon line, and the tone of their manifesto was set by the title Ransom gave to his own piece: "Reconstructed but Unregenerate." They were Faulkner's contemporaries and among his earliest and most admiring readers, but as apologists for a peculiarly Southern tradition they underplayed his quarrel with our nation's irrepressible fractures, and he always kept his distance. For the South that the Agrarians imagined was in essence a land without black people. They wrote slavery out of its history, seeing it as but an aspect of the region's past and not its organizing principle, and their readings of Faulkner scanted the importance his work gave to both it and the Civil War itself.

In Faulkner criticism the canonical version of that argument came in a book by Warren's friend, colleague, and collaborator Cleanth Brooks. As young faculty members at Louisiana State in the 1930s, they had founded the *Southern Review* and edited a foundational classroom anthology called *Understanding Poetry*; later they each moved to Yale. Their way of teaching a poem required a student to abstract it from its social matrix, a close reading that concentrated almost exclusively on questions of form—voice, irony, metaphor, paradox. They pushed biography aside, history too, and it's never been difficult to see the connection between what became known as the New Criticism and the Agrarians' desire to look away from the central facts of the South's past. Of course no practice is ever so pure as its theory, and in *William Faulkner: The Yoknapatawpha Country* (1963) Brooks took far more account of the historical context of Faulkner's work than he ever did with a seventeenth-century lyric. Nevertheless, he read for structure and symbol above all, and flinched whenever Faulkner asked his readers to look hard at that past, retreating instead into generalities about "man" and time and community. Nor did Brooks himself finally look hard enough at his subject, at the things the novelist could not or would not say.

Faulkner's students haven't stopped investigating his representation of human consciousness or the intricacies of his prose. But such readings in themselves are no longer adequate, and I'll suggest why through a comparison to the British writer Joseph Conrad. In 1977 the Nigerian novelist Chinua Achebe published an essay called "An Image of Africa" in which he upended eighty years' worth of commentary on Conrad's 1899 "Heart of Darkness." That short novel had often been read as a critique of European imperialism. "The conquest of the earth," Conrad's narrator Marlow said, "is not a pretty thing when you look into it too much," and most readers heard the deadly understatement in the character's voice. They took the story as an attack on the savagery of nineteenth-century colonialism, and it did in fact shape public awareness of the atrocities on which Belgian rule in the Congo depended.

Achebe argued, in contrast, that the tale lent a tacit support to the politics it appeared to condemn. It equated blackness with evil and emptied the African continent of its peoples and histories by depicting Marlow's steamboat journey upriver as a voyage back into the earliest days of the earth itself, a primitivist trip into the continent's supposedly empty heart. At the level of its language, in its choice of words and metaphors, the story depended on a racism engraved within English itself, and Achebe suggested that we should simply stop reading it. The paradox is that his argument has only made Conrad's work seem all the more central, all the more interesting. It marked out a field of investigation that has turned "Heart of Darkness" into a locus of continuing debate about the relation, the inextricability, of imperialism and modernity itself. Many later readings have therefore explored the story with an eye to its internal contradictions, using Conrad to consider the limits of what can and cannot be thought in a given culture at a given time.

Faulkner learned a great deal from Conrad, above all how to nest one narrative, one voice, within another. And our reading of the Mississippian has undergone a similar metamorphosis. No single work of Faulkner criticism has had so decisive an effect as "An Image of Africa," but an accumulation of scholarship has indeed changed the way we see him. Figures like Brooks were of course aware of Faulkner's context, of how much his work depended on his precise historical moment. But they moved swiftly past the local and saw him instead in terms of some abstract "human condition." A more recent and historically grounded criticism has returned him to that moment. Scholars have examined his relation to the literary marketplace, to Cold War culture, to Hollywood, and to the many writers, like Toni Morrison, whose work stands in agonistic relation to his own; they have studied his account of labor, and gender, and the environment. They have in particular looked closely and often skeptically at his treatment of race: his portraits of black characters and the ventriloquism with which he presents black speech; his depiction of slavery and of the intersection of sex and servitude; his way of registering what Morrison herself defines as the "Africanist presence" in American life.

At the height of his career in the 1930s and '40s, Faulkner was seen as a moderate on the South's racial questions, and many white Mississippians viewed him with suspicion. He thought World War II would bring a long-overdue shift in the country's social structure by forcing "the politicians . . . to make good the shibboleth they glibly talk about freedom, liberty, human rights." Nevertheless he remained a white man of the Jim Crow South and did not always rise above it. At times his words both can and should make us uncomfortable, though perhaps more with the man than the work—which I know begs a question. Yet that only makes the business of reading him more urgent. He stands to us as Conrad does to the study of imperialism, with our understanding made ever more urgent by Faulkner's very limitations. And by "us" I don't mean the South alone. Faulkner's early readers saw a quarrel in his work between Sartoris and Snopes, the Old South and the New. Today that seems like pocket change, and the story he offers us instead is that of the nation itself.

One day in the late fall of 2010 I sat in the Luxembourg Gardens in Paris, at the edge of a circle of grass, looking out through the trees at the wrought-iron fence that marked the park's edge. There was a gravel path at my feet, a dappling of shade on the greenery, and behind me I could hear the faint thunk of a tennis ball in the distance and the voices of men playing *boules*. I was trying to finish a book that year, spending most of my time at a study center a few streets away, but my mind wouldn't work that morning and I'd walked off into the garden's hush. It was one of my favorite places in the city, and I knew it had been one of Faulkner's as well.

He had first come to Paris in August 1925, sailing on a freighter from New Orleans and landing in Genoa before crossing the Alps to the north. He was twenty-seven and unknown, a would-be writer who had just finished his first novel, *Soldiers' Pay*, but didn't yet know if the New York publisher to whom he had sent the book would take it. The firm was called Boni and Liveright, and it specialized in the consciously modern; its list included both T. S. Eliot and Faulkner's own mentor, Sherwood Anderson, along with a writer two years his junior named Ernest Hemingway. Paris in the 1920s has become a place of fable, one of the capital cities of American literary history. Gertrude Stein had lived in the rue de Fleurus, just a few blocks away from the bench where I was sitting, the walls of her apartment lined with Picassos and Cezannes; and in the very summer of Faulkner's visit, Hemingway was at work on *The Sun Also Rises,* just a bit to the south on rue Notre-Dame-des-Champs. Faulkner met neither of them during his two-month stay. He met nobody, and when he saw James Joyce in a café he did not dare to speak. Instead he spent as much time as possible in the Gardens themselves, telling his mother that "I sit and write there, and walk around to watch the children, and the croquet." Nothing he wrote in Paris has lasted, but five years later he would set the final page of *Sanctuary* in the park's "gray light," with the dead-eyed rape victim Temple Drake sitting in the "sad gloom" of its trees.

That was Faulkner's only trip to Europe until he won the Nobel Prize a quarter of a century on. But I wasn't thinking about him as I sat there—I was thinking instead of the news from home. Each morning I opened up the *New York Times* on my computer, and for the last few weeks one of my regular coffee-time pleasures had been a column on its op-ed page called "Disunion." It was 150 years since Lincoln had been elected president, and the paper had decided to follow the week-by-week course of the war that followed, with different historians providing bulletins on what had happened. Adam Goodheart, for example, had described what he called the "Last Ordinary Day," a week before the 1860 election, when Colonel Robert E. Lee was still a member of the United States Army, stationed in Texas and worrying about Comanches. In other installments I read about the election's immediate aftermath: about the doubts and fears that Herman Melville tried to capture in his poetry, and of Lincoln's fascination with a map that showed the relative density of the South's slave population.

But something else filled the news at the end of 2010 and set off a strange disturbing echo. There had been an election back home, and my side had done badly, losing a political momentum that only lately had appeared unstoppable. For a year I had been reading about something called the Tea Party, a movement I found hard to understand: radically conservative and populist at once, suspicious of the federal government in general and of its recent actions in particular, the Affordable Care Act above all. The Tea Party borrowed its name from a 1773 tax revolt in Boston, and some of its cadres had taken an old Revolutionary War–era motto as their own: "Don't Tread on Me." They talked among other things about nullification, a nineteenth-century theory that claimed an individual state had the power to reject a federal law; I had thought that was a dead letter, a belief that had vanished even before the Civil War. Now it seemed back, and the more I read, the more the Tea Party appeared to speak not of colonial New England, but rather of the South in the age of disunion; to put a libertarian hood on something much older and more troubling. *Butt out of our business:* the issues seemed all the same, as if our time rang off the world of 1860, and nothing had ever stopped or changed or gone away. So I began to listen harder, listen more; and yet I followed that echo by paying attention not to the American present but rather to its past, reading about the Civil War with a depth and a passion that the period had never before aroused in me.

I began with a few books on particular battles, borrowed from the city's superb American Library, in the shadow of the Eiffel Tower. I soon found, however, that I was more interested in the memory of the war, in our different attempts to define what it meant, and buried myself in the eight hundred pages of Edmund Wilson's *Patriotic Gore* (1962). Wilson describes the various ways in which the war's participants and observers had written about it, beginning with Harriet Beecher Stowe in the 1850s and ending in the early twentieth century with Oliver Wendell Holmes Jr., who as an officer in a Massachusetts regiment had been wounded three times. Wilson wrote about Lincoln's speeches and the stories of Ambrose Bierce; about Confederate poets and the postwar attempts of the South's supposed statesmen to justify themselves. He showed how the conflict had changed the American language, making it ever more lean and plain and visceral, and all studies of the war's literary aftermath must start with him still. After that I picked up Robert Penn Warren's *Legacy of the Civil War* (1961), written for the conflict's centennial, and then David Blight's *Race and Reunion* (2001), which told me how the North had lost the peace. Drew Gilpin Faust's *This Republic of Suffering* (2008) showed how the nation had dealt with its dead, both their physical bodies and their memories; George Fredrickson's *Inner Civil War* (1965) detailed its psychic effect on a generation of New England intellectuals.

Then early in 2011 the Library of America published a volume called *The Civil War: The First Year Told by Those Who Lived It*, the first of a series of four. I snatched it up the day it appeared on the library shelves, gulping down such things as the report of the South Carolina diarist Mary Chesnut on the attack on Fort Sumter and Colonel William Tecumseh Sherman's letter to his wife about the Union debacle at Bull Run. Living abroad had made me far more consciously interested in my own country than I had ever been before, as though distance had given me new eyes. It made me realize that I needed to look more closely at our history and our literature, to sort out what I thought about the American past. That meant writing about it: an act of citizenship as much as scholarship, an American book by someone whose academic specialty had until then been the British novel. I would read everything; I would—why not?—rewrite *Patriotic Gore* itself. Or so I told myself, until one day I realized that I could say anything I wanted to about the Civil War by taking up a writer I already knew: a dialectic in which I could use the war and the novelist to read each other.

A dialectic implies a synthesis. But I prefer to think of myself as telling a story, a critical narrative in which Faulkner's chronicle of his imagined land will find itself entwined with our country's history, and with other voices too: the diaries and letters of the war years, and the memoirs of the generation after; other novelists as well, and then the historians who in trying to make sense of it all seem to tell us as much about their own moment as they do about the war itself. One voice has been especially present as I've sat up over this preface. James Baldwin's "Stranger in the Village" (1953) describes a winter's stay in an isolated Swiss hamlet called Leukerbad. I have known that essay almost as long as I've known Faulkner's own work, and I never reread it without a sense of profound discomfort, an uneasiness with American life and my own cushioned place within it.

Baldwin knows that he's a stranger in the Alps, the first black man most of the villagers have ever seen. But he is not a stranger in America, despite the best efforts of its white citizens to treat him as one. For the history of our shared country, he argues, is the history of the way white people have tried both to recognize and to deny the humanity of their black neighbors. The problem all white Americans must confront is that of learning how to live with him in order to live with themselves, and though Baldwin never mentions Faulkner his conclusion might have been written with the older novelist in mind: "For even when the worst has been said, it must also be added that the perpetual challenge posed by this problem was always, somehow, perpetually met." Always met because never quite avoided, because that "problem" has stood, more often than not, at the center of our political life. In his greatest books Faulkner accepted that challenge. He faced it, fought with it, fought with himself too. Never adequately, as we will see; not in ways that would satisfy us today or that could satisfy Baldwin then. Yet his very blind spots and uncertainties have lessons for us, and that challenge remains itself without end.

Hence my title, *The Saddest Words*. There are two of them, and they come from *The Sound and the Fury*, Faulkner's first great novel. In that book an alcoholic Jefferson lawyer named Jason Compson, the son of a Confederate general, tells his own son Quentin that *was* is the saddest word of all. Something that *was* is fixed and unchangeable, forever in the past, an event—a mistake—that can be neither altered nor redressed. The very thought of what he can't undo in his own family life has been enough to send him to the bottle. Though no reader stops with that family, we push beyond to history itself, an entire past that can never be made right. And his son will find a sadder word. Away in New England and planning to kill himself at the end of his first year at Harvard, Quentin will think that *again* is even sadder than *was*, saddest of all. For the term suggests that what *was* has simply gone on happening, a cycle of repetition that replays itself, forever. That's how it is in Faulkner's South: a land where the dead past walks, not *was* but *is*, and burning always in one's mind.

What *was* is never over. There have been moments in our history, brief ones, when the meaning of the Civil War has seemed settled. This isn't one of them, not when the illusion that this country might become a postracial society lies in tatters. *Again.* That's precisely why Faulkner remains so valuable—that very recurrence makes him necessary. How should we read him today? My answer begins on a July day in 1863, with history rather than fiction, and in Pennsylvania, not Mississippi: with Robert E. Lee, the Confederacy's greatest icon, and the biggest battle ever fought in North America.

ONE

Gettysburg, at Not Yet Two

A t sunrise on the battle's second day the general stood on a low ridge to the west of the Pennsylvania town and looked out over a shallow valley of fields and orchards. The place itself lay below him: a county seat of twenty-four hundred people, and of no strategic importance whatsoever. But a dozen country roads ran into a knot at Gettysburg's center, and the day before some of his troops had gone blundering up one of them and into a waiting body of enemy cavalry. Robert E. Lee had heard the guns when he was still miles away, and by the time he reached the field it was already too late; a skirmish had become a general engagement almost before he knew it and certainly before he wanted it. Still, he had gotten most of his men there first, ahead of the other side's advance, and by the end of the day had put his headquarters atop a hill that his opponents had held that morning, on the grounds of a Lutheran seminary. The school's main building had a high cupola and would have made a good lookout, but it had now become a field hospital, its wide halls filled with the wounded men of both armies. The general wouldn't allow himself to disturb their groans and instead took a spot under a tree outside, his aides clustered around him, and raised his field glasses into the dawn.

There was another ridge a mile away to the southeast, and it too was low: not a hard climb, not at all, not unless the people on top were shooting at you. His soldiers had driven the Federals back upon it the day before, pushing them off Seminary Ridge and then hitting them from the north as well, harrying them through the streets of the town itself until in the fading light the bluebellies had found a refuge on its heights. Lee had won the day, he could call it a victory, and yet it was a disappointment too, for the Union's battered forces had been just one short hill away, and he had told his lieutenants that he wished to take that hill, if practicable. It hadn't been; the chance was lost. They would have to fight again, and in the day's first light he could see through his glasses that the enemy's tattered lines had begun to fill. New regiments, brigades, divisions, had come up and fallen into place on the opposite crest, extending the front his men would have to face. His own strength had also grown in the night, as one commander after another pushed along those country roads, but their job would be harder than he'd expected. Those people were waiting for him on what was called Cemetery Ridge, and that was where he would have to attack them.

And now it was the steaming third day of both July and the battle alike, and the enemy was still there. On the second Lee had sent one prong of his army to the north and another to the south, but his commanders couldn't coordinate their attacks and neither of them had the speed the assault required. They had marched and countermarched, hoping for surprise, and the main blow had not been launched until late in the afternoon. It smashed an enemy corps and his troops had given him three brilliant murderous hours, but though he gained some ground the day had to count as a failure. The opposing army still held that ridge and had even been reinforced; despite their casualties, their ranks had continued to swell. His own reserves were thin by comparison, and yet his faith in his soldiers remained unshaken. They would strike once more, and so that summer morning Lee was on horseback and moving among the men whom he would ask to walk across that open rolling mile and into the center of the enemy lines. He expected to have about 15,000 of them, including his one fresh division, three full brigades from his own state of Virginia. They were in place early, concealed in the woods to the south of Seminary Ridge, and as he rode slowly past each company he removed his hat in salute, a courtly gray-haired man in his fifties, and weary.

He believed that no soldiers had ever had such grit and courage, and those soldiers in turn believed in him, in his genius and righteousness; and in consequence they believed in the inevitability of their own success. A string of victories—Second Manassas the previous summer, Chancellorsville that spring—had made defeat inconceivable, and they spoke of their enemy with open contempt. They could win any fight Lee planned, simply because he had planned it. But that belief wasn't shared by everyone in the Army of Northern Virginia. Lee's senior corps commander was a burly, saturnine South Carolinian named James Longstreet. He would be in charge of the third day's assault, and he had not wanted to fight at Gettysburg at all. Lee was always aggressive, forever seeking the daring and decisive Napoleonic strike. Longstreet preferred defensive battles. He wanted his opponents to come to him, to bloody themselves upon his lines and then suffer the crushing force of a counterattack. He saw the opposing ridge as impregnable and the day before had said so, suggesting that instead of attacking they swing the army around to the south; they could put themselves between the Federal forces and Washington City, and make the enemy fight on a field of their own choosing. He still thought they should do it, and his scouts told him that the way remained open. Lee felt, in contrast, that after two days of hard fighting he couldn't ask his men to withdraw from the ground they'd won; it would shred their morale, whatever the logic of Longstreet's argument. He could not, however, change the shape of the land before them, and as the two men studied the field that morning Longstreet swept his arm toward the enemy position on Cemetery Ridge, toward the stone walls that would shelter the Union riflemen and the hills from which the Federal cannon would fire, and told his commander that no army of their size had any chance at all to take and hold it.

But the decision was not Longstreet's. Nor perhaps was it finally Lee's. The fighting began at one in the afternoon with an artillery barrage directed by a twenty-eight-year-old colonel named Edward Porter Alexander, an engineer from Georgia who had trained at West Point and a veteran of every major battle in the war's eastern theater. His guns had destroyed the Yankee charge at Fredericksburg the winter before, and though his nominal command was only a battalion, he now took charge of the artillery for Longstreet's corps as a whole. Alexander would survive the war and live on into the twentieth century, unrepentant and yet without nostalgia for his youthful cause. He believed that the South had indeed possessed the constitutional right to secede, but he also thought that the steamship, the railroad, and the results of the war itself had put new limits on the sovereignty of individual states. He made his peace with the peace and left a memoir that stands as one of the Confederacy's most comprehensive and clear-eyed records. Yet so long as the war lasted he was a wily and formidable foe. At Gettysburg he had eighty guns under his direct command and on July 3 was up at three in the morning to put them into position, sheltering them in the trees as much as he could. The orders he had received were simple. Two cannon would boom a signal and he was then to open fire all along his front and do his best, as he wrote, to tear the enemy limbless. And when that was done—when he judged that he had silenced the Union artillery—he would send a courier to Major General George Pickett with word for the Rebel infantry to advance.

Alexander thought a show of some twenty or thirty minutes should be sufficient and hoped he wouldn't need more, for "I had not the ammunition to make it a long business." His guns had worked for hours the day before, and though he had refilled their limber chests as best he could—round shot and grape, canister and shell—the reserves had run low, and they were too far from the army's Virginia base to have any chance of a new supply. Then just before the cannonade began he got a note from Longstreet. The general wrote that if in Alexander's belief the enemy was not either driven off or "greatly demoralize[d] . . . I would prefer that you should not advise Gen. Pickett to make the charge. I shall rely a great deal on your good judgment." Those words both shocked and scared him. They appeared to leave the battle in his hands, as if the campaign now depended on his own cold assessment of what he saw and not on the inspired leadership of Robert E. Lee. The army, it now seemed, would advance or not, would fight and die or not, on the word of a mere colonel.

The Union artillery immediately answered Alexander's opening shots, and between them they so covered the field with smoke that no clear view—no confident judgment—was possible. He could estimate his own success only by the rate of the enemy's returning fire, and he feared that they might as a ruse let their guns go quiet. Yet the Federal cannon did not slacken. They made the ground shake and the sky rain sound, and there were more of them than Alexander could count. Just a few minutes' work told him it would be "madness to send a storming column out" into their face; was that decision really his? At 1:25 he wrote Pickett that the barrage had not yet been successful. But it was too late. Pickett himself had already asked Longstreet for permission to move forward; the older man turned his head aside, unable to speak, and Pickett took that pained silence for assent. His soldiers needed time to form, however, and Alexander was still waiting for them to step out of the woods when Longstreet rode up and learned just how little ammunition he had left. Now it was the general's turn to be shocked, but though Alexander recognized that Longstreet needed only the slightest encouragement to call off the attack, he could not bring himself to speak. Then the Southern troops swept by them and out into the open field, dragged forward, in the words of Lee's biographer, "by the very ticking of [the] watch to the inevitable hour" of their defeat.

Nobody ordered what became known as Pickett's Charge. Or so Alexander's memoirs suggest, in presenting it as something that on that hot July afternoon no one felt able to stop. Not him, though he may have had the most accurate estimate of the field. Not Longstreet, who didn't want to attack and knew that his forces would fail; nor Pickett, the dandy known for his long perfumed hair, who dreamed of glory and believed they would succeed. Not even Lee, who had planned the attack and yet did not give the final command, did not say *now*. It is as if the very moment of its conception had called the battle's future into being, a disaster ordained by the hastening motions of time itself.

Gettysburg broke the Confederacy as an offensive force. The South still sent raids beyond its borders, but it never again had the strength to invade the North. Still, the fight's consequences were not immediately clear. Longstreet expected a counterattack, which did not come, and the next day both sides remained in position and marked a somber Fourth of July, static as the rain poured down and covered the living and the dead with mud. On that same Independence Day, a thousand miles away in Mississippi, the Union general Ulysses S. Grant received the surrender of an enemy army at the riverfront citadel of Vicksburg; after a seven-weeks' siege the starved Confederates stacked arms in front of their fortifications, and the Union took control of what Lincoln called "the Father of Waters." That night Lee began to withdraw from Pennsylvania, using his cavalry and the weather alike to screen his retreat to the south, a logistical marvel that ten days later allowed him to escape back into the safety of Virginia. His army crossed the Potomac where the river narrowed above Harpers Ferry; and in Washington the president was so angered by the ineffective Federal pursuit that it almost seemed the Union had not won.

Southern newspapers at first called Gettysburg a victory. Soon enough, however, Lee's defeat began to seem of strategic importance, and in time the low stone wall on Cemetery Ridge that some of Pickett's men reached before their final repulse became known as the high-water mark of the Confederacy. A brigadier named Lewis Armstead, with his hat stuck on the end of his sword as a guidon, had gotten there with perhaps a hundred of his men and was then—so the tale goes—shot down in the act of capturing a Federal cannon. In time that march toward the Union guns, with the gray lines in perfect step and the casualty figures at 60 percent, would become a legend, and the Rebels' courage against the odds would seem, to those who believed in it, to justify the nobility of what almost immediately became known as the Lost Cause. Some of those boys *had* reached the wall—some of them had gone over it. If only there had been more of them, if only the past were not yet the past!

------·+·------

EIGHTY-FIVE YEARS LATER A great American novelist wrote a page that can stand as a gloss on Alexander's dilemma.

The novel William Faulkner published in September 1948 was called *Intruder in the Dust*, and it was far from his best. He had begun it only that January and had written it quickly, sending it off just three months later; quickly, and for the money. Faulkner's critical reputation in the 1940s was creeping skyward, in Europe especially, but his sales were low, kept down by both his books' reputation for obscurity and their often scandalous subject matter, incest included. He'd made up for that with an explosive productivity, publishing thirteen books in thirteen years; many of them drew on the short stories that, in deliberately simplified versions, he had already sold to magazines. But that period had ended with *Go Down, Moses* in 1942, and there had been nothing new in the six years since. He had been too old to enlist when America entered World War II; nevertheless, it had stalled him, drained him, and so had a punitive contract as a Hollywood scriptwriter.

Almost all his work was out of print at the war's end, and yet by 1948 his position had changed. He still needed money, but Malcolm Cowley's *Portable Faulkner* had received front-page coverage in the *New York Times Book Review*, and the anthology's success had gotten a few of his earlier novels reissued. The new book would help. For *Intruder in the Dust* was a mystery, and Faulkner's deliberate reliance on a familiar genre had kept off the formal difficulties of his earlier work. It sold a quick 15,000 copies, and the movie rights went for $50,000; he would never again have to worry about an American audience.

The novel's protagonist, Lucas Beauchamp, is a black man who's been framed for the murder of a white one, but his true crime, in the eyes of Yoknapatawpha County, is that he acts as if color doesn't exist. Lucas's maternal grandfather was one of the county's earliest white settlers, a planter named Carothers McCaslin who fathered children upon his slaves, and even upon those slaves who were themselves his children. Faulkner had traced that fictional family history for four generations in *Go Down, Moses*, and there and in *Intruder in the Dust* he presents Lucas as both a successful farmer and oddly proud of his ancestry: a man who's gotten his white cousins to acknowledge their kinship. Yet his moral force and confidence make him suspect in this segregated world, and he's known to have quarreled with the murdered man. The county sheriff assumes his guilt, but also thinks a lynching would be bad for public order and manages to keep him safely in jail; meanwhile, the garrulous lawyer Gavin Stevens follows out the few clues that Lucas can provide about the way he's been set up.

The novel has moments of real excitement, including a confrontation over the dead man's open coffin. But what most readers remember is a bit of high-flown language, a moment of dream-like stasis in which Gavin stirs Lucas's own case into the white South's collective memory of that decisive Pennsylvania day. "For every Southern boy fourteen years old," he says:

> not once but whenever he wants it, there is the instant when it's still
> not yet two oclock on that July afternoon in 1863, the brigades are
> in position behind the rail fence, the guns are laid and ready in the
> woods and the furled flags are already loosened to break out and

Pickett himself with his long oiled ringlets and his hat in one hand probably and his sword in the other looking up the hill waiting for Longstreet to give the word and it's all in the balance, it hasn't happened yet, it hasn't even begun yet, it not only hasn't begun yet but there is still time for it not to begin against that position and those circumstances which made more men than Garnett and Kemper and Armstead and Wilcox look grave yet it's going to begin, we all know that, we have come too far with too much at stake and that moment doesn't even need a fourteen year old boy to think *This time. Maybe this time* with all this much to lose and all this much to gain.

Gavin doesn't mention Gettysburg here. He doesn't need to. The names of the generals are enough to summon the whole story, Longstreet and Pickett, and then the four brigadiers, two of them soon to die. Now, in reading these words, I want to pause and qualify: that instant exists not for every Southern boy of Faulkner's era, but rather for every Southern *white* boy, the boys for whom those names evoke a kind of Valhalla. That's clearly what Gavin, and beyond him Faulkner, actually means. Except maybe it is true for *every* Southern boy, or partly true, insofar as the war, or the aftermath of the war, seems to have snapped the threads of time itself, so reluctant has their society been to accept that war's verdict. Jim Crow keeps it true. This novel describes a world in which, as in Faulkner's real-life Mississippi, black men shouldn't be seen out after dark in some parts of the county; as though the antebellum slave patrols were still active, still riding the midnight roads. The old ways have lingered, do not yet know they're dead.

Indeed the very grammar of the passage suggests their continuing life. Gavin speaks in the present tense. The guns *are* laid and ready, his sentences come loaded with gerunds, and some of his constructions are proleptic ones, anticipating an event that is just about to happen. *Still not yet.* But they are also spiked with negatives, an invocation of an alternate future that is in fact an alternate past; maybe this time everything will be different. Whenever he chooses, that fourteen-year-old boy has access to a moment in which history becomes hiatus, when the Confederate debacle has not yet begun, is not yet inevitable. There's still time for Alexander to speak, for Longstreet to shake his head and decide that this time he will, for once, disregard Lee's order. Maybe delay will change things. Or maybe this time the Union lines will falter, and the South will win its gamble; "the golden dome of Washington itself" might fall, and a new world open out, forever. Maybe. The teenager Faulkner imagines will want to arrest that onrushing moment, to linger precisely because he can't help but know that the clock beats on even as Gavin's invocation works to stay it. He knows it's going to begin, knows the troops will step from the woods and the flags unfurl in the breeze; that mile-long march will start, and with every step the Union cannon will rip a new hole in the line. The Confederacy has come too far to let it all stop now, but the future those white boys have willed into being is not the one they would choose.

The passage offers the most delusional bit of romance in all of Faulkner's work, and I want to say two more things about it. The first of them has to do with Gavin's sense of the past. His words stand with a whole school of Confederate historiography, one marked by a predilection for the counterfactual, an eternal fascination with *what if*: a school that lived—lives—more in conversation than on the page, in the country stores of old or the coffee shops of today, wherever men gather to muse or to rage. Of course the character himself sees the war's ever-recurring present, that immediate access to the past, as a good thing; something for a boy to dream on in an idle hour, a bit of sustenance waiting for whenever he wants it. But Gavin is hardly the only one of Faulkner's characters to believe that the boundary between past and present remains porous, and for most of them the experience isn't nearly so positive. History swims up whether or not they want it to, not a blessing but a curse, the involuntary memory of a past, or a pain, that can never be quite faced or conquered: a trauma in the clinical sense of the term. So in a later book, *Requiem for a Nun* (1951), Gavin claims that "The past is never dead. It's not even past." His words grow out of a secret in the life of his extended family, a crime from which other crimes have followed. Nevertheless, they are usually taken as a statement about history in general and that of the American South in particular: a statement that carries the weight of that July day and that central conflict in our nation's history. *The saddest words.*

The second thing cuts deeper. As a piece of rhetoric, Gavin's speech exemplifies a crucial aspect of Faulkner's own imagination and style, one that

Jean-Paul Sartre described, in writing of *The Sound and the Fury*, as a "frozen speed at the very heart of things." For time in this passage appears at once to accelerate and yet pause. In a 1955 interview the novelist said that he always tried to imagine a knot in his characters' lives that required him, first, to figure out "whatever must have happened before to lead [them] to that particular moment," and second, how they would act afterward. Before and after, not during: Faulkner typically moves both his readers and his characters toward some climactic event and then works away from it, but about that moment itself he often says nothing at all. Gavin offers us an image of men on the verge of action, but though we know what's to come we never see them walk into the Union bullets. And this moment from *Intruder in the Dust* finds its parallels throughout Faulkner's oeuvre, in which many determinative moments go similarly undescribed, the violent ones in particular.

No scene in *Light in August* shows us Joe Christmas's murder of Joanna Burden. In *Absalom, Absalom!* we hear only the muffled report of Charles Bon's shooting, his death at the hand of his best friend and prospective brother-in-law Henry Sutpen, and never see the leveled pistol itself. "Something is going to happen to me," Temple Drake thinks in *Sanctuary*, but then the narrative skips and what was going to happen already has. She's now bleeding into her dress, and in the space or time—the pages—in between she's been raped. These events are implied, discussed, referred to, their causes and consequences explored to exhaustion. They are everything *but* directly depicted, and so it is with Faulkner's treatment of the Civil War itself. He will offer vignettes of the Mississippi home front, describing a few isolated skirmishes or raids, and other references to Gettysburg lie scattered through his books. But he never comes closer to describing it than he does in Gavin's account of its yet-suspended outcome, and the war as a whole remains his missing center: an all-determining absence, a gap hardwired into the novelist's very imagination.

Two of Faulkner's books do, admittedly, make that war into a dramatized present and presence, and my story will draw upon them repeatedly. One of them is the sublime and maddening *Absalom, Absalom!*, a novel that offers a version of Yoknapatawpha County's history from the antebellum years and on through Reconstruction. It always circles back, however, to Bon's shooting in the war's last days, at the gates of the Sutpens' claustral plantation. The other is *The Unvanquished*, which began as a linked set of frankly potboiling and half-comic short stories about a Confederate colonel named John Sartoris, as narrated by his young son Bayard. The two books are coincident in time. Faulkner began his work on *Absalom, Absalom!* in the spring of 1934, but almost immediately interrupted himself to write the four opening tales in the Sartoris sequence, all of them first published in the *Saturday Evening Post*, his most steadily remunerative market for short fiction. He returned to that material once the novel was done, early in 1936, and quickly produced the last three stories in the sequence; and anyone reading them together will feel that the lesser and lighter work must have relieved more than his bank balance, must have given him a bit of air or sense of space.

Yet the war is always with him, even when it's not his explicit subject, and in defining its place in his work I will treat his many volumes as a single enormous text in which one can move at will. For that I have some warrant in Faulkner's own thinking. Late in his career he spoke of wanting to write what he called his "Doomsday" book: a synthesis, half gazetteer and half history, of his imagined land. Faulkner often finished stories in one novel that he had started in another, and explained away any inconsistencies by claiming that with time he had gotten to know his people just a little bit better. Sometimes a minor figure in one work became a major character in another, a practice he learned from Balzac, and many of those characters seem to have existed in his mind well before he had completed a single story about them. Rather than offer full readings of individual novels, then, I'll take the course of the war and its aftermath as my template for a narrative arc that runs from the 1830s until the 1930s: unstitching Faulkner's own elaborately layered chronologies and rearranging them into something like linearity, into a coherent if fictional history. I will show the Yoknapatawpha world that streamed into that war and the one that flowed out of it, inserting it into our nation's narrative, and in the process I will look far beyond Faulkner's own pages.

Bits of family and regional history; a reading of other fiction about the conflict and a consideration of the period's letters and journals; accounts of battles and of my own visits to battlefields; a look at Civil War historiography, and at war memorials too: all these will have a role in my story, one that enacts a steady movement between Faulkner's books and the war itself, each of them providing a context for the other. I'll visit Vicksburg and Shiloh, the marble tablets to the Union dead in Harvard's Memorial Hall, and of course the novelist's own town of Oxford, Mississippi. Another part of my work will involve a reading of the historians that Faulkner himself read, and a look at the way the conflict was taught in the local schools during his childhood. And while this book is not a biography, I will also keep an eye on Faulkner's own circumstances: his family background, his finances and his marriage, his work in Hollywood and the wider public life that opened after he received the Nobel Prize.

Walt Whitman claimed that the real war would never get into books, and yet in the very act of writing those words he also showed they were wrong; the book of journal entries that contains them, *Specimen Days*, offers one of our most profound accounts of the war's human costs. What he meant was that neither fiction nor poetry had yet found the capacity—the language— it needed to deal honestly with those costs. Readers from both North and South wanted an epic. They wanted Homer or Walter Scott, and a generation on would complain that there was no American Tolstoy. What they got instead were Whitman's own extraordinary elegies and then a lot of novels in which Yankee officers marry Southern girls and work together to heal the country; the sardonic brutalities of Ambrose Bierce followed a bit later. Most of the period's fiction remained too decorous to describe the odor of suppuration or the bullet in your neighbor's eye, and none of the young men who would become the war generation's best novelists had fought, not Twain nor Howells nor James. The example of *Specimen Days* implied that anyone who wanted to understand that struggle should look elsewhere, should look to documentary accounts above all, and in the early 1960s Edmund Wilson's *Patriotic Gore* showed us just how. Noting the absence of great fiction from the war period and its immediate aftermath, Wilson argued that the conflict's most valuable imaginative record could instead be found in speeches and diaries and memoirs; in the cadences of Lincoln, the tart social detail of Mary Chesnut, the terse clarity of Ulysses S. Grant.

Still, Faulkner's own work suggests something more complicated, something for which the distance of half a century and more was required. Great fiction about the Civil War will never be about just the war itself, in the sense of battles and campaigns. The real war lies not only in the physical combat, but also in the war after the war, the war over its memory and meaning. Or as the former slave Ringo says in *The Unvanquished,* during a Reconstruction-era quarrel over voting rights, "This War aint over. Hit just started good." For Faulkner the actual fighting lacks the emotional turmoil, the sense of a riven soul, on which his best work depends. That comes later, in the long years of furious immobility that follow upon and have been made by that war. The critic Daniel Aaron puts it memorably in *The Unwritten War,* the 1973 study that remains Wilson's best successor. What interested Faulkner was not the struggle but its "aftereffects ... [he] read the War's meaning not in its heroes and battles but in the consciousness of a people." But that is too simple. What came before matters too, and to understand the war's moment we need to look far into its future and its past alike. We need to read each in relation to the other, and in both formal and thematic terms that's not simply what Faulkner offers but what he requires. So in a 1909 "summer of wistaria" a boy in Jefferson can still breathe "the same air in which the church bells had rung" on a Sunday in 1833, and watch a long-dead stranger ride into town.

Those words come from *Absalom, Absalom!* (1936), written a full seventy years after the war's end. And before going further I need to pause over that book for a moment, need to get the acrid, estranging difficulty of its prose into our mouths. The boy is named Quentin Compson, the oldest son of an old Jefferson family, and many of the novel's first readers would remember that they had met him before in *The Sound and the Fury.* There he had drowned himself in the Charles River at the end of his freshman year in Cambridge, stricken by a doubled despair: first over his sexual desire for his own sister, Caddy, and then by his inability to keep her from surrendering the "minute fragile membrane of her maidenhead" to another man, his inability to preserve his family's honor. In this novel, however, he has been summoned, just before he heads north, to the house of a Jefferson spinster, an old woman who wants to tell him a story:

> From a little after two oclock until almost sundown of the long still hot weary dead September afternoon they sat in what Miss Coldfield

still called the office because her father had called it that—a dim hot airless room with the blinds all closed and fastened for forty-three summers because when she was a girl someone had believed that light and moving air carried heat and that dark was always cooler, and which (as the sun shone fuller and fuller on that side of the house) became latticed with yellow slashes full of dust motes which Quentin thought of as being flecks of the dead old dried paint itself blown inward from the scaling blinds as wind might have blown them.

That's the book's first sentence; the second one is even longer. What hits us first are the adjectives, that stretched-out string of six words to modify "afternoon," and four of them monosyllables, so that it seems to take forever before we reach a noun and a verb: *they sat.* Time comes here before person or place, the only thing moving in this static world is the dust, and Faulkner will repeat two of those adjectives—*hot* and *dead*—before the sentence reaches its end. Each of those recapitulations forms part of a triad, moreover, and the novel will insist on that pattern; the birds make a "dry vivid dusty sound" and Rosa Coldfield speaks in a "grim haggard amazed voice." The wistaria outside her window has bloomed twice that summer, its odor "sweet and oversweet," and this prose has the same overheated fecundity, its modifiers piled recklessly, rank with too much meaning. Quentin sits listening to Miss Coldfield until the very sound of her voice appears to "renege" into the image of a man. Synaesthesia; and then that man "abrupt[s]"—the adjective made verb—onto the earth as if spewed from a crack within, a man whose story contains all that is ruined in her own life and in that of their region as well. And Faulkner's language looks equally riven, broken and flowing at once, its words thrust into paradox and bent into new-use. *Absalom, Absalom!* uses the fractured mind of a boy who seems already half-ghost to present the family history of "the son who widowed the daughter who had not yet been a bride." No one can read it quickly or even entirely with pleasure, but anyone who can hear its flowered dissonance will know that such books are why we read at all.

The Civil War did not produce a great novel, or at least not one that its soldiers and widows could cherish; but then few survivors of the Napoleonic period were alive for the publication of *War and Peace* some sixty-five years after Austerlitz. It's often noted that *Absalom, Absalom!* and *Gone with the Wind* came out the same year. Faulkner hated the "moonlight and magnolia" tradition to which Margaret Mitchell's bestseller belongs, and claimed he should get twice what she had for the movie rights. He added that his own book was about "miscegenation"; there were no takers. What's less often recognized is that the dozen-odd years of his greatest achievement—the end of the 1920s boom, the years of the Depression and of America's entry into World War II—stand as an exceptionally hot moment in our country's long-running argument over the origins and meaning of the Civil War itself.

In an 1861 speech the Georgia politician Alexander Stephens, who would soon become the Confederacy's vice president, referred to slavery as the "Corner-stone" of the new nation, one founded on the principle of a God-given inequality. Yet few scholars of Faulkner's day would have agreed with him. In 1927 the Progressive historians Charles and Mary Beard argued that the war was but an epiphenomenon of the great struggle between agriculture and capital; inevitable perhaps, but only an aspect of a much larger conflict between two fundamentally incompatible economic systems. A decade later the Chicago-based Avery Craven put the opposite case. The fighting had been unnecessary, the fault of weak and fallible men on either side, who had whipped each other into a high-tempered frenzy. The one thing those historians agreed upon, however, was that slavery itself had very little to do with the war at all. In Craven's words, it provided a mere symbol of more consequential "sectional differences" and one that played but a "minor part in the life of the South and of the Negro."

Those years were marked too by the work of the Virginian Douglas Southall Freeman, whose four-volume, Pulitzer Prize–winning biography (1934–35) of Robert E. Lee codified that soldier's image for a new generation. Freeman's Christian gentleman made no substantive mistakes even at Gettysburg, but the historian followed that study with three volumes on those who sometimes did, the men he called *Lee's Lieutenants* (1942–44). Faulkner had both studies on his shelves in Oxford, and his evocation of the moment before Pickett's Charge seems clearly indebted to them; the Confederacy may have reached its high-water mark many decades before, but the heights of Confederate hagiography coincided with the novelist's great period. And there were other voices as well. For a generation the Reconstruction period had been read through the eyes of the Columbia historian William Archibald Dunning and his students, who opposed black suffrage and saw the state governments that depended on it as necessarily corrupt. Reconstruction belonged to carpetbaggers and buffoons, and the white South had been right to rise up against disaster. Dunning's followers buttressed their arguments with long pages of statistics and legislative details, but their work nevertheless stands as the scholarly counterpart to such exercises in white supremacy as Thomas W. Dixon's wildly popular novel *The Clansman* (1905) and the film that D. W. Griffith based upon it, *The Birth of a Nation* (1915). In the 1930s, however, another scholar began to push for a different understanding of the era. It would take many years and many changes in the course of American life before his argument was widely accepted, but W. E. B. Du Bois's *Black Reconstruction in America* (1935) belongs to this moment as well.

All these will have their place here, along with Lincoln's oratory, the diaries of Confederate women, and the letters of a slave-owning family from Georgia that are gathered in *The Children of Pride*. I will look too at the memoirs of generals and their aides, the local color stories of Thomas Nelson Page and Charles Chesnutt, and of course at the secession debates and ordinances of the different Southern states. For this book provides an account not only of Faulkner's work but also of what I might call the rhetoric of the Civil War itself, of the ever-changing ways in which it has been conceived over time. Those ways provide a register of the national psyche, and what we think about that war at any given moment serves above all to tell us what we think about ourselves, about the nature of our polity and the shape of our history.

The Civil War seemed to break the history of Faulkner's region in two. It drew a bright line between past and present, and left "the deep South dead," as he put it in *Absalom, Absalom!*, "and peopled with garrulous outraged baffled ghosts." Yet that past persisted for its white inhabitants in a legacy of military defeat and loss, and for its black ones in an enduring poverty and injustice. "*Tell about the South*": that's what the other Harvard students say in that novel to Quentin Compson. "*What's it like there. What do they do there. Why do they live there. Why do they live at all.*" Quentin's answer will fill a whole winter's night in 1910, taking the form of a story that he tells to his Canadian roommate, Shreve McCannon. He will remember his wistaria-haunted meeting with Miss Coldfield and look back not only to the war, but also to the decades that led to secession: to the reduction of the wilderness into the apparent order of a plantation by the "demon" Thomas Sutpen, Henry's father; to slavery and the sexual crimes it made possible; and on to a diminished present that seems forever frozen in place. In that South, Rosa Coldfield can claim that there is no such thing as memory because memory requires a sense of the past and for her it is all still present, fifty years that form a single moment of unending pain. Or as Quentin himself will put it, "*Maybe happen is never once but like ripples maybe on water after the pebble sinks,*" ever-spreading concentric circles that might then bounce back from the shore. But for him those ripples will never quite fade. "Happen" continues on, forever, and the more Shreve listens to the Mississippian talk, the more it seems to him that to be from the South is to live in an atmosphere that is "always reminding you never to forget."

But what exactly is it that the Southerner remembers? Let me propose two very different answers, to each of which I'll return in this book's later chapters. In a classic 1882 essay the French social theorist Ernest Renan argued that national identity grows above all from a sense of a shared past, a common purpose and history; we could even say, in the words of Lincoln's first inaugural address, that it requires the "mystic chords of memory." Renan also suggested, however, that "historical error" is a "crucial factor in the creation of a nation." People need to remember but for that very reason they also need to forget, and to forget above all the "deeds of violence which take place at the origin of all political formations." That was especially true in Renan's own France. The precarious social peace of the country's Third Republic depended upon a selective amnesia, an attempt to forget the blood of this upheaval or that, from the Revolution of 1789 to the 1871 suppression of the Paris Commune, consigning them to the pages of history rather than feeling them on the fevered pulse of memory.

Faulkner's South, in contrast, seems as if it can't forget anything. It accepts reunion only insofar as it can recall itself as a place apart, and yet that memory, paradoxically, is also a form of forgetting. For in the first decades after the war the white South remembered its defeat above all; it saw itself as the victim of a rapacious conqueror, forgot its own acts of aggression and indeed atrocity, and thought of slavery only as something now lost. And the white North had its own ways of forgetting too. Twenty years after the war the *Century* magazine ran a famous series of articles called "Battles and Leaders of the Civil War" that concentrated on the war's military aspects alone, putting all political questions aside in the name of national unity. The Blue and the Gray began to knit themselves together once more: they remembered those mystic chords, and in time the Civil War itself would provide the tonic. But they stand as a binary in which black Americans, as David Blight has argued, found themselves excluded and forgotten.

My second answer has to do with Quentin Compson's belief that "happen is never once," a sense of recurrence that provides a more pointed version of Gavin Stevens's idea about Southern teenagers. In *Absalom, Absalom!* Rosa Coldfield tells Quentin about a day in 1865 when she stood outside the closed door of an upstairs room in a Yoknapatawpha County mansion. On the other side of that door lay a dead Confederate soldier, a man with whom Rosa was half in love even though she had never even seen him. Nor will she see him now; all she'll get is her hand on the closed coffin. "I heard an echo, but not the shot," she says; "I saw a closed door but did not enter it." She may know what's behind that door and yet she can also only imagine it; she stays outside, removed, and for almost fifty years will strain toward a knowledge she cannot quite have. One doesn't need to be much of a Freudian to see this moment as a version of the primal scene or to recognize that the link between sex and death might be especially strong in a region where so many handsome young men got killed. The past is inevitably the site of trauma, but Faulkner goes further—the past *is* trauma, insofar as it is the past, the unrecoverable time when things began. It is a place, a time, to which Rosa paradoxically has no access, however much it haunts her; haunts her to the precise degree that it remains unmastered. Nevertheless, that door will open. At the end of the novel Faulkner will make us walk with Quentin as he climbs toward it, up the stairs of that same dark house on a summer night in 1909, and we will follow him beneath its lintel to face the wounds of the Southern past.

But Faulkner wasn't only a Southerner. He was also an American and as such, as a white man from his time and place, he lived with his own version of what Du Bois described as a double consciousness. "One ever feels his two-ness," Du Bois wrote, "an American, a Negro; two souls, two thoughts . . . two warring ideals in one dark body." Faulkner's twoness was of course a different one, and his account of what he called "the human heart in conflict with itself" would take many forms. Yet one of those forms was surely his awareness of himself as a regional figure within a larger nation that saw that region, as Shreve does, as an alien place. Faulkner identified himself with his region, but he also judged it: a place that, like Quentin, he would always insist he did not quite hate. For his work does not speak of his region alone, and it is in his account of the Civil War's inner meaning and legacy that he stands above all as a national voice.

———————

MY EXPLORATION OF THESE questions falls into three major parts, each tending toward a different rhetorical mode. The first, "Twice-Told Tales," draws most heavily upon biography, while the second, "Yoknapatawpha's War," lies closest to history and will, among other things, look at Faulkner's representation of emancipation. The last part, "Dark House," leans toward criticism and also examines his understanding of racial identity. Still, these are but tendencies. My practice in each section remains mixed, and taken together they offer a roughly chronological account not of Faulkner's career so much as of his imagined land itself: its conception and settlement in my first unit, Reconstruction and the landscape of Civil War memory in my last.

In offering that account, however, I find myself laboring under a peculiar consciousness of my own. In his essays of the 1950s Faulkner often evoked the kind of elderly "undefeated" Southern lady who seventy years after the war "would get up and walk out of *Gone with the Wind* as soon as Sherman's name was mentioned." He had his own great-aunt Alabama in mind, but the type is general throughout his work and some of those women would have hesitated to have me at their dinner tables. Because I'm a Yankee, though not as the term is understood in my own native New England. Words never have a single meaning, or, as Faulkner himself said, they don't ever quite fit what they seem to say. To me that name denotes a particular ethnic heritage within my home region, and above all in its northernmost states: those deep-rooted families of English ancestry who swallow their *r*'s and stretch out their vowels in wood-smoke and flannel. I'm not one of those Yankees—but then in New England we don't often distinguish between Tidewater and Piedmont, the Delta and the red clay hills. Up here it is all the South to us, and down there I am indeed a Yankee, someone who, as a hotel clerk in Corinth, Mississippi once told me, has come a long ways.

That statement masks a question. Why? What are you doing here? It reminds me that I'm an outsider, and an outsider, moreover, with the full panoply of Yankee prejudices. I believe, with Frederick Douglass, that "there was a right side . . . in the late war" and a wrong one, and I have squirmed at the kind of Civil War museum that tells me the white South fought for "home." There are even places at Gettysburg that make me uncomfortable. The South Carolina memorial there insists that the conflict's motivating force lay in the "sacredness of States Rights." It was dedicated in July 1963: a way to mark the battle's centennial, true, but also at the height of Southern opposition to the civil rights movement. Mississippi's own Gettysburg monument is worse—it went up a full decade later and speaks of a "righteous cause." But Faulkner's work allows for that discomfort. He imagines an audience that includes people like those Harvard students in *Absalom, Absalom!* who want Quentin to tell them about the South, and their questions are as urgent today as ever. For if you believe as I do that the determining drama of American history is the quarrel over slavery, then you will be at once drawn to and suspicious of the uncanny otherness of that not-quite alien land.

The third day at Gettysburg was the hottest yet in the summer of 1863, humid and with the temperature stretching up through the eighties. The Confederates stepped off into the sweatiest part of the afternoon and would have felt every ounce they had to carry. I made my own walk toward the Union lines under more temperate conditions, on a dry morning in June and carrying nothing more than binoculars and a water bottle. The Rebel front was something like a mile long, with the regiments to the north under the command of Johnston Pettigrew and Isaac Trimble; Pickett's name is traditionally used for the charge as a whole, but his own division covered only the southern portion of the line. The ground between the two armies was mostly agricultural, and the troops would have had to walk through whatever crops had not already been trampled. It was also undulating, full of dips and hollows; as the march began, many of the soldiers could see exactly where they were going and could be seen and shelled in turn, but in the middle they were able to find a bit of cover. I took my own position in the woods at the far end of Pickett's own, and from there I saw nothing but grass and a dirt road rising ahead of me as I stepped from the trees and began to climb a gentle hill. The soldiers here would have been safe for a minute, shielded from the Union view. The Federal forces were shielded too, however, and when Pickett's men got to the top of that hill they walked unsuspectingly into a raking artillery fire from their right.

The march had been planned to converge on a copse of trees in the center of the Northern lines, and each Confederate commander had to think of what the others were doing, had to make his men walk obliquely across the field in step with troops whom they could not always see. About two-thirds of the way across they encountered a highway called the Emmitsburg Road, with its bed sunk deep below the surface of the fields. That gave a bit of shelter—or would have if it hadn't been lined on both sides by fences. A lot of Southerners were shot by Yankee sharpshooters as they tried to scramble over them; others were hit as they stopped to throw the fence rails down and make the way easier for the units behind them. But Pickett's now-diminished force got through, and his men gathered themselves to rush the last few hundred yards to the low stone wall that ran in front of those trees, the wall behind which the Union guns were waiting.

I didn't feel the freedom to cut through Gettysburg's fields and pastures myself, so I kept to the farm lane until I reached the Emmittsburg Road, then walked for ten minutes along its rolling course to where a smoothly trodden path led up to the Federal position. From here on the Confederate troops would have been exposed almost every foot of the way, though just before the end there were a few scrub-covered bumps behind which a man could lie out of sight and reload. At Fredericksburg the previous December Lee had stood on a bluff above the cannon-smashed town and watched as the Northern infantry marched up through the ruins toward the wall where Longstreet's men lay ready. The Rebel arms had sliced through them, but the Yankees had regrouped and come again, and again, and on his hilltop Lee had looked out at the spectacle, with its mixture of discipline and slaughter, and said to his staff that "It is well that war is so terrible—we should grow too fond of it." Now the situation was reversed; indeed, the waiting Union forces spoke of "giving" their enemies Fredericksburg, and not only with rifles. I stepped through a gap in the wall and turned to face the other way, back toward Seminary Ridge, with my hand resting on a cannon. Guns just like it would have been double-loaded with canister that day—tin cylinders filled with musket balls that ripped open as they left the muzzle, a shotgun four inches across.

The two lines here were at their closest point, and from where I stood there was a neatly mown way back to the other side, back to the grand equestrian monument that the state of Virginia had put up in 1917. I raised my binoculars and brought the statue into focus: forty feet high, with a representative group of soldiers in bronze around its base and Lee himself on a granite plinth above, mounted and bareheaded. In 1863 he had ridden forward from that spot to meet the defeated men who streamed back toward him. Longstreet was nearby as well, and Alexander, and a British observer who heard everything they said and wrote it up for the magazines. "All this will come right in the end," Lee told the soldiers retreating past him, and to his distraught generals he added that it was all his own fault. But for now "all good men must rally." Except they couldn't. The general ordered Pickett to reform his division in expectation of a Union advance and was interrupted as he spoke. *I have no division now.*

My own day would eventually take me back to my car in the Confederate wake, across that field and past Lee's statue and through the tour groups clustered around it. I had another stop first, though, and turned to the north, walking past more artillery batteries and a series of markers noting the position of the Union's different regiments; past other equestrian statues too, these to the victorious generals like the Yankee commander George Meade, or Winfield Scott Hancock, who to stiffen his troops had ridden slowly up and down the lines in full sight of the Rebel guns. I walked through a hundred yards of trees, then a parking lot full of out-of-state SUVs, past a bus stop, and out onto a busy road; crossed it, and went up a drive and into a cemetery where some months after the battle Abraham Lincoln had spoken for two minutes. Or two cemeteries, rather—the town's own, from which the ridge takes its name, and then adjacent to it the newly established grave-yard for Federal troops at whose dedication the president spoke. Nobody now knows just where he stood on that November day; nobody even knows where the speakers' platform was erected. Good arguments have been made for spots in either cemetery, but probably it doesn't much matter. What matters are the words, and two old myths about them have been conclusively demol-ished. One held that Lincoln had written his speech in the train on the way to town, even scribbling it down on the back of an envelope; the other that the address was little noted at the time. But the president had already put it through several drafts before he left Washington, and it was widely reported and discussed in the days after its delivery, before it was driven from the head-lines by the news of Grant's latest victory, at Chattanooga in Tennessee.

Nevertheless it *was* controversial, for it relied on what Garry Wills has called an act of "open-air sleight-of-hand," in which the crowd had an old political assumption lifted from its pocket and a new one slipped into its place. Wills argues that the speech remade America by redefining the pur-pose of the war. In his first sentence Lincoln insisted that at its founding the country had been "dedicated to the proposition that all men are cre-ated equal," and in his last line he resolved that the battle had been fought to ensure "a new birth of freedom." It appealed to the Declaration of Inde-pendence rather than to the imperfect Constitution and suggested that the restoration of the Union as it was would no longer be enough; the North now fought for emancipation, which had become something more than the "military measure" that the president had proclaimed at the start of that year. Of course, many of his listeners knew that already, or hoped for it; but in his own state of Illinois the Chicago *Times* attacked the speech as a "libel" on the Founding Fathers and a misstatement of the cause for "which our officers and soldiers gave their lives."

I think Wills overstates the light-fingered quality of Lincoln's words or perhaps mistakes its nature. The genius of the speech lies in its abstraction. His country may be "engaged in a great civil war," but he never names the sides; there is no reference at all to North or South, Union or Confederacy.

He does not, in fact, mention an enemy of any kind; it's almost if the struggle were with some disembodied and perhaps natural force. He says nothing about slavery, nor does he specify the war's causes and origins. The "unfinished work . . . the great task remaining before us" goes undefined, and so does the purpose for which the dead had given their "last full measure of devotion." Not that his audience needed to have those things spelled out—he told the North about the North, and in Wisconsin and New York alike they knew exactly what he meant. And yet there *is* something strange about his words, for in his very refusal to specify he seems also to be speaking to the country as it once was and would be again: the whole country, whose president he had been elected to be. The abstraction allows those splintered-off states to step back inside, and in the years and wars that followed, his statement of collective endeavor would come to embrace the erstwhile Confederacy as well.

So it seems to me now, when I read his words on the wall of the Lincoln Memorial, its stones quarried from every corner of this land. But the cemetery at Gettysburg itself says something very different. Something that gave a shock to my Yankee naiveté, so powerfully had those words cast their unifying spell. I walked past the graves of troops from Massachusetts and New Jersey, Minnesota and Vermont, and realized that I had made one of Renan's historical errors. I had forgotten to remember what was obvious then and should be still today. Lincoln spoke over the Union dead only. "The brave men . . . who struggled here" and whose blood has already consecrated its ground—those phrases referred only to those on the Federal side, the ones who died for Lincoln's own cause. None of the soldiers Faulkner imagines as standing "ready in the woods," none of the men who made that walk across the field, the ones for whom in his prose it was still not yet too late—none of them are here. For there are no Confederate corpses in Gettysburg's National Cemetery, and the Southern dead lay instead outside, in mass graves dug on the battlefield itself. Many of them were exhumed after the war and taken back to their home states. But for Lincoln's first audience they were that unmentionable enemy, and had no claim on the nation they had denied.

PART ONE

Twice-Told Tales

TWO

Old Man Falls

Maybe happen is never once. So Faulkner wrote in *Absalom, Absalom!*, and his world is, accordingly, one in which the past seems instantly and immediately available, not once but whenever you want it or even if you don't. That's what his characters think, anyway, and the idea of that recurrence doesn't stop with them—it's also an integral part of his approach to narrative itself. Most things that happen on his pages get told twice, three times, four, and never quite the same way. Sometimes he returns to the same story within a single novel, looking at it from different points of view, circling it, embroidering or enriching what had seemed at the start like a simple anecdote. *The Sound and the Fury* provides a good example, with four versions of the same family history: three in the first person, in the voices of Quentin Compson and his younger brothers, and the final one written in the third person and concentrating on the lives of the family's black servants. At other times, however, Faulkner might use a new book to go back to some old characters, revisiting a tale in one book that he had first developed in another. And I am going to tell one of those stories myself. It's one that he himself told twice, and in looking at that repetition, in threading it throughout this chapter, I'll take us deep within what Faulkner has to tell us about the Civil War: into the questions his characters ask about its causes and its memory; its consequences, conduct, and its permanence, too.

One of the first characters he invented for his mythical land was a Mississippi planter called John Sartoris. He appeared in *Flags in the Dust*, the initial book in the Yoknapatawpha cycle, and later in *The Unvanquished*; a dashing Confederate cavalry commander who is name-checked in a dozen other works as well. I say "appeared," but Faulkner set *Flags in the Dust* in 1919 and Sartoris has been dead for more than forty years by then—dead, and yet always present in the minds of his survivors and indeed in the memory of Yoknapatawpha County as a whole. Anyone in Jefferson you could tell his story. He came out from South Carolina as a young man in the 1840s, he bought land and slaves and built a house four miles north of the town's courthouse square; a widower with one son whom he christened Bayard, lifting the chivalric name out of Walter Scott. By 1861 he had become a power in the county and the state alike, and rich enough when secession came not only to organize and lead the region's first regiment of Confederate volunteers, but also to pay for it. He took his soldiers north, and there his fictional regiment became a part of Lee's Army of Northern Virginia.

The novelist imagined him as both courageous and competent, but Faulkner also made him arrogant, a man quick to let other people know what he thought of them. Volunteer regiments on both sides of the war elected their own officers; Sartoris had quickly grown unpopular, and in 1862 was voted out of his colonelcy and took himself back home. This time he raised a body of irregular cavalry and kept it out west. His men would form up for a raid and then disappear back to their farms, not fighting so much as stealing horses and nipping at the edges of General Grant's advancing army, as the Yankees tried to figure out the best way to take the riverfront citadel of Vicksburg. Sartoris made himself a nuisance, with a price on his head, and after one such raid he began to argue with his best horse thief, Zeb Fothergill, about the merits of the last mount they'd lifted from the Union army. And so they decided to race. There was a bridge a mile ahead, on the far side of a rise, and the two men left the rest of the troop behind and lit out, neck and neck at first and out of sight in a moment. The soldiers could see their dust in the distance, however, and after a bit they saw two separate patches of it and knew that the Colonel was going to win. Then he disappeared, dropping down to the river, and when his soldiers caught up they found he had captured a whole company of Union cavalry all by himself.

Here's how it happened. The Colonel came up over the crest and was in the middle of an enemy camp before he even saw it, riding down between the cookfires where the soldiers were gathered, with their horses picketed and their stacked rifles a dozen yards away. There was no time to turn back, but he probably wouldn't have even if there were; and the Federals were just as startled as he was. So Sartoris pulled his pistols and started to yell, telling his troops who hadn't yet arrived to surround the Yankees in front of him, threatening to shoot anyone who moved while continuing to move himself, pacing his horse through the fires and spreading as much confusion as he could. Then Fothergill rode up, and a few minutes later the rest of Sartoris's band. Still, there were too many prisoners to handle, too many to march off to a Confederate stockade. Instead, the Colonel's men held the disarmed Yankees close all day and when night fell put a guard on the horses, while pretending to watch over the Union troops as well; trying not to laugh as Sartoris allowed them in ones and twos to slip off into the dark.

That story—that version of the story—can be found in a novel that itself exists in two versions, one that Faulkner wrote as *Flags in the Dust* and then published in a much abbreviated form as *Sartoris*; the novel appeared in its original form only in 1973, a decade after the novelist's death. I'll have more to say about it later, in considering the origins of Faulkner's "postage stamp" of ground, but for the moment I'll stick with the story, or rather with the way the story is told. John Sartoris might loom over its every page, but *Flags in the Dust* is not precisely a Civil War novel. Faulkner splits its interest between two of the Colonel's descendants, each named Bayard. One is the Colonel's son, a banker and now himself an old man; the other is the banker's grandson. Young Bayard has newly returned from France, having flown World War I fighter planes in an international squadron, and in peacetime has found nothing more or better to do than drive fast and drunk over Yoknapatawpha's bumpy roads, trying to kiss the wheels of the wagons he passes.

So *Flags in the Dust* is at once a Lost Cause and a Lost Generation novel, in which the seeming purpose and heroism of the Confederate past squats over an apparently meaningless present. Yet how much, really, does that past have to offer? The story of the Colonel's great deed comes to us through the mouth of his last surviving trooper. Old Man Falls is an object of Bayard's— old Bayard's—charity, who every few months comes visiting, fetching the "odor ... [and] spirit of the dead man into that room where the dead man's son sat." The banker is always good for some tobacco and a bit of cash, and he also provides a reliable audience for the stories that the soldier doesn't so much tell as tell over, stories forever retold and repeated. Late in the novel the old man calls up the tale of the horse race once more, reliving those "gallant, pinch-bellied days," but this time Bayard has a question. He shakes the ash from his cigar and asks, "What the devil were you folks fighting about, anyhow?"

The second version of the Yankees' capture comes in *The Unvanquished*, and it's told to us in the first person by Bayard Sartoris himself: Bayard as a boy, living with his grandmother and their slaves on the family plantation while his father is off at the war. The anecdote appears in the volume's second story, "Retreat," but there's no race this time. A series of accidents allows the boy to join up with his father's troop, and he's riding at the Colonel's side when Sartoris decides to let his own horse have his head and run. The stallion shoots out ahead "exactly like I have seen a hawk come out of a sage field and rise over a fence." Again there's the lip of a hill, and the boy in pursuit sees his father's mount appear to pause in mid-stride on its very brow, the Colonel standing in the stirrups and waving his hat in the air. Then Bayard too is over the top and coming down toward the river and the bridge and the Union troops below, with Sartoris snapping his pistols and yelling to his absent men to surround them.

To the boy the whole episode seems impossible to accept, too incredible for his mind to take in: that moment when their horses seemed to stop, and to float for a heartbeat "in a dimension without time," as though the scene were "beneath rather than before us... the muskets all stacked carefully and neatly and nobody within fifty feet of them; and the men, the faces, the blue Yankee coats and pants and boots," sixty soldiers caught by a lot of noise. Soon the rest of Sartoris's troop come piling over the hill, looking every bit as surprised as the enemy, and the rest of the anecdote goes very much like the version in *Flags in the Dust*. It's a nice bit of professional writing, magazine writing, but as such it's also highly conventional. The gullible Yankees get fooled by the clever Rebel underdog, a kind of joke in which nobody gets hurt and the larger issues of the war are held at arm's length.

Conventional—because to Faulkner's audience the Colonel's brand of audacity and luck was already familiar, not only from fifty years' worth of popular fiction, but also from the library of Confederate memoirs and biographies. The Virginian John Singleton Mosby spent the later years of the war leading an independent partisan band rather like Sartoris's own, but in June 1862 he served as a scout for J. E. B. Stuart on the latter's famous ride around the entirety of the enormous Army of the Potomac. The Union forces were within an easy strike of Richmond; Stuart's exploit confused their commanders and brought Lee the intelligence he needed to fight them. In the memoirs he wrote in old age, Mosby includes a newspaper clipping of the period that describes his solo capture of a wagonload of stores. Then a bugle call told him that a Yankee company was moving on his new treasure; he charged while shouting to his "imaginary men to follow," and the Federals broke. And in the West, the Tennessee cavalry commander Nathan Bedford Forrest managed at least once to bluff a much larger force into surrender; while in a nighttime raid one of his lieutenants scattered a Yankee camp by having each of his sergeants call out commands as if to a company as they rode through the campfires.

Faulkner knew these tales, or ones like them. After the war Forrest became a founder of the Ku Klux Klan. But an exculpatory account of the general by the Agrarian Andrew Nelson Lytle appeared in 1929, the same year as *Sartoris*, and the novelist always presented Forrest as a figure out of legend, the trickster who was said to have once ridden his horse through the lobby of the Gayoso Hotel in Memphis. In writing of John Sartoris, Faulkner drew on a well-established set of literary formulae, on his mastery of both Confederate legend and the rhetoric of commercial fiction alike. That's what made his stories acceptable to the *Saturday Evening Post* in the first place, and though he spoke contemptuously of such potboiling work, he could when necessary summon the conviction to make an honest job of it.

Old Bayard will listen to Will Falls throughout *Flags in the Dust*. He will look at a pair of his father's old boots and remember the time the Colonel was surprised by a squadron of Union cavalry on his own front porch and got away by affecting a limp and pretending to be an idiot. He will hear once more about that horse race, and the capture of that Yankee company, and will ask his question. *What the devil were you folks fighting about?* And the

answer Old Man Falls gives him will have a long echo. "Be damned ef I ever
did know."

———— • ————

To ask what those folks were fighting about isn't quite the same as asking why they fought or what they fought for. I think we can recognize that
the Union and the Confederacy had a very different understanding of what
the war was over. Anyone meditating over it needs to distinguish between its
causes, its purpose, and its meaning, and also needs to acknowledge that our
sense of those things has inevitably depended on our own historical location.
Still, Bayard's phrasing is open-ended enough to suggest all that, especially in
the way it touches on the war's origins. It points toward both its fundamental
cause—the slave interest that, in Lincoln's words, was somehow behind it
all—as well as the complex of both local and ideological allegiances that led
people without much interest in that interest to join the Confederate side.
And the answer he gets from Old Man Falls will point in several directions
as well.

On the one hand, that answer comes from the ground level, the private's
view of the war—damned if I know, ours not to reason why. Yet as the archi-
val work of James M. McPherson and Chandra Manning has shown, most
Civil War soldiers had a quite precise understanding of what they were fighting about, even if that understanding differed widely from soldier to soldier
and changed as the war itself changed. At the time few of them expressed
anything like Will Falls's uncertainty. Instead, an Alabama private wrote in
1861 to his wife that without the whole Northern "set of Psalm singing" abolitionists, he would "never have been soldiering," while in the same year an
Iowa sergeant noted in his diary that the slave owners had started the war "to
secure the extension of that blighting curse." Each side blamed the other, and
each imagined they fought for liberty. But they defined that liberty in radically different terms. Northern troops emphasized its universality; Southerners tended to see it as a question of their own individual rights, including an
unfettered right to property. But the South had another motivation as well,
and many of its soldiers seemed also to fight out of fear: fear of a future, as a
lieutenant from Louisiana wrote in 1864, with "all of our property confis-

cated . . . [and] our slaves stationed in every town with guns in their hands." For such a writer the war had moved beyond its original motive and bearing; what he saw as the Union invasion of his homeland had made the fight more purely and simply a defensive one.

But there's another way to hear Old Man Falls's response. It's that whatever he once believed no longer seems an adequate explanation for so astounding a period, that the war's meaning now seems occluded or forgotten. Some former Confederates wrote their memoirs with a sense of incredulity at their own actions. The Gettysburg artillery commander Edward Porter Alexander has moments like that in his *Fighting for the Confederacy*. He had a long and prosperous postwar life and the honesty to admit his relief that, when all the battles were over, he was still alive to enjoy himself. The Louisiana-born Supreme Court justice, Edward Douglass White, took a larger view. In his teens he had been both a Rebel officer and a Yankee prisoner, and while he remained a white supremacist he also came to believe that secession had been a catastrophe. In old age and with the United States now a world power, he was heard to mutter, with horror, "My God, if we had succeeded." Madness, and petrifying, and impossible to believe: how could one have ever even thought of it?

What were you fighting about? They fought, as individuals, for all the reasons that men do fight: because they were afraid not to, because their friends were going, or they needed a job, or they wanted to impress a lover or to get away from one. Some fought to protect their own homes, or perhaps to preserve their economic interests; to prove themselves, or from conviction, or maybe because fighting looked better than farming. Some enjoyed violence, others the rush and speed of a gallop. In a letter of September 1863 William Tecumseh Sherman assessed the people he faced along the Mississippi, and singled out a particular class of young men as "the most dangerous set . . . this war has turned loose upon the world . . . splendid riders, shots, and utterly reckless." They didn't care about slavery, or land, or anything much except horses; they hated Yankees, but didn't otherwise bother with the questions of cause or consequence; their very heedlessness made them deadly. And Faulkner himself created such a character in *Flags in the Dust*, a figure known as Carolina Bayard, the Colonel's blue-eyed younger brother, who goes to war in a "spirit of pure fun" and has no "political convictions" whatever. Sherman thought such men would all have to be killed; and Faulkner's character accordingly gets himself shot one day in Virginia, riding into a Union commissary in search of a bottle of anchovies.

They fought for every reason imaginable. But let's stick with a few of the political justifications for that irrepressible conflict. Nowadays we think we know what they were at bottom fighting about, just as anyone reading the secession debates of 1860 and 1861 must recognize that they thought they knew then. South Carolina was the first state to secede, just six weeks after Lincoln's election, when on December 20, 1860, a convention called for the purpose voted unanimously to sever its ties with the Union. A purely sectional party had gotten its leader elected to the nation's presidency: a party, they said, that represented only that portion of the country which denied any right to property in slaves; and a man who dared to hope that slavery itself might someday stand in the course of ultimate extinction. The new president had always claimed that he had no desire "to interfere with the institution" in the states where it already existed. But few Southerners believed him, and they were probably right not to.

Mississippi was the second to leave, on January 9, 1861. The brief ordinance with which it did so is drily legalistic and offers no reason for the state's decision. But the public "declaration"—the word is deliberate—with which its secession convention explained itself is considerably more pungent: "Our position is thoroughly identified with the institution of slavery—the greatest material interest of the world.... [A] blow at slavery is a blow at commerce and civilization." Like South Carolina, the state argued that a force hostile to that institution had now taken control of the government; its "unhallowed schemes" had destroyed any chance that the two sections might live together in peace. And in Georgia that March, as we have already seen, Alexander Stephens announced that the "Corner-stone" of any secessionist polity rested "upon the great truth, that the negro is not equal to the white man; that slavery—subordination to the superior race—is his natural and normal condition." Stephens suggested that the men who framed the Federal Constitution had fudged on that; they thought slavery was probably wrong, but "knew not well" what to do about it. The seceding states knew better. He saw slavery as a positive good, and the South's new constitution would put to rest any quarrelsome questions about it by stating that no "law denying or impairing the right of property in negro slaves shall be passed."

Not every Southern state was so quick. Virginia called a secession convention that January, but its first vote on the issue failed by a two-to-one margin. Then in April, and with all South Carolina watching, an old firebreather named Edmund Ruffin touched off a cannon aimed at Fort Sumter, a few miles offshore in Charleston's harbor. Secession itself was not yet war, and the South had professed a desire to go in peace, even as it formed an army and seized the Federal installations and arsenals on its soil. Sumter had only a symbolic importance, but the lightly garrisoned fortress had long refused a demand to surrender, and shelling it seemed at first as much a piece of political theater as an act of war. The cannonade lasted for two days. Then Sumter took down its flag, and the war came. Lincoln called for 75,000 troops to suppress the rebellion. They would have to march south through Virginia on their way to battle, and that in itself made the Commonwealth reverse its vote. Refusing to serve as a staging-area for an attack on the other slave states, Virginia seceded on April 17, 1861, just three days after Sumter fell.

The Confederacy had hoped for and probably needed the Old Dominion to join it. In population the state was the region's largest; the mills and ironworks of Richmond made it one of the few with an industrial base; and its prestige as the cradle of the Founding Fathers would help legitimize the new nation. Several of the other Southern states had therefore sent "secession commissioners" to the Virginia convention, men whose job was to explain their position and make the case for sharing it. Indeed, such ambassadors were common throughout the South; Mississippi, Alabama, and South Carolina all sent them to each other. What they said at the time provides the most reliable index we have of Southern sentiment about the causes of the impending storm; that is, what they said at home, rather than to their Northern neighbors, or in the years that followed. So in Richmond the Mississippian Fulton Anderson equated abolition with the "degradation of the Southern people" and urged Virginia to resist its "infidel fanaticism." Outside interference with the peculiar institution threatened to destroy the Southern economy; most of the region's capital was invested in human property, and that property secured its debts. That interference stood moreover as an insult, and not only to the owners of people. For as the journalist J. D. B. DeBow wrote in December 1860, even the South's non-slaveholders still had *the status of the white man.*

Mississippi's commissioner to Georgia thought abolition would lead inevitably to "civil, social, and political equality with the negro race" and claimed that he would rather see every white woman and child dead rather than subject to that defilement. *What the devil were you folks fighting about?* That's not a question those commissioners would have thought to ask. They simply believed that they knew. You don't question an inevitability or argue with an earthquake, and to them secession and war were as much a natural event as a political one, however much they might have to explain or justify it. Bayard's question belongs to the 1920s and not to 1861. It's Faulkner's question; John Sartoris may know what he's fighting about, but the creator who gave him that confidence isn't nearly so sure.

And meanwhile the North had its own story to tell. Many people in New York and Pennsylvania, Ohio and Indiana, thought at the start that it might be enough to restore the Union as it was: to bracket, for the moment, all the many years of argument over runaway slaves and the extension of servitude into the new territories of the West. Put secession down; and then take those issues up once more. Only a minority believed as yet in ending slavery entirely, and in consequence some abolitionists weren't sure that the war was worth fighting—not for such a limited goal. Then mounting casualties forced the realization that the fight for the Union must also become a fight for abolition itself. The cause of the quarrel must be done away with, lest it start all over again; and the Emancipation Proclamation gave the North a new sense of conviction, a belief that it was fighting *for* something, rather than simply *against* it. Still, it's the South's story that matters more here. Its actions lit the match, and the explanation of the war's origins in which most of us believe today matches the one that many of its own leaders gave at the time. The Civil War was not fought to end slavery, not at first. But it was fought to preserve it.

That wasn't the only narrative the region had to offer, however, and even as it pointed to slavery's motive force, South Carolina also provided another explanation for secession, one with deep roots in the nation's political life. The doctrine of states' rights held that the Federal Constitution had been a compact between sovereign powers: they might have joined together for the common good, but each state nevertheless preserved its independent existence and "separate control over its own institutions." It was none of Washington's business if an individual state wanted to hold some portion of its people in bondage. Pushed to an extreme, this theory held that a state had the right to nullify any Federal law it believed unconstitutional; and if it thought that Federal actions were a tyrannical infringement on its liberty, it had the right to leave that compact, the right to secede. South Carolina had in fact threatened to secede before, over the tariff—tax policy—in the early 1830s; the threats faded when President Andrew Jackson ordered warships into Charleston's harbor. Still, the rhetoric of states' rights stretched back into the early days of the Republic. Even Vermont had appealed to it, in refusing to enforce the Fugitive Slave Act, and it would continue to be invoked throughout the South long after the war's end had settled the question of secession.

Not all Southern leaders accepted the most radical forms of that doctrine. Robert E. Lee was still a member of the United States Army in January 1861, when he wrote to one of his sons that the North's actions had indeed given the South a legitimate sense of grievance. He would do anything necessary for redress—and yet thought it "idle to talk of secession" as if the Constitution allowed it. The proper word was "revolution." States' rights were, however, the ground on which the Confederacy's president, Jefferson Davis of Mississippi, staked the argument of his inaugural address. The new federation illustrated "the American idea that governments rest on the consent of the governed." Davis had been a congressman and a senator; he had led a regiment in the Mexican-American War and in the 1850s had served in the cabinet as secretary of war. He had a reputation for honesty, and many Southerners believed him when he said that Lincoln's administration was a perversion of the principles for which the nation had once stood. In consequence, some of its "sovereign States" had formed a new union, one determined to stand against the aggression of the other. He hoped to avoid a war, but if it came he did not expect any "considerable diminution in the production of the staples which have constituted our exports." Davis's prose is always sententious, loose and clogged at once; he has none of Lincoln's pith or vigor. Still, he makes his case, and another of his claims would endure in the popular mind as well, whatever its truth: the Northeast was a "manufacturing or navigating community," but the South belonged to an "agricultural people."

In practice, the only states' right anybody was willing to kill or perhaps die for was the one on which the white man's wealth and status depended, the right to hold slaves. Davis himself ran a plantation just south of Vicksburg called Brierfield. There were some two hundred enslaved people upon it, but the place was dwarfed by his brother Joseph's neighboring property. They were among the state's wealthiest citizens, and yet Davis never spoke of slavery as the war's cause. An 1864 editorial in the *Richmond Examiner* quotes his claim that "We are not fighting for slavery; we are fighting for independence," and the paper itself argued that while slavery had provided the war's immediate "occasion," it was not in itself the cause. This simply begs the question. Was there some other purpose for which that independence was needed? Why had this issue, and no other, provided an occasion? Lee at least was honest about the South's purpose, but high-minded statements of principle are almost always a mask for self-interest, and the *Examiner*'s language became standard in the years that followed. Davis used it in his own two-volume history of the war, writing in 1881 that to "whatever extent the question of slavery might have served as an *occasion*, it was far from the *cause* of the conflict." Alexander Stephens argued in his own memoirs that the institution had simply given secession its best opportunity. The war had really been fought to preserve the original principles of the Federal Constitution, and Stephens went so far as to claim that he had been misquoted in his "Corner-stone" speech.

The *Examiner*'s column was probably written by the paper's editor, Edward A. Pollard, who in 1866 determined the course of Confederate historiography with a book called *The Lost Cause: A New Southern History of the War of the Confederates*. Few now read its 700 pages; everyone knows its title. It stands as a proper name, shorthand for the antebellum South, the war itself, and also for the whole complex of attitudes with which they were regarded, the years of mingled nostalgia and mourning that followed. Faulkner himself uses the phrase in *The Unvanquished*. Bayard's grandmother, Rosa Millard, invokes it even before the war is over, calling the Confederacy "a holy cause, even [if] ... a lost cause"; the indefinite article suggests that she isn't quoting anything but has found that language on her own, a description but not yet an ideology. And the mythology that Pollard's title summons would shape the Southern understanding of the war for many decades to follow. The United Confederate Veterans insisted that the South's surrender "in no way ... established the wrong of the cause for which they fought," and in 1897, the year of Faulkner's own birth, they demanded schoolbooks that would present such truths to their children. Twenty years later there were calls to reject any text that suggested the South had fought for slavery. Few people by then were willing to admit that their ancestors had killed to defend a defunct and irretrievable system. The twentieth century required some more seemingly principled justification, and in consequence states' rights assumed a greater if retrospective importance, one that also fit the goals and methods of Jim Crow.

Faulkner had been assigned such textbooks as a boy, and his work acknowledges the pull, in his time, of the rhetoric of the Lost Cause, with Colonel Sartoris on his horse and Gavin Stevens thinking of Gettysburg at not yet two. But the novelist also and more consistently evokes its frozen enraged futility, the dead still air around Rosa Coldfield in *Absalom, Absalom!*, thus dramatizing his own quarrel with a past from which he can never quite escape. What were you folks fighting about—or maybe fighting with? For Faulkner does fight *with*, fights with memory above all, and one way to understand him is to consider an argument that Robert Penn Warren made in *The Legacy of the Civil War* (1961), when his standing as a voice of the South stood second only to Faulkner's own. Warren claimed that at the moment of its death "the Confederacy entered into its immortality." It died young, and its very brevity had forever fixed its image. It was a ghost, and unalterable, it was for the white South the sense of loss itself, and it could not be put in its place, put away as though it were over and done with. Which is, of course, what most historians try to do, and what Faulkner himself could not. His past is never past. He remembers what his world believes it has lost. Yet he also remembers what it did, and in a way that makes him a more reliable guide to the period than were many historians of his day.

Today we explain the war in terms that match those used in 1860 and

1861, but that hasn't always been the case, and I've already noted that the years of Faulkner's own great books were a particularly muddy time in our understanding of that conflict. Leave aside the certainties of Confederate hagiography, with their celebration of Southern gallantry and dash, the virtue of Lee and the genius of General Thomas "Stonewall" Jackson. The question many readers of those volumes had to face was how the South could have lost in the first place, and indeed one myth held that it hadn't. Southern armies had not been beaten on the battlefield; they had simply, in the words of Lee's last message to his troops, "been compelled to yield to overwhelming numbers and resources." But even a reader of less clearly partisan books might have shared Bayard's sense of bafflement.

Let me go back, for example, to the work of Charles A. Beard, whom I mentioned in my last chapter. He was one of the most influential American historians of Faulkner's day, a scholar who argued that ideas, events, and individual actions were but the foam on history's current, and largely irrelevant to its flow. What counted for him were the largest and most impersonal of forces, economic forces above all, as if he were a latter-day naturalist, the social sciences' equivalent of Emile Zola or Theodore Dreiser. In 1927 he published the best-selling *Rise of American Civilization*, co-written with his wife Mary. Slavery mattered little to them, for they saw events from such a distance as to make it but one of several systems of labor. Nor did states' rights. Jefferson Davis would have agreed with the Beards that the war had pitted the "capitalists, laborers, and farmers of the North" against the South's "planting aristocracy." But no one at the time would have shared their belief that "the fighting was a fleeting incident," that it simply sped the inevitable mechanism through which one group replaced another at the center of the nation's power. The "revisionist" historian Avery Craven, in contrast, saw nothing inevitable about it at all, arguing in *The Repressible Conflict* that the actual war was the product of a temporary hysteria, and need not have happened. Democracy's safety valves had failed. Lincoln didn't have the experience a president needed to steer through the first months of the crisis; he made too many blunders, and the abolitionists were such fanatics. If they hadn't pushed so—if the people involved had been utterly different—everything could have been adjusted or finessed. Leaving us with what?

The Beards gave no place to human agency or contingency; Craven too much. Still, they chime with each other in underplaying the role of slavery itself, as if embarrassed that so venal a system could have produced such destruction. Craven even argued that the enslaved did not suffer from slavery per se; their oppression grew, rather, from their employment in a plantation system that remained somehow separable from the institution itself. Those arguments suggest that the participants' own actions and beliefs, their understanding not only of events but also of their own lives, were at once misguided and irrelevant. Such views condescend not simply to the enslaved, but to anyone who lived through those years; and in that, they seem no more certain what all the shooting was about than Old Man Falls himself. Yet there were other issues too that might have left Faulkner's people confused, other questions about the past that would have made the war's meaning seem less clear in 1920 than it was in either 1860 or today. Let me name just two of them, with the promise that I'll come back to each in my later chapters.

The first is Reconstruction or rather its eventual failure, its failure to reshape the social landscape of the former Confederacy as fully as many had hoped. In some ways the dozen years of the Reconstruction era seemed to run the war and its aftermath into one, because the fighting wasn't over when it was over. Emancipation so provoked some areas of the South as to lead to the mass murder of black people on a scale unknown in the antebellum period, when human beings had a cash value; to pogroms that were excused with the term "race riot," as if the violence had been spontaneous and on all sides. In 1870 black men gained the right to vote, one ensured in theory by the all-too-fitful presence of Federal soldiers. The freedmen's political participation was often violently suppressed, however, and by 1877 the troops were gone, the postwar Republican governors had left office, and each state had been "redeemed," with white supremacists and old Confederates again taking power. The voter rolls were not purged at once, but they were purged, and the region's African-American citizens lost most of their new gains in property and civil rights alike. The region had fought off the equality that Mississippi's secession commissioners so feared, as Faulkner himself would show in the last stories of *The Unvanquished*. Many parts of the South were still desperately poor, and its new governments still had their enemies in the North and at home, but on its own territory the white South had in some sense won.

Each section blamed the slaughter on the other, and in many ways the hatred of the postwar years surpassed that of the fighting itself. But they had to learn to live together, and the price of comity was the Federal willingness to bring Reconstruction to a halt. So my second bit of dissonance lies in the rhetoric of reconciliation itself. For one of the ways in which the nation came to function was by agreeing that the troops on both sides had been brave, that the Blue and the Gray had each fought for causes in which they sincerely believed. In time that agreement established so marked a moral equivalence between the two sides that even an old trooper might wonder why so much death had been necessary; perhaps it had indeed been an accident. Of course, not everyone accepted that equivocation. No former slave could, no veteran of the United States Colored Troops, nor indeed anyone who stood at the edge of Boston Common and really looked at the sculptor Augustus Saint-Gaudens's memorial to the Fifty-Fourth Massachusetts, the war's most famous black regiment. Nevertheless, "the most vigorous advocates of reconciliation believed," as the historian David Blight has written, that for harmony's sake "they had to banish slavery and race from the discussion." They had to separate the war from its causes and indeed from its consequences. Reunion required amnesia. *Damned ef I ever did know.*

FAULKNER TOLD THIS STORY twice—the fast horse and the Colonel's bold gamble, the little rise before the stream, the impotent Yankees on the other side. The prisoners crawling off in the night. One version takes the form of an old man's memory, a legend that is perhaps distorted by time and the telling. The other offers a participant's second-by-second account, a boy's wide-eyed amazement at the deeds of his heroic father. The old man says that it happened on "as putty a summer mawnin' as you ever see," and for Bayard too it takes place in some eternal summer, when the Union army isn't yet an everyday presence in northern Mississippi and the war is not yet lost. But neither account can be dated with any precision or graphed onto the actual events of the war. The date doesn't really matter, and yet there is one sense in which the question of time matters profoundly. Old Man Falls tells his story in 1919 in a novel published in 1929; young Bayard's adventure is set in the early 1860s in a book published in 1938. The first version of the tale comes last. Or maybe the second one is earlier, set earlier anyway, and putting these two books together gives us the kind of temporal disjunction, so familiar from the rest of Faulkner's work, when one moment seems to fall into another, and the future knocks the bottom from the past.

The Unvanquished doesn't ask the inconvenient question that old Bayard puts to Will Falls; for the boy, the war is simply the setting of his childhood, and he has neither sought an explanation for it nor needs one. Yet most readers today *will* question—and be troubled by—the role played in this scene by Bayard's best friend, a black boy exactly his own age called Ringo; a friend who is also one of the Sartoris family slaves. The two of them have "fed at the same breast and had slept together and eaten together for so long that Ringo called Granny 'Granny' just like I did," so close that Bayard can no longer quite tell where one of them leaves off and the other begins; he even believes they've reached a point where he's no longer white and Ringo no longer black. But the book itself always remembers. Most of Ringo's speech is presented phonetically, as Bayard's isn't, and his role in this particular story is largely comic. He too is riding along with the Colonel when they encounter the Yankees, but his half-blind horse goes crashing off through the trees, and Bayard can hear him "hollering and moaning and hollering" the whole time that they're taking the soldiers' surrender.

Faulkner's model here lies in the work of the Virginian Thomas Nelson Page, who in the late nineteenth century found a ready audience, in New York's *Century* magazine and elsewhere, for a series of sad sweet tales about the Old South, apologias for a world made palatable by the presence of contented black folk. Page's stories pushed the business of reconciliation by suggesting that Reconstruction itself had been unnecessary. His South is a place without masters, for the whites who represented the old order have either died or left the land, while his black characters have remained, as if bound to it still, living on in uncertainty and loss and testifying, in dialect, to the grace and rectitude of the antebellum world. For "Dem wuz good ole times." *Their* fictional masters were always kind, and are missed by the new freedmen who recall them for us. Page's minstrelsy set the pattern for what became known as "plantation" fiction, with stock characters like the faithful Mammy and the loyal "servant." Such figures were familiar presences in the folklore of Faulkner's childhood, and in the second half of the 1930s *Gone with the Wind* would do its awful best to keep those characters current, presenting them as big-hearted, touching, and faintly absurd. Faulkner's own work both follows and breaks that pattern. Ringo's commitment to the Sartoris family and through them to the Confederacy seems total, but the Colonel also claims that Ringo is smarter than his own son. He has the head for business and the ambition that Bayard lacks, and we will later see that Faulkner gives him the book's shrewdest comments on the questions of race and Reconstruction. Nevertheless, he begins as a type and can grow past it only by disappearing from Yoknapatawpha itself, from a world that would have no place for an intelligent and resourceful black man. In *Flags in the Dust* he does not even figure in Old Bayard's memory.

Flags in the Dust and *The Unvanquished* offer between them two different and in some ways incompatible versions of a single cavalry encounter. I could explain those differences away by noting what Faulkner wrote in a prefatory note to *The Mansion* (1959): he's fully aware of the discrepancies between that late book and the earlier incidents from which it grows, and he wants us to take them as a mark of life, a sign that the characters have gone on developing in his mind. He's now lived with them longer and knows them better than when they first showed up in his pages. So in returning to the Sartoris family and thinking through the white boy's Civil War childhood, Faulkner saw that he would need a companion, someone with whom to get in trouble; and it was both historically probable and thematically useful for that other boy to be black. But that note to *The Mansion* won't quite cover the Colonel's exploit; it doesn't explain the variations in Faulkner's two accounts of it. He presents the same essential action from different though equally admiring points of view, and yet we don't go more deeply into the Colonel as we move from book to book. Each version has its own emphasis, but we don't learn more about its protagonist from Bayard than we do from Old Man Falls. Instead Faulkner offers us an incident, an anecdote, and above all an image: John Sartoris poised on top of the hill and deciding in something less than an instant just how he will brazen it out. It's just—just!—that the novelist himself has different ways to tell the story, different versions of the same myth, as though derived from different sources. Yet they are both valid, and so would a third one be if he had ever decided to write it: a frozen moment of rather mischievous heroism that he can summon at will, that's available whenever and for whatever purpose he wants it, or needs it.

What can Faulkner tell us about the Civil War? How does our sense of the one inform our understanding of the other? We've already found that his questions, his characters' questions, can make us ask our own; Bayard's conversation with Old Man Falls is only one example. We will have others, and moments too when the issues he skips over or takes for granted, like Ringo, will open a seam in our understanding. Yet let me put dates and documents aside for a moment and stick with the fiction. Sartoris sits his horse on top of that hill, he sits it twice because happen is never once. Things return, continue, repeat, and need to be told and told again and yet again. The Confederacy is forever lost, and present, and maybe the biggest thing of all that Faulkner can show us about the war, or that the war can show us about him, is the fact of that recurrence itself.

THREE

The Family and the Town

Ripley, Mississippi, sits an hour's drive to the northeast of Oxford, a county seat just big enough for a Walmart and a hospital. It has a checkerboard center of regular blocks and two-story buildings, with wide streets and a courthouse square, but there are more parking places than customers for the few shops still open, and I didn't see a spot for a coffee or even a Coke when I drove through one July afternoon. A hot afternoon—I suppose I could call it that, but it wasn't, not for there, low nineties only, not even enough to make the air shimmer. I went past a line of storefront law offices and made a few turns, feeling my way and keeping an eye out for the railroad tracks, knowing that they would eventually take me where I wanted to go. Then at last I saw the sign for Cemetery Street and bumped over the rails, with a Pizza Hut off to my right, and rolled into the town's bleak and treeless graveyard. The grass was burned brown, and dusty, except in one small plot, fenced with wrought iron, where everything still glowed green. Family graves, and low to the ground, all but the one in its center, the one I'd come to see: a statue atop a pedestal, and more than twenty feet high from the ground to the top of its subject's balding head. There was a Confederate flag stuck in the ground before it, and a single word, in raised capitals, on its plinth: "FALKNER."

William Falkner, the ancestor for whom the novelist would be named; he added the "u" as a twenty-year-old, in a gesture of independence. Colonel William Falkner, on whom his great-grandson would model John Sartoris; modeling him so closely, in fact, that in some ways the fiction can serve as a guide to reality. I knew the tracks would bring me to his monument, and I knew it because in *Flags in the Dust* Sartoris's own statue gazes toward the railroad he built to connect Jefferson to the world outside; a frock-coated figure, looking even in death at the thing he'd made. So it is here. William Falkner built a railroad of his own and called it the Gulf & Chicago, a grandiose name for what was little more than a local line. He used convict labor to lay the tracks in the years after the Civil War, and today his effigy stares out to the place where the trains still run. Falkner had planned that monument long before he was shot down on a Ripley street by a former business partner. The novelist would give his character the same fate, in *The Unvanquished*'s last chapter, and to understand the country that the second William Faulkner called into being we need to know something about the place and the people he came from, beginning with the man that the family called the Old Colonel.

He was the first Falkner in Mississippi, and grew up poor in Tennessee and Missouri before arriving, in his teens, on what was still almost the frontier. Somehow he learned enough law to make himself a creditable attorney, but he also found more sensational ways to make money: in 1845, when he was twenty, he took down a murderer's jailhouse confession, had it printed, and sold it beneath the gallows. By 1850 he owned five slaves and a house in Ripley, the seat of Tippah County, and he did a varied business, buying and selling both land and people in addition to his legal practice. Yet Falkner was a townsman, not a planter. His slaves weren't field hands but either household servants or merchandise, though that didn't keep him from asserting the planter's usual privilege. In 1858 he took an enslaved woman named Emeline as collateral for a loan, and he was probably the father of the girl to whom she gave birth a few years later.

Certainly the child bore his name—Fannie Falkner—and such "shadow families" would provide a recurring theme in his great-grandson's fiction. *Go Down, Moses* (1942) is the chief example, but a short story set in the 1920s, "There Was a Queen" (1933), tells us that the longtime Sartoris housekeeper, Elnora, is also Bayard's half sister, "though possibly but not probably neither of them knew it." The hedged phrasing suggests the novelist's likely awareness of his own mixed-race cousins, even as its double negatives preserve a plausible deniability. Faulkner must have known the kitchen gossip—known its probable truth—and yet knowledge is one thing and recognition another.

Some of the white families in the fictional Yoknapatawpha do acknowledge their "black" relatives; they admit to the link even if they won't sit down at the same table. Faulkner's did not. He wrote of such connections but neither he nor his parents lived them. Fannie Falkner graduated from the newly founded Rust College in Holly Springs, an hour's drive to the north of Oxford, and married a man who became a college president. Yet each passing decade made that side of the past ever easier to ignore, and in the twentieth century there does not appear to have been any contact at all between the two branches of the Old Colonel's family. Which doesn't mean that the novelist didn't think or wonder about that parallel line of descent. His parents or grandparents might never have had somebody like Elnora at work in the house, but he was always drawn to the outer edge of the sayable, the stories nobody quite wants to tell or to hear, and his own family's history may suggest one reason why.

William Falkner was respected and feared in Ripley, but he was not much liked. His neighbors described him as a man whose "Bowie Knife and Pistols are constantly about his person," and he used them, killing two other men in arguments and then talking his way out of the consequences. Still, he took the lead when the war came. Ripley's population stood then at just under seven hundred. Falkner helped organize its young men into a militia company called the Magnolia Rifles, and got himself voted colonel of the regiment to which it was assigned. The Second Mississippi went north to Virginia, and in July 1861 they stood well at the first battle of Bull Run, with his men taking four guns from a Yankee battery. He hoped his success would lead to a brigadier's star, but he was never popular with his men and lost his post the next spring, at the annual election of officers. Lacking a command, Falkner rode back to Mississippi and formed a unit of irregular cavalry. At the start, his Partisan Rangers had about six hundred men, but their numbers quickly fell, and at this point the history and the fictional legend diverge. The Old Colonel never captured a company of Union cavalry on his own, and though Sartoris serves until the end of the war, Falkner resigned his commission in 1863 on the grounds of ill health. Then for a time he vanished, and a biographer speculates that he might have spent the war's last months running cotton through the Federal lines. Because one thing is certain: when the fighting was over and Confederate bonds were worthless, when Mississippi's towns had been turned into charcoal and the price of land had fallen to nothing, William Falkner had cash.

In *The Unvanquished* Sartoris rebuilds the plantation house the Yankees had burned and sets a window with a few panes of colored glass from the South Carolina mansion where he was born. Falkner had no such ancestral home. He didn't have a line to continue but rather a family to found, and in the postwar decades railroads and not cotton became king, the period's most consistently lucrative investment. He began with a little spur of track that went north from Ripley into Tennessee, where it joined the east-west line of the Memphis and Charleston. His first train ran in 1872, and two years later Falkner's net worth stood at more than $100,000. It's hard to say just how much that would now be. Different economists use very different multipliers, anywhere between 30 and 200, depending on whether one looks primarily at inflation or at the relative cost of good and services. The most conservative estimate would therefore put a comparable fortune at upward of $3 million today, but Falkner's was probably much more and that was only the start. He went on laying track and buying land all through 1870s and 1880s, growing ever richer and ever more quarrelsome too. He was generous and shrewd but also vain and sharp-tongued, and he enjoyed taunting the one man in the county who had more money than he did, a tight-lipped skinflint named Richard Thurmond. They had known each other for years, but one day Thurmond decided he had had enough. In November 1889, just after Falkner had gotten elected to the state legislature, the two met on Ripley's square, and Thurmond shot him in the head. There were plenty of witnesses; but then as now, it was hard to make a jury convict a white man with money.

The weathered, lichen-crusted marble of Falkner's funerary statue shows him as handsome, with deep-socketed eyes and a Vandyke that reminds me of Dickens's. He was a tall man as well; the order for his coffin specified six feet two, and most of his descendants were built to his scale. The novelist was not. William Faulkner stood barely five feet five, but none of his ancestors would take a larger or more explicit place in his imagination than the great-grandfather who died before his birth: not his grandfather, John Wesley Thompson Falkner, and still less his own father, Murry. Yet the boy was captivated by something more than the Old Colonel's military exploits. For William Falkner was a man of action who was also a man of letters, and he had done something much more original than shoot Yankees and make money. He had written a novel, an engaging picaresque romance called *The White Rose of Memphis* (1881), in which his characters move through a South that is apparently innocent of both slavery and war. It sold an astonishing 160,000 copies, and he followed it with a book of European travels. His namesake would never have that kind of commercial success, but when the young Faulkner said that he wanted to write, he added that he was following in a family tradition.

The Falkners had moved from Ripley by the time the novelist was born. The Old Colonel's oldest son, J. W. T. Falkner, had gone to the state university in Oxford, forty miles and one county to the west, and later opened his own law practice there; the fictional Jefferson draws the Sartoris family history from Ripley, but almost everything else comes from Oxford itself. The second Falkner was called the "Young Colonel" despite having no military experience at all, but he was every bit the businessman his father had been, opening a bank and starting Oxford's telephone exchange: a dozen enterprises and more, including three terms in the state senate. Murry Falkner had neither that ambition nor ability. He hoped to run the family's railroad, and when William, his oldest son, was born in 1897 he was working at the depot in the nearby town of New Albany. But J. W. T. Falkner sold it out from under him, and in the early years of the twentieth century Murry failed in a series of small businesses before finding an administrative sinecure at the University of Mississippi.

William Faulkner was five when his parents moved to Oxford, and he would live nearly his entire life within the same square mile. There was his grandfather's house a block south of the town square, now demolished and replaced by a gas station; and the gingerbread-trimmed place, still standing, that his parents soon got nearby, on a deep lot with a barn and a pasture. There was the brick house on the university grounds that came with his father's job, and the apartment on the road to the campus where he lived when he was first married and at work on *As I Lay Dying*. And then there is Rowan Oak, the tumbledown antebellum mansion in the middle of the woods that he bought in 1930 and slowly repaired and improved and enlarged. The woods are still there, thirty acres between the center of town and the university; if they weren't now deeded for preservation they would, it's said, be the most valuable bit of land in the state.

In Faulkner's boyhood Oxford had a population of just under two thousand, roughly two-thirds of them white. The county as a whole had about twenty-two thousand, but the races were more evenly balanced; 45 percent of its citizens were black. To a visitor and maybe even to its residents, the town's most notable feature was and is its courthouse square. Yet I don't think those residents fully recognize just how regionally distinctive it seems to someone from another part of the country. In the New England county seat where I grew up, the Federal-period courthouse sits on a hill at the head of the main street, along the top of a T-shaped intersection. In the one where I live now, the courthouse broods, in massive neo-Romanesque, over the downtown's major crossing. The Lafayette County courthouse, in contrast, doesn't hold down a prominent corner or take up a side of Oxford's square. It isn't even *on* the square, but *in* it, defines it: a colonnaded building, shrouded by trees and surrounded by benches, in the center of a grassy oval. That oval is itself set within the four sides of an asphalt frame, with two lanes of traffic running counterclockwise around it, a kind of filled-in roundabout that creates a focus for civic life. It's a common form of city planning in that part of the South, and perhaps Oxford's is unique only in its liveliness; even now, when the main roads into town are lined with big box stores, you can have a pretty good social life simply by walking around the square a few times each day. In both Faulkner's time and his pages alike almost anything anyone needed could be found there: hammers and plow-lines and kerosene, groceries and dry goods, a hotel and a drug store with a soda fountain, and then a couple of banks, with the lawyers' offices on the galleries above, reached by an outside staircase. The banks remain, and of course the lawyers, and the dry goods too in the form of Ralph Lauren and Ole Miss sweatshirts. But the South's best independent bookstore has replaced the pharmacy, and there are more restaurants now, and certainly more bars than in the days when Mississippi was legally dry and everywhere wet.

Faulkner first drew a map of Yoknapatawpha County for a foldout in

Absalom, Absalom! and a second one for *The Portable Faulkner* in 1946. But he never supplied a detailed plan for the center of Jefferson itself, showing it as little more than a cluster of arrows and captions, bunched around a crossroads. Nevertheless, he relied on Oxford's actual streets in plotting out his apocryphal town, and I want both to fill in its details and to note the biggest way in which Jefferson departs from its model. For Faulkner decided not to give his town a college, even though the university sits less than a mile to the west of the square; some of his characters will go to school there, but he always suggests that Oxford lies some fifty miles from his imagined land. He wanted Jefferson to stand as a more typical Mississippi community, with its economy based upon cotton and isolated from the world outside. Lafayette County was agricultural enough, but Oxford drew students from throughout the state and a faculty from across the South, if not yet from the nation as a whole. It was always a more sophisticated and more prosperous place than the Jefferson he made from it, and the university's presence in his hometown would have an incalculable effect on his life and work.

The old established white churches lie in a residential neighborhood between the campus and the square, including St. Peter's, the Episcopal parish where Faulkner was the most nominal of members. Oxford had been set out in a grid around the courthouse, with the grandest houses directly to its north and south, his grandfather's among them. But Union troops burned the town in 1864, and only a few of them date from before the war; Faulkner's own Rowan Oak lay just far enough away from the town center to survive. Commercial development was heavier to the south, as it still is, but most of the town's other working parts lay to the north. The jail was a block off the square, and the cemetery to the northeast; each would provide the novelist with a setting. The station was off to the west, near the university, where in the 1920s six trains stopped each day, for service to Memphis and New Orleans.

That was the white Oxford, the one Faulkner lived in. Black people entered it regularly, though almost always as servants: laundresses and cooks, coachmen and gardeners. The square was common to all, and yet African-Americans had to step from the sidewalk when a white person passed, bowing their heads and avoiding eye contact; in stores they waited until every white was served before stepping to the counter. But there was also a black Oxford. Freedman's Town began a few blocks northwest of the courthouse, a district of unpaved roads and "small grassless plots" half a mile square, and with its own churches and schools. White women almost never went there. White men would sometimes drive a family servant home, but often their presence was feared, for they might also come looking for violence or whiskey or women, for something whose taking would assert their own supremacy. Children moved more easily, and as a boy Faulkner often went to Freedman's Town with Caroline Barr, the woman he called Mammy Callie, to whose memory he would dedicate *Go Down, Moses*. She lived on his parents' property, in a cabin at the back of their lot, but her grown children lived on those unpaved roads, along with a niece who ran a juke joint. The young Faulkner walked through Oxford alongside her, and in hearing what she heard and seeing what she saw, he developed both a precise ear for African-American speech and an appreciation of the black church that would later shape his fiction.

But there's one thing that no one knows if he saw, something horrific in the Oxford streets. Nelse Patton was a bootlegger who had been in and out of the county jail for years. In the late summer of 1908 he was in again—but he was such a familiar figure that he was also out, an African-American trusty who was allowed to run errands. The evidence holds that on September 8 he was sent to carry a message from a white inmate to his wife and got drunk along the way. The woman grew afraid and reached for a gun; Patton had a razor and cut her throat. He ran, but a shotgun blast caught him, and a posse then returned him to the jail, where the sheriff locked him in and hid the key. It wasn't enough: a former United States senator got up a mob, and over the next few hours they used crowbars and sledgehammers to break through the prison's brick walls. Patton was shot in his cell. Then he was scalped and castrated, dragged through the streets, and hung in front of the courthouse. His body stayed there all the next day, just a few blocks from the Falkner house; in going to school the boy would have needed to walk out of his usual path to avoid it.

In 1935 Faulkner told an editor at *Vanity Fair* that he had never seen a lynching and so couldn't describe one. The first part of that statement was probably true, whether or not he had passed Nelse Patton's body in the street. But he had already described several lynchings in his work and would go on to imagine more of them, scenes that provide our most frightening fictional images of the hysteria from which they grow. "Dry September," which appeared in *Scribner's* for January 1931, begins with the news that after "sixty two rainless days" a Jefferson spinster has been "attacked, insulted, frightened" by a black man. None of the white men gathered in the barbershop on a Saturday evening know exactly what has happened—"Except it wasn't Will Mayes." That's what the barber Hawkshaw says, and that's enough. For Mayes's name is now associated with whatever happened, if anything happened, and in trying to separate him out, to insulate him, Hawkshaw has guaranteed his death. Nobody—nobody white—can resist what happens next. Nobody wants to be known as what one man in the barbershop calls a "damn niggerlover." Nobody wants to "accuse a white woman of lying," for even if nothing happened, the barbershop says, the best way to ensure that nothing ever will is to act, now. Later that night a car will speed out of Jefferson with Will Mayes inside and then come back without him.

Rumor and innuendo, a world in which hysteria lives in every throat and the collective temper is always already on fire. The story is one of Faulkner's best, and I can still remember the sense of paralyzing fear with which I first read it. But more frightening still is the letter that Faulkner published in a Memphis newspaper the very next month. One of the *Commercial-Appeal's* black readers had written to thank the white women of Mississippi for organizing an anti-lynching society. In reply, Faulkner sent in a rambling, incoherent, and apparently unmotivated screed that effectually contradicted the story he'd just published. "No balanced man can . . . hold any moral brief for lynching," he writes, and yet mobs, "like our juries . . . have a way of being right." For try as he might he cannot remember any case, outside of fiction, in which "a man of any color and with a record beyond reproach, suffer[ed] violence at the hands of men who knew him." Did he have his own story in mind? None of this letter's factual claims are true, and nothing can extenuate its disgrace. That was the conclusion of the two Mississippi-based scholars who first wrote about it, Neil R. McMillen and Noel Polk. For them the letter showed just how much "in his personal, communal life" William Faulkner shared the values of his white neighbors and community. Some of those neighbors—some of his relatives—would later brand him with the same epithet that the man in the barbershop uses. In daily life, however, there was in the 1930s very little to choose between them. What a reading of that vicious letter finally suggests, McMillen and Polk conclude, is how very far Faulkner needed to come—how hard he had to fight with himself—before he could write *Absalom, Absalom!* and *Go Down, Moses.*

I would say more. Faulkner could not see the racial ideology of his world—could not even really *think*—except when writing fiction. He could stand outside that ideology only by first assigning it to a character. He inhabited those beliefs by inhabiting another person. Then he saw them clearly, and in that act he became better than he was. Another way to say this is that Faulkner could not have written so clearly of mob psychology in "Dry September" without knowing it from within, without feeling or recognizing the force of its communal roar. One of his few adequate pieces of nonfiction is a loose autobiographical sketch called "Mississippi" (1954), an essay written in the third person, as though it were about somebody other than himself. There he describes the "middleaged novelist" as a man who loves his "native land . . . even while hating some of it." Loving the river and the hills, the fields and the voices, but hating "the intolerance and injustice": hating, among other things, the fact that black people "could worship the white man's God but not in the white's man church"; hating above all the irrevocable evil of lynching itself. There the novelist recognizes that its victims are chosen simply "because their skins were black" and feels the sting of shame. I spoke in my preface of a civil war within Faulkner himself. In reading these words I wonder if it was only Mississippi that he hated.

———

WHAT DID CHILDREN IN Faulkner's native state learn about the Civil War? In his childhood there were still old soldiers on the Oxford streets whose missing arms had left them with empty sleeves, and each of his paternal grandparents became a leader in the groups that commemorated the Confederate cause. J. W. T. Falkner organized the local branch of the Sons of Confederate Veterans, and his wife Sally was president of her chapter of the

United Daughters of the Confederacy. In 1906 a statue to "Our Confederate Dead" went up on the edge of the university's campus. All but three of its undergraduates had joined a company called the University Greys in the spring of 1861, and the all-male school had then closed for the war's duration. As a unit they fought at Bull Run and afterward in Lee's Army of Northern Virginia; and in 1863 every one of its surviving members was either killed or wounded at Gettysburg. The speaker at the memorial's dedication announced that in all of human history no other group had "fought such a great fight for the sake of principle alone." That was a lie, unless you believe that slavery was a principle. Most Civil War monuments in the South belong to one of two historical moments. The first began around 1890, with the erection of an enormous equestrian statue of Robert E. Lee on Monument Avenue in Richmond, and ran into the first decades of the twentieth century. Their apologists claim that memorials like the university's served to commemorate a war generation that was itself dying out, a way to mark the old soldiers' passing. Yet their construction both coincides in time and remains inseparable from the increasing sway of Jim Crow and the disenfranchisement of black voters, and they stand as an assertion of white supremacy, white domination. The second period only underlines that truth. For a new wave of building took place in the 1960s, when that statuary increasingly and explicitly asserted that the war was fought for "states' rights." The phrase itself served as code for an opposition to civil rights and as such was used by Ronald Reagan in his 1984 presidential campaign.

Still, one Civil War monument wasn't enough for Oxford. In 1907 a statue was placed in front of the courthouse as well, a musket-bearing soldier atop a pillar, this one representing the entirety of Lafayette County. Both monuments stand today, and the one in the square would play a crucial role in Faulkner's own fiction, so persistent a point of reference that in his pages it almost seems a feature of the natural landscape, rather than the product of human choice. And the Falkner family found other ways to recall the war as well. The Young Colonel liked to talk about his father's experiences in Virginia and the things he himself had seen as a boy; and he had his equivalents of Old Man Falls, hosting occasional reunions of the Partisan Rangers, feeding them up on whiskey and barbecue, and letting their voices roll. The novelist kept the memory of those old men in their "shabby grey uniforms," though he also said that he learned even more from "the maiden spinster aunts which had never surrendered." There were other memories too. Caroline Barr had her own stories, and from her the boy heard of the terrifying violence to which black people were subjected in the postwar years, the years when she went in nightly fear of the Ku Klux Klan.

Today we often draw a distinction between history and memory. Each of them tells stories, each attempts to shape an interpretation of the past, but in doing so they draw on fundamentally different kinds of materials. *I was there; I saw it, felt it, believe it; this is what it was like, this is what my parents told me, this is what we say where I come from.* That's what memory tells us. It relies on testimony and sometimes brushes the facts aside in its claim to represent the voice of authentic experience. I say "the facts," as if deciding on them were simple; but in this context the phrase simply means any kind of contradictory evidence, anything that challenges the primacy of one's own subjective experience and beliefs. *That's not how I see it.* But history tells us not to be so simple. It draws on written documents and it explores anomalies, and while some of its sources may lie in individual memory it will treat that memory as just one bit of evidence among others. It tests my memories against yours, and both against those of a third party, a fourth, depending always upon a plurality of voices; and then tests itself against the dates and figures and texts of what one might call the public record. The paradox is that memory too can stand as an object of historical inquiry: an investigation into how and why and when people came to believe or recall some things about the past and not others.

Much of what the young Faulkner learned about the Civil War took the form of memory. The statues, stories, and civic organizations provided a collective narrative shaped and shared by the white South of the period, though maybe he got just enough from Caroline Barr to know that not everyone accepted that narrative or saw themselves within it. But he also went to school, and I wanted to know just what his teachers would have taught him. In my last chapter I mentioned that groups like the United Confederate Veterans claimed that the region's textbooks should present their own version of the South's reasons for secession, and in the early years of the twentieth century most states in the former Confederacy established special governmental commissions to approve and purchase those books. Few Northern states thought that necessary, leaving such decisions to the local board of education instead. Mississippi's own commission was established in 1904, with a law designed to give the state a uniform series of textbooks, ostensibly so that students in Tupelo or Biloxi might learn the same things as those in Jackson. It also stipulated, however, that "no history in relation to the late civil war between the states shall be used in the schools in this state unless it be fair and impartial."

What might such a fair and balanced textbook be like? One of the approved volumes was a 1900 work by Franklin L. Riley called *School History of Mississippi*. Riley taught in the university's history department and served as the longtime editor of the *Publications of the Mississippi Historical Society*; his own scholarly work included a volume on Robert E. Lee. The copy of the *School History* that I read had gone through many hands by the time I got it, on loan from a local historian. He left it for me at Oxford's tourist office, a small brick house just off the square. In Faulkner's day the building had served as the law offices of his friend Phil Stone, and memory held that in an earlier generation Nathan Bedford Forrest had used the place to organize the local branch of the Klan. Now it was filled with light and travel posters, and a teenager behind the counter handed me the book with a smile. Its cloth cover, embossed with the state seal, was faded but looked as though it had once been green. Many of its pages were foxed and some of them torn, and as I sat with it over a sandwich in a nearby café I thought about the name on its flyleaf. The book had once belonged to a woman named Ruth Alvis of Waterford, a hamlet twenty miles to the north of Oxford; census records list her birth in 1891, and as I started to turn the pages I wondered if she had known the novelist. Then I found the right chapter and began to read a narrative remarkable for all that it left unsaid, remarkable despite or maybe precisely because of Riley's drily factual prose.

His summary of the positions taken by the different political parties of the 1850s is lucid enough, and he doesn't vilify either the abolitionists or the new Republican Party. Riley's Confederate partisanship is subtler than that and depends on the skill with which he uses omissions to shade the truth.

His Mississippians are all fair-minded. So he notes that the state was "greatly agitated over the slavery question" but makes it sound as if the institution's continued existence had been a subject of debate within Mississippi itself. In 1860 public interest hung on the question of "how the State could continue in the Union and be made secure in the enjoyment of her rights," while leaving the nature of those rights unspecified. Secession follows as the logical consequence of Lincoln's election, and though Riley finds space to describe the state's new flag he doesn't quote from the secession convention's statement of the reasons for its decision: "Our position is thoroughly identified with the institution of slavery." Instead he depicts that choice as if it were both divorced from its causes and the last stage of a natural process, as inevitable as that statue in the courthouse square.

His treatment of the war itself is rather abbreviated, for though the state mounted a "gallant resistance," the fighting in Mississippi offered very little in the way of contingency, the not-yets and what-ifs that Faulkner himself had evoked in describing the battle of Gettysburg. It was instead dominated by Grant's strategic genius and the Union's consequent success, without the Eastern conflict's back-and-forth. By way of compensation, Riley emphasizes the war's destruction, especially that wrought by Sherman, and gives disproportionate weight to a few minor Confederate successes, including some real-life cavalry raids of the kind led by John Sartoris in *The Unvanquished*. But he completely ignores the many thousands of black Mississippians who joined the Federal forces. The Emancipation Proclamation affected every one in the state, black or white, but it gets just half a paragraph, less than Riley gives to the effect of the Union blockade on the Confederacy's diet and clothing. Still, "when the South was forced back into the Union at the end of the war it was generally believed that the institution of slavery was dead."

Generally suggests something less than full acceptance, and yet Riley doesn't explore the ways in which the state tried to maintain that institution. In fact, the chapters on Reconstruction are far more problematic than his treatment of the war itself. He wrote them in collaboration with the Mississippi-born historian J. W. Garner, and I'll consider them in greater detail, along with Garner's own history of that period, in a later chapter. But let me note one detail. In the "Meridian Riot" of March 1871, "a number of Negroes and a white justice of the peace were killed.... The affair grew out of political conditions existing in that town." The nature of those conditions remains undefined, but in fact the Meridian riot was the last stage in a plot to overthrow the town's duly elected Republican government. There was violence on both sides, but that of the white supremacists was organized and the Klan played a role in it; about thirty black men were killed, the white mayor was put on a northbound train, and at the end the town did indeed have new rulers.

Events are once more cut off from their causes. They need to be reported, but only in the blandest of terms; they aren't to be examined or analyzed. Riley's school history offered its first readers a few necessary facts and dates. But it also tried to suppress any questions they might have had, and the longer I sat over it in the sun-drenched café, with the noise of college students around me, the more dizzying it seemed. The book is accessible to a bright middle-schooler, and it's possible that Faulkner encountered it in the seventh grade. His instructor that year had a particular interest in state history, and in later years the novelist would both ask the questions the textbook elides and observe its strategic silences. Among the things Riley might have taught him was that public school teachers were sometimes "visited" by the Klan; for the taxes meant to support those schools were "very burdensome" to the people. The young Faulkner could also have learned that by 1873, when Reconstruction enabled a few black men to enter political life, the "greed of the colored people for office ... was astonishing." And black students would have learned that too, for when a white school had worn through its textbooks they were inevitably passed on to the black schools in the state's segregated system.

However, a book like Riley's merely reinforced the lessons that Faulkner's generation had already learned. Much of his library at Rowan Oak has been preserved, and on its shelves is a 1905 novel called *The Clansman*, by a onetime Baptist minister from North Carolina named Thomas W. Dixon. It's signed and dated by Annie Chandler, his first-grade teacher, and though nobody knows just how the book came into his personal library, it may have been a gift or a school prize. Annie Chandler, the daughter of an Oxford doctor, lived in a large white house south of the square, its grounds surrounded by a wrought-iron fence that served to keep her intellectually disabled brother Edwin from wandering into the street. Edwin Chandler was just a few years older than Faulkner, and the future novelist was disturbed by the way other children teased him. Decades later he sometimes took his infant daughter Jill to visit the man; by that time the house and the fence and Edwin himself had helped to inspire *The Sound and the Fury*. His publishers struggled to sell even a few thousand copies. But *The Clansman* sold a million, even before D. W. Griffith filmed it as *The Birth of a Nation* (1915).

The Clansman begins just after the Civil War's end—an early chapter takes place at Ford's Theatre—and uses the fear of black men to justify the erosion of civil rights in Dixon's own Jim Crow world. The novel stands as a travesty of a popular postwar genre, the romance of reconciliation, in which marriage between a Northern man and a Southern woman provides a symbolic healing of the nation's wounds; the best example is probably John W. DeForest's *Miss Ravenel's Conversion from Secession to Loyalty* (1867). Here the romance is reversed, with the North depicted as both feminized and weak. For the girl is a Yankee, the daughter of a fiercely vengeful Republican congressman, and the boy—the boy is a delicate young man driven by what he calls injustice to found the Ku Klux Klan. North and South reconcile over the body of black America. The congressman admits his mistakes, and at the climax the Yankee girl feels an exhilarating joy at the knowledge that a vengeful "squadron of white-and-scarlet horsemen" stands ready in the woods. We read of the terror imposed on the South by "black hordes of former slaves, with the intelligence of children and the instincts of savages," and one of the book's villains is described as "a man of charming features for a mulatto," someone who combines the finely cut lips of the "Aryan race" with the yellow eyes of the jungle. But Dixon never mentions the white father from whom, in the years before the war, those lips must have come. That's not the kind of sexual crime that interests him. Instead he imagines a moment in which four men break into an isolated house and tie a white woman to her bed, allowing their leader, Gus, to fasten "the black claws of the beast" into the creamy throat of her nubile daughter. After it's all over, the two women clean the room, so that nobody will know their shame, and then walk to the nearby

Lover's Leap, where together they step "into the mists and on through the opal gates of Death."

Gus's inevitable lynching always stood as the highlight of *The Clansman*'s stage version; Faulkner probably saw it when it came to Oxford in 1908, playing at a theater owned by his grandfather. By that time most American historians had judged Reconstruction a failure. Emancipation may have been the right thing to do, but they thought the country had gone too far in granting political rights to the freedmen. They argued that it led to corruption and incompetence, and, in Riley's words, to the disenfranchisement of the region's "more prominent and influential citizens," who then needed some extralegal means to restore their position. *The Clansman* is something worse than awful, far clumsier as fiction than the crudest of today's bestsellers, and utterly naked in its ideological push. Some cities banned the play, and yet Dixon's work is but an overdrawn version of what passed for respectable white opinion in many parts of the country. Young white boys in Mississippi loved it; so did many of those in Massachusetts.

FOUR

Postage Stamps

Elizabeth Prall was a New York bookseller. She had long dark hair that she kept pulled back from an elfin face, and though she came from Michigan she had made her way in the city, working in her thirties as the manager of the big Doubleday store at the corner of Fifth Avenue and Thirty-Eighth Street, and buying a brownstone in what's now called Soho. One of her tenants there was a scholarly playwright named Stark Young, who'd been born into the remnants of Mississippi's plantation aristocracy. His father had practiced medicine in Oxford, and he later wrote of his family origins in a best-selling novel called *So Red the Rose* (1934). But for the moment he was the drama critic at the *New Republic*, and in the fall of 1921 he asked his landlady if the bookstore could use a new clerk. For Young had a friend sleeping on his couch, a slightly built young man with a mustache whom he knew from back home. The fellow wanted to be a poet but hadn't published much; he was giving New York a try and needed a job. Prall hired William Faulkner at eleven dollars a week, enough to get a room of his own in Greenwich Village. He started just before Thanksgiving and was surprisingly good at the work, his soft voice working especially well with old ladies, selling them the books they hadn't known they wanted. Regular hours bored him, however, and after a few weeks he slipped off back south. She probably thought that was the end of him—only to find him, three years later, standing again at her door.

But it was a very different door. For Prall had gotten married in the meantime, and her new husband was one of the period's most sudden and unlikely of literary successes. Sherwood Anderson had spent most of his adult life in business, running a paint factory among other things, and failing at much of what he tried. A man with a nose like a wedge and graying unkempt hair, he was over forty by the time he put together the stories that made him famous. *Winesburg, Ohio* (1919) came with a map of the imaginary town from which the book took its name, marked with the location of the newspaper office and the hotel, the fairgrounds too, and showing its houses as all shaded by trees. But behind each of Anderson's walls there lived a "grotesque": men and women who had snatched at some overarching principle—thrift or passion or profligacy—and bent their lives crooked in following it. The book's sense of disenchantment fit the postwar world; so did the overdrawn simplicity of its prose, and its success left Anderson free to live wherever he wanted. He met Prall in New York, and they married in the spring of 1924, after he divorced his second wife in Reno. They settled in New Orleans, taking an apartment in the Pontalba Buildings on Jackson Square, in the heart of the French Quarter. On one end the square was bounded by the city's Roman Catholic cathedral of Saint Louis, and on the other by the Mississippi River itself. The Pontalba Buildings lined either side, long four-story structures in red brick and wrought iron. They dated from the 1840s and were then in a state of elegant disrepair; now they are tourist sites, with their ground floors given over to cafés and souvenirs.

Anderson's range was narrow, but for a while in the 1920s he stood as one of the country's most influential writers, publishing a book a year and speaking all across the country for $500 an evening. At the start of the decade he helped the young Hemingway find his stripped-down style, and now he would help Faulkner too. The Mississippian was by then the author of a book of poems, and in November 1924 he presumed on his acquaintance with Elizabeth Prall to go down from Oxford and call. He admired Anderson's work and knew it well, the 1923 *Horses and Men* in particular. And something about him must have impressed the older writer too, for Anderson almost immediately wrote a sketch of his new acolyte. "A Meeting South" described a "very small and delicately built" young man called David, who walked around town with a jug of homemade whiskey in his pocket. He was a poet, an admirer of Shelley, and liked to tell stories about his father's Alabama plantation, where its black workers boiled sugarcane down into molasses. "David" claimed too that he had served all through World War I with a squadron of British fighter planes and had broken his legs in a crash. His cheekbones had splintered as well, and now he had a silver plate set beneath the skin of his face.

Faulkner's father had no plantation; nor did the young man have a plate in his head. Still, he liked to say he did, liked to suggest he had flown in battle, and it's possible that Anderson even believed him. What's certain is that the older man enjoyed having someone to yarn with. Faulkner would go out to Jackson Square after lunch and sit on the curb, waiting until Anderson appeared, and then the two of them walked through the music of the New Orleans streets, tossing ideas from one to the other and inventing characters out of the people around them. Though what made Faulkner himself seek Anderson out? It wasn't just the man's fame, or even his work in itself, the intrinsic merits of stories like "Hands" or "I'm a Fool." No, what drew Faulkner was the particular nature of Anderson's achievement. But to define that achievement I need to tell a story about American literature in the decades after the Civil War and about the role of the country's different regions within that literature: a story that begins with the appalling book with which I ended my last chapter, Thomas W. Dixon's *The Clansman*.

———·—·———

THE PLOT OF *THE CLANSMAN* enacts a politics. It establishes a white supremacist order on which North and South can agree, and the novel's very language embodies that same politics. For its white characters all sound alike. Dixon doesn't attempt to represent their speech phonetically, to distinguish the differing accents of each region; they all speak what we might call a standard English, correct in its grammar and orthography, and unmarked by any local idiom. His black characters are another matter: "Dr. Cammun, u'se been er pow'ful good frien' ter me—gimme medicine lots er times, en I hain't nebber paid you nuttin." It's doubtful that many people actually spoke like that—but then realism is the last thing on Dixon's mind. He makes their speech depart from an imputed linguistic norm in order to embody a racial hierarchy. These people haven't mastered the language. Their grammar is imperfect and their pronunciation slurred, the speech of those whom he depicts as somewhat less than human.

All this seems entirely transparent, and Dixon's practice was hardly unique in the literature of his day and after. Still, many writers who drew on non-standard speech did so in far more complicated and flexible ways. Faulkner himself often represented his black characters' speech phonetically, but he was never consistent about it and sometimes changed just a single word—"throwed" rather than "threw"—allowing its tang to capture both the accent and the idiolect of a particular person. Moreover, he used such variations in the speech of his poor white characters too: "kilt" for "killed," as the hill folk of *As I Lay Dying* will have it. But even the Harvard-bound Quentin Compson says "Yessum," and in fact Faulkner's rendering of regional speech depends much more on colloquial diction than on anything else. So a pot of turnip greens is "mighty spindling eating," and his characters almost always "reckon" rather than "guess."

After the Civil War such dialect writing became inseparable from what was called "local color." The term originally comes from painting, where it has a precise technical meaning: local color refers to an object's natural color, undistorted by shadow or bright light. Things as they are: a red apple against a matte surface. But the phrase also had a colloquial meaning and in the nineteenth century became synonymous with genre painting, with scenes of the everyday and especially those an outsider might take as typical of a given place. Local color in American prose accordingly concentrated on small towns and ordinary people, on stories and sketches of a deliberately modest scale. As such it seems at odds with the postwar tenor of American life, a world away from the bustle and noise, the glamour and squalor, of the country's ever-booming big cities. And yet that is precisely if paradoxically why it stands as the period's most characteristic, and most important, form of short fiction.

The movement's cultural charge was complicated and at times contradictory, with individual writers each pursuing a different end, but it did as a whole attempt to register the range and diversity of American life. The Civil War had made people newly aware of the country's size and scale. It wasn't just that the army had put them on the move; they had also learned to depend on the news from faraway places. Railroads and telegraphs increasingly spliced the country together, allowing quick communication over once unheard-of distances. They made it ever easier to acquire some knowledge of the country's different regions, even as they threatened to erode the distinctions between them. The stories that filled such monthly magazines as *Harper's* and the *Century* both participated in and resisted that process: stories of coastal New England and the Louisiana bayous, of midwestern roads and the Tennessee mountains. On the one hand, these stories brought the news from one small corner of the country to another, and therefore played a role in the business of postwar reconciliation. Yet they also helped fix local distinctions in place. They defined and preserved a sense of regional difference, and in the South that included the experience of ruin and defeat, as if in the absence of its peculiar institution the place itself remained more peculiar than ever.

Many of these stories attempted to capture regional speech, and some of them did indeed rely on the phonetic spelling of dialogue in a way that served a reactionary purpose. The Atlanta newspaperman Joel Chandler Harris collected African-American folklore with an assiduity that rivaled that of the Brothers Grimm, but the Uncle Remus through whose voice he presented those tales exists only to edify and entertain a white audience. I have already mentioned Thomas Nelson Page, who in the stories of *In Ole Virginia* (1887) used the conventions of local color writing to provide an apologia for the Lost Cause. Stories like "Marse Chan" or "Meh Lady" rely on a white narrator, a traveler, who in riding through the devastated South inevitably encounters an aged and lonely freedman, still clinging to the land on which he had been a slave. The narrator coaxes him into speech, and Page then makes that freedman offer a nostalgic account of the old order, in dialect, for a white listener. His voice—his life—finds its meaning through its subordination to the normative speech of his white audience; and these stories, like Chandler's, use that voice to justify both the social order of the antebellum world and, more crucially, that of the Redeemed South as well.

Each writer was popular—as popular in their time as they are shunned today—but their blackface narration received an effective rebuke in the work of Charles W. Chesnutt. He was born in Ohio, yet his family's roots lay in the small free black community of North Carolina, and his parents returned to the South in 1867, when he was nine. He listened and he read, he absorbed a world of folktale and legend, and in 1887 sold a story called "The Goophered Grapevine" to the *Atlantic Monthly*: the first of what became known as the "Conjure Tales" and the first story the magazine had ever published by an African-American writer. Chesnutt took the structure of his work from Page, but used his own form against him, subverting his message in a series of quietly devastating stories about life under slavery. He too framed his work through the voice of a white narrator, an Ohio businessman known only as "John," who has settled in North Carolina and wants to hear about black life in the Old South. "Uncle" Julius McAdoo was once enslaved on the same property and now works as a gardener; he has many stories to tell, most of them painful, stories that trouble him still. But Chesnutt never makes his dialect into an object of fun—the character's speech carries his history, and John learns to listen more for instruction than for some confirmation of what he already believes, to listen for an explanation of some bit of local lore or custom. At times he finds Julius's tales rather quaint; no modern reader does, and Chesnutt instead suggests the limitations of the Ohioan's own point of view. For in telling us of "hants" and sorcerers and people turned into such things as a wolf or a tree, Julius McAdoo also shows us the world of men and women whose lives have been distorted and destroyed by servitude. This freedman lives in a place far removed from the superficially similar plantation fiction of Page or Harris; and no one who reads Chesnutt closely can go back to their lies.

Most local color writers would have joined Chesnutt in disavowing Dixon's or Page's attempt to establish a linguistic hierarchy. In an age of increasing standardization, they refused to believe that all Americans should speak alike, and they saw themselves as recording those folkways that might be in danger of vanishing. Or perhaps of being forgotten. For local color stories were often set in the nation's cultural backwaters, places that history had left behind, enclaves cut off from the all-incorporating rush of modernity itself. The canonical example is Sarah Orne Jewett's *Country of the Pointed Firs*, and I want to pause over it, as I will over two other classics of American regional writing. Understanding them will help us understand the role that a regional setting, a regional identity, both does and doesn't play in Faulkner's work;

will help us understand the place in our literature that he himself would hold. Jewett's book was first published as an 1896 serial in the *Atlantic Monthly*, at the very end of local color writing's great period: a work that in capping its tradition also worked to transform it. Most of what's lasted in the genre does, as I've suggested, take the form of short stories, fragmentary glimpses into daily life, and Jewett herself published many volumes of them, almost all set in her native Maine. Here, however, she produced a suite of tales and sketches, closely woven and yet seemingly loose, in which every episodic page is integral to the whole. Scholars have always argued about whether it's a novel or a collection of stories, but to most readers the question will seem irrelevant. The book is its own thing, and perfection.

A nameless first-person narrator travels down east to a village called Dunnet Landing, a summer visitor who knows the region but comes from away, perhaps from Boston, where Jewett herself spent half the year. Certainly that narrator has a life elsewhere, though we learn nothing about it beyond the fact that she wants to do a bit of writing. She boards at the house of Almira Todd, a widow and a wise woman, famous for her knowledge of herbs and remedies, and over the course of the season sinks into Maine's local life, learning its ways and hearing its stories. She will be told about boats, and fishing, and the interrelation of different families across the generations, and also of those who live alone, by choice, on the small islands offshore. She will learn the region's speech, listening to small boys and retired sea captains and, above all, to her landlady. "No, dear, we won't take no big bo't," Mrs. Todd says as they plan an excursion. "I'll jus get a handy dory ... I don't want no abler bo't than a good dory, an' a nice light breeze ain't goin' to make no sea." Dunnet Landing knows madness and loss and a closed community's need to keep silence. Nevertheless, the narrator finds something sweet in its cool sequestered life, and readers will recognize a bit of pastoral in her appreciation of country wisdom, the quaint endurance of a fading past. And they might also remember the German critic Walter Benjamin's claim that there are only two kinds of storytellers: the person who knows all the lore of her region, and the one with a journey to tell about. Jewett's book, at once delicate and profound, depends on a dialogue between the two, between "Almiry" Todd and its traveling narrator.

Both Jewett and Chesnutt set their work on the nation's margins and yet in doing so extended their reach by inventing a character from the world outside, an intermediary, as a way to enter and depict a region they knew intimately. For local color writing faced a danger: its material might prove of merely local concern. It looked to populations on some cultural or geographic border, or located its subjects in an economic hinterland; many of its writers were women, whose work depended on a precise notation of their sisters' too-often circumscribed lives. And this important strand of American literature has seemed at times but to cling on the borders of the canon as well. Yet the magazines that published local color stories were anything but marginal in their interests and audience. They were read throughout the country but edited in New York or Boston or Philadelphia; edited in the belief that the eastern seaboard provided our national norms. The same journals also ran stories by Henry James about Americans abroad and William Dean Howells's accounts of middle-class life in the city; and each kind of fiction took a part of its meaning from its juxtaposition to the other. A tale in the *Atlantic* might serve to validate what was, in literary terms, an unknown region, such as Chesnutt's North Carolina; and in doing so it both challenged and affirmed the assumptions of those who saw their own lives as reflected in Howells.

The urbane narrators of Jewett and Chesnutt helped make their regional speakers—regional informants—available, and yet such normative voices also worked to contain and control those speakers. Few local color writers would go as far as Mark Twain did with *Huckleberry Finn* by making the vernacular into the voice of the narration itself. But mentioning Twain opens another issue as well. For local color writing lay in tension with a very different conception of American literature: not just the tension between the rural on the one hand and the urban or cosmopolitan on the other, or even between the local and the national; but rather that between the purposefully modest form of the short story and the novel's claims to importance. It was in tension, in short, with the idea of the Great American Novel. The phrase was coined in 1868 by the Civil War veteran John W. DeForest, just a year after he published his own *Miss Ravenel's Conversion*; and the concept, like that of local color itself, both grew out of and was inseparable from the nation's great struggle. DeForest called for a novel that would capture the entirety of American life, one that tried to cover it all. He admired Nathaniel Hawthorne and admitted his greatness, but he also believed his concerns were narrow; to DeForest, Hawthorne seemed to speak to and of New England alone. Harriet Beecher Stowe he found clumsy, while recognizing that she had the necessary ambition; and he didn't mention Herman Melville, whom nobody then read. In the years that followed, Henry James would make fun of DeForest's idea even as he sought his own form of greatness, setting much of his work in Europe and looking back at an America wiped clean of regional distinctions. Most of his compatriots had a different question, though. How could one combine an attention to the local, to the particularities of this place or that, with the ambition made necessary by the country's very range and sprawl?

Jewett looked to an ever-fading past, to the America that was; Dunnet Landing seems so beautifully preserved precisely because the postwar world has no place for its boatbuilders and sailing captains. Her protégé Willa Cather turned to the future instead, to the country in the process of becoming, and her sense of regional life and regional literature offers something profoundly different and significantly larger than the work of her local color predecessors. The prairie towns of *O Pioneers!* (1913) and *My Ántonia* (1918) are every bit as isolated as Jewett's Maine, but that's because they're new. They lie on the verge of the national life in both senses of the term: along its edge, and yet also ready to enter, something about to be more; and her people are always in motion. The key text here is Cather's 1915 *Song of the Lark*, a book about a girl with a voice. Thea Kronborg is a minister's daughter in a small Colorado town called Moonstone, a place where everybody has come from somewhere else—Sweden, Germany, Michigan, Mexico. She is forceful and dreamy and odd, and yet the place has a tolerance for individuality, a recognition that not everyone is cut to pattern; and when the town's piano teacher decides that Thea has talent, her mother pushes her to practice. At seventeen she receives a small legacy that lets her travel east to Chicago. The young person from the provinces goes to the great city, where she can find a better teacher, a bigger chance; it's the classic theme of the nineteenth-century European novel, only there it's usually a young man and the city will kill his soul.

Thea has better luck, better luck than Balzac's Rastignac or her Chicago contemporary, Theodore Dreiser's Sister Carrie, and though she does fall in love, what really seduces her is the music itself. She pays for her keep with a job in a church choir, and when her piano teacher hears her sing, he encourages her to train her voice and not her fingers. Adventures follow: a growing confidence and a touch of local fame; a broken heart and then the boat for Europe, where her real lessons begin. At thirty she returns to America and takes the stage in New York as Wagner's Sieglinde, no longer Thea so much as Kronborg, *die Kronborg*, and a triumph. Still, Cather knows what success has cost her, what the young woman's commitment to her vocation requires. Her parents die while she's abroad, she no longer has anything in common with her siblings, and at times her loneliness seems to eat her raw.

But she does remember the high plains and snowy peaks of her Colorado home, she carries Moonstone with her, and she dreams of her father on the night before she fully comes into her song. Her origins sustain her, they feed her will, and though Thea can no longer live in the place from which she started, she has nevertheless been made by it, by everything she has seen and known. And now she will claim the world. It is a fairy tale. Or perhaps an allegory, and the richest account of an artist's education in all American literature. Of course opera singers do claim the world, in the form of their repertoire, singing in several languages and sometimes on several continents as well. Thea Kronborg will travel far, just as Cather herself moved beyond her local origins to become a connoisseur of America's varied cultures; her greatest books are set in New Mexico, a place she didn't discover until she was almost forty.

Most regional writers did not, however, have Cather's extraordinary sense of optimism, her belief that the land itself is a promise—and here I will return us to Sherwood Anderson himself. His own small town of Winesburg offers something far more harrowing than either Jewett or Cather, an air of crawling unease that makes me want to look over my shoulder whenever I read of its quiet Ohio streets. Winesburg's residents include a man hounded by rumors of homosexuality, a doctor who's worn the same suit for ten years, and a farmer who believes that God has struck him mad, but still longs to do His bidding. The older people remember the Civil War and recognize that they don't fit the new world that has grown up after them; the young men play baseball and hope that some job or woman might give their life a meaning that never seems to arrive. Each of the book's stories concentrates on a different person, but some characters continue from tale to tale, above all a quiet curious boy called George Willard. His mother Elizabeth runs the local hotel and prays that he might be spared a life as drab as her own, a life different from what she believed, as a girl, she was promised. Not that anything in her adult existence seems terrible. Nothing in Winesburg is terrible, and the town itself is without either the poverty or the violence of Faulkner's Yoknapatawpha. And yet it is all unendurable, dull and stupid and unending. Elizabeth Willard wants George to get himself off to the city, to be "brisk and smart and alive"; he wants only "to go away and look at people and think." But then he does that already as a reporter for the local paper, a post that takes him through every cramped house and shop in the town, a witness to the sadness of other people, strangers in their own village.

His own sadness comes when his mother dies after a few months of "hungering . . . along the road of death," an old woman at forty-one. George sits up with her corpse and thinks of a girl he knows; under its sheets Elizabeth's body looks long and young and graceful, and he starts to his feet in shame. A few months later he will leave Winesburg behind, making it "a background on which to paint the dreams of his manhood." Those are the book's last words, and they ring a bit false; nothing Anderson has said makes us believe that the city might offer anything more than the broken fantasies of small-town life. His people are desperate and lonely and their minds at once furious and immobile. Yet though they are bound by their provincial circumstances, Winesburg isn't Dunnet Landing or Moonstone. It isn't dwindling or booming, and it's in no danger of losing its own individual identity precisely because it has never actually had one. It's just a small midwestern town, and by definition generic, a place like any other. There isn't even a local accent. Winesburg is nowhere, and anywhere, and everywhere, which may indeed be the source of its own particular terror.

———·——

MAYBE ANDERSON BELIEVED FAULKNER'S stories about World War I. Maybe. The Southerner's family knew better. They knew that in the summer of 1918 Billy Falkner had enlisted as a pilot in the Canadian branch of the RAF, adding a *u* to the family name in the process, and gone to Toronto for training. They also knew that the war ended before he could finish his course and that he was back in Oxford that December, wearing a smart uniform, affecting a limp, and boasting to anyone who would listen of having flown upside down in a Sopwith Camel. Faulkner never gave an entirely satisfactory answer as to why he chose this particular kind of military service. He could, after all, have simply joined the American army, but his biographer suggests he was looking for a way to avoid enlisting as a private, the only rank to which this high school dropout was entitled. Pilots, in contrast, received a commission at the end of their course, and then too he was drawn by the glamour of aerial combat. Knights of the air, duels in the sky—these startling new machines looked like the vehicles for an old kind of heroism, a contemporary cavalry charge in which men fought one-on-one, and survival seemed to depend on one's skill alone. Still, there was another reason why Faulkner wanted to put Mississippi behind him. The young woman he loved had gotten married to somebody else.

Two relationships dominated Faulkner's teens, one with a boy and another with a girl. The girl was called Estelle Oldham, and Faulkner had known her since they both were six. She had a china-doll face and a slender frame that seemed made for good clothes, and they grew up on the same block, inseparable both in school and outside it. When she was sixteen, her parents sent her away to the Mary Baldwin Seminary in Virginia, and in her absence Faulkner both left school and began to drink. She was gone just a year, but when she came back she moved into the vivid social world of undergraduate life at the University of Mississippi. Faulkner was desperately in love with her and yet he had no plans for a profession; he could not follow her into that new whirl of parties and dates and dances. Estelle's parents were ambitious, and she soon got engaged to a lawyer named Cornell Franklin. But she couldn't stop talking about running away with her childhood sweetheart, and on the very morning of her wedding, in April 1918, an aunt offered to help call it off. She went through with the ceremony anyway and then moved with her new husband to Honolulu, where he had a position in the Judge Advocate General's office; later they set up in Shanghai.

Faulkner wasn't in Oxford for Estelle's wedding, and her family wouldn't have welcomed him if he had been. Instead he was in New Haven, Connecticut, on a visit to the friend who in had in many ways replaced her, a lawyer's son named Phil Stone. Stone was a few years older than Faulkner and peculiarly overeducated: he had gotten undergraduate degrees at both Mississippi and Yale, and then repeated the process at their law schools. But what really interested him were books. He read Swinburne and Keats, subscribed to *Poetry* and the *Little Review*, and followed Ezra Pound and T. S. Eliot almost from the moment of their first publications. In 1914 an Oxford girlfriend introduced him to a teenager whom the other children in town already knew as a storyteller. Stone needed a hobby and was soon passing on everything he'd learned in his Yale English courses, putting Faulkner through a course of study that more than made up for his absent schooling. They read Balzac together; in 1924 they would read the banned *Ulysses*, with Stone giving him a smuggled copy. Phil Stone spent ten years supplying Billy Faulkner not only with books, most of them ordered from the New Haven shop where he kept an account, but also with the little magazines in which the day's most interesting new work appeared. He was convinced from the start of Faulkner's genius and saw himself as his mentor; the role has even earned him a biography of his own, subtitled *A Vicarious Life*. Nor was their friendship limited to books. Stone's father kept a hunting camp at which Faulkner was a regular guest, and the young lawyer was also a skilled poker player; both pastimes would appear throughout the novelist's work, in *Go Down, Moses* especially. Stone liked women too, which in their world meant brothels. The younger man went along but preferred to wait downstairs, observing the madam and her customers.

He was writing verse before he met Stone, however, and in 1919, after his return from Canada, he had a poem accepted by the *New Republic*. Its forty lines are a Yeatsian stew in which the speaker moves through a forest of "singing trees" in pursuit of a girl with "lascivious dreaming knees"; Faulkner, who always liked allusive titles, called it "L'Après-Midi d'un Faune." But most of his poems got rejected, and his life after his military escapade resembled that of any artistic undergraduate who hasn't yet found his métier. The University of Mississippi allowed him to register as a "special student." He took French and Spanish, studied Shakespeare, and built sets for the college's drama society; he joined a fraternity and contributed to the student newspaper and the yearbook. None of it seemed to settle him. Faulkner's manners were distant and formal. He wore his RAF uniform whenever he thought he could get away with it, and sometimes carried a cane; other students referred to him as "Count No 'Count." He did a number of odd jobs in these years, house-painting included, living with his family while earning at least a part of his keep; and in the fall of 1921 he went up to New York and found himself working for Elizabeth Prall. But there was another position waiting for him, less interesting though with more time to write, and that December he went home to begin three years in charge of the university's post office.

Faulkner's life at the P.O. is one of the legends of his biography. He hired two friends to fetch the mailbags from the train station, but instead of distributing it they spent their time playing cards; occasionally he would close up for a round of golf. Nevertheless, the job provided him with an extraordinary opportunity, and he was just irresponsible or maybe just purposeful enough to take it. The essays of writers like Henry James and Virginia Woolf offer us an almost complete inventory of their reading. Faulkner left nothing like that. He wrote little outside of his fiction, and his interviews are sketchy at best about what exactly he had picked up and when: *Moby-Dick*, yes, but otherwise just "the Flauberts and Conrads and Turgenievs." He spoke admiringly of Cather but never mentioned a particular novel, and he said nothing about his readings in history. Much of his literary background can be reconstituted from Stone's notes, but beyond that it's rarely safe to assume he had looked at a specific book. And yet it's never safe to assume that he hadn't. Every bit of mail destined for the university's library or its faculty came through his hands, every book and magazine in the great years of modernist experimentation, and often enough he stopped them on their way and used them to continue the education he had begun with Phil Stone. Sometimes he didn't bother to deliver them afterward.

Inevitably there were complaints, and finally an official investigation charged that he spent too much time reading on his own to keep the counter open and that he had even written a book while on duty. Faulkner resigned before he could be fired, and we might say he managed to keep the job until he no longer needed it. He left on Halloween in 1924, telling a friend that at least "I won't ever again have to be at the beck and call of every son of a bitch who's got two cents to buy a stamp." The charges were all true. He *had* produced a book on the government's dime, a collection of poems called *The Marble Faun*, and though he had to subsidize its publication, it was scheduled to come out at the end of the year from a small but reputable Boston house. It received no attention whatsoever, and at the New Year he went back down to New Orleans and his new friendship with Sherwood Anderson.

Thirty years later he would write his own account of their relationship. He got a room in the French Quarter, just off Jackson Square and down a street called Orleans Alley that ran alongside the city's cathedral; today it's known as Pirate Alley, and the building he lived in, its floor plan unchanged, houses the most charming of the city's independent bookshops. "Anderson talked and I listened," he wrote of the afternoons they spent on foot in the city, the Ohioan always in bright clothes better suited for the racetrack. They spun fantasies, one of them about a swamp-dwelling descendant of Andrew Jackson, "half-man half-sheep and presently half-shark." Sometimes they met again in the evening, only this time with a bottle. And as they walked Anderson would offer lessons in writerly dissatisfaction. He said that you might call a piece done when you couldn't see how to make it better, but that didn't mean it was ever good enough. Because the older man thought Faulkner had a problem. He had "too much talent. You can do it too easy, in too many different ways. If you're not careful, you'll never write anything."

No one aside from Phil Stone would have said as much at the time, and Faulkner's earliest pieces give no indication at all of the scale of that talent. Biographers sometimes claim to find a key to his aesthetic or his psyche in his apprentice work; critics might trace a line or metaphor out into his maturity. But nothing he wrote before his first novel, *Soldiers' Pay* (1926), would be worth reading if it weren't for what came later; and even that book and its successor, *Mosquitoes* (1927), would be long forgotten as well. The articles he contributed to the university newspaper in Oxford are no better than most student journalism, and as late as 1926 he tried to write a heroic allegory about "young Sir Galwyn" of Arthgyl, with his horse all "caparisoned in scarlet and cloth of gold." He was not a precocious writer. Hemingway did better younger, F. Scott Fitzgerald too; as an undergraduate T. S. Eliot was already making Victorian poetry into something entirely new. From his teens on Faulkner was always at work, but his poetry remained a sampler of other people's voices, and in prose he took years to find his proper material and cadence.

Still, there are moments in the sketches and stories he produced in New Orleans in which he does begin to sound like himself. In the first months of 1925 he contributed both to the *Times-Picayune*, the city's leading newspaper, and a literary monthly called *The Double-Dealer*, a journal founded on the seemingly paradoxical principle that it was possible to be both Southern and modernist at once. Its offices were just outside the French Quarter, and in 1922 it had run one of his early poems; other contributors included Allen Tate and the young Robert Penn Warren, along with such non-Southerners as Djuna Barnes and Anderson himself. Faulkner gave the *Double-Dealer* a set of rather precious vignettes that appeared at the start of the year, prose-poems depicting some of the city's conventional types—priest, longshoreman, whore. But the *Times-Picayune* paid better and the work he did for it had a stronger thrust. A sketch from that April described the statue of Andrew Jackson, in his eponymous square, as marked by a "terrific arrested motion," three words that could have come out of *As I Lay Dying* or *Absalom, Absalom!* An "idiot" in a story from the same month holds a narcissus tightly in his hand, his eyes "clear and blue as cornflowers, and utterly vacant of thought," just like Benjy Compson in *The Sound and the Fury*. And later that year "The Liar" begins with four men on the gallery of a country store, spitting tobacco out into the landscape as one of them begins to tell a story.

In one of his *Double-Dealer* pieces Faulkner imagines the Crescent City as a tourist might see it, describing it in conventionally gendered terms as "a courtesan, not old and yet no longer young, who shuns the sunlight that the illusion of her former glory be preserved." Dim and tarnished, with incense in its air: New Orleans was a seductive place, and all the more so for being jaded and worn. The city's economy depended on its port—the oil came later—and in the 1920s the city was still the South's largest, with its population edging up above 400,000, swelled by both Italian immigrants and new arrivals from its surrounding fields of cane and cotton. Louis Armstrong had already moved to Chicago by the time Faulkner arrived, but New Orleans remained loud with street corner trumpets, its nightclubs swung, and Prohibition was nominal at best. Faulkner liked it. He liked most cities—New York, and Memphis, where people from Oxford went to shop and to sin, and later Paris. New Orleans had an intricate past, with a flick of danger in its mixture of languages and cultures, an attractive place where you couldn't always tell just who was who. It was bustling and langorous and crooked, a Caribbean capital with good food and better music; and it was also the only city in the South with an interesting literary heritage. George Washington Cable came from a slave-owning family and had fought for the Confederacy before experiencing an almost religious conversion to the cause of civil rights; Kate Chopin was originally from Saint Louis but had married a New Orleans cotton broker. At the end of the nineteenth century they each used the conventions of local color writing to explore the borders of racial identity; and both had been frank enough to outrage their own white world.

But Faulkner hadn't come to New Orleans to stay, however much he enjoyed himself there. He wanted to use the city quite literally as a port of departure and hoped to catch a freighter bound for Europe. Nevertheless, he lingered into the early summer, talking with Anderson and working on what would become his first novel. He called it *Mayday*, a signal of distress; and while the title wouldn't last, the feeling would. Published as *Soldiers' Pay*, it presents us with two deliberately inscrutable characters. One is a war widow in her twenties. Margaret Powers has married a lieutenant she barely knows, and though she enjoys her vividly remembered honeymoon, she has just decided to break with him when she gets the news of his death. She is benevolent but dangerous, a puzzle to herself, and far more lost than any of the book's ex-soldiers. The other character is a wounded pilot called Donald Mahon. His face is hideously scarred, he's going blind, and he says little more than "Carry on." Margaret meets him on the train and helps take him back to the small Georgia community where he grew up; back to his minister father and the shallow belle to whom he was engaged. Faulkner gets a grim comedy out of the townspeople's attempts to read Mahon's blank, ruined face, and he does suggest their utter incomprehension of the pilot's experience. But the book is broken-backed. It never fuses the story of a Lost Generation with its satire of small-town life, and the place itself remains abstract. The scholar Cleanth Brooks suggests that Faulkner's Charlestown, Georgia, might as well be in New Hampshire, and, however readable, the book lies to the side of his principal oeuvre.

Faulkner worked on the novel through the spring of 1925 and then submitted it to Boni and Liveright, a new house with a name as the most au courant of New York publishers. Horace Liveright was willing to take risks. He published Sigmund Freud and Hart Crane, along with John Reed's memoir of the Russian revolution, *Ten Days That Shook the World*; he did the American edition of Eliot's *Wasteland* and that October would release Hemingway's *In Our Time*. Anderson too was one of his writers and said, in Faulkner's version of the story, that he would recommend the book so long as he didn't also have to read it. In fact, he had already seen Faulkner's early drafts and told Liveright that he had "a hunch this man is a comer." A year later, though, he added that the young writer might be a "bit like a thoroughbred colt who needs a race or two before he can do his best." A comer, but also still figuring out how to run: Anderson loved horses and often wrote about them, and in this case his judgment was accurate. That July Faulkner at last caught his freighter to Europe. He spent five months abroad, much of it in Paris, as I've already noted, trying to write a book about a young American painter in France. He left it unfinished, a novel about a world he didn't know at all. On his return he started another one about literary life in New Orleans, a loose and talky thing set aboard a pleasure boat on Lake Pontchartrain. He called it *Mosquitoes*, and some of its characters were recognizable versions of his friends, Anderson included; funny if you're in on the joke, but little more.

By that time their relations had cooled. Faulkner was still doing it too many ways; he hadn't decided what kind of writer he wanted to be, and yet he now began to outgrow his teacher. The older writer had gone past his peak. His sales remained strong but he never matched the artistic success of *Winesburg, Ohio*; his stories are still read, but none of his novels have any presence today. Faulkner gave one of them a sharpish review and wrote a parody of Anderson's work as well; and the older writer turned against him. Elizabeth

Prall said they were too much alike for the friendship to last, but Faulkner later called Anderson "the father of my generation," of Hemingway and John Dos Passos as well as himself, and he always remembered one lesson in particular. For as they walked through New Orleans they talked about the relation of their own local origins to the national life, about the place of regional writing in American literature as a whole. Anderson was all Ohio, and self-conscious about it in a way that, for Faulkner, marked a limitation; nothing but *Winesburg* quite escaped its origins. His teaching was better than his practice, however, and what Faulkner learned from him was that to be a writer "one has first got to be what he is, what he was born." And that was enough—it didn't matter where you were from, for no one place was more central than any other. "You're a country boy," Anderson told him. "All you know is that little patch up there in Mississippi where you started from. But that's all right too. It's America too." Just touch it right and the entire continent would open. Faulkner would discover that he could define the world only by first defining his home. He would enter his bid for greatness by becoming the most intensely local of American writers.

SARAH ORNE JEWETT WRITES about her Maine villages in order to make us see. She's always aware of the world outside, and she writes to explain her people to an audience from elsewhere, to that *Atlantic* subscriber for whom her narrator is a stand-in. Her hard-bitten midwestern contemporary Hamlin Garland was born on a Wisconsin farm and found a different way to stand outside his origins. The stories in his 1891 *Main-Travelled Roads* rely on protagonists who have returned home after a long absence. They've been in business elsewhere, or maybe in the war; the farm or the village has changed, they need to find their footing, and Garland uses them to give the reader both a native's understanding and a set of exploring, disillusioned eyes.

Faulkner did something else. He wrote of Mississippi, and really only of Mississippi, and yet he also made a decisive break with any remnants of the local color tradition. He describes his world with an unrivalled exactitude, the wheel ruts and the courthouse square, the dogs gathered for the hunt and the cabins back in the hills. He does make his readers see, and yet that's not his purpose and he hardly seems to care if we do. Quentin Compson's Harvard classmates may ask him to "tell about the South," but when he speaks he's only incidentally aware of his audience; he's not explaining it to them but rather to himself, and at a certain point his utterance remains unspoken. Books like *Light in August* (1932) and *The Hamlet* (1940) do, admittedly, seem full of people explaining things to each other, bits of family history or the details of a famous Yoknapatawpha County murder; yet none of them are outsiders and when they speak it's to tell of something they all already half-know. Faulkner would transcend local color by seeming to forget that there is anything *but* the local, as if he had shut a door between himself and the world outside and grown strangely unconscious of anything but his own little patch of ground. Oh, of course his characters know about that other world—they go to Memphis or New Orleans or even New England, and some of them run away to Texas. But nothing that happens there ever really counts; it's just a rumble of thunder at the outer edge of hearing.

His most important work exists in the apparent contradiction between a letter he wrote in 1944 and an interview he gave a dozen years later. In the mid-1940s the critic Malcolm Cowley began to work on an anthology called *The Portable Faulkner*; it was published in 1946 and helped spark the revival of interest in the novelist's work that culminated in the Nobel Prize. Faulkner affected indifference but he took an active interest in the project, and their correspondence offers the most valuable set of his letters we have. "I'm inclined to think," he wrote to Cowley, "that my material, the South, is not very important to me. I just happen to know it, and dont have time in one life to learn another one and write at the same time." The claim seems outrageous—so outrageous that it's worth taking seriously. To understand it, though, we'll need that later statement too, a sentence drawn from his 1956 interview with the *Paris Review*. Faulkner told the journal that when he began *Sartoris*—the book we now call *Flags in the Dust*—he found that "my own little postage stamp of native soil was worth writing about and that I would never live long enough to exhaust it, and by sublimating the actual into the apocryphal I would have complete liberty to use whatever talent I might have to the absolute top."

Evidently Faulkner still had a few stamps to sell. The words are often quoted and seem at first like a simple application of Anderson's advice about his "little patch" of ground. Put them alongside his letter to Cowley, however, and this classic defense of American regionalism actually tells us more about its dangers. Every place may be worth writing about, and Faulkner's immersion in his own bit of native soil had given him a necessary frame of reference, a place he could take for granted. Yet that postage stamp doesn't have anything special or intrinsically valuable about it. He makes no claim for its particular worth and certainly has no interest in defending the idea of a distinctively Southern way of life. It's just that it's his. He knows its shape and speech and soil, knows how to work it; knows it well enough to know when it alone is not enough. For novels aren't collections of facts and the "actual" doesn't really much matter. Jewett and Garland and Chesnutt had wanted to get their settings right, and yet a precise account of the landscape or a transcription of regional speech is never on its own enough, not if the actual is to become apocryphal, a legend or "keystone in the Universe."

If the local is all we've got, then it can't be allowed to set a limit on ambition, as it had seemed to the writers and readers of the late nineteenth-century short story. The local has to become something more if one is to use one's talent to the top, it needs to hold everything, questions about the nature of time and consciousness along with a set of particular manners and mores. And for that, he thought, there was nothing at all necessary about the South's presence in his work; another place would do as well, if only he had time to learn it. But he didn't, and what he had, all he had, was the region that was already his. He told Cowley that in writing *Absalom, Absalom!* he didn't share Quentin's compulsion to explain his home. That pained need belonged to the character, "but he not I was brooding over a situation," and doubtless Faulkner needed at some level to trick himself into believing it. We don't have to, and certainly he never wrote so powerfully—so magnificently—about anywhere or anything else.

"Art is no part of southern life." So he said in an unpublished essay from 1933, and two years later the Kentucky-born poet and critic Allen Tate argued that "we lack a tradition in the arts; more to the point, we lack a literary tradition. We lack even a literature." Neither of those statements was quite true, and if either man had stretched his mind back into the 1880s he would have found some predecessors, two writers who defined the creative possibilities provided by the Civil War itself, even though their own work could not fully exploit them. Albion Tourgee fought for the Union and then served for a decade as a judge in North Carolina, working on behalf of Radical Reconstruction, battling the Klan, and earning his enemies' respect for his honesty and courage. He described those struggles in an 1879 novel called *A Fool's Errand*, one of the day's bestsellers, and in 1896 appeared for the plaintiff in *Plessy v. Ferguson*. He lost that case, and the Supreme Court's decision established the principle of separate but equal public accommodations on which the Jim Crow South depended. I've already mentioned George Washington Cable, who began his literary career with a volume of local color stories called *Old Creole Days* (1879). He was one of the first American writers to work in dialect, a Presbyterian teetotaler who nevertheless became a friend and an inspiration to the irreligious Mark Twain. Cable found his particular subject in the border—the sexual border as well as the social one—between the old French society of his native New Orleans and its many *gens de couleur libre*, its free people of color. Eventually his essays about racial justice made it impossible for him to stay in the South, and in 1885 he settled in Massachusetts.

Tourgee was a political activist who wrote; Cable, in contrast, was a contemplative forced by conscience into public life. In 1882 the latter gave a commencement address at the University of Mississippi, in which he argued that the South's reliance on slavery had produced an "estrangement" from the world of imaginative literature. The region's entire intellectual energy had been marshaled in the institution's defense, and in consequence its society remained "fixed, immovable, iron-bound. . . . No moral question was open for public discussion." But the very aspects of Southern life that had kept it from developing a literature of its own were precisely the ones that now most called for it. So in speaking to the Mississippi graduates Cable suggested that it was time for a sustained look within. The men and women of the white world needed to study the effects that slavery had had on their own minds, to examine the flaws "in our views and . . . our temper."

Cable's speech was well received; whether any of his listeners took it to heart is another question. Tourgee's view was both wider and more combative. "The South as a Field for Fiction" appeared in an 1888 issue of *Forum*, a New

York–based journal of opinion with a reformist edge, and began by noting that Southern stories had become popular in Northern magazines; Tourgee had Thomas Nelson Page's plantation tales in mind above all. For by the 1880s most white Americans saw slavery as a dead letter, a merely political question that the war itself had settled; they believed that the country had reached closure; it was time to accept the past and move on. Tourgee would have none of it. That belief ignored the fact that "two centuries of bondage [had] left an ineradicable impress on master and slave alike." The North might forget that burden; the South could not. The past was always there, and to the South's black citizens that past was the site of "unimaginable horrors. . . . Every freedman's life is colored by this shadow," and the further away it got, the more bitter its legacy would seem. There could never be compensation enough for that, and yet for a writer that suffering offered a wealth of material, "richer and far more tragic than the folk-lore" recorded in the tales of Uncle Remus. He imagined that the South's literary future lay in the historical novel and thought some of that literature would be written by the children of Confederate soldiers. But some would be written by the children of slaves.

These were not local issues, not peculiar to Mississippi or North Carolina. They affected the region as a whole—what the antebellum world had called the "section"—but they were also national, a dilemma that in the twentieth century would give the literature of the South its cultural valence and centrality, the reach and ambition and range of the greatest American novels. Faulkner himself always claimed that he never did a lick of research, never opened a book with the idea of finding something inside it to use. That's not entirely true, but Cable's commencement address wasn't published until 1955 and despite its Oxford origins it's unlikely that Faulkner knew it; or the Tourgee article either, for that matter. The questions they raise about slavery's enduring presence had barely begun to be explored by the time Faulkner started to publish. Nevertheless, they define a program for the region's literature, and their analysis was one that he in particular came to share. Probably he would have laughed at that idea. He wasn't what he called a literary man, a man of letters like Cowley, or at least he didn't want to be seen as one; he was just a storyteller, or even, sometimes, a farmer. He didn't write about history but about old soldiers and former slaves, lawyers and shopkeepers and

FIVE

Inventing Yoknapatawpha

Yoknapatawpha began with a tall tale about a con artist. Faulkner typically composed in longhand, writing in a minute but legible script on unlined legal-sized paper; he numbered the sheets and kept the left-hand side empty, a space for interpolations and revisions. Most of his pages show the expected mess of scratched-out sentences and inserted phrases, but some of them are uncannily clean; he famously said that he didn't change a word of *As I Lay Dying*, and while that was hardly the truth the novel's final version *is* surprisingly close to its first one. Afterward he did some though not all of his own typing, revising as his fingers hit the keys. Late in 1926, and living once more in New Orleans after the publication of *Soldiers' Pay*, he wrote a title at the top of a sheet and then moved into a new story. He called it "Father Abraham":

> He is a living example of the astonishing byblows of man's utopian dreams actually functioning; in this case the dream is Democracy. He will become legendary in time, but he has always been symbolic. Legendary as Roland and as symbolic of an age and a region as his predecessor, a portly man with a white imperial and a shoestring tie and a two gallon hat, was; as symbolic and as typical of a frame of mind as Buddha is today.

The lines are overwrought but Faulkner must have liked them; they sit unrevised on both his handwritten page and the typescript. The title character is a man named Flem Snopes: Father Abraham only insofar as he's the founder of a tribe, a swarm of nephews and cousins and in-laws and their cousins too, who over the years will settle with his help into running blacksmith's shops and dirty picture shows and every kind of business in between. The title is parodic, sardonic, and so are the references to Roland and the Buddha. But they do show that Faulkner is already turning this place into myth and looking for its typical or even archetypical figure, someone to replace the courtly gentleman with the shoestring tie.

Phil Stone later said that he'd given Faulkner his theme here, claiming that the real story of the modern South lay not in its racial questions but rather in "the rise of the redneck." At this distance we may doubt that, or at the very least insist on the relation between them; nevertheless, this is where Yoknapatawpha got its start. Not that Faulkner had named it yet. "Father Abraham" opens with Flem sitting in the window of a bank he now apparently controls, but then falls back in time to the end of the nineteenth century and a hamlet known as Frenchman's Bend; back to the place "where the light of day" first found him, twenty miles to the southeast of the town Faulkner already called Jefferson. Those names would stay, and he would take that of the county itself from a stagnant little river that flows through the actual Lafayette County, a few miles south of his Oxford home. Maps now show it as the Yocona, but the Chickasaws who once held that land did in fact call it the Yoknapatawpha. Faulkner later claimed that he got the name from a term meaning "water runs slow through flat land," but his etymology has been challenged. The word in fact suggests an earth ripped open, which has its resonance too.

"Father Abraham" shows Flem newly returned to Frenchman's Bend after a trip to Texas, accompanied by a man named Buck, "a soiled swaggering man in a clay colored Stetson," who carries a pistol in one pocket and a package of gingersnaps in the other. With them is a string of calico horses, spotted things roped together with barbed wire and as "wild as rabbits, deadly as rattlesnakes." The local farmers all own mules; horses carry status, everybody wants one, and nobody believes he can afford one. These uncontrollable animals will go cheap, however, and between them Buck and Flem set up an auction—two dollars, five, maybe eight. Only it's never clear who actually owns the ponies, who's making the money. Is it a partnership, are they Flem's, or do they maybe belong to Buck, and he's going to take all the cash away with him? Who's responsible for one villager's broken leg, the consequence of trying to catch the beast on which he's spent his last dime? Each man puts it all off on the other, and Faulkner will never answer these questions. The scam clearly delights him, though, and he would return throughout his career to scenes of financial chicanery, to the elaborate plans one man lays to defraud another.

In literary terms the story comes out of what's called frontier humor. The best-known examples today are triumphs of exaggeration like Mark Twain's *Roughing It* (1872) and his "Celebrated Jumping Frog of Calaveras County" (1865), but collections of such stretchers were common in the second half of the nineteenth century: adjective-rich and often heavy-handed attempts to fix an oral form in print. Yet this one also had a biographical origin. Faulkner's paternal uncle John was a hard-bitten lawyer and political fixer, a fierce segregationist who never thought much of either his nephew or his work. Still, in the early 1920s he sometimes used the young man as a chauffeur, and in one village they saw just such an auction, a line of spotted unbroken horses wired together for sale. One of the beasts got up onto a boarding house porch after it was cut loose and ran along its length, driving Faulkner himself inside. In the story it sprints into and through the house, surprising a man in his underwear and then meeting the landlady on the back porch; she's carrying "an armful of yet damp clothing" and breaks a washboard across the horse's face without any effect at all.

Faulkner never finished "Father Abraham." He took the anecdote about the Texas ponies to its conclusion, began a new chapter, and then stopped. But he never abandoned it either, and he would never shake himself loose of the Snopeses; would never really want to. He revised the tale of the auction into a short story called "As I Lay Dying," a title he liked so much that a few years later he used it again for the novel; the two share a few minor characters but no more. The story failed to sell, and so did four or five other attempts at the same material, until in 1931 he got *Scribner's* to take a version named "Spotted Horses"; this one was told in the first person by the man in his underwear, a traveling sewing-machine salesman called V. K. Suratt. By then Faulkner was at work on other Snopes tales as well, and in 1940 he stitched some of them together into *The Hamlet*, an expanded version of "Spotted Horses" included. He wasn't yet done with them, though, and in the late 1950s he followed their story out in *The Town* and *The Mansion*: the chronicle of a family from "the land and yet rootless . . . cunning and dull and clannish . . . [like] mold on cheese, steadfast and gradual and implacable," and munching down everything in its path.

"Father Abraham" wasn't published until 1983, a fragment found among Faulkner's papers; no one would read it in preference to *The Hamlet*, and yet it's astonishing how much of Yoknapatawpha it already contains. There are moments of description as fine as any he ever wrote—a cold dinner eaten "beneath the moth swirled lamp"—characters he would always come back to, and above all the entire geography of his imagined land. Frenchman's Bend and Jefferson, the hill country and the county seat, the two poles of this world. Faulkner begins in the country, in a district without a single black farmer, a place of Methodists and Baptists, poor whites who grow cotton in the bottomland and corn for whiskey in the "pine clad hills." The Bundren family in *As I Lay Dying* comes out of that landscape, taking their mother's corpse to Jefferson for burial, and *Sanctuary* begins there too, in the ruins of what's called the Old Frenchman's Place, an empty, crumbling plantation house from the lost time before the war. Indeed, by 1930 Faulkner had almost everything about Yoknapatawpha's history and its people already in his head, a world that existed in its entirety long before he could set it down. But "Father Abraham" wasn't enough, he needed the social mix of Jefferson too, and after 14,000 words he put it away and turned toward town.

His friendship with Anderson had foundered by then. Restless and unsettled, Faulkner moved back to Oxford at the New Year, and in February 1927 wrote his publisher, Horace Liveright, that he was at work on both a novel and a collection of stories about "my townspeople"; later he described the novel as the book to which his "other things were but foals." He called it *Flags in the Dust*, and we have already seen it in part: the story of a Mississippi family whose history is a grander version of his own. The novel begins in 1919 with old Will Falls stumping into the bank on Jefferson's courthouse square, bringing with him the memory of Bayard Sartoris's Confederate father, of a past and a family tradition that nobody seems able to escape. Some time later

Bayard climbs to the attic of the house the Colonel rebuilt after the war and opens a chest that's lain shut for decades, the smell of cedar rising around him, and "a legion of ghosts . . . at his shoulder." He takes out an elegant rapier and a heavy cavalry sabre; a set of dueling pistols, an officer's coat and the derringer his father wore under his sleeve; and finally a family Bible, in which he writes the name of his grandson John and the date of his death, a flier shot from the sky in the last months of the Great War. It is, he thinks, a "good gesture," but no more; time always wins anyway. And meanwhile Young Bayard, John's twin, lives in a heedless frenzy of bottles and fast cars, while wondering if he's quite as brave as a Sartoris should be.

The first thing Faulkner ever finished about Yoknapatawpha, then, is a book about the memory of the Civil War. But *Flags in the Dust* is more than that, more too than a family history. For one thing, the Snopeses are here as well. We are a generation on from the horse auction; Flem has long since moved to Jefferson and to old Bayard's "profane astonishment" become vice president of the Sartoris bank. His cousin Byron is now the bank's cashier and writes obscene letters in his spare time to a young woman in town called Narcissa Benbow; and she in turn will marry Young Bayard, though without ever seeming to like him. Faulkner's early critics made far too much out of the opposition in his work between the Sartoris and the Snopes families, starting with a 1939 essay in which George Marion O'Donnell argued that while the Sartorises "act always with an ethically responsible will," the Snopeses are motivated by self-interest alone. The tension between them, the argument claims, presents a "universal conflict" in which a traditional order is threatened by an inhospitable modernity. A reader would, however, need to be a romantic indeed to find anything like that in Young Bayard; his alcoholic failure hardly requires the Snopeses or even the modern world.

Still, these are the people, the families, with which Faulkner began. Their opposition wound the clock. Afterward it might run of itself, and the conflict between them in no way contains or defines the vivid corporate life of Jefferson and its surroundings. Yet even if we downplay their importance we can't forget that they set him ticking, and that opposition does indeed track a movement in Southern political history, in which patrician landowners were replaced in power by more populist and more openly racist figures; in which a business-minded New South appeared to push an agricultural society aside. *Appeared*—for as we have already seen with the Nashville Agrarians, the white South liked to believe that its old order had remained somehow separate from the world of the marketplace. That was one of the stories it told about itself in Faulkner's era, and at times he told it himself, looking on dyspeptically at the twentieth century's "row after row of small crowded jerry-built individually owned demiurban bungalows."

But he knew other stories too, and to insist on this one is to miss the ever-increasing importance of race in his sense of the region's history. That is not, however, something that a casual reader might have predicted from *Flags in the Dust* alone. William Faulkner used racial epithets almost every day of his life, and as a young man he accepted the whole social order of the Jim Crow South; in 1931 he even told an interviewer that "Southern Negroes would be better off under the conditions of slavery than they are today." Many white Southerners talked like that. Only one of them wrote *The Sound and the Fury*, and yet when he was talking Faulkner was, as we have seen, all too often caught by the conventional thought and language of his time and station. He *allowed* himself to get caught—would revert, or regress, or become what he himself called "a native of our land and a sharer in its errors"; errors he saw but could not resist. Yet something happened when he faced a fictional page. The pen made him honest, and from the beginning he skinned his eyes at the racial hierarchy in which a part of him never stopped believing.

The black characters in the early Yoknapatawpha novels are as clearly individuated as his white ones, and Faulkner is always a close observer of manners and social codes. At one point in *Flags in the Dust* Young Bayard hires some African-American musicians to serenade his sweetheart and afterward offers them a drink from his jug of corn. Their lips can't touch the same rim, however, and nobody has a cup, so he takes the breather-cap off his car's engine: "It'll taste a little like oil for a drink or two, but you boys wont notice it after that." We notice it, though, a moment when those codes push beyond absurdity and into the grotesque. And Faulkner wants us to—that's why he invented this incident. For he himself noticed such practices often enough to think them worth setting down; in fiction he was able to stand outside his Oxford, his Jefferson, and see the behavior his people take for granted, the things they don't even question. It's inconceivable, to young Bayard, that he might simply pass the jug, and who knows what Faulkner the man would have done with a bottle in his hand? But this moment exists for a reason, and what counts is the novelist's decision to stress it, to employ that breather-cap in place of the cup his plotting could so easily have provided.

Other moments bring us into the kitchen run by the Strother family—the Sartoris servants, descendants of the Colonel's slaves. Faulkner imagines what they might say when there are no white people around to hear, and at times his use of dialect seems as egregious as anything in Thomas Nelson Page, loaded with "gwine" and "cullud" and "mouf" for mouth. Or is it? Almost all Southern writers of his period, white or black, used that vernacular, one whose details included word choice and grammar as well as orthography. It figures in both Richard Wright and Zora Neale Hurston, right down to "mouf," though Wright himself argues that such linguistic conventions are part of the minstrelsy forced upon the black artist. I don't think any serious novelist at work today would write the kind of dialogue one finds in *Flags in the Dust*: "Him en Isom off somewhar in dat cyar." There is, however, a more interesting and important issue behind that now-embarrassing bit of phonics, with its effort to capture an accent's variation from some imputed norm. For by what right has Faulkner put himself in that kitchen at all? The cultural politics of our moment have at times suggested that the attempt to represent or to speak for the other, through the other, stands as an unwarrantable act of appropriation. It claims material to which one has no title, and in this case involves a scene at which someone like Faulkner himself could not, by definition, be present. Should the white writer have the freedom to depict black speech or black lives at all?

The novelist himself would probably have said that his work needed to include such voices and such characters; his account of Southern life would be entirely implausible if he *didn't* have the Strothers talking in the kitchen or working in the garden. That argument—one cast in terms of realism—is unlikely to convince anyone who doesn't agree with it already. There are better ones, though, beginning with the simple point that the novelist could not have depicted the power relations in his society as fully as he eventually did without employing such characters. *The Unvanquished* shows the different ways that the white and black people on the Sartoris plantation meet the moment of emancipation; *Light in August* the brutality with which the local police search for information, and the fear with which Jefferson's black community sees them. But there is an even more powerful argument. For if a writer like Faulkner—if a white writer today—were *not* to write about Americans of other races, then he would in effect have segregated his world even more completely than Jim Crow itself ever dreamed possible. Such a writer might have the best of intentions, in his reluctance to seem as though he were speaking for others. Nevertheless, his work would present a vision of society as an all-white fantasy, indeed a white nationalist's dream.

The question isn't whether or not Faulkner has a right to this material. It's one of execution. Just how does he present these characters? What are the conditions—the assumptions, the prejudices—that shape his portrait? Can we trust his ear, and does he depict these people in different terms than he does his white ones, erecting a hierarchy of representation that replicates that of the social world around him? These aren't questions that can be settled in the abstract. They must be tested moment by moment, and always with reference to particular passages and incidents. Here it's worth noting what I take to be Faulkner's sense of his own limitations. At times he dips briefly into the minds of his black characters, allowing us to look at them as they look at the world around them. But he doesn't use a Joycean stream-of-consciousness in depicting their inner lives, and he never imagines a black narrator, as he did with the many white voices that speak to us in *As I Lay Dying*, characters whose first-person interior worlds we inhabit fully. That's a choice, and one I think he made because he didn't trust himself to get such a narrator right.

What he does instead is to give us a close description of a character's physical presence, a description that works to convey an inner life. The best example is Dilsey Gibson in *The Sound and the Fury*. That novel's first three sections are first-person interior monologues, one in the voice of each of the Compson brothers. It then switches, in its fourth and last section, to an omniscient third person, and with the narrative emphasis itself shifting to the black family whose lives march alongside those of their white employers. Dilsey is the family matriarch, and the Compsons' cook. We see the clothes she wears, the "man's felt hat and an army overcoat, beneath the frayed skirts of which her blue gingham dress fell in uneven balloonings"; we watch her build a fire in the kitchen, an old woman stacking "stovewood into her crooked arm." Later she walks to church, a figure of authority, and slowly these details build into a complex account of her life, of her relation to the two families that depend upon her. And we will listen to her as well, her voice always terse and utterly focused on the job at hand. At one point, exasperated by a fuss in the house before breakfast, she tells her grandson Luster that she doesn't "want nobody else yelling down dem stairs at me twell I rings de bell." Her speech may be represented phonetically, but she is in no sense a figure of fun, and her words belong to *her* rather than to a social type. Her grandson speaks with the same accent, but far more volubly, and with a teenager's jumping excitement; her daughter Frony with a nervous awareness that white people are watching them.

Yet the novel also offers us a more complicated account of black speech. At church that day—Easter Sunday, 1928—Dilsey hears a sermon by a minister visiting from Saint Louis, a sermon that in effect he delivers twice. At first he sounds "like a white man. His voice was level and cold," but the more he speaks the more the congregation recognizes how skillfully he uses that voice, and they admire its "virtuosity." Then he pauses, holds still for a moment, and starts over with everything changed. He switches registers and this second voice has the "sad, timbrous quality" of a saxophone, as "different as day and dark from his former tone." "Brethren," the preacher says, and then he rings out clear, "Breddren en sistuhn." This second sermon, in a key that the congregation recognizes as their own, seems all the more effective because of what has come before. But the novelist never suggests which one is the preacher's "natural" voice, never offers a clue. Language is social, contextual—it is not in fact "natural." Faulkner usually depicts the speech of his white characters with standard orthography—their word choice and phrasing are a different matter—but up in New England the oldest Compson boy, the Harvard student Quentin, is described as talking "like a colored man." The few Northern black characters in Faulkner's work speak an English that seems indistinguishable from his white ones.

This argument can take us only so far. During the 1930s a number of pioneering Northern social scientists did field work in Mississippi. One of the best was Hortense Powdermaker, whose *After Freedom* (1939) provided a close account of the black community in the Delta town of Indianola. Most of its men were laborers and farmers, and its women domestic servants, but she also described its small middle class of teachers and undertakers, insurance agents, doctors, and of course ministers too. Faulkner shows us nothing of that. The black residents of his apocryphal county all fill stereotypical roles, working the jobs in which white Mississippians most often saw their black neighbors: maids and washerwomen, stablehands and sharecroppers, men sitting on the square and ready to run an errand. Each named character may be particularized, but still they speak in the mumbled accents of literary convention; and no black child in all of Yoknapatawpha ever seems to be in school. Still, nothing in Faulkner's work is simple, and even at his broadest he is in one crucial thing closer to Charles Chesnutt than to Thomas Nelson Page. The clichéd language he gives to his characters matters less than the fact that he always imagines their voices and lives as having an existence that lies outside of and separate from that of the white world around them. Dilsey Gibson's life is not subsumed into that of the Compsons, or the Strothers' by the Sartorises. He shows us, through the things these characters talk about and the judgments they pass, that their plans and desires are never fully determined by those of the white families for whom they work. They have their own lives to make, their own world and ambitions. That may seem a small point to us now, and yet it's also a starting point, and one that many of his white contemporaries could never quite grasp. Each of his major novels would go further.

We don't know exactly when Faulkner began to write *Flags in the Dust*, when he put "Father Abraham" aside. Nor do we know when he made the most consequential decision of his career, the decision to draw over and over again on the same physical and human geography. He had read Balzac with Phil Stone, and the linked stories of *Winesburg, Ohio* are an obvious model for his proposed book of tales about his "townspeople"—but just when did he realize what he was doing? Faulkner didn't keep a notebook or diary in which we might trace the conception or development of a particular work. Henry James recorded the dinner-table conversation that gave him an idea for a story; Virginia Woolf wrote in her diary that she wanted to put her parents on paper at last, and the result was *To the Lighthouse*. With Faulkner we have the obvious biographical parallels between John Sartoris and the Old Colonel, and a few acknowledged links between his characters and their "originals," like that between Benjy Compson and Edwin Chandler, the intellectually disabled brother of Faulkner's first-grade teacher. Scholarship has given us others, but much of his work seems sourceless still, and his comments about the idea of Yoknapatawpha all date from after its house was built.

We do, however, have his manuscripts, with their false starts and canceled chapters, and know that this novel's opening pages gave Faulkner trouble. He hadn't yet found Old Man Falls, and instead of the old trooper's garrulous memories he offered an inert account of the Sartoris family history: "Sartoris. Bayard Sartoris: A fatal name. There is death in it." Faulkner is feeling his way here, taking his first steps in this imagined land, and the trail is a hard one; no path is entirely wrong, but some of them are not yet right. In style and structure *Flags in the Dust* remains the easiest of the Yoknapatawpha books, but no reader should begin with it. Or maybe Faulkner himself shouldn't have begun with it. The novel has too many characters and too many plots, and some moments are predicated on books he hadn't yet written. *Who are these people?* And why does he write as if we should know them already, know the old country doctor, Peabody, or the talkative sewing-machine salesman, Suratt? It's as if the whole of the excessively peopled world that already lived within him needs to be put on the page at once; as if Faulkner thinks he'll never have another chance to get it all down. New readers will find the book baffling, but those who have read a few of his other novels already won't mind its flaws. They'll have met many of its characters before and might even know how some of its loose ends get tied.

Faulkner would always risk the confusion of citing himself. *The Sound and the Fury* contains a sentence about "old Colonel Sartoris" that not even the few readers who already knew about the character could understand; a decade later *The Unvanquished* would make it clear. Faulkner finished *Flags in the Dust* in late September 1927, just a few days after his thirtieth birthday, and was confident enough when he sent it to his publisher to add some instructions for the typesetter. Horace Liveright's answer came at the end of November. The book had no story at all, and nobody at the firm thought they should publish it. In fact, "we're frankly very much disappointed by it. It is diffuse and non-integral with neither very much plot development nor character development." There wasn't even enough structure to allow for revision. Faulkner owed the firm money, and they wanted to keep him tied in case his next book was better; still, they'd release the manuscript if he wanted to try another house. But Liveright advised against it: *Flags in the Dust* could only hurt what little reputation he already had.

———————

THAT'S ONE VERSION OF Yoknapatawpha's origins. Here's another. For the next few pages I'm going to pretend, as Faulkner did, that his imagined land is a real place. I'll pretend it has a coherent history and chronology of its own; that its characters are people, members of families that endure for generations, and with their biographies jumping from book to book. But I'll skip any titles for now, and I'll let Faulkner himself disappear as well; because after all, real people don't live in books but are found instead in what I'll call documents. This account of Yoknapatawpha's invention charts the county's history in the years before the Civil War, and it begins with a Chickasaw thief named Ikkemotubbe—no, a Chickasaw chief. But thief first, and a murderer too. He was the nephew of his people's great chief, the man who in their language was called The Man, but Ikkemotubbe had what they called a bad eye and nobody trusted him. So his tribe, The People, weren't sorry when he disappeared down the river to New Orleans; indeed, The Man was always hoping for news that his young relative had gotten himself killed. Instead, the city's waterfronts and saloons taught Ikkemotubbe what little he didn't already know about crime. The first steamboat appeared on the Mississippi in 1811, and when Ikkemotubbe took it back up the river he brought with him a little gold box full of a rare delicacy, a special New Orleans salt. He gave a bit of it to his uncle, who began to act strange at his food, and died. He gave some more to his cousin, the heir; and then Ikkemotubbe himself was The Man. Only he preferred to say it in bad French: Du Homme, or Doom.

So he stole a kingdom, and soon he had a white wife, the daughter of a West Indian planter. He also had slaves, winning the first of them at cards on the steamboat north, and began to cultivate some of his land, as the white people did, growing cotton for sale in the market. Doom got more slaves, women among them, and there too he did like the white man; so he had his own children among his slaves, and sold them. But his real business was land. The Man did not own the Chickasaw lands. They were possessed but not owned, like one's hand or heart; they were his, and yet not to sell; they had never been his to sell. Still, it was easy enough for the white people to act as if they were, and so Doom discovered that he could sell the land for money; perhaps The People were too afraid of his special salt to stop him. Yet at the very instant of the sale the land ceased to have ever been his, as if the alienating chink of a coin had canceled his ancestors' past.

Nobody knows when Doom started to sell his heritage, and one of the first bits to go wasn't actually sold but instead swapped for a horse. White men began settling in what became Yoknapatawpha County just before the turn of the nineteenth century, coming down from Tennessee and into the western part of the wilderness known as the Mississippi territory. At first there were just three of them: Samuel Habersham, a medical doctor and incumbent of the Chickasaw Agency established by the new American government; his groom, Alexander Holston, who would soon open a tavern; and Louis Grenier, a Huguenot who brought in the first slaves and laid out the river-bend plantation that after his death would be called the Old Frenchman's Place. More settlers soon came but there was no town as yet, just the trading post and a few houses, and then a bit of excitement provided by a man named Jason Compson. He rode up the bandit-infested forest path known as the Natchez Trace in 1811 on a quick little horse and with his saddlebags empty. But the horse was enough. He matched it in races against the mounts of The Man's young men, and then he traded the beast to Doom himself for a solid square mile of land near the center of what would soon be a town. Compson's Mile would have its columned house and formal gardens, its slave quarters too: and Compson's son became the state's governor; the governor's son, a Confederate general.

Doom was white enough to help other white men cheat The People of their land, and he sold more of it before the Indian Removal Act of 1830 forced him to sell the rest. Some of it went to a man called Carothers McCaslin, whose hardscrabble plantation lay fifteen miles to the northeast of the little settlement around the Indian agency. But old Carothers left his heirs something besides the land. His twin sons, Theophilus and Amodeus, kept a half-literate record of the plantation's life in a set of clumsy ledgers: the names of their slaves, their births and deaths, and at times their purchase prices. That too was a legacy, and in the decades that followed some members of his family would find it impossible to accept the story those ledgers told. Of course, all plantations kept such books. These, however, appear to be the only ones from Yoknapatawpha to have survived the Civil War, and so we know the names of the people Carothers McCaslin held in bondage. For though many thousands of black people lived and died in the county in the years before the war, few of them left any trace in the records. Yoknapatawpha's history in those years—or rather the few surviving facts of that history—is a white man's history. We don't even know, from those early days, the full names of the white women that men like McCaslin and Compson married; "Mrs. Compson" is all the documents give us.

Carothers McCaslin died in 1837, just as the last of the Chickasaws were forced onto the Trail of Tears and walked west to Oklahoma. By then the settlement had a name and its place as a county seat. Yoknapatawpha had been organized out of the last Indian land cessions. The place grew, and in 1830 Jefferson had a blacksmith, a rudimentary courthouse and a jail, six stores, three churches, the Holston House hotel, and maybe thirty houses. One of the shopkeepers was a man named Goodhue Coldfield, and his otherwise unremarkable family history suggests the region's pattern of settlement; in this, Yoknapatawpha is a mirror of the old Southwest as a whole. Coldfield's grandfather had been a Virginian, but his father had moved west into the new territory of Tennessee; then he himself had gone west again, coming into an even newer land with a scant wagonload of stock. Few of Yoknapatawpha's white settlers brought much with them; Compson made a fortune with his horse, but he had nothing to start with besides luck. He prospered, and Goodhue Coldfield hung on; we know their names because they and their descendants remained. But most people who came through Yoknapatawpha didn't make money and didn't stay put; in the next generation they moved west again, to Arkansas or Texas or eventually California.

Down to the south there were a few established towns on the high bluffs along the great river, places like Natchez, where the woodland Trace to Nashville began, prosperous and long-settled and surrounded by plantations. There the Indians had been pushed aside a century before, and the district had been French and then Spanish and even English for a while before becoming American. Money, some of it, had had a chance to grow old, and a few of the planters counted their slaves in the hundreds. But northern Mississippi was above all a place for new men. Still, every so often a prosperous planter's son would arrive from Virginia or South Carolina and take up new land. John Sartoris fit that pattern: a gentleman, with ancestors and capital behind him.

Sartoris didn't come into the county until the 1840s, however, and by then Ikkemotubbe was just a memory. But the chief made one last sale before he was gone. One Sunday morning in 1833 the men sitting with their feet on the railing of the Holston House gallery looked up to see a stranger. He was called Thomas Sutpen, a big man with a short red beard that looked like a disguise, and whose eyes in his tanned terra-cotta face were at once visionary and alert, ruthless and reposed. He was about twenty-five and wore two pistols and knew how to use them; a few days later he showed that he could ride at speed and still put a bullet into a playing card from twenty feet out. After that nobody asked questions, though the town did wonder where he went each day and why he kept his room locked. But the Chickasaw agent through whom he worked was too discreet to say anything, until one night Sutpen woke the County Recorder and used his last dollar to register his deed to a hundred square miles of the best virgin land in all of Yoknapatawpha.

After that he disappeared; and when he came back two months later Sutpen brought with him a French architect and a covered wagon full of slaves. The slaves were French too; at least they spoke a language someone eventually recognized as a form of French. They must have come from the West Indies, but Jefferson simply thought they were wild, men who worked naked in the swamp, and unlike any black people the place had ever seen. And if they did come from the islands, then their very presence was a crime, for the Constitution itself had already put a stop to the foreign slave trade. Still, the county worried less about that than about how he'd paid for them. Jefferson was beginning to be a little bit scrupulous, to care about respectability. Nobody knew where Sutpen bought his slaves; nobody knew how he'd gotten the money to pay Ikkemotubbe; and no one in the bar at the Holston House would ever know. Which left them free to imagine him riding out to the Mississippi itself, boarding a steamboat with a handkerchief to cover his face, and then using those pistols to help him load his pockets. So there was a touch of sulphur about him from the beginning, and that only increased once he began to raise a new Pandaemonium. The French architect drew his plans, and Sutpen worked alongside his slaves, all of them naked and covered with mud against the mosquitoes, as he tore a plantation out of the unbroken land. It took two years to build his mansion, but in 1835 he put in his first crop. Sutpen's Hundred, he called it, and the place would make him the county's biggest planter and one of its richest men.

Until the house was built he kept the architect a virtual prisoner in what was still a swamp, a man trained in Paris. But he did once loan him out, sending him into Jefferson to design a new and larger courthouse and to lay out its square. The Frenchman marked off four broad avenues and put the courthouse at the crossing. He gave the town something simple and true, a plan so clear that it still worked a century later: school and church and bank and jail, each in its ordered place. Still, even that wasn't enough to make the town trust Sutpen. Jefferson's men rode out to hunt his land and came at night for the other sport he gave them. He would pit his slaves against each other in a bare-knuckle match without rules, and sometimes the planter himself stepped into the square his spectators formed. Sutpen stripped to the waist and fought his own property, covered with blood and gouging at the other man's eyes. Nothing else was ever known against him, but though he was in the county for ten years before anyone heard of John Sartoris, he always remained an interloper.

The town swelled, and by 1860 it seemed finished and whole, with its streets and houses and people too, almost a thousand of them. The courthouse sat in a grove of trees and had even acquired a portico, its marble columns shipped from Italy to New Orleans and then up the Mississippi. The square was formed of two-story buildings on all sides, shops at street level and then the doctors and lawyers in their offices above. No train just yet, and so the white gold of the cotton fields had to be brought by wagon to the Tallahatchie

River, on the county's northern border, where it waited for the next steamboat south. And gold it was, even if it did eat the soil. A few years' growth and profit would exhaust any cotton field, and maybe only Sutpen had enough land, had always more ground to clear and new fields to break. For cotton was king. Senator James Hammond of South Carolina had said so in Congress and dared anyone North or South to stand against it, though in Yoknapatawpha no one ever wanted to, no white man anyway. The Compsons had their mile, and Sartoris his spread to the north of town. Sutpen had married the daughter of Coldfield the shopkeeper and had two children by her, with the boy at the state university in Oxford. And out at McCaslin's, old Carothers's twin sons were getting old themselves, white-bearded bachelors known as Uncle Buck and Uncle Buddy. The brothers ran their land on a system that would have gotten anyone new to the county in trouble. They lived in a log cabin and kept their slaves in the big plantation house their father had built, locking the front door each evening while knowing that every one of them went immediately out the back for a night's worth of devilment. Those slaves were supposed to be working out the cost of their freedom, but none of them had ever yet worked enough, and maybe that's why Yoknapatawpha accepted it.

Jefferson was complete. Then one day in 1861 John Sartoris stepped onto the courthouse balcony wearing the first Confederate uniform anyone in town had ever seen. He swore in his new regiment, a band of untried men who knew they were ignorant and hoped they were brave, and prepared to take them up north to Virginia; north, and over the precipice that they thought was an apotheosis.

———————

"APOTHEOSIS" IS FAULKNER'S WORD, not mine, and so is "precipice." They come from his description of secession in the oddest of all his books, *Requiem for a Nun* (1951), which intercuts a play about the mid-twentieth-century murder of a child with a historical narrative about Jefferson itself, from its first settlers to the present. I've drawn many details from it in the pages above and borrowed some of its language as well, burying the quotations in my own prose. I've taken fragments from other works too: lines from stories like "Red Leaves" about Yoknapatawpha's Indians; a great deal from *Absalom, Absalom!* and some from *Go Down, Moses*; a few words from Faulkner's 1946 Appendix to *The Sound and the Fury*; everything in which he defines the early history of this imagined place. That place has such a presence in American literature—such a presence in our minds—that it seems to have existed always and inevitably. But go back to 1928. Go back to Horace Liveright's rejection of *Flags in the Dust* and his advice that Faulkner not offer the book elsewhere, and nothing about his achievement looks so certain. Yoknapatawpha could have died right there if Faulkner himself hadn't had the strength to fail again, to fail better, and go on; and maybe that book's rejection was a good thing. For it gave him the sense of anguished liberation, formal liberation above all, on which his greatest works depend.

"One day," he wrote, "it suddenly seemed as if a door had clapped silently and forever to between me and all publishers' addresses and booklists and I said to myself, Now I can write. Now I can just write." In the spring of 1928 he put the word "Twilight" at the head of a page, a working title, and in a time when hope itself appeared to have died he began to write a short story about a little girl and her three brothers. The four Compson children have been told to go outside and play, sent away from the house to keep them from knowing what's going on inside, where their grandmother has just died. They hop around in a creek, they argue and boast, and then the girl, Caddy, climbs a tree to look in at the window of the dead woman's room, trying to see what's happening, while her more timid siblings stand below, peering up at her wet and muddy drawers.

He worked, he remembered, without allowing himself to form a plan or to think about where he was going; worked without any sense of strain or trouble. But even in "Twilight"'s opening pages Faulkner had already moved beyond or away from that kernel of narrative. He tried at the start to tell the story through the first-person interior monologue of a character who cannot connect a cause with its effect or distinguish past from present, memory from his current actions. That was the youngest Compson brother, Benjy, the "idiot" implied in the lines from *Macbeth* that eventually gave him his title: life is "a tale / Told by an idiot, full of sound and fury, / Signifying nothing." That version proved a failure, or so he later said, and he therefore tried to present the family's story again through the voices of Benjy's two brothers, Quentin at Harvard in 1910, and Jason back in Jefferson in 1928. But it "still wasn't enough," and so he let "Faulkner try it," with that fourth and concluding section, the one that gives us Dilsey; and then threw up his hands.

Faulkner always believed in risking failure; believed in the precipice. Still, the self-mythologizing story he came to tell about the composition of *The Sound and the Fury* is so clearly a *story*, albeit a good one, that we can afford to be a little suspicious. Certainly he himself was. The words I've quoted about that door clapping shut come from a 1933 introduction to the novel that went unpublished at the time. A dozen years later, an editor at Random House named Robert Linscott came across it in the publishing company's files and asked to use it; Faulkner refused, saying he had "forgotten what smug false sentimental windy shit it was." Similarly, there must have been some lost early drafts or sketches for the short-story version of this material, some ur-"Twilight." The book's surviving manuscript is heavily reworked in places, but its pages nevertheless show that he already knew both where he was going and that he was indeed at work on a novel. Still, there's no mistaking his sense of exhilaration. Liveright's rejection must have cost him something, but it also freed him; nobody with an eye on the market would have written this novel, not even in that 1920s height of modernist experimentation. *Flags in the Dust* did not yet have a publisher but he had already gone far beyond it, and when he was done he described the new work as if somebody else had written it: "the damndest book I ever read. I don't believe anybody will publish it for ten years."

The Sound and the Fury will have its proper place later in my narrative. For now, however, I want only to suggest that Faulkner's work in writing it was a form of desperate play; it was what he did when he should have been trying to revise or place its predecessor. Instead, he gave the manuscript of *Flags in the Dust* to an Oxford friend named Ben Wasson, who'd become a playwright's agent in New York, and asked him to shop it around; at least that way, he claimed, he would save on postage. Wasson collected eleven more rejections before the book was finally accepted, in September 1928, by Harrison Smith, an editor at Harcourt, Brace. Yet that acceptance was not straightforward. At just under 150,000 words *Flags in the Dust* was far too long; the publisher wanted it trimmed by 40,000 words—well over one hundred printed pages—and wanted it in less than three weeks.

Faulkner caught a train to New York, but when he sat down to chop his own pages he felt as if he were killing them. He couldn't do it, and so Wasson took on the job, telling him that the problem was that "you had about six books in here. You were trying to write them all at once." Wasson's revision sliced some minor characters and cut back on others; the result was at once tighter and less coherent, gappier in presenting its characters' motivations and yet somehow smoother in the telling. The stripped-down version passed. Now called *Sartoris*, it was released in January 1929, and the reviews confirmed Ben Wasson's judgment; the New England regionalist Mary Ellen Chase wrote in *Commonweal* that it had "the faults of a style and a method crammed with virtues." A few weeks later Faulkner signed a contract for *The Sound and the Fury* with Smith, who had left Harcourt to start his own firm in partnership with the English Jonathan Cape. It would take twenty years and then the Nobel Prize before the business side of Faulkner's career ran smoothly. But Smith was willing to chance the future, and he served as Faulkner's editor through *Absalom, Absalom!* in 1936.

The masterpieces that now began to tumble out of him came so immediately and bewilderingly on each other's heels that few readers at the time were able to absorb them. *The Sound and the Fury* was published at the end of 1929 and met with baffled awe and low sales. A new book, a great book, appeared in each of the next three years: *As I Lay Dying, Sanctuary*, and *Light in August*. Their virtues were easier to see but so for many readers were their faults—did they really need to be so difficult, so violent, and so strange? Yet Faulkner's reviews were never dismissive and their terms of attack treated him as someone who mattered. Collections of stories came out in 1931 and 1934, and a novel about stunt pilots called *Pylon* in 1935. *Absalom, Absalom!* followed and then he skipped a year; after that *The Unvanquished, The Wild Palms*, and *The Hamlet* were released in annual succession, and finally *Go Down, Moses* in 1942.

The books of those thirteen years hold the core of Faulkner's achievement. No American writer has written so much enduring work so fast, not even Henry James, and the period also includes many months as a Hollywood scriptwriter. The books came so quickly, in fact, that in my next chapters it will make little sense to pause over the details of his biography, and as I move into his account of the Civil War my treatment of him will seem to abandon chronology. Or rather the chronology it obeys is that of history itself, rather than of Faulkner's career as such, and I'll look at what he says about the war without much regard for when he says it. I'll return to his life only in this book's third section, when the details of composition become important and his depiction of the Yoknapatawpha world approaches his own period once more.

One essential change in Faulkner's condition does, however, demand attention. Estelle Oldham returned to Oxford in 1927. She had visited several times in the decade of her marriage, but now she was back in Mississippi for good, worldly and with a sloe-eyed chic that made her seem both out of place and more alluring than ever. Her union with Cornell Franklin had been shaky almost from the start. Estelle was theatrically high-strung and intelligent, a beauty and yet far from the docile, conventional presence Franklin wanted; she could play that role when she wanted to but she rarely did, and he soon turned to other women instead. Divorce had been on both their minds for years, and the final decree was granted early in 1929; Estelle kept the children. The woman Faulkner had always seen as unattainable might now be his at last, and meanwhile their relationship, though perhaps still unconsummated, was on the edge of becoming a local scandal.

Everyone in Oxford assumed they would marry. Everyone assumed they would have to, and a letter Faulkner wrote to Harrison Smith suggests that they did have to; not because of pregnancy but the sake of his own "honor and the sanity—I believe life—of a woman. This is not bunk; neither am I being sucked in." But it may have been bunk. The letter has often been read as suggesting both Estelle's fragility and Faulkner's own reluctance, his second thoughts and sense of being trapped; and yet he wrote to Smith in the hopes of touching him for a loan. He wanted $500—more than the advance on *The Sound and the Fury*—and it was in his interest to sound as desperate as possible. Faulkner had earlier stuck Liveright with a gambling debt, and he would write to his publishers in a similar vein and for similar purposes throughout his career.

William Faulkner and Estelle Oldham were married on June 20, 1929. No adult relationship could match the dreams of his adolescence, and their union was never untroubled. He was already an alcoholic, a binge-drinker and prone to blackouts; Estelle soon became one if she wasn't already. They had a difficult honeymoon, at Pascagoula on the Gulf Coast, with Faulkner claiming to prefer bourbon to the bedroom, and her parents were no more pleased with the idea of him as a son-in-law than they had been ten years before. Writers were disreputable even when, as soon happened, their work appeared in the *Saturday Evening Post*. In 1930 Faulkner used the proceeds from such magazine sales to buy the house he called Rowan Oak, and it became a home for Estelle's son and daughter. His sense of fantasy and ability to listen made him good with children, and he was an attentive stepfather. They had a daughter of their own in 1931; she arrived prematurely and lived for little more than a week. A second child, Jill, was born in 1933 and remembered a household marked by "lots of storming up and down the stairs," with her parents performing their grievances both for and at each other, her mother's bright despair and her father's murderous silences. At times he pretended, and with utter conviction, to be a simple farmer; she a helpless Southern belle. Faulkner spent long periods in California working as a Hollywood screenwriter and other stretches in New York, and yet he never imagined living anywhere but Oxford until Jill married a man from Virginia and had children of her own. But he was not always faithful, and in 1935, while working at Twentieth Century-Fox, he began an affair with Howard Hawks's secretary. It lasted for fifteen years, and with time there were other women too. Nevertheless, the marriage survived, sustaining and destructive in equal measures, and for each of them necessary. They endured.

PART TWO

Yoknapatawpha's War

SIX

The Precipice

The morning news had carried flood warnings for New Orleans, and an old man in Jackson Square told me that the river was already running high, going higher. There'd been a week of heavy rain to the north and now it was all moving down, but the desk clerk at my French Quarter hotel laughed when I asked if I needed to worry about it. Every day brought flood warnings, she said, and so I got my car and went north out of the city, with the highway raised on concrete stilts over a swamp, all stumps and greenery and yet with nothing at all that looked like land. I skimmed the flat and marshy edge of Lake Pontchartrain and at Baton Rouge, eighty miles on, left the interstate for Highway 61. Port Hudson was next, the last Confederate town on the big river to fall, in July 1863, a week after the great fortress at Vicksburg had surrendered to Ulysses S. Grant. After that came the turnoff for the spot of hell called the Angola State Penitentiary, and then the road moved out of the bottomland into an unfrozen January of forest and gray stubble, and dove over the border into Mississippi. Natchez was another hour along.

At dusk that evening I walked down the little town's main street to a bit of park on the heights above the river. There were benches and a gazebo, and a railing to lean on, and I could see that here at least the floods would be no trouble. For Natchez sits on a vertiginous bluff, and the Mississippi itself was almost two hundred feet below, down a twisting road that led to the docks where, in season, the modern facsimiles of old paddle wheelers would tie up to let their tourists off. It was different on the other side, however, back across the border and into Louisiana once more. There the land lay flat and open and empty, an alluvial plain just right for cotton; and two days later the river would indeed spill from its western banks and spread its silt for miles. Such floods had made the place rich: its soil, its plantations, its slave owners. Before the Civil War the region had over three hundred planters who each kept more than 250 people in bondage; many of them owned land on both sides of the river and stocked—that's the word they used—each separate property with a hundred persons or more. But the white masters rarely lived on those plantations themselves, building grand houses either in or near the town instead, and giving them names that might have come out of English novels, Dunleith and Auburn, Melrose and Elgin. Other families got rich not by growing cotton but by selling it. For Natchez was also a busy port in the years before the war, fetching in bale after bale from the surrounding counties and sending it downriver, down to New Orleans and then out across the Gulf of Mexico to the mills of Lancashire and Lowell alike.

By American standards it was already an old town when the war came. The French had built a fort there at the start of the eighteenth century and swapped massacres with the local Indians, killing them all in the end, while appropriating their tribal name for that of the place. Settlers and bandits had gone up and down the four hundred miles to Nashville along the Natchez Trace, and flatboats had tied up in the days before steam at what was known as Natchez-Under-the-Hill, a raucous, violent waterfront settlement that the river itself eventually washed away. Legend holds that in 1860 the place had more millionaires than anywhere else in the entire United States, a claim that's probably unprovable but still perhaps true, at least on a per capita basis or at least on the per capita basis of the white population, itself a distinct minority. Not all of those millionaires supported secession. They didn't trust Lincoln but they believed that the quarrels of the 1850s weren't over slavery per se so much as its spread into new territories of Kansas and points west. Surely Washington wouldn't interfere with the institution in those states where it had always existed? So they told themselves, believing that their own fortunes were safer within the Union than in a new nation that risked the chance of war.

Yet the lust for new acreage was unquenchable, and when the war came the town's planters did indeed support the Confederacy. The land may have been rich but cotton was greedy and swallowed its nutrients down; and the soil was friable too, prone to erosion, and seamed through with gullies. The young Frederick Law Olmsted visited the place in 1854, surveying what he named the "Cotton Kingdom" on assignment for the *New York Times*; he was still in his early thirties, and a few years away from beginning the work that would make him the country's greatest landscape architect. Olmsted found that some of the area's plantations were already abandoned, their "hillsides worn, cleft, and channeled like icebergs," a desert after just ten or twenty crops. He thought the fields could be saved and restored if their owners would only pay to have them terraced, but with "fresh land in Texas at half a dollar an acre, nothing of this sort can be thought of." Land was cheap, and slaves expensive. A planter needed a quick cash crop to protect his investment in other people's flesh, and nothing was quicker than cotton. So new land was always being broken, and more was always needed.

For a while the river itself seemed to offer an answer to the planter's dilemma. I stood on the bluff and looked down at its gray and dimpled surface, quiescent now and with just a single convoy moving upon its face, half a dozen barges lashed together and pushed downstream by a tug. Yet even today the traffic could run heavy on what the historian Walter Johnson has called the "river of dark dreams," and in the 1850s some of the Cotton Kingdom's princes had dreamed that its stream could lead them to an overseas empire in the Caribbean. The Mississippi flowed south, out of the continent's heart, and both its steamboats and the plantations along its banks were funded by the most sophisticated financial instruments of their day: a set of interlocking capital-intensive industries whose debts and bonds and mortgages were in part secured by human property. It flowed out to the Gulf of Mexico, and though the ships loaded with Mississippi cotton would then head north, that whole huge valley had an even larger hinterland to the south. Going down that river might open a new world.

Cuba had slaves already; it grew sugar and could grow cotton: why should our manifest destiny lie only in the west? Why not southward too—why not take even more of Mexico than the slave-owning president James K. Polk had already seized, and grab the whole continent below the Rio Grande? A senator from South Carolina saw the river as "expanding its waters in the wide gulf" and spreading its own brand of democracy throughout the Caribbean. In 1854, and with Washington winking its approval, a former governor of Mississippi named John Quitman tried to organize an invasion of Cuba by the frontier mercenaries called "filibusters"; two years later the Nashville-born William Walker attempted to conquer Nicaragua for slavery. Both efforts failed. The peculiar institution would indeed have to spread west if it were to grow at all, but by the end of the decade the Kansas territory looked closed to it, and the Republican Party was on the rise, with its opposition to any expansion of slavery at all. In 1860 Lincoln did not get a single vote in Mississippi, but then he wasn't on the ballot either; his party knew better than to waste money on any play for the deep South.

Natchez had a comparatively easy war, easy for everyone but the black people who were lynched there in the fall of 1861, after the town's planters heard rumors of an uprising. The exact number still remains uncertain, but estimates run to forty or more. The place surrendered to Federal gunboats early in 1862, and though some outlying plantations were later burned, the center of town remained intact. Union troops staged an intermittent occupation, and Grant established a headquarters there once Vicksburg fell. And afterward the city stayed prosperous, at least for Mississippi. Cotton bolls still opened in the sun and still needed to get to market; there were factories and textile mills, bank buildings sheathed in marble, downtown churches that each filled their block, a historical society and even a synagogue. Natchez had big bones—bigger bones than it now needs. For today most of its industry is gone, the population is scarcely larger than in 1930, and what Natchez survives on is the simple fact that it did survive. Its antebellum houses had not been burned. Pillared halls and wrought-iron fences, high ceilings and live oaks: Natchez lives off the tourism brought by its architecture and gardens, a kind of southern Newport where the big houses are open for business.

A lot of that business happens during the hoop-skirted fantasia known as the Natchez Pilgrimage, a few weeks each spring and fall when a sliver of the town's white population dresses up as its own ancestors and shows the place off to busloads of visitors. But I hadn't come for that, and when I drove a few miles out from the center of town to a spot called Longwood, I found I'd have the guided tour to myself. Most historic houses in Natchez are pretty much what you'd expect: square-built in red Federal brick or white Greek

Revival, with a deep two-storied porch on the front. Longwood is different. It was put up a little bit later, the dream-palace of a man named Haller Nutt, a planter who had developed an especially profitable strain of cotton. He owned almost seventy square miles and several hundred other people, and what he built was a flamboyant frivolous octagon, six stories high and with four gingerbread verandas on each of its first two floors: Moorish Revival perhaps, or a slightly squashed pagoda, or maybe a wedding cake, with milky confectionary dripping down its ruddy sides. The windows are Palladian, but nothing else is, and least of all the white lantern that tops it, as fanciful as a steamboat's pilothouse: a lantern that is itself topped with a bulbous red dome and then a gold-painted finial.

Inside, the octagonal footprint is preserved, with each floor meant to have eight great rooms off a central rotunda, and open to the light falling from above. Preserved—but never finished, and in fact only a few rooms on the ground floor were ever furnished. Longwood's bricks were molded and fired on site by slave craftsmen, as was the norm, but most of its interior walls remain unplastered, and above the first story neither the woodwork nor the doors were ever installed. One tours a building site, a shell of great bays and odd recesses; walking through, I felt as if I had stepped into a bit of Piranesi, an incomplete and yet all-enveloping maze. On an upper floor I came upon some empty barrels and tubs that looked as if they had once been used to stir mortar; I stared up through the rotunda and found my view blocked by scaffolding, but scaffolding too rickety and tattered to be used in any repairs today. For construction on Longwood did not begin until 1860, and though Haller Nutt himself opposed secession, when the war began the crew of artisans and carpenters he had hired from Philadelphia simply dropped their tools and left. I thought of Ecclesiastes, of human vanity and its fleeting dreams, and listened as the guide told me how visitors a century later could still find the workmen's hammers and planes.

———————

MY DRIVE HAD BEGUN in New Orleans, the city where with Sherwood Anderson's help Faulkner had found his subject; and after walking Natchez's nighttime, ghostly streets I would go on to Vicksburg and then to Oxford.

Natchez was more than a stopping point, however, more even than the great mansions that stood upon its precipice. Or its two precipices, really. The place hung high above the river, but it also stood on the edge of history as well: the precipice that the South first saw as an apotheosis; the precipice, in Faulkner's words, of secession itself. Natchez was finally but a house-proud advertisement for the iniquity that some of its inhabitants still thought of as a lost world, a lost cause. But that wouldn't have been enough to make me stop if there hadn't also been a literary connection.

I've already mentioned Stark Young, who got Faulkner his crucial job in Elizabeth Prall's New York bookstore. Young was born in 1881, and spent the new century's first decades teaching at Amherst and elsewhere, while also publishing poems and plays. In middle age he moved to New York and began to write fiction that drew upon his own family history as a descendant of the Natchez cotton barons. His first novel was published in the same year as *Soldiers' Pay*, and his fiction was in every respect more conventional than Faulkner's own. It had no influence at all on the work of the younger writer, but he was a generous mentor and friend, and he proved that a Mississippian could make a literary life. His most successful book was called *So Red the Rose*, a novel that followed his maternal ancestors through the war years. They were a sprawling intermarried clan called McGehee—Young uses their actual names—and in their different branches owned land and slaves from south of Natchez on up to the Tennessee border. Scribner's released it in 1934 and moved an astonishing 400,000 copies. That's just a fraction of what Margaret Mitchell's *Gone with the Wind* would sell just a few years later, but it dwarfs any royalty statement that Faulkner himself ever saw.

Young set *So Red the Rose* on the various McGehee plantations near Natchez, and most of its four hundred pages are passed in talk—talk of family matters, of courtships and marriages, but also of the presidents and senators and generals whom one McGehee or another has known as friends. But in all that verbiage the McGeehees' many hundreds of slaves barely even figure as a backdrop, just a few men and women in the house. Young never shows us the work of the fields. Nor are there long scenes of battle, and for many chapters the war is present only in letters and newspaper reports. The McGehees may be touched by death at a distance, but the rhythm and even the plenty of their lives continue as before. Then in 1864 a detachment of black Federal soldiers arrives, a plantation is burned, and their world changes forever. Young doubtless means this to be affecting, but the novel seems naked in its nostalgic appeal to the old order. *So Red the Rose* really does believe in the grace and beauty of the antebellum world, and yet it can only maintain that belief by leaving a great deal out; it makes no mention at all of the area's 1861 lynchings.

Much of its storytelling seems clumsy, with too many characters for anyone *not* related to keep them all straight, and at times it's impossible to tell which of them belong to which generation. Young offers neither Mitchell's clear narrative arc nor Faulkner's formal intricacy, and yet for all his weaknesses he does provide one crucial thing that they don't. The novel opens in the summer of 1860, and he allows his characters to talk seriously about the coming crisis, to ask what it all means and to consider what is to be done. They measure the attractions, dangers, and probabilities of secession; they debate its constitutionality and wonder about Lincoln's intentions; they weigh cotton's economic might against the power of Northern industry, and even worry about the growing strength of midwestern wheat. His characters all speak from deep within the planters' ideology, with its assumption of an unquestioned racial superiority. But few of them agree with one another about anything else, and there's often a split between the generations, in which one can trace the growth of a Confederate consciousness. Old Hugh McGehee believes in the Union and opposes secession; his son Edward thinks that while staying in might be more profitable, freedom is "beyond all price."

The book's characters will come to recognize that they are living at the end of time, their time—as fits a writer who later translated Chekhov. And young Edward will be killed at Shiloh. When the novel begins he's a student at the Louisiana Seminary, a military academy whose superintendent is a former army officer named William Tecumseh Sherman. The students have begun to drill, they carry arms, and they expect that both Mississippi and Louisiana will secede. Meanwhile, Edward's father, Hugh, has a kind of sympathy for Colonel Sherman's awkward position; the Ohio-born commandant has been said to like the South and seems no friend to abolition. Yet he remains a Union man, his brother is a Republican senator, and over these pages hangs the memory of both Sherman's later actions, and his words to a Louisiana colleague that Christmas, just before he resigned his position and went north: "You people speak so lightly of war. You don't know what you are talking about." The South had courage but courage alone was not enough; the North had it too, he said, and also had factories at a time when Southern manufacturers could hardly make "a yard of cloth or shoes." The section might know some early triumphs. That much Sherman admitted, but then its resources would fail and "your cause will begin to wane."

Young wants to persuade us that the McGehees' was indeed a seigneurial life, something out of a Rusian novel, like the Rostovs on their country estate in Tolstoy's *War and Peace* or Turgenev's gentlefolk worrying on the eve of change. Still, even he admitted that that life carried a high moral price, while believing all the same that it offered its beneficiaries a sense of grace and ease. But Faulkner doesn't have the same romantic stake in defending the Old South as a system. His myth lies elsewhere, in his sense of a dim hot airless past that weighs upon the present. He feels no need to stage the controversies of 1860 and nowhere provides anything like Young's detailed account of the South's thinking about secession. For him it is simply something that happens, happened: inevitable, irrevocable, and as little worth debating as a hurricane.

That is, in fact, how secession was depicted in the textbooks Faulkner read as a child; Franklin L. Riley's *School History of Mississippi* presents that moment with the same sense of inevitability, and Riley too ignores the long and sometimes quarrelsome discussion that preceded the decision itself. Still, the omission remains surprising, a lapse in the novelist's attention to his region's history. His own Lafayette County saw plenty of argument on the issue, though it was eventually led by a "fire-eater" named L. Q. C. Lamar, a former congressman who arrived at the state convention on secession with a draft of the necessary ordinance already in his pocket. After the war Lamar went back to Washington and died as a lion of the Redeemed and supposedly reconciled white South; Oxford's main street is named for him even now. Yet Faulkner's Jefferson contains nobody like him. Oxford was a small town in 1860 and few of its adult residents had been born there, but it already attracted ambitious people from throughout the South. Lamar had come from Georgia to teach law at the university, while Jacob Thompson, a member of President James Buchanan's cabinet, had grown up in North Carolina. The actual town had political weight—it was part of a larger world. The imaginary Jefferson doesn't and isn't; it remains but a single stamp snipped off from the rest of the sheet. For Faulkner simply isn't interested in the actualities and contingencies of public life—in what stands for him as the froth on the stream of Yoknapatawpha's psychic history.

What the devil were you folks fighting about? Faulkner never gives an answer. His account of the Civil War's first days has no room for that question, and what draws him instead are scenes of men massing for a common purpose. April 16, 1861, and his character John Sartoris stands on the balcony of the Yoknapatawpha County courthouse to sign in his troops, a unit numbered "Two in the roster of Mississippi regiments." I've already quoted from Faulkner's description of this moment in *Requiem for a Nun*, but it's worth going back to that ceremony, and the date he gives for it is nicely chosen. Fort Sumter had officially surrendered on the fourteenth, and the next day Lincoln had called for 75,000 volunteers to suppress the insurrection. On the sixteenth the new Confederate Congress passed a Conscription Act, but the intrepid colonel we have seen in *The Unvanquished* has been at work already. The men standing before Sartoris have come together as a "voluntary association," watched by the assembled town—fathers, sisters, and sweethearts lining the four sides of the square—as a Baptist minister prays over them and a recruiting officer from Richmond swears them in. Faulkner is both simplifying and exaggerating here, racing the engine of Confederate heritage. Confederate regiments were supposed to number near a thousand men at the beginning of the war, and a town the size of Oxford might then have yielded a few companies at best. The actual Second Mississippi was formed at Corinth, a rail junction to which any number of militia units from around the state had been ordered for training, including W. C. Falkner's own Magnolia Rifles.

Only one man on that square yet wears a uniform—Sartoris himself, with the very cleanliness of "his pristine colonel's braid" suggesting the blood and the dirt to come. Again Faulkner's description emphasizes the moment's pageantry, and its febrile but oddly impersonal rhetoric depends on our knowing this place already; he only needs to point his finger for his world to spring into being. Jefferson isn't so much described here as invoked, and Sartoris is only a name; yet that name carries the weight of all its other appearances in Faulkner's fiction, from *Flags in the Dust* on. For we are meant as we read to remember all that we know about him: family, friendships, enmities, habits, history. Watching him here makes us recall everything that we've already learned about him in Faulkner's earlier books, even if in some sense it hasn't yet happened. We know that he will fight at Bull Run and then lead a troop of partisan cavalry; that after the war he will start a railroad and get himself murdered. We know his son Bayard, and the rest of his family too, and in reading we think of the changes the years will bring, just as we might in seeing an old friend's childhood photograph. It's the same with Faulkner's other recurring characters. Each cameo appearance of a Snopes or Compson calls up their major roles, and to my mind he does this more effectively than even Balzac, who often buries the reappearance of an important figure like Rastignac in a list of other characters.

Sartoris's men take their oath, and then the regiment marches off to Virginia and is gone. But their exhilaration will ring hollow, for the future is already determined, the future of a region:

> ... whirling into the plunge of its precipice, not that the State and the South knew it, because the first seconds of fall always seem like soar: a weightless deliberation preliminary to a rush not downward but upward, the falling body reversed during that second by transubstantiation into the upward rush of earth; a soar, an apex, the South's own apotheosis of its destiny and its pride.

Doomed at the moment it believes itself most free, its end encompassed in its origin, as Sherman indeed had foreseen. It will, however, take some time for that sense of soar to turn into fall, and meanwhile the town seems, like Stark Young's Natchez, to hang motionless in both time and space, "static in *quo*," and with the war just a rumor as from some dreamlike and distant place. Jefferson sleeps, a few quiet streets of children and old men, waiting for the war to arrive, for the unsuspected plummet to come. But come it will, and leave "the deep South dead."

I've taken those last words from *Absalom, Absalom!* and the family drama in that novel provides Faulkner's most haunting if oblique account of a world that has put itself on the lip of a precipice. In his great house, a dozen miles out of town, the demon Thomas Sutpen has three children. The oldest of them is without a last name. She is coffee-colored and known always by a diminutive, Clytie and never Clytemnestra, though she has that queen's fury and endurance; the daughter of a woman, her name unrecorded, whom Sutpen brought to Yoknapatawpha in a wagonload of "wild negroes" from the islands. The other two are his get on Ellen Coldfield, whose father was a Jefferson shopkeeper. First Henry, the son and heir of a plantation the size of a dukedom, and then the girl, Judith; but Judith is the strong one, and fascinated by her father's bare-knuckled fights with his slaves, while Henry turns away to vomit.

In the fall of 1859 Henry left Sutpen's Hundred for the state university at Oxford: a country boy, awkward and unmannered, but rich. And there he made one good friend, a Francophone law student named Charles Bon, of New Orleans. He was a few years older than Henry himself and "actually a little old to be still in college and certainly a little out of place" in that almost rural and undistinguished schoolyard; a long way in every sense from the charming decadent entrepôt he called home. That's the story Quentin Compson hears one evening in 1909, at the end of what Faulkner calls a "summer of wistaria," when the flower's smell mingles with that of his father's cigar and the fireflies light the dusk. Before he goes north to Harvard the boy needs to learn the history he already half-knows, to piece the old stories into something as near coherence as possible. So Quentin listens as his father adds to what an old woman named Rosa Coldfield had told him that afternoon about her sister Ellen and the monster she had married. Mr. Compson tells his son that at Christmas Henry brought Charles Bon out to Sutpen's Hundred: a handsome man and rich himself, equally at ease in a silk dressing gown or with a blade in his hand; feline perhaps, but pantherish, always elegant and always dangerous. Bon came at Christmas and then again at the end of school the following June, in that "last summer of peace and content"; and those few

brief days were enough, without either party having spoken, for all Yoknapatawpha to know that Judith Sutpen and Charles Bon were engaged. So Ellen
Sutpen had said, and apparently the two of them believed it as well. For in the
one extant letter between them, a piece of local history that Mr. Compson
now produces, and written from "a gutted house in Carolina" at the end of the
war, Bon told Judith that they have waited long enough.

They have had to wait. Thomas Sutpen was gone during Bon's second
visit, but he was at home in December 1860, when Henry brought his friend
to Sutpen's Hundred once more. There was only one thing to talk about in
the South that winter, but it wasn't secession so much as the question of what
would come after. South Carolina had already left the Union. Mississippi
would be next, and in the interval or interregnum between them Sutpen
called Henry into the library on Christmas Eve and told him that his sister could not marry his best friend. Yet what could forbid such a seemingly
desirable match? Sutpen must have had his reasons, though no one claims
to understand them, and by Quentin's day Jefferson has speculated about
them for half a century. In fact, the novel will posit a series of explanations,
each apparently more powerful than the last, but by this point in *Absalom,
Absalom!* we have yet to hear any of them. All the county knows—"the tale
came through the negroes"—is that the father and son had quarreled and
"Henry had formally abjured his father and renounced his birthright" and
ridden away with Bon in the night. Though Mr. Compson adds one thing
more: Henry must have told his father that whatever he knew about Bon
could not be true. He must have called his father a liar. Yet the simple fact
that Sutpen took those words and did not deny them was enough to tell the
boy that the charge *was* true. Nevertheless, he rode off with his friend, out to
the river and on to New Orleans, and unable to speak for fear of what Bon
might answer.

The young men probably hid themselves somewhere, Mr. Compson says,
though they did stop in Oxford to sign on with the company of infantry then
forming at the university. They were no longer seen on campus, however, and
didn't join "the gallant mimic marching and countermarching" of their fellows in training, emerging only when their unit moved north. Faulkner has
a particular formation in mind here, a group of soldiers known as the Uni-

versity Greys, who became Company A of the Eleventh Mississippi Infantry. They fought throughout the war in the eastern theater, at Bull Run and Gettysburg, and the regiment as a whole numbered less than a hundred when it surrendered at Appomattox. But Faulkner doesn't use that name for Henry's company. The Eleventh formed part of the same brigade as the Second Mississippi, the regiment commanded in fact at Bull Run by the novelist's great-grandfather, and in fiction by John Sartoris and afterward by Thomas Sutpen himself. The novel needs to keep father and son apart, though, and so Faulkner puts the college's unnamed unit in the war's western theater. Bon and Henry will fight at Shiloh and later join in the long retreat before Sherman's army in Georgia, their brigade headed at first by Quentin's grandfather.

They retreat again up through the Carolinas, and there in the spring of 1865 Henry Sutpen will see his father for one last time. Father and son talk once more, as they did that Christmas five years before, one final conversation, and afterward Henry and Bon ride off together again, the two friends heading west through the defeated South, riding over the ruined land toward Mississippi and Sutpen's Hundred. They keep pace with each other until they reach its gates, and then Henry surges forward, turns, and shoots his sister's beloved down. And disappears, no one knows where, or why, not until that night in 1909 when Quentin Compson will enter the past's closed door. But this we do know: father, son, and fiancé may seem to fight on the same side, and yet *Absalom, Absalom!* is above all the story of a house divided.

———·•·———

WALT WHITMAN CLAIMED THAT the real war would never get into the books, but he thought of those books in terms of fiction or poetry and believed that the language of his day could not tell the literally visceral truth. It couldn't describe the carnage, and about that he was mostly right. Yet it's perhaps a mistake to look in "the books" of the period for an account of the Civil War as such. How could any literary version compete with the narrative arc traced by the conflict itself? The illusions of its opening months, followed by long years of battle, never quite decisive; the combat lasting until the slavery that was somehow the cause of it all had been wiped away, at least in name; and then the stillness at Appomattox, followed immediately by the assassination of the era's tragic hero. No novelist could have matched that, not even Tolstoy, and none of the war's historians have had Gibbon's or Macaulay's vivid force. There are other kinds of books, however, the books those historians themselves read, the "speeches and pamphlets, private letters and diaries, personal memoirs and journalistic reports," in Edmund Wilson's words, that captured the Civil War's drama as no novelist or poet has even now. Those documents provide in themselves an extraordinary literary record and are especially vital in capturing what's called the "Secession Winter" of 1860–61, the months between South Carolina's decision that December to leave the Union and the April attack on Fort Sumter. "Fiction is so flat, comparatively," as the patrician Confederate diarist Mary Chesnut put it, and no single novel about the war has ever offered the immediacy—the sheer thrill and suspense and trepidation—of an immersion in the letters and diaries of the day.

That was Wilson's argument in *Patriotic Gore* (1962), his still-unmatched account of the period's literature. Wilson's early books established him as the nation's most prominent and authoritative literary critic: books like *Axel's Castle* (1931), a study of the modernist moment that looked at Joyce and Proust among others; and *The Wound and the Bow* (1941), in which he argued that artistic genius was enabled by psychic damage. He wrote about the history of European socialism in *To the Finland Station* (1940) and then in the 1950s began a series of *New Yorker* essays that examined the language through which the Civil War had been defined. The book he made from them amounted to an encyclopedic eight hundred pages and among other things showed that the terse pith of Lincoln's prose had forever changed America's political speech. In particular, he gave renewed currency to Grant's memoirs and established Chesnut as one of the greatest of American diarists. Wilson limited himself to those who were alive during the war itself and mentioned Faulkner only in passing. Nevertheless, his emphasis on the war's literary documents has helped me bring the novelist into focus, and in these next pages I'll follow his lead in using the period's documentary record to define the rhetorical territory Faulkner inherited, and to characterize the voice and timbre of the war's first months in particular.

No one has yet equaled Wilson's work. But we know more than he did, and in large part because he provided a spur to further scholarship. He did not, for example, have full access to Chesnut's diary, whose most pungent moments had been trimmed from the editions available to him; C. Vann Woodward's 1981 study of her manuscripts restored them to us. Nor did Wilson know *The Children of Pride* (1972), a 1,400-page collection of the letters written between 1854 and 1868 by the various members of a Georgia family. Charles Colcock Jones was a Presbyterian minister who owned more than a hundred slaves and raised rice, cotton, and cattle on his three plantations just down the coast from Savannah. As a young man he was called the "Apostle to the Blacks" and wrote a simplified catechism held to be especially useful both in converting slaves to Christianity and in persuading them of their biblical duty to obey. Jones believed that there was indeed a clear scriptural authority for slavery, but the work regimen on the Georgia coast wasn't as punishing as that of Mississippi's cotton monoculture, and he allowed the people he called his "servants" to plant their own gardens and raise produce for the market, whose profits they kept. At the start of the conflict he and his wife Mary had three adult children: a second Mary, herself married to a clergyman; Joseph, an army surgeon; and Charles Jr., a Harvard-trained lawyer who after the war published an important collection of African-American folklore.

The Joneses' papers include vivid accounts of the chaos and confusion of the 1864 siege of Atlanta and of Sherman's subsequent March to the Sea. I'll return to those in a later chapter, but let me begin with a moment from 1856. James Buchanan has just been elected to the presidency, and the twenty-five-year-old Charles Jr. writes to his parents that for the next four years they "may hope for peace and prosperity. Beyond that period we scarce dare expect a continuance of our present relations." In the next election, he predicts, each part of the country will vote as a solid bloc, and if the free states win, the South must find the courage to make no concessions at all. Three years later the father describes those Northerners who applauded John Brown's attack on Harpers Ferry as cowards; if they are so opposed to slavery, "Why do they not arm and come to the field in open day?" But each of them thinks that Lincoln will triumph, and Charles Jr. fears that one state or another—he names South Carolina—may then force them into the horrors of an "intestine war." His father isn't so worried. The withdrawal of any Southern state from the Union will lead to the withdrawal of all, but on what grounds, he asks, could the free states possibly attack? Surely a claim to self-governance is no casus belli.

Charles Jr. establishes a law practice in Savannah and even serves a term as mayor. Daughter Mary has "such an abundance of nourishment" after the birth of her first child that she needs for relief to nurse one of the newborn slaves. They speak of books and meals and the state of the crops, ask after their relatives, and report on especially good sermons. But the national fate is always before them. Georgia seceded on January 19, 1861, and a week later Mary wrote her mother to ask how she felt about living in a foreign country. The Joneses may wonder what will happen, yet they have no doubt at all about what they will do. They are as firmly and immediately committed to the Confederate cause as Faulkner's own characters. Charles Jr. regrets the Union's demise; nevertheless, the slave states must separate themselves from those who blight the land with "hissing tongue and noxious breath." North and South may share a common parentage, but he has read J. G. Herder, the eighteenth-century German theorist of national origin and identity, and claims that after two centuries the climactic differences between one region and another have split the white race in two. Each section now has an utterly different sense of morals and religion and can no longer even agree on what counts as honor or truth.

Lincoln's inaugural address in March 1861 puzzles him, with its claim that the election has changed nothing: "It means this, and it means that; and then it may mean neither." Sumter falls, and he grows busy with a local militia company, worrying about the placement of howitzers for the city's defense. The South, he says, is a land of purity and high purpose; Washington in contrast but a swamp of "unmitigated rascality." His father, meanwhile, believes that Providence has favored the South in giving it Lincoln as a foe. His fanaticism will drive the border states into the Confederacy, and it's no wonder God favors their cause, for Christianity "finds no lodgement in the soul" of the Republican Party. The Joneses never doubt their own rectitude, and they are almost entirely without a sense of humor. Yet as the letters pass between them, the quotidian details of their lives become as utterly absorbing as those in a Victorian novel. Death and birth, sickness, and love too; nor does war put an end to personal ambition. Charles Jr. delights in his promotion to colonel, but he also complains about the price of nails. Brother Joseph is eventually sent to investigate medical conditions at the overcrowded Andersonville Prison; he returns in shock at the deliberate cruelty with which the South treats its captured Union soldiers and yet can do nothing about it. Even then, however, he doesn't doubt the Confederate cause; none of them do, not until the war is over and Mary's husband, Robert Mallard, writes of his struggle to reconcile his belief in God's justice with the victory of what he still sees as a "cruel and wicked foe."

The Joneses recognize the full moment of their times; they register the weight of the events around them. Yet they don't know that they are also living within a story, and nothing they write to each other seems calculated for effect. With Mary Chesnut it's just the opposite. She peppers her diary with references to Dickens and Thackeray, she sees herself as a woman with a part to play, and wants to make it a good one in every sense of the term. Chesnut was in her late thirties when the war began, with decades of devoted reading and letter-writing behind her. That experience had taught her how to shape a narrative, to work a moment of comedy or melodrama, and she sketches some of the Confederacy's great personages—Jefferson Davis in particular—with the ambition and even the wit of a Saint-Simon, the great seventeenth-century diarist of the French court at Versailles. For that she had good opportunities. Her husband, James Chesnut, had been a United States senator, but resigned his seat immediately after Lincoln's election and went home to help draft the secession ordinance for his native South Carolina. He did not expect a war and offered to drink all the blood that would be shed over the Union's breakup, claiming it wouldn't even fill a wineglass. Those words are perhaps the one excessive gesture of his life; he was coolly efficient and urbane, his emotions ever in check, and spent much of the war as one of Davis's aides. Meanwhile Mary Chesnut became, and with some amusement at her own position, a kind of lady-in-waiting to her old friend Varina Davis, the Confederate president's wife.

They are attendant lords, the Chesnuts, and yet on paper at least she feels none of the courtier's need to restrain her tastes and quirks and hatreds. Her angriest moments are also her most splendid:

> I wonder if it be a sin to think slavery a curse to any land. [Massachu-setts senator Charles] Sumner said not one word of this hated insti-tution which is not true.... God forgive us, but ours is a *monstrous* system and wrong and iniquity. Perhaps the rest of the world is as bad—this *only* I see. Like the patriarchs of old our men live all in one house with their wives and their concubines, and the mulattoes one sees in every family exactly resemble the white children—and every lady tells you who is the father of all the mulatto children in every-body's household, but those in her own she seems to think drop from the clouds, or pretends so to think.

Chesnut thought, reflexively, that much of the blame attached to the enslaved women themselves. In her eyes they were prostitutes, who had seduced their owners, rather than the victims of systemic sexual exploitation and rape; and perhaps she had to believe that in order to go on living in the world of her birth. Abolitionists like Sumner knew better, but she does at least have the honesty to see the role that sexual license played in that monstrous institu-tion, the honesty to see its attraction for the white men of her time and place. Chesnut looked at the "thing we can't name," the relations most Southerners denied, the crime they might whisper about to others, but in public pretend not to see. And they would go on denying it right up to Faulkner's own day and after. Neither Stark Young nor Margaret Mitchell—let alone such pre-decessors as Thomas Nelson Page—would depict those patriarchs in all their iniquity. Faulkner did. He too saw his native land as cursed, and for much the same reason as Chesnut herself; he too, as we will see, would locate much of slavery's evil in the power it gave "our men" over the sexual fate of the black women around them.

This passage now stands as her most famous, but anyone who read the versions of her work published in 1905 and 1949 as *A Diary from Dixie* would not have seen it; the first of them cut it entirely, and it was bowdlerized in the second. Chesnut kept her diary throughout the war, albeit with some

Major Robert Anderson, had moved his men at Christmas 1860 from the easily taken Fort Moultrie to the heavily fortified Sumter, built on a man-made
island in the middle of the harbor itself. Eventually the new Confederate government decided to starve the small garrison out, and in mid-April sent an
ultimatum: lower the flag or have it shot to shreds. James Chesnut was one of
the men who rowed over with the message, something his wife records only
by way of noting his return to the fashionable boarding house where they
waited out the crisis and the fact that he wants his dinner. She herself believes
that the war could have been avoided if only that "green goose Anderson"
hadn't moved into Fort Sumter. South Carolina would have stood alone and
in time gone back to the Union, but his actions have united the cotton states
in militancy. "And so we fool on," she writes, "into the black cloud ahead of
us," as though she too saw that Faulknerian moment when soar becomes fall.

The fort was told to surrender by four o'clock on the morning of April
12; she hears only silence after the church bells strike and begins to hope that
there will be no war. Then a cannon booms and she climbs to the roof in
her dressing gown to watch the sky light up. At first the Carolina artillery
seems mere "sound and fury." The gunners soon find their range, however,
and the fort begins to burn; its own cannon are ineffective in return. The
newspapers claim that Richmond and Washington are "ablaze," but she discounts it; at most, she thinks, they blaze with excitement. Chesnut's writing
here has an almost pointillist quality. She records the stray details she's seen
and heard, rumors and news and the confusion of other people's opinions,
and almost all of it reported without comment: spritzed onto the page, and
often in sentence fragments. Chesnut hates slavery but nevertheless believes
in secession. Yet when a friend speaks of having God on their side, she simply
asks "Why?" She is too worldly—and too flippant—to think of the South
as a sacred cause, and she proves more interested in gauging the war's effect
on Charleston's black population. "Not by one word or look can we detect
any change in the demeanor of the negro servants." Her husband's valet sits
at the door, as sleepily respectful as ever, and seems not to hear the cannon.
Their slaves never acknowledge that something momentous is happening,
and Chesnut notes that the whites continue to talk politics before them as
if they were tables or chairs. It all makes her wonder if "they are stolidly stu-

pid or wiser than we are, silent and strong, biding their time?" And then she
notes the arrival of tea and toast.

"So we took Fort Sumter," she writes, and meanwhile all the "agreeable
people" in the South seem to have arrived in Charleston for the show. To
most of them it's still a game, and Chesnut herself continues to note her troubles in training a new maid and her pleasure in talking to a handsome man.
The mails still run between North and South, and so she reads the New York
papers and laughs at what they get wrong; she sets down the table-talk of
this dignitary and that, and enjoys reminding people that the elegant General P. G. T. Beauregard, Sumter's Louisiana-born conqueror, had only lately
been a captain. She is frivolous, self-dramatizing, and petty, but always,
always brilliant. "We have risked all," she wrote that February, when the business of secession was still new, and the South now had to pick up its cards and
be canny and bold. She accepted the wager—but that April she nevertheless
found herself wondering, as she looked out on a beautifully kept spring lawn,
if she still lived in the same world as she had just a few days before.

Chesnut finds her Northern equivalent in the letters of the twenty-two-
year-old Henry Adams. In the summer of 1860 the young man returned to
America from Europe, where he had, among other activities, reported for a
Boston paper on Giuseppe Garibaldi's Sicilian campaign, which overthrew
the Kingdom of Naples in the name of united Italy. His father, Charles Fran-
cis Adams, would soon be appointed Lincoln's minister to Britain; the young
man went along as his private secretary, doing essential diplomatic work
but still wondering, as he always would, if he should have fought instead. In
Washington that winter he became a caustic witness to the process of secession. He writes his brother in December that President Buchanan divided
his time "between crying and praying; the Cabinet has resigned or else is
occupied in committing treason. Some of them have done both." He dines
regularly with William Seward, the secretary of state, who always pockets an
extra after-dinner cigar, and has a kind of sympathy for Mrs. Stephen Douglas, the wife of Lincoln's great rival, for "her husband is a brute—not to her
that I know of." And every other page has something about Fort Sumter. In
January 1861 Anderson and his men are still receiving their mail and South
Carolina hasn't yet cut off the groceries, but Adams hopes for a fight, and one

that he believes the North must lose, "in order to put the South in the wrong. If Major Anderson and his whole command were all murdered in cold blood, it would be an excellent thing for the country."

Adams had as acid a voice in his twenties as he did when he wrote *The Education of Henry Adams* in his sixties, and he sees himself as the shrewdest young man alive. Probably he was, and his clipped yet rounded sentences always make me laugh. Still, there's a more reliable account of the Union's sentiment in the diary of a New Yorker named George Templeton Strong. He was a civic-minded lawyer—trustee of Columbia College, president of the New York Philharmonic—whose greatest service came on the United States Sanitary Commission, which at first supplemented and then essentially ran the army's medical corps, raising money and providing nurses, doctors, and supplies to hospitals at the front. New York didn't have Boston's abolitionist fervor; its banks made too much money off slavery, and the city's large immigrant population feared the competition of free black labor. But Strong himself was a firm Republican, and all that fall and winter he watched the nation's spectacle, the South's confident weightless soar, with a mixture of fascination and alarm. At the start the threats of secession seem just that, threats, and "the attempt to bully us is barefaced. . . . The crack of the plantation whip is too audible." But he soon believes that disunion must come, and recognizes that the South's once-exaggerated claim that the Republican Party was simply the political wing of abolition has by now become true.

Strong writes that the South's folly has done more for the abolitionist cause than "a regiment of John Browns"; like Chesnut, he blames the other side for strengthening the resolve of his own. But he thinks the North should let the seceding states go; a forward-looking Congress will be well rid of them, and any Confederacy will soon dissolve in anarchy. At the end of January he feels a bit of encouragement—Kentucky and Maryland look firm, though Virginia now seems less so. Wall Street, acting as Wall Street always does, has even begun to wonder if secession might be good for business. Capital will desert the South, and the trade of its ports move north; "but money cannot pay for our national disgrace." By February war looks inevitable, and he predicts that within a year the Union will put slave regiments in the field and breach the Mississippi levees in order to drown New Orleans. Then

Sutpen has abjured his father and waits in hiding with his friend Charles Bon for the struggle to start. And meanwhile a detachment of their fellow soldiers from the university, mounted and with their body servants in a forage wagon, has gone all around the state with the company flag, its different pieces of colored silk "cut and fitted but not sewn." They have ridden from town to town and plantation to plantation, visiting the house of each soldier's sweetheart so she can take a few stitches in the banner they will carry into battle. Wagons move slowly, though, and Mississippi is not small, while hospitality would demand a meal or a cup at each stop; so the simple facts of time and distance make me doubt this tale of a ceremonious progress. In fact, the official history of the Eleventh Mississippi says nothing at all about it, though it does describe the presentation of a flag to another company raised in Oxford. The University Greys were an upper-class unit, its members drawn from throughout the state. Even its privates took a personal servant with them to the front, a slave to cook and care for their clothes. The Lamar Rifles were in contrast recruited within Lafayette County itself, many of them the sons of Oxford's merchants and professional men, and received their colors at a pageant in which each state of the new Confederacy was represented by a local girl in white. Such standards might indeed be made collectively, at something like a sewing bee, but Mr. Compson's story appears all moonshine, as fits that talkative alcoholic lawyer. Though at this moment in *Absalom, Absalom!* it's not just the character who's embroidering. Faulkner claimed to dislike the fanciful tissue, the clichés of moonlight and magnolia, in which other novelists wrapped their versions of the Southern past, and in this novel especially he would tear through it. Yet even here he can romance with the worst of them.

Henry and Charles will next appear at Shiloh, in April 1862, a year after the actual University Greys went into camp at Corinth, in the state's northeast corner, and were assigned to the Eleventh. The tall and bearded William Falkner was encamped at Corinth too: a "fine figure of a man," in the words his great-grandson would use for Thomas Sutpen, who at the start of May 1861 was elected colonel of the Second Mississippi. A few days later the two regiments went north by rail to Virginia, and along with units from Tennessee and Alabama became the Third Brigade of the Army of the Shenandoah; Falkner led the brigade for a day before he was replaced by Bernard Bee, a

West Pointer who had resigned his commission to fight for the Confederacy. For a while they bounced between Harpers Ferry and Winchester in the lower reaches of the Shenandoah Valley, facing but not fighting a small Union army, and suffering more from disease than anything else; military camps were by definition insanitary, and few soldiers from rural districts had developed much immunity. Then in mid-July they marched out of the valley and took the cars for the thirty-mile trip to the great camp at Manassas Junction.

Falkner's unit reached the front on Saturday, July 20, not long after another Shenandoah brigade had arrived, this one headed by a former instructor from the Virginia Military Institute named Thomas Jackson. The shape of the next day's battle was determined first by the winding stream known as Bull Run and then by the low hills to its south. Bull Run has steep banks and was in places heavily wooded; its fords were widely scattered, and it was spanned by just one bridge. Federal troops had to cross from the north. They could not mount a wide unbroken front, and the action funneled toward what was known as the Henry House Hill, after the family whose home was destroyed by the battle's artillery. Falkner's brigade began the morning as part of a line that managed to slow a heavy Union advance, but not long after noon it was scattered by a fresh assault led, among others, by William Tecumseh Sherman, now a Union colonel and commanding a brigade of his own. The Southerners fell back, retreating up the slopes of the Henry House Hill, where Bee tried to rally the remnants of his command by pointing to Jackson "standing there like a stone wall." The name stuck, though Jackson always claimed that it referred to his troops and not to himself. But walls can break waves, and the Union advance broke on this one.

General Joseph Johnston's official report on the battle mentioned Falkner as one of a dozen colonels whose performance was worth noting. Bee would doubtless have added something about his regimental commanders if he had lived to write a report of his own, but he died of wounds the next day and there's nothing else about the Second Mississippi in the *Official Record*'s account of the fight. The Memphis *Appeal* said more. Falkner apparently had two horses killed under him and took a slight wound in the face; he wore a black plume in his hat and at one point General Beauregard himself was heard to cheer him on. Still, the Old Colonel's namesake wouldn't have been interested in more details, not to put on the page anyway. The novelist had little interest in tactics, in a battle's moment-by-moment flow, and about John Sartoris's day at Bull Run he writes nothing at all. He merely tells us that the character was there; that's it. Faulkner uses the names of battles in the same way that he uses Sartoris's own in *Requiem for a Nun*. He simply drops them in and expects that the proper noun itself will be enough to summon up a part of his reader's mental furniture. The referent points, that is, to the history that people in his world already knew, and part of my own purpose here is to make that history clear to a reader today. Not military history per se, not the details of a day's fighting, a general's orders, or the movements of this unit or that; though with Gettysburg he does, admittedly, count on a knowledge of Pickett's Charge. No, what matters instead, what mattered for Faulkner, is the way that each of the war's great battles stands as a site of memory. Their very names carry a cultural significance, nominating a collection of particular meanings, marking a stage in the conflict or calling up some especially charged emotion.

Bull Run made the Union recognize that the war would be long and hard. Some officers knew that already, the hot-tempered Sherman among them, but public opinion had held that the war would be easy and McDowell's troops marched out of Washington to the cheer of "On to Richmond." Their loss and above all their chaotic retreat, in which entire regiments seemed to dissolve, was due in part to the fact that they were at best half-trained, a volunteer army sent into battle by a country hoping the crisis could be quickly resolved. Of the war's great captains only Sherman figured on the Union's side at Bull Run. The South made a better show. Almost every commander who would count in the Army of Northern Virginia was there with the exception of Robert E. Lee himself. Stonewall Jackson became a legend, and J. E. B. Stuart's cavalry earned him his first long draught of fame. Indeed, the South was so excited by its triumph that it forgot how narrow the margin had been. Victory confirmed the Confederate belief in Yankee pusillanimity—any single Rebel soldier could whip a dozen of the enemy. Some newspapers thought the battle would bring the war to an immediate close; Southern independence was assured. One of Mary Chesnut's friends told her, however, that Bull Run might well become the South's ruin, lulling it into a "fool's paradise of conceit" even as the Federals' shame woke "every inch of their manhood."

I began this chapter with a visit to Natchez and the ghostly shell of a house called Longwood, where after the war the descendants of the slave owner Haller Nutt lived in the imprisoning dust of the few rooms they had been able to furnish. Let me finish with another Mississippi house, this one fictional, an airless box on a Jefferson street, the home of Sutpen's father-in-law, the storekeeper Goodhue Coldfield. Faulkner describes him as a harsh-voiced, righteous man, the only conscientious objector in town, and in the spring of 1861 he refused to let his younger daughter, Rosa, look on as the first Confederate units marched by. In his shop he refused to sell anything at all to soldiers, or their families, or to anyone who had ever spoken in favor of secession. Not a straw hat or bit of salt meat crossed his counter, and eventually he had to close up. Afterward he sat in the parlor window, his Bible at the ready, aiming the book's "old violent vindictive mysticism" at any passing unit. Then one day he went up into his attic, nailed the door shut behind him, and threw the hammer out the window. Bull Run mattered. But for both Lafayette and Yoknapatawpha counties alike there would be more consequential battles to come.

SEVEN

The Real War

Faulkner imagined Yoknapatawpha County as a territory of twenty-four hundred square miles and about fifteen thousand people, 60 percent of them black. Those are the figures he put on the map he drew for *Absalom, Absalom!*, and he dotted his postage stamp with farms and plantations, from Sutpen's Hundred in the county's northwest to the erosion-laced acres of the Bundren family in *As I Lay Dying*, away down in its opposite corner. But in all that space he planted just two settlements, two clusters or communities of people. One is Jefferson, in the county's dead center. The other he called Frenchman's Bend, a hamlet along the Yoknapatawpha River about twenty miles to Jefferson's southeast. It's a tiny and impoverished place, a crossroads that boasts little more than a cotton gin and a general store, a boarding house and a blacksmith's shop. And yet this little village, as I said two chapters ago, is where Yoknapatawpha County itself began: the setting for "Father Abraham," the first story Faulkner ever tried to write about his apocryphal land.

But this is where Yoknapatawpha began in another sense as well, for Faulkner also defines it as the site of the county's original land grant, the tremendous antebellum plantation of a Huguenot called Louis Grenier. The man himself never actually appears in the Yoknapatawpha cycle; he's but a point of reference, a figure from the lost past, who vanished with the Civil War. Nevertheless, his nationality gave the spot its name, and the ruins of his great house are known to the whole county as the Old Frenchman's Place, a pillaged, tumbledown shell surrounded by vine-clogged gardens. For Grenier had no heirs, and after the war his former slaves were driven off by the poor whites who came down to the Bend from the Tennessee hills. The house lay open to anyone who wanted a piece of it, with its walnut staircases chopped up for firewood by people who didn't even know the Frenchman's name. There was, however, one thing they did all know about him: the old story, as Faulkner writes in *The Hamlet,* of the money he "buried somewhere about the place when Grant over-ran the country on his way to Vicksburg."

There are two names in the words I've quoted, two proper nouns, and one of my concerns in this chapter lies in the relation between them: in the questions of strategy that determined the course of the Civil War in Faulkner's home state. I come to those names through his work, however, and so my story also rests on the way that that history helps shape his fiction: his plots and his characters, his representation of the war itself, and the weight of memory too. But the names first. Ulysses S. Grant, of the Army of the Tennessee, the Union major general who "over-ran the country"; the verb implies that he did it all on his own, as fits so legendary a figure, and yet it also suggests a swarming horde, rats maybe, or locusts. And then Vicksburg. I've already touched on that river town's importance. Still we need to look at the place more closely, at the history for which its name provides a shorthand. Most of what happened in wartime Mississippi was determined by the Union's desire for that small city, and mastering the events that led to its fall in 1863 is essential to understanding what Faulkner wrote about the period; doing so, however, will require some slipping and sliding between the world and the fictional page.

In 1860 Vicksburg had about forty-five hundred inhabitants and lay on the outer edge of a sharp tight bend in the Mississippi River, almost equidistant between Memphis and New Orleans. Like Natchez, it sat on a high bluff along the river's eastern shore, but its location on that bight gave the town a strategic importance that Natchez lacked. Its guns commanded the great stream, and so it didn't really matter that by the middle of 1862 the Union had already captured both Memphis and New Orleans, not so long as the Confederacy still held the town in the middle. Vicksburg broke the Federal line. It gave the South access to the rich and largely untouched agricultural lands to the west, to the foodstuffs and cotton of Arkansas and Louisiana. Seize Vicksburg, and you control the river; seize Vicksburg, and you cut the rebellion in half. It took Grant almost a year to get there, however, after a long series of feints and failures, and one of those failures happened in Faulkner's home territory. Late in 1862 the general moved his army into Lafayette County, pushing a Confederate garrison out of Oxford itself and establishing his headquarters there, while setting up a supply depot in Holly Springs, thirty miles to the north. He planned to come down on Vicksburg from the northeast, a march of two hundred miles that would have made the town's waterfront batteries irrelevant. But just before Christmas a Confederate cavalry raid swept through Holly Springs in a surprise attack, burning more than a million dollars' worth of the Union's accumulated stores and forcing Grant to abandon his plans. He didn't control the countryside firmly enough to risk that march, and in January he fell back to Memphis.

Meanwhile the residents of both Lafayette County and its fictional counterpart got used to the Union's foraging missions, to the almost-daily presence of soldiers looking for hams and horses. Oxford's leading citizens had their houses turned into hospitals, the mythical Frenchman buried his gold, and in *The Unvanquished* young Bayard Sartoris's grandmother, Rosa Millard, stands with a watch in her hand, counting off the minutes as the household practices packing a trunk with the family silver and hiding it in the orchard of the Colonel's plantation. After the war almost every big house in Faulkner's work will have its legend of hidden wealth, and many of his characters spend their nights digging in the hopes of uncovering that treasure, with the novelist playing their greed for laughs. None of them ever find it, and the Sartorises themselves will lose their silver to a Yankee raid: to an army so encumbered by captured loot that when Grandmother Millard asks for her cutlery back they simply give her a wagonload.

A SUMMER AFTERNOON, AND the "sunimpacted" earth behind the smokehouse has baked itself dry, so dry that it sucks down the water with which two twelve-year-olds are trying to make a "living map," scratching a furrow in the dirt to represent the Mississippi River and pouring in bucket after leaky bucket. It's a hopeless job, keeping that stream full or even just damp, but the desperation fits their purpose. For they are playing at war, and alongside their trough they've put a pile of woodchips to represent that far-off place called Vicksburg. They fill the little ditch, fighting for time, and hoping to get the battle started before the water all drains off. Bayard, the white boy, usually takes the role of General John Pemberton, the state's Confederate commander. Ringo, the black boy, has to settle for Grant. But they switch off every third turn, for Ringo won't play unless he too gets a chance to be the Reb.

This is the opening moment of *The Unvanquished*, and it's important to note that Faulkner doesn't start with what Bayard calls "the cannon and the flags and the anonymous yelling" of battle. Instead, he begins with children at play, and in doing so asks us to concentrate on the relations between black and white on the Sartoris land. For that's what the war is about, and what matters here isn't the fighting as such but rather the way in which it will affect those relations. The boys bring another bucket, and another, and are then interrupted by the man who suddenly stands over them—Loosh for Lucius, as Ringo is short for Marengo. He asks about their game, and then laughs and stoops to sweep the chips away. "There's your Vicksburg," he says, "and I tell you nother un you aint know. . . . Corinth." His words announce defeat at what the boys know are Mississippi's two most strategic points, and they make the younger slave stand still, looking at Bayard even as the white boy tries to keep playing, tries to fight off his own fear. Because Bayard trusts Loosh, despite that laugh. He trusts the grown-ups whom he has known all his life, and he also believes what his father, the Colonel, has told him: word of mouth will sometimes carry the news from the slave quarters of one plantation to those of another before it can reach the planter's own house. Many of the period's letters and diaries do in fact stress how much the South's largely illiterate black population knew about the war, how accurately informed they were about its every stage. Then the boys hear a shout and turn to see a smoke-colored stallion pacing up the lane, bringing Colonel Sartoris himself on an unexpected visit, his gold braid now dusty and his buttons tarnished.

The Colonel confirms Bayard's fears: Loosh does know something about how the war is going. But Sartoris thinks he can use that knowledge, and tells the family's cook, Louvinia, Loosh's mother, that she needs to watch him, and closely. His actions will tip them off about any marauding Yankees, and Sartoris adds, with a note of good-humored brutality, that "even if he was her son, she would have to be white a little while longer." Those words suggest that the Colonel knows something too. He knows that slavery itself is about to die—but not yet, and for the moment he counts on Louvinia to collaborate with the system that holds her in bondage. He wants her to be the "faithful servant" of Confederate mythology, to identify her interests with his. And Faulkner suggests that some of the family's other slaves will make that identification willingly, in a way that grows increasingly problematic as *The Unvanquished* moves from chapter to chapter. Ringo wants to play the Confederate Pemberton in his game with Bayard, and to the white boy the pair of them are so close, having "slept together and eaten together for so long" that he wonders whether the terms "white" and "black" even apply anymore. Only a white child could ask that question, though, and Bayard gets to play the Rebel twice to his friend's once.

Still, there are more things than Loosh to watch here, and two of Faulkner's formal decisions tell us a great deal about his sense of the Civil War as a subject. The first is the impossibility of dating this scene, of making any clear connection between these fictional events and a particular historical moment. The novelist tells us that Bayard was born in 1850 and is twelve years old in "Ambuscade," *The Unvanquished*'s first chapter. That suggests a setting in the late spring or early summer of 1862. The Union army captured the rail junction at Corinth, in the state's northeast, at the end of May that year, and in late June Yankee gunboats began an intermittent shelling of Vicksburg itself. Their artillery was ineffective, but still the rumor spread that the town would fall. Is that what Loosh means in scattering those woodchips? Pemberton did not, however, take command in the state until that October, and the boys play as if Vicksburg were under siege. That points us to the summer of 1863. Grant invested the town in May, and it surrendered on the fourth of July, when there was no news at all from the long-established Union garrison at Corinth.

I could explain this collage of Confederate disasters by supposing either that Loosh is wrong or Faulkner forgetful. Yet I think the confusion is deliberate. Faulkner has purposefully spliced together two very different years in the war. Jefferson seems undisturbed by Federal forces in the opening pages of *The Unvanquished*, and indeed the fighting hadn't fully reached northern Mississippi in the spring and summer of 1862. The war still lay at a distance, a faraway rumble rather than a fact of daily life, and in Lafayette County the routines of the women and children at home were in many ways undisturbed; there was plenty of food and they weren't yet subject to Federal raids and requisitions. Then 1863 brought chaos, with Union armies marching back and forth across the state and brigades of Yankee cavalry ripping up its railroads and riding down its spine. Faulkner fudges the dates to give us both things at once, two historical moments in a single incident, blurring the years to capture the psychological truth of the Confederate home front. To young Bayard that still faraway war seems stretched out, both static and perpetual, as well it might to a boy of twelve. Time hangs suspended, and yet so does a sense of enduring crisis: the war isn't a sharp and sudden blow but something ongoing and continuous, not a battle but a siege. Vicksburg. But the Colonel will confirm that Vicksburg has indeed surrendered, and with that surrender will come a new time of ever-faster change, faster fall.

That's one of the formal decisions Faulkner made, a decision about the relation between history and fiction. The other is more purely novelistic and concerns young Bayard's own point of view. Faulkner allows his first-person narrator some vocabulary that a child simply wouldn't have, along with occasional moments of adult retrospection, and over the book's seven chapters he does age from twelve to twenty-four. But at the start he's still a boy, and the war seems distant in more ways than one—still a game, something played with bits of wood and buckets of water. Colonel Sartoris has come and gone, talking all night before riding back to his command. And soon after the Yankees themselves will arrive, in the form of a scout sitting "on a bright bay horse and looking at the house through a field glass." He is the first enemy soldier Bayard has ever seen. The boy is startled to discover how much this demon looks like a man, and then without a word he and Ringo run inside and take down the loaded musket over the mantelpiece.

Hiding in the honeysuckle along the drive, Bayard steadies the gun's barrel across Ringo's stooping back, each determined to shoot the "bastud," and neither of them understanding just what this Yankee presence means. It's something to do with freedom, that much they know—but the boys aren't sure if the Union wants to bring it or take it away, and they don't yet realize that it won't mean the same thing to each of them. Bayard's finger sits upon the trigger, and "the sights came level and as I shut my eyes I saw the man and the bright horse vanish in smoke." They hear the horse scream, and what follows makes the war seem like a game indeed. Or a comedy. When the smoke clears they are sprinting back to the house with what looks like the whole Union army after them, and they've barely scrambled under Grandmother Millard's armchair, "her skirts spread over [them] like a tent," when an angry sergeant enters, shaking the abandoned musket, and accuses her of having ordered the boys to fire. There are no children here, she claims, only to be told that Bayard's aim was good. "Broke his back and we had to shoot him," the soldier says, and Faulkner allows both his narrator and his readers a heartbeat of fear before he magics it away. "Best damn horse in the whole army. The whole damn regiment betting on him for next Sunday." Then a Union colonel arrives, someone whom even this well-starched Southern lady recognizes as a gentleman. He accepts her denial—he takes her at her word even as he stares at her widespread skirts. The Union army has many horses and losing one isn't going to slow their advance; but it is such a pity, he tells her, that you have no grandchildren, as if the page itself were winking.

Plot and genre and tone: which of them determines the others? War means fighting and fighting means killing, as the Confederate cavalry commander Nathan Bedford Forrest once said, and an incident like this can only happen around its edges. Or maybe the fact that Bayard's gunshot has no final consequences works to keep it on that edge. Move that musket ball a few inches and it would be easy to imagine the Yankee vengeance; move that ball, and every word of this story would be different. For Bayard at twelve, the war isn't yet fully imaginable, and the business of *The Unvanquished* lies in bringing him into a deeper understanding of its nature and meaning. A part of that process depends, however, on his growing recognition of what he cannot in fact imagine, of experiences he cannot enter. "We had heard about battles and fighting," he says in a later chapter, "and seen those who had taken part in them," but he's been taught to believe that war is a dazzling spectacle of galloping horses and crashing artillery. He can't match that image to the everyday presence of Jefferson's veterans, men who have come home with-out an arm or a leg. Yet Bayard does learn something as he hides beneath his grandmother's skirts. He learns what war is not. Not what it is, and Faulk-ner's choice of a boy's point of view allows him to find his subject in the war's very absence.

"The real war will never get in the books"; let me quote Whitman one last time. The words come from *Specimen Days* (1882), and they make me wonder how the poet saw that unforgettable book of his own, a collection of jour-nal entries in which he described his time on the wards of army hospitals, bringing what help he could to the wounded. For him "the real war" stood as a problem of representation. The literary language of the time was simply too well-clothed to make its readers imagine the face of battle. It couldn't strip itself down to the gobbets and pus of wounded flesh. By Faulkner's day that language had changed, but as a historical novel *The Unvanquished* stays within the conventions of its period setting. It's a war novel that works around its own limitations by reminding us that its account of the conflict is by no means the real war, the whole war, a book that invokes all the things Bayard hasn't seen and doesn't understand. Faulkner was hardly the first writer to do this, however, and I want to pause here to look briefly at two attempts from the Civil War era itself to find a language in which to write about war. Each offers an understated and indeed antiheroic rhetoric, but while one is a popular classic the other offers a grim taste of the future, of the way combat would be described in the twentieth century and after.

"You have heard from a great many people who did something in the war; is it not fair and right that you listen a little moment to one who started out to do something in it, but didn't?" That's Mark Twain at the start of "The Private History of a Campaign That Failed," a sketch of his own alleged expe-riences in the early summer of 1861; alleged, because no trace of the Confed-erate unit he describes has ever been found outside his own pages. Still, the facts are never the point with Twain. The piece's emotional acuity is another matter. It ran in the *Century* magazine for November 1885, a year after *Huck-leberry Finn* had made him the most famous writer in America, appearing as part of the magazine's "Battles and Leaders" series, an ironic counterpart to its articles on Gettysburg or the Seven Days, its general's-eye view of this fight or that. Twain was no leader and admits that the story he tells is in many ways trivial. And yet, he adds, any record of the war would be incomplete without the voices of people like him, of those who planned to fight, and then didn't.

Twain's Missouri was one of four slave states to stay in the Union, and in the first months after Sumter it saw something like a Civil War of its own. The secessionist governor tried to muster the state's militia for Confederate service; Federal troops forced their surrender but met with a riot when they marched their prisoners through Saint Louis. Twain's hometown of Hannibal leaned South, and in the war's early days it served, he says, as the recruiting ground for a volunteer unit called the Marion Rangers: young men with few political convictions and nothing much else to do, who marched off with a sense of fun and laughter to train in the woods. That lasted about an hour. Then they got bored. It was a dark night and all "the play . . . oozed out of it"; the remaining weeks of their training were a regime of "dull trudging and . . . depression." No one would take orders from anybody else or knew whether a sergeant outranked a corporal, and they almost never set pickets or sentries. Twain rode into camp one night without being challenged, "and the enemy could have done the same."

Not that he ever saw an enemy. The essay wrings a sly if overdrawn comedy out of its narrator's own fecklessness, until one night a man on horseback appears in the forest path, as indistinct as mist but seeming as if at the head of a troop. Guns flash, and the man falls; "my first feeling was of surprised gratification; my first impulse was an apprentice-sportsman's impulse to run and pick up his game." But surprise almost immediately turns to sorrow. The entire unit, horrified by their new knowledge of war, works to stanch the man's blood. But all they can do is offer a few encouraging words as he dies, and they then discover that he was just a solitary civilian traveler, and unarmed. Twain risks one last joke. His own bullet couldn't have killed the man, for "I had never hit anything I had tried to hit, and I knew I had done my best to hit him. Yet there was no solace in the thought."

The "Private History" captures a moment when the country didn't yet know how serious the war would be; by the time it did, Twain himself had left the Confederate army far behind. His brother Orion was a Union man, with an appointment as secretary to the governor of the Nevada territory. He

and dead to shame." They could only be kept from boarding—from running further—at the point of a bayonet. His unit disembarked and climbed up the steep road from the water and on into the night, past hospital tents lit by candles. In the morning he walked through what had lately been a forest, its every tree reduced to splinters, and the ground covered with abandoned supplies. Bodies too, and then one man still living, his skull opened by a bullet and with froth crawling down his cheeks. They could see his brain, and a soldier asked Bierce if he should kill him for mercy's sake; "I thought not; it was unusual, and too many were looking." Later he walked through some woods where the fallen leaves had been set aflame by sparks, and he found he could distinguish the burned corpses of the men killed by gunfire from those of the wounded men who had then been roasted alive. The former had an "unlovely looseness of attitude"; the others had died in such pain that their hands had contracted to claws. Then Bierce's regiment formed its line, and other lines in gray came toward them, dissolving in smoke and noise; and the two armies broke and broke on each other again, like water sloshing in a bowl, until silence fell and he could see a chaplain walk across the field.

His sketches and stories remain undervalued to the degree that they are in fact sketches and stories, yet they provide his generation's most probing account of battle, its closest approach to "the real war." Such tales of disillusionment remained the prerogative of Northern writers. That was the luxury of victory; the beaten South still needed to believe in glory. Nevertheless, Bierce's mixture of blunt physicality and bitter comedy suggests a new way of writing about combat. The poetry and memoirs of the Great War would approach it. The novel wouldn't fully master that mordant idiom until after World War II, an idiom to which the pronoun in Bierce's title seems utterly crucial: "What I Saw of Shiloh." These incidents, he writes, "necessarily group themselves about my own personality as a center." He knows when the fighting scared him or when an enemy line quailed in the face of his own, but makes no claim to describe the battle as a whole or to define its tactical errors and triumphs. None of the Confederate units he faces have names or numbers, and he never knows who commands them, as a historian might. What *I* saw: this single sergeant, not his brigade commander, nor the men who died in the forest, nor even the soldier next to him. Bierce's title insists on his own version of these events—its validity, its relevance—and yet in doing so implies that other people's experience may have an equal value. Faulkner's John Sartoris had one war; Thomas Sutpen another. Even young Bayard, playing with woodchips—even he has his own war, and it's as entirely present to him as anything his elders feel or fear. There is no one real war. But perhaps only someone who saw as much of it as Bierce could say so.

IN APRIL 1952 FAULKNER walked over the field at Shiloh with a younger writer named Shelby Foote. He came from Greenville, on the Mississippi River, and had been an admirer since the 1930s, when he had read the Yoknapatawpha books along with his friend Walker Percy, who would win the National Book Award for his 1961 novel, *The Moviegoer*. Foote had just published a novel of his own about the battle, splitting its narration between half-a-dozen first-person voices, and was about to begin work on a three-volume history of the war itself. The two men walked from point to point, picking out where particular regiments had formed and positing that a patch of blackberries now filled the spot where a Union brigade had been encamped. Then Foote found a piece of wood that weighed about the same as a Confederate musket, and charged the blackberries, with Faulkner looking on in approval.

Shiloh spoke to Faulkner. It was the nearest major battlefield to his Oxford home, and he put more of his characters there than he did at any other fight. Bayard Sartoris, for example, has a cousin named Drusilla Hawke whose fiancé dies in that struggle, leaving her to what her own mother calls "the highest destiny of a Southern woman—to be the bride-widow of a lost cause": a fate she declines to accept. Henry Sutpen and Charles Bon join in the battle as well, their company of university students now part of the regiment led by Quentin Compson's grandfather. Bon has become an officer while Henry remains a private, but they still march together and use each other's Christian names, and on the second day one of them gets hit—shot through the shoulder and then carried to the rear on the back of the other. I say "one of them" because *Absalom, Absalom!* allows that it could have been either. Jefferson has always believed that Bon was the wounded man. That's the story Quentin gets from his father, the official version—and one that Quentin and his Canadian roommate Shreve reject as they tell things over in their Harvard dormitory. Henry took the bullet, Shreve says, and asked Bon to let him die on the field—a way to avoid whatever his father had told him that Christmas at Sutpen's Hundred.

And Colonel Compson is wounded there too, and goes back to Jefferson "to get used to not having any right arm." These references all take the same form. Faulkner never spends more than a few sentences at a time on the battle, but when he does the first thing he notes are the casualties. There's a reason for that. The Confederacy's killed and wounded at Shiloh came to just under ten thousand men, almost 25 percent of its army; in raw figures the Union lost slightly more out of a significantly bigger force. The human cost of Bull Run had shocked both sides, but the bloodshed at Shiloh beggared anything in the American past; so did the size of the armies. Bigger battles would follow, and with more deaths, but Shiloh set the pattern. Bull Run said that the war would be a long one; Shiloh showed what that meant.

The battlefield today is an exceptionally beautiful piece of ground, on a wide bend in the Tennessee River and with the national cemetery sitting on a bluff above the water. There are open fields that could double as fairways if they weren't lined at either end with cannon; the winding roads dip suddenly into the shadiest of glens, and the woods are full of deer. In 1862 it was farmland, and especially known for its peach orchards; the trees were in blossom as the shooting began. The fighting itself, in Bruce Catton's words, "was not one battle but a vast number of intense and bewildering" smaller ones, a seemingly patternless melee, and yet in retrospect its overall shape looks clear. A Confederate army commanded by Albert Sidney Johnston attacked the Union encampment at dawn and pushed the Yankees back toward the river. The Rebel leader himself died from a wound in his leg, but not before many Federal units had dissolved in fear; these were the men Bierce saw huddled below the bluff when he reached the battlefield at the end of the day. Then the Union line steadied and began an artillery barrage that halted the Confederate charge. That night a heavy rain fell, and Grant received the reinforcements he had been waiting for, more than twenty thousand fresh troops under the command of Don Carlos Buell; and in the morning they pushed the Confederates off.

What matters for our purposes isn't the course of the battle as such, but rather an understanding of why the armies met there at all, one that will allow us to see the shape of the war in Faulkner's Mississippi. The conflict in the east was dictated by the proximity of Washington and Richmond. The Union capital lay on the edge of the Confederacy and was vulnerable to an attack from the northwest, as Lee showed in twice bringing armies over the Potomac. Richmond was just a hundred miles away, but it sat behind a screen of rivers and was much harder to reach. Still, the Federal command believed that once Union troops got there the war would be over, and so they marched south in 1861, twice in both 1862 and 1863, and then again in 1864; and all but the last of those assaults were turned back.

The North's objectives in the west were not at first so clear, and the distances far greater. In February 1862 Grant captured a pair of forts in northern Tennessee. His expedition had begun as a bit of local tactics, but he stretched his orders and gave the Union both its first hero and control of two major rivers. The Cumberland ran through Nashville, which fell without a fight; the Tennessee made a U-shape through the middle of the state, with its bottom in northern Alabama, and grazed the borders of both Georgia and Mississippi. Grant wanted to press on while the Confederates were in disarray, but his superiors ordered him to wait at Pittsburg Landing for Buell's reinforcing army. Together they would march on the rail junction at Corinth, twenty miles away in Mississippi's northeast corner; but in the meantime Grant's unsuspecting army lay open to Johnston's preemptive assault.

This is a severely telescoped account of a complex situation, one developed at length in the superb narrative histories by Catton and Foote, among others. At the end of May the Union occupied Corinth and took control of Mississippi's major railroads, and in July Grant began to plan an assault on Vicksburg. But that small city wasn't only impossible to take from the water, it was also surprisingly hard to reach by land. It sat at the confluence of the Mississippi and Yazoo Rivers, and the wedge of country between the two streams, stretching off to the town's northeast and then on up to Mem-

phis, was low, swampy, and impassable. It was called the Delta, and though
it contains some of the richest farmland in the world, much of it was as yet
uncleared; roads were few and the forest thick. High ground along the river
began at Vicksburg and ran south to Natchez and beyond, but it also sliced
down on a diagonal from a range of hills to the east. Oxford lay tucked
within those hills, about twenty-five miles from the Delta's edge, and Grant
planned at first to march his army south along them. In November, as I've
already noted, he put his supply depot at Holly Springs, a county seat just
under the Tennessee border. The Confederates retreated before him, and his
army moved into Oxford itself on December 2.

The Union's plans did, however, depend on maintaining its lines of supply and communications to the north. Food and ammunition had to travel
by wagon or rail, and orders required the telegraph. Grant's army needed to
hold the roads, but in mid-December he found himself savaged by a pair of
cavalry attacks. Nathan Bedford Forrest had already made himself a legend
with his daring escape from Fort Donelson on the Cumberland River, the
site of Grant's first great victory. He broke the Union lines and led his men
out across a flooded stream, riding chest-deep in the icy water, and was soon
known as the "Wizard of the Saddle." Now he took 2,000 troopers on a raid
through Tennessee, cutting both the railroad and the telegraph on which the
Federals depended, and freezing his enemy in place; it took almost two weeks
for the wires to be restored and more for the track itself. At the same time the
Confederate general Earl Van Dorn mounted an attack on Holly Springs,
where the depot's commander surrendered without a fight. Grant now had
neither supplies nor a supply line; his army would have to take a different
path, and he retreated to Memphis for the winter.

Yet before he left Oxford he found a new way to provision his men. At the
start of the war Lincoln believed that many Southerners, outside of the slaveholding elite, would cleave to the Union if given the chance. So the army's
job was to fight other soldiers. It did not make war on civilians and would
respect private property; early on some Federal commanders even returned
runaway slaves. Meat and grain and hay might need to be requisitioned,
houses too, but strict accounts were to be kept and compensation offered.
But the Confederacy commanded a broader and deeper loyalty than Lincoln

had expected, and by the middle of 1862 his policy had run thin. That July the president got a letter from occupied New Orleans in which a prosperous Rebel complained about the struggle's threat to private property, and Lincoln had finally had enough. Exasperation pushed him toward sarcasm—should he prosecute the war with "elder-stalk squirts, charged with rose water?" Grant took the hint. Ordinary citizens would now feel the war's hard hand, and after Holly Springs he sent out wagons to seize food and fodder, picking clean a wide swath along the road that ran from Oxford to the Tennessee border and beyond.

His army could live off the land, at the expense of a civilian population that had shown itself to be hostile. For his enemies weren't just soldiers. They were also the people who fed them, whose labor kept those troops in the field; and that December Grant discovered how to provision his army even as he kept the South from supplying its own. It was a lesson both he and his lieutenant William Tecumseh Sherman would draw on in the future, and one he shared with Oxford's townspeople, who came to gloat after his supply depot had been burned, asking him what he would do without any food for his men. He told them about the wagons and watched their expressions change; but "their friends in gray had been uncivil enough to destroy what we had brought along, and it could not be expected that men, with arms in their hands, would starve in the midst of plenty."

Those words come from the *Personal Memoirs of U. S. Grant*. Even during the war Grant was known for the concision and clarity of his written orders; nobody receiving one, his subordinates said, ever had a doubt of its meaning. Lee in contrast preferred to give his commands orally, often in the form of a suggestion, and at times that made their burden uncertain. Grant had had no plans, at first, to write about the conflict, and he declined the *Century*'s initial suggestion that he contribute to its series of "Battles and Leaders." But in 1884 he lost what capital he had; he had put his money into a brokerage house, trusting a partner who in fact ran it as a Ponzi scheme. The general, now a bankrupt, took the magazine's offer, beginning with an article on Shiloh. And he soon found that he had another reason to keep writing. He was a heavy smoker, with a fondness for cigars—and now learned that he had throat cancer. Grant had always been a devoted husband

and father, and feared he would leave his wife destitute. He needed to make money, fast, and began to write at speed against the most absolute of deadlines: two volumes that covered his life from West Point to Appomattox. Much of it he dictated, with his three sons acting as fact-checkers, but at the end he could no longer speak. His throat was too cracked and constricted even to form words, and he squeezed the last pages out in pencil, his physical agony requiring a regular dose of cocaine. Grant was still revising in his last weeks, and the tenacity and indeed courage with which he stuck to the job and finished has made readers ever since describe it as his last victory. He died in July 1885, with the book in press, but by then he knew that Julia Grant would not have to worry about money. The *Personal Memoirs* was published by a firm called Webster & Co., whose controlling partner was Mark Twain. They offered him 70 percent of the profits, and the first printing was more than 300,000 copies.

In a note to his doctor written just before his death, Grant said that he had become "a verb instead of a personal pronoun. A verb is anything that signifies to be; to do; or to suffer. I signify all three." Those sentences are terser and perhaps more eloquent than anything in the memoirs themselves, and yet the book has their quality. For it is above all record of action, of a man *doing*, though not in any obvious way. The obvious way belongs to Bedford Forrest. Shelby Foote, in both his history and the fictional *Shiloh* (1952), describes Forrest as sabering a path through a knot of Federals as he guarded the Confederate retreat, taking a bullet in the hip and then swinging a Yankee across the back of his saddle to serve as a shield as he galloped back to the Rebel lines. That could come from a movie, and there's nothing like it about Grant either in person or on the page. But his memoirs do provide a limpid, laconic account of decisions made and forces set in motion, of contingencies and consequences, along with a good bit of gin-dry wit. Grant's preferred uniform was a soldier's blouse without gold braid and marked with the barest indication of his rank. So it is with his prose: the modesty is real and yet never masks his power.

Quotation is necessary here, and almost every page could serve; but let me stay with Shiloh. In the afternoon of the battle's second day Grant was near a Confederate position, "and seeing that the enemy was giving way everywhere else, I gathered up a couple of regiments, or parts of regiments, from troops near by, formed them in line of battle and marched them forward, going in front myself to prevent premature or long-range firing." Grant breaks his action down into its constituent parts, defining its cause and qualifying as necessary, and he no more skips a stage than would a well-written set of instructions. Troops must be formed before they can march, and though it's odd to see a general out in front, his every motion has an explanation. The general led his makeshift formation to within musket range, then stepped back as the troops charged and broke the enemy line. Two compliments come to my mind here, one for the man and the other for the writer. The first belongs to one of his soldiers, who said that "Ulysses don't scare worth a damn." The second is from Edmund Wilson: "never has a book so objective in form seemed so personal in every line."

The Vicksburg campaign provides the climax of Grant's first volume, as Appomattox does of the second. But capturing that town would not be as easy as it is in young Bayard's game, when Loosh simply sweeps that pile of woodchips away. Grant needed to get his troops past its artillery, south to a point from which they could come up behind it, and at one point his engineers thought about rerouting the Mississippi itself, cutting a canal and hoping that the river would find a new course. Later he sent steamboats to explore the narrow bayous to the north, hoping for a landing on the Yazoo; Rebel woodsmen dropped trees into the water behind his troops as a way to block their return. None of the Federal plans worked, not until the winter floods receded and they found a path down the Louisiana side of the great river. The army could then be ferried back across into Mississippi—but for that Grant needed boats, boats that would have to steam down by night from the north and run the Vicksburg batteries. They were easy targets, with the river lit up by Confederate bonfires, and yet all but one of the lightly manned flotilla made it, their decks packed with water-soaked bales of cotton and hay to protect their boilers. And then Grant was ready. He crossed on April 29 with 20,000 men; soon he had 40,000, and by the end of the campaign there were 70,000. At the start he took plenty of ammunition but almost no food—Holly Springs had taught him he wouldn't need it—and he had no secure lines of either supply or communication. Sherman thought the plan was risky and even foolish; but his Atlanta campaign shows that he made a good pupil.

"Grant" may be a verb, but it or the name of any other general also stands as a figure of speech, the synecdoche by which we designate the forces at his command. His landing was hardly unopposed, but Grant shrugged the Confederates off and now stood at last on dry ground, on the same side of the river as the enemy. That enemy was formidable, but he did not doubt the ending. Still, Vicksburg itself wasn't his first objective. The army swarmed out in three separate columns, darting and fighting and feinting, but always tending east, for there was a second Confederate force at Jackson, in the state's center, with reinforcements coming in and ready to march to Vicksburg's relief. Grant drove them off and then turned toward Pemberton, who had left his fortifications in the hopes of coming up on the Federals from behind. The city—the river—perhaps the war—was really lost and won at the short sharp battle of Champion Hill about twenty miles west of Jackson. Pemberton suffered heavily and withdrew, and a siege became inevitable.

In 1954 *Holiday* magazine offered Faulkner $2,000 to write an article about Vicksburg. That was good money, even for a Nobel Prize winner, but he turned it down. He spent a few days in the once-beleaguered city, walked its streets and went over the battlefield, but wrote that he had "no feeling" for the place. A reporter should do it, he thought, or maybe somebody from Vicksburg itself, someone who owned it as he did Oxford. Shiloh meant something to him, he could see the flags and hear the yells, but Vicksburg didn't carry the same burden of meaning; it stands in his work as a necessary reference but he never put any of his characters there. And in going over the battlefield myself, on a still clear January morning, I could see why the place had left him silent.

For one thing, the town no longer sits upon the Mississippi. In 1876 a flood sent the river pouring through the narrow neck of land opposite the old town center. An oxbow remains, and the port is still busy, but Vicksburg itself now squats above the narrow Yazoo, and what Lincoln called the Father of Waters is two miles away. It's hard today for a visitor to imagine why the place was once so important; certainly no one would fight for it now. But in 1863 its defenses were as formidable as anything in the South. They ran for miles, completely ringing the town and with a thousand yards of open ground between the town center and its outer fortifications: a high crescent of ramparts and trenches and rifle pits, with cannon staring down from the sky, and an obstacle course of fallen timber on the slopes the Union would need to climb. Grant tried twice to take the town by storm before he decided to "out-camp the enemy" and began to dig trenches of his own; the Union works eventually covered fifteen miles.

The ground around Vicksburg is humped and broken; I'd call it corrugated except that its irregular folds seem to run in all directions at once, and in none of them very far. Some of those folds were made by the war's shovels and shot; others by time and water and the action of the land itself. And I find it all hard to read, hard to follow the course of the siege in the way that I can with a battlefield like Gettysburg or Shiloh. Geography may define Vicksburg's strategic importance, but the landscape offers no clear narrative, no opening move or moment of climax, no Pickett's Charge. I drive from point to point, climb an earthwork, walk through a gully that was once a trench, and then move on to repeat those actions elsewhere. Sometimes there's a monument, placed without much regard for what happened at that particular spot; the one commemorating the troops from Texas looks like the entrance to a stadium. Here lay a Union battery that for seven weeks threw shells into the town; over there was Pemberton's headquarters, and at some quite separate place is the little hump of ground on which he spoke to Grant about the terms of surrender. It's marked by an upturned cannon, stuck in the ground like an obelisk and half-hidden, now, by the trees. It is all disjointed and illegible, and yet that very illegibility speaks to the sheer scale of the battlefield in both time and space. For by its very nature the action of a siege happens in many places at once and nowhere in particular.

The Union dug its trenches. The Yankees gashed the ground, cut troughs so wide that four men could walk abreast, and brought their sunken roads closer and closer to the Confederates' own. The plan was to blow down the walls between them and then boil their way through, and in the meantime there were hand grenades. In the town itself people grew hungry. Some soldiers raided civilian gardens; others deserted. Grant's army was too strong for any relieving column to get close, and the Confederate attempts to do so were at best halfhearted, as if they had already accepted the results. Finally Pemberton did as well, on July 3, and with his army facing imminent starvation he posted a white flag.

The formalities filled a day, and then the woodchips were scattered at last. Grant took and paroled more than thirty thousand prisoners, watching as his well-fed men pulled loaves of bread from their packs to share with the hungry Confederates. Throughout the siege there had, he writes, been a good deal of friendly verbal sparring between the lines of men trying to kill each other, and the Rebel pickets had even passed along a daily copy of the Vicksburg newspaper; at the end it was printed on wallpaper. So once his troops entered the town "the two armies fraternized as if they had been fighting for the same cause." His men did not cheer their own victory, and he thought there was even "a feeling of sadness just then in the breast of most of the Union soldiers at seeing the dejection of their late antagonists." And far away in Pennsylvania, Pickett's troops marched toward Cemetery Ridge, Mississippi's University Greys and the Old Colonel's old regiment among them. Thomas Sutpen fought there too, at least in the pages of *Absalom, Absalom!*, and received a commendation for valor written in Lee's own hand.

THE WAR CAME TO Oxford twice, and twice to Faulkner's Jefferson. After a while, of course, it was always there, in the empty sleeves and missing legs, there in its very absences: the absence of men and coffee and new clothes, the absence even of ink. A few years in, and the townspeople had to write their letters in pokeberry juice. There were Union patrols, and skirmishes, and then the Confederate irregulars like John Sartoris who brought the war with them whenever they came home. But twice the war came in the form of actual fighting, and the second time, in 1864, it was serious enough for the town to be burned in both fiction and history alike. Still, Jefferson and Oxford aren't quite the same place, and in describing the war's first visit there's a difference between what actually happened and the darkly unheroic comedy Faulkner made of it.

Holly Springs sits only one county to the north of Oxford, another town oriented around a courthouse square, and with a rich stock of surviving antebellum houses. But it barely exists in Faulkner's world, getting just a sentence in *Flags in the Dust*, an almost parenthetical reference to Van Dorn's 1862 raid on Grant's supplies; and even there the writer moves its date from December to midsummer. He returned to that exploit in *Light in August*, however, and in the process both simplified and intensified his version of history. Grant had put his headquarters and supply depot in different towns, but Faulkner makes them one. He locates them both in Jefferson, in effect layering Holly Springs onto Oxford, taking liberties with the past as if to suggest that whatever of importance had happened in northern Mississippi had happened in his own imaginary kingdom. The change turns Jefferson into a more important place in Civil War history than Oxford was itself. Or maybe not. Because to Faulkner the raid's meaning lies not in its effect on the Union campaign, but in the way it cripples the mind of a Confederate soldier's descendant more than half a century later.

Light in August is the most sprawling of his great books, a multi-plotted novel that would seem Victorian if it weren't for the freedom with which it breaks chronology and switches point of view. Faulkner sets its three major lines of narrative at the end of the 1920s, but he allows a space for family history, for tales and memories that stretch back beyond the war, and one of the book's stories belongs to Gail Hightower, the erstwhile incumbent of Jefferson's Presbyterian Church. Hightower lives in a dream of the Confederate past, and his life has been dominated—his marriage and ministry destroyed—by one thing: his memory or imagination of his grandfather's death in "Van Dorn's cavalry raid to destroy Grant's stores in Jefferson." Faulkner describes that grandfather as a profane old lawyer, fond of cigars and whiskey, the kind of man who would have enjoyed that foolhardy prank of a raid, the soldiers riding "with the grim levity of schoolboys" through a hundred miles of occupied territory and into a garrisoned town. Earl Van Dorn had failed as an infantry commander, and this escapade stands as his one moment of military glory. Grant had some warning, but noted that the Rebels had "traveled as fast as the scouts who brought the news," and the place was taken while most of its defenders were still in bed. The raid succeeded only because it was impossible, and the Confederates then turned the Union's food and clothing into flame. "The sky itself must have been on fire," the fictional grandson says in his fever-dream of the past, and he asks us to savor it, "the shouting of triumph and terror, the drumming hooves . . . the troops galloping past toward the rallying bugles." But the men were hungry, they had ridden a long way with never enough to eat, and some of them pulled up by a henhouse. Old Hightower had just entered when a shotgun crashed.

That's the story his grandson hears as a boy from a family servant, once their slave. How she got it he never quite knows, and yet it's "too fine to doubt." Soldiers are supposed to get killed in battle—but in a chicken coop? Hightower has never gotten over the incongruity, a joke played by God himself, and yet its very absurdity makes his dream of Confederate glory seem all the more paradoxically present. It fixes him in a vanished time of what might have been and never was. But there's a more worldly joke here too, for, Holly Springs aside, Van Dorn was in actual fact best known for raids of another kind. Old Hightower may have liked whiskey but his commander liked women, and a few months after he burned Grant's stores a jealous husband put a pistol to his head. So in making up the Hightowers, Faulkner had a classic bit of bawdry in mind: both the general and his soldier get killed while breaking into another man's henhouse.

Grant's 1862 occupation of Lafayette County had a comic side of its own. Jacob Thompson was an Oxford lawyer who had served both in Congress and as Buchanan's secretary of the interior. He resigned with secession, and the northern papers denounced him and the other Southern department heads as traitors, men who had wrecked their own government from within; feeling against them ran far higher than it did against mere senators and generals. Thompson went to Toronto in 1864 as the head of the Confederate intelligence services, carrying a satchel full of gold, and was later rumored to be involved with John Wilkes Booth; the assassin had a hotel receipt from that city in his pocket when he died. Nothing was ever proven, but when the war was over Thompson left the country and spent a few prudent years abroad. In 1862, however, he was a mere colonel, and on leave in Oxford when Grant began to overrun the county. His house there was one of the grandest in town, sitting catercorner from the more modest grounds of Robert

Shegog; seventy years later Faulkner would buy the Shegog place and call it Rowan Oak.

Thompson had expensive tastes and knew that Union soldiers sometimes destroyed the houses they occupied. To protect both his own valuables and those of his friends, he made his home into a depot for the town's silver, piling it up in his back office and hanging a sign about smallpox on the front door. Then he stationed a few slaves outside and told them to weep, as a way to complete the illusion—which fooled the Union not at all. Soldiers had already begun to break the house's windows and to write on its walls when Grant stopped the looting and turned the place into a hospital. Then he went into Thompson's office himself: not for the silver but rather in search of any incriminating letters. Gentlemen are not supposed to read each other's mail, and Thompson affected outrage; but the house and the silver survived until the Union's second visit in 1864.

Faulkner didn't let the Sartoris family escape so easily. In the second chapter of *The Unvanquished*, "Retreat," the Colonel is at home when a company of Union cavalry rides through the gate in the hopes of capturing him. He sends Bayard to get his horse ready and stalls the bluecoats by pretending to be a "born loony. . . . Yankee cussing him for idiot fool." And Sartoris gets away with it, riding off just ahead of a bullet. But the Yankee firebugs have been at work already. Yellow smoke comes foaming out of the windows and the sky is full of noise as the flames begin to take the house down to its chimneys. Then Bayard sees Loosh walking up from his cabin, a bundle on his shoulder, and ready to follow the soldiers. "I done been freed," he says, "I don't belong to John Sartoris now," and he has, moreover, told the Federals where the family silver lies buried. That's not yours, Grandmother Millard says—that's the Colonel's, and who are you to give it away? Loosh's reply has all the eloquence of a spiritual. Young Bayard may not hear it that way but the reader does, and the man's words retain their force. "Let God ax John Sartoris who the man name that give me to him," Loosh cries. "Let the man that buried me in the black dark ax that of the man what dug me free." Rosa Millard is one of the most tenderly seen characters in all of Faulkner's work; nevertheless, this moment makes me want to tell her something. *How dare you.*

EIGHT

Freedom

How dare you. But those are our words, not Faulkner's, and still less those of *The Unvanquished's* characters. Not even Loosh would ask that, not quite, for all that we feel, and are intended to feel, the justice of his claim. "I belongs to me and God," he says; not to John Sartoris, not any more. For the moment of emancipation has come at last, and Grandmother Millard seems to accept it. She knows, at any rate, that she cannot keep him from leaving with the Yankee troops who have burned her house; cannot keep him from taking title to himself. Her concern lies only with the family silver now, a form of property that can't walk off on its own. Still, newly freed slaves did often claim a right to the products of their labor: to the land they had cleared and planted, the cotton and the livestock, and sometimes to the master's house as well. Why not the silver too? Their work had created the white man's wealth, and they knew that one of the things freedom offered was the right—and perhaps the retrospective right—to be compensated for that work. They knew that their bondage was nothing less than theft. Their ancestors had been stolen from Africa, and in America their own lives and labor; as he crosses into the future, Loosh is simply taking what should always have been his already.

Not that Rosa Millard can see it that way. Loosh may claim himself but no more, and besides, it's not as if the silver will be his. The Yankees will take that, melt it into bullion or maybe just let it sit; it won't help him, and revealing its hiding place seems to her like an act of pure vengeance. Yet Loosh does walk off with something besides the bundle on his shoulder, for he is followed by his wife, Philadelphia. "Dont you know he's leading you into misery and starvation?" Granny asks, and Philadelphia replies that indeed she does. She doesn't believe what the Yankee soldiers have said about the new world ahead of them: "But he my husband. I reckon I got to go with him." Traditional marriage has its own conception of mastery and obedience, and she will not escape from those. Nevertheless, she decides to obey that law rather than the one that binds her to Sartoris. She determines her own fate, as a slave cannot; she may submit but she will no longer be owned.

The Unvanquished offers several accounts of freedom's arrival, of black men and women exercising their new power of choice. But this is the only one in which slave and master face each other with such immediacy, and I want to compare it to some very different versions of liberation's moment. "Retreat" first appeared in the *Saturday Evening Post* for October 13, 1934, and was then revised for its 1938 book publication. In the years between, the Works Project Administration gathered several thousand brief oral histories from those once enslaved throughout the South, including some 450 in Mississippi. Most of these stories remained unpublished until the 1970s, and they need to be used carefully. For one thing, virtually all the interviewers were white, and in reading you can sense their subjects' caution; for another, the WPA insisted on a supposedly phonetic transcription of their testimony, which managed to be both inaccurate and belittling at once. All the subjects were in their late seventies at least, and many were older; most had been children during the war, and so their memories were shaded by youth on the one hand and age on the other. Much remains vivid nonetheless, and especially their accounts of the moment when the rumors of freedom became reality.

The news was not always unmixed; Jane McLeod of Oxford remembered that the Yankees "took everything the cullud folks had same as they did the white folks," food above all; though she also recalled that the bluecoats encouraged them to help themselves to their mistresses' finery. One man enjoyed playing as a boy with the canteens of the Federal soldiers who came through his district, but his father "went off wit' 'em ... [and] never did come back." At times a Northern officer, a stranger with a line of gold braid around his hat, gathered a plantation's slaves together and told them they were free; more often the slave owners made the announcement themselves. Cato Carter from Alabama remembered that his former master proclaimed,

"You is free to do as you like 'cause the damned yankees done 'creed that you are." Some whites tried to hide the news, even after the war was over, or threatened anyone who wanted to leave; some Union troops acted like the press-gangs of old and took all the men for soldiers. Emma Johnson of Marshall County, just to the north of Faulkner's own Lafayette, recalled burying pots of food so the foraging Yankees wouldn't get it, and remembered seeing the Confederate general Earl Van Dorn on his way to burn the Federal stores at Holly Springs, and then Grant the day after. But her most vivid memory was that "Old Master never did tell us we was free. He called us up to tell us, then everytime he would start to tell it, he would bust out and cry. He never did tell it."

These descriptions carry an inherent drama, and though Faulkner could not have known the WPA interviews he must as a boy have heard such tales on his own; perhaps from Caroline Barr, whom he thought of as a second mother, in the conventional sentiments of his day, and who told him and his brothers about her own life in slavery. What strikes me in reading those interviews, however, is how very different they are from this incident in *The Unvanquished*. Many of the men and women who spoke to the WPA had had to wait for the adult world to present them with a future: to wait not simply because they were slaves but because they were still children at the moment of emancipation. Hence the tableau they so frequently describe: the white man speaking in the center of a circle or maybe standing on the gallery and talking to the people gathered in the yard below. They were told of freedom, but few of them were able at six or eight or even thirteen to seize it for themselves. Loosh's situation is very different. To Bayard and Ringo he looks like one of those who "went off wit'" the Yankees. Yet while his departure may be mediated or even made possible by the presence of Union troops, those soldiers play no role in his confrontation with Rosa Millard. Loosh takes his freedom. It isn't given to him. He takes it now, without waiting, and his fleeting talk with Rosa isn't one between owner and slave so much as between two strong-willed and obdurate people.

Misery and starvation—that will be their fate, Rosa says, and for many of those who followed the soldiers her words would prove true enough. That's the world into which Loosh and Philadelphia will step when they leave the

Sartoris land, and we'll soon look at its terms and conditions. But what about the world they leave behind? Faulkner shows us little of the punishing regime by which black lives were governed under slavery. The casual terror of the lynchings he described in stories like "Dry September" and "Pantaloon in Black" belongs to his own day, to the Jim Crow world of the 1920 and 1930s. A slave held by the Chickasaws becomes a human sacrifice in "Red Leaves"; both *Absalom, Absalom!* and *Go Down, Moses* define the sexual exploitation of black women by white masters. Yoknapatawpha's world is violent enough—and yet in writing of the pre-1865 South Faulkner never depicts a slave auction or a family broken by sale. Nor does he describe a whipping, still less the salt and pepper that were often rubbed into the skin the leather had broken; none of his people have a tree of scars upon their back. One of Charles Chesnutt's characters is required to wear a ham around his neck after he's accused of theft. He hangs himself, in madness and shame, and the story involves a grotesque visual pun on the biblical curse by which slavery was often justified. Nothing like that happens on the Sartoris place. Slavery there is made to look almost innocent, and not just because it's seen from a white child's point of view. For Faulkner depicts the plantation as though it were nothing more than a well-run manor house, with master and servants bound together by affection, loyalty, and a sense of mutual obligations. They form an extended family, the Colonel at its head, and in drawing on that patriarchal image Faulkner is absolutely in accord with the dominant ideology of young Bayard Sartoris's time.

Or perhaps the dominant beliefs in the white historiography of his own. We will never know enough about what Faulkner himself actually read. Yet maybe he didn't actually have to open the work of the Georgia-born historian Ulrich B. Phillips in order to absorb its argument. Phillips's *American Negro Slavery* (1918) stood for a generation as the canonical view of its subject, one that presented an image of slavery as benign, labor on a human scale and with "little of that curse of impersonality and indifference which too commonly prevails in the factories of the present day." For Phillips, master and slave lived in a realm of mutually understood obligations. They knew what to expect of each other, and their relations were a matter of custom in which each found meaning and purpose. Each white family provided a model of conduct to emulate, one reinforced by a "vigor of discipline which democracy cannot possess." Just let that euphemism sink in. Such views are easy to caricature. The ideological screen through which Phillips saw his material kept him from consulting African-American sources, and W. E. B. Du Bois gave the book a devastating review; its "curiously incomplete . . . idyllic picture" says little about the slaves themselves and instead concentrates on the "economics of slaveholders." Nevertheless it has endured, even as its every judgment has been challenged: a point of departure for later scholars, an old understanding forever in need of correction. And Phillips's work survives for another reason too, though not as an account of how slavery worked. It stands instead as a picture of how the slaveholders' descendants believed that it had worked: of how, half a century on, they hoped and wanted and imagined it to have functioned.

At times those descendants included Faulkner himself—who in other books and even in other parts of *The Unvanquished* itself knows better. But he has to handle his material carefully in order to sustain the kind of illusion that Phillips provided. Almost half the white families in Lafayette County held slaves, though most of them owned six people or less; only four had more than a hundred. John Sartoris is depicted as a substantial planter, one of Yoknapatawpha's leading men, and he would need to be, in order to pay for his regiment's initial outfit. Look closely, however, and it seems that there are just six slaves on his place: an old couple, Joby and Louvinia; their two sons, Loosh and Simon, along with Loosh's wife Philadelphia; and Simon's son Marengo, Bayard's playmate. I say six, but Simon himself appears for only two sentences in the book's last chapter, which is set long after the end of the war. He's described as having gone north with Sartoris, as his body servant, and yet he doesn't ride back through the gates on the Colonel's visits home. Faulkner never thinks to include him in Sartoris's reunion with his family in 1865, and his wife, Ringo's mother, never has a name or even a sentence devoted to her.

The only reason for Simon's purely nominal existence is to keep us from wondering about Ringo's parentage, to stop us from asking if he might be Bayard's brother as well as his friend; for the fact that he too calls Rosa Millard "Granny" does suggest a family bond between white and black, and a sense of common purpose. These characters all work around the house, with Loosh the only one who resembles a field hand, and though there are a couple of slave cabins, Faulkner never suggests that there is another body of men and women on the place whose labor produces the cotton and the corn to pay for Sartoris's soldiers. This isn't a plantation—it's a farm. The details of John Sartoris's military service are often taken to resemble those of Faulkner's own great-grandfather, the lawyer William Clark Falkner. What's less commonly noted is that Sartoris also resembles his model in the size and scale of his prewar property, for census records show that in 1860 Falkner too owned six slaves.

One mark of its relatively modest scope lies in the fact that there's no man on the Sartoris place—that is, no adult white male. The Confederacy feared its slaves, feared their potential for unrest and disorder, for violence. Somebody needed to stay home and keep rebellion down, and an 1862 conscription act exempted one white man for every twenty slaves a plantation might hold. Many planters took that exemption for themselves or their sons, confirming the popular belief that it was a rich man's war and a poor man's fight. Others hired an overseer, ideally someone quick-fisted and physically tough, but in wartime often a man unfit for other work. Of course, a small place was in itself no guarantee of kindness—only of an intimacy that could make the violence all the more personal when it came. Nevertheless, the Sartoris land seems to run on its own, with the crops made and the smokehouse full. The Colonel's mother-in-law—Rosa, Grandmother, Granny—exercises a gentle discipline, which mostly consists of washing both Bayard's and Ringo's mouths out with soap whenever she catches them cursing. Otherwise she gives her orders calmly, expecting the obedience she receives, and puts up with a reasonable amount of grumbling in return. These details helped keep the readers of the *Saturday Evening Post* firmly on the Sartoris side, and Faulkner's all-too-forgiving depiction of slaveholder paternalism finds its counterpart here in the myth of the faithful servant, the slave who stands by his or her master, and resists the Yankee temptations. "Fore God, Miss Rosa," Philadelphia says; "I tried to stop him. I done tried."

Such men and women did exist and so doubtless did a few such masters. Even the moment when Ringo helps level a musket at a Union trooper isn't entirely unfounded. Early in the war J. E. B. Stuart wrote from the Shenandoah Valley that "one of the enemy was killed by a negro" under his command, not a soldier but probably a servant or teamster. Still, the fact that he put the incident in his official report suggests he saw it as remarkable; if it had been the norm, the Confederacy would hardly have needed what was known as the "Twenty Negro Law." The WPA narratives record some masters who taught their slaves to read, and others whose lash was never still. As a girl in Oxford, Lucindy Hall Shaw saw a woman beaten to death by an overseer and buried where she fell. One of the most detailed accounts of the time comes from a man named Louis Hughes. He was in his thirties when the war ended, and at the end of the century, while living in Milwaukee, wrote and published an autobiography called *Thirty Years a Slave* (1897). Hughes had been a cook and butler in northern Mississippi on the plantations of a man he called Edmund McGee; land records suggest that the name was in fact McGehee and that he belonged to the cousinage Stark Young wrote about in *So Red the Rose*. But Hughes's picture of the clan is rather different. Some of "Boss" McGee's slaves were whipped for the crime of literacy, others for not meeting their daily quota of picked cotton, and at times they were made to whip each other. They were beaten on a whim or for the most fleeting of facial expressions; Hughes's wife was beaten for saying that an earlier punishment had made her lose a baby. Nor did a slave's relative status help save him, for McGee didn't spare the salt when Hughes himself was whipped.

We're shown nothing like this in Yoknapatawpha. The county's biggest plantation and probably its largest slave-holding is that of Sutpen's Hundred. But Faulkner never thinks to describe its working life and never counts the number of Thomas Sutpen's slaves, even if *Absalom, Absalom!* does make me imagine that he would be quick to use the whip—and would use it himself, without handing the job to an overseer. Then again, having read of the eye-gouging brutality with which Sutpen fights and beats his slaves in the ring, I suspect he wouldn't often need it.

HE WAS BORN AROUND 1807 in the mountains of what would become West Virginia, in a place where the only possessions that mattered, in Faulk-

ner's words, were whatever one could "eat or swap for powder and whiskey."
The land itself was so poor and so plentiful that it wasn't worth the effort to
fence or claim any particular piece of it, and the differences between men that
counted were those of strength or courage, a dead eye and a fast hand. That
was the coin of status, not birth or coins themselves: a rough white man's
democracy, in which "the only colored people were Indians and you only
looked down at them over your rifle sights." Then young Sutpen's mother
died and for no reason that he could remember his family began to move,
to tumble down the mountains, human flotsam washed out to the brackish
lowlands around the mouth of the James River. There he met a shock. This
new world looked entirely bounded, with the land parceled out and the lines
of both ownership and race forever fixed and neat.

That's the story Sutpen tells in *Absalom, Absalom!* to Quentin Compson's
grandfather. He wants one man at least to know of his origins, and he takes
his opportunity when they are out one day in the Yoknapatawpha wilderness. The French architect he brought along in his wagonload of slaves has
run off, hoping to find his own freedom, and the county's young men have
gotten some dogs together and gone out to chase him down. It's a long story,
and Sutpen spins a bit of it as they work through the mud of the bottomland and then some more as they sit on a log and wait for the dogs to find;
the end comes at night around a campfire in the open air. The future Confederate colonel tells it to the man who thirty years later will become a one-
armed brigadier; the brigadier gives it to his son, who passes it on to his; who
tells it himself to his Canadian roommate Shreve in the bitter cold of a New
England winter, and in speaking to Shreve will speak to us as well. Stories
become legacies, and this one takes us into the deep past and the deep psyche
of the American South, the story of a child coming into the knowledge of a
racialized world.

Space and time in Faulkner are always interchangeable, and Sutpen was
never sure just how far his family's journey lasted. The seasons overtook them
on the road; one of his sisters got pregnant and became a mother before they
lost sight of the mountains. At some point he saw his first slave, an enormous
man in the door of a country tavern with the boy's drunken father hoisted
on his shoulder. They finally stopped along a river where black men worked

over crops he had never heard of, with white overseers on horses to watch them. And down in that flatland the young Sutpen discovered that there was a "difference between white men and white men" that couldn't be measured by the standards of his native hills. He discovered the power that possession conferred, and he decided that he wanted it. *How* he discovered it is material for another chapter; "happen is never once," as Quentin thinks, and we will come back to this part of his story. Sutpen wanted money and land, he wanted his own slaves, and so in 1823, at the age of maybe fifteen, he took himself to the West Indies.

The next thing Sutpen claimed to remember, or at least to tell, was standing by the window of a house under siege, an overseer himself now, and firing a musket into the Haitian night. There was a girl with him, and another man, her father; they passed the emptied muskets back to her and she handed them each another and then reloaded as they aimed out into the dark. And all around them the sugar cane burned, its caramel scent intensified by the bitterness of history itself, the history of an island that, in General Compson's words, seemed "set aside by Heaven . . . as a theatre for violence and injustice and bloodshed and all the satanic lusts of human greed and cruelty." It burned for a week and then Sutpen put his gun down and went out into the night to meet a line of black faces, and "subdued them." That's how he describes it; that was the start of his fortune. The solitary white man stared down the dark mob and conquered. He doesn't say how. Force of will, perhaps—that's how it would work in Hollywood or indeed in the imperial romances Faulkner read as a boy. He got more from Joseph Conrad in particular than his sense of how to handle a frame tale or a flashback, and this moment owes something to *Lord Jim* (1900), in which a lone white man stands as the law itself to the villages along a Borneo river. But another of Conrad's books comes to mind here as well, for in his mixture of grandiloquence and greed Sutpen has more than a bit in common with the ruthless ivory-hunting Mr. Kurtz in "Heart of Darkness" (1902).

This moment in *Absalom, Absalom!* begs a great many questions. Under its old name of Saint Domingue the island had been the richest of all France's colonies, with its wealth dependent on slave-grown sugar. What, however, is a white overseer doing on an island in which, after an uprising during the

French Revolution, slavery itself had been abolished? An island whose black population had successfully resisted Napoleon's attempts to reimpose that institution? A lot of answers to those questions have been proposed over the years, but for now it's enough to say that Faulkner's use of a Caribbean setting locates the United States within a larger slave economy—indeed a slave empire, however varied its governments—that ran from Virginia down to Brazil. The Mississippi fed into that empire from the north and in turn fed dreams of an endless American expansion. But Haiti turned that dream to nightmare. Haiti mattered in the mind of the American South precisely because it was the one place where a slave rebellion had succeeded.

"In her youth the St. Domingo stories were indelibly printed on her mind." So Mary Chesnut wrote in the fall of 1861 about her mother-in-law, a woman in her eighties, and felt no need to add the details: the hundreds of white soldiers hanged in retaliation for the French having buried their own prisoners alive; the 1804 massacre of those Europeans who had not already fled the island, over three thousand of them. Haiti was the white South's dread and its name a synonym for horror. Everybody in Chesnut's world knew its particulars, or at least they knew what had been done to the whites, turning away from the atrocities committed by the French themselves. Denmark Vesey of Charleston in 1822, Virginia's Nat Turner in 1831—the rebellions they led had no chance of anything beyond a local and temporary success, but they carried Haiti's echo and were suppressed with extraordinary violence. The fear of "servile insurrection" lay behind the prohibition on teaching the enslaved to read, lest they encounter abolition's heresy, and the slave patrol hunted through the darkness, punishing anyone caught without a pass and sometimes even those who had them; there were night riders in the South long before the Ku Klux Klan.

Yet what the white South feared above all were black men with guns. That's what John Brown had hoped to produce with his 1859 raid on the federal arsenal at Harpers Ferry; and in 1863 Lincoln wrote that "the bare sight of fifty thousand armed, and drilled black soldiers on the banks of the Mississippi would end the rebellion at once." It didn't; the slave power had always worried about retribution and faced those worries with a terrible retribution of its own. When the young Sutpen steps outside we can see him, in American terms, as fighting off the South's great fear and suppressing a field hands' rebellion; or perhaps he's calling Loosh to order, controlling his people in a way that the masters of the Civil War era weren't always able to do. And maybe we can read beyond this moment and into the anxieties of Faulkner's own time. Jim Crow remained largely unchallenged in Mississippi when *Absalom, Absalom!* was first published in 1936, but anybody who read the book with even a touch of historical knowledge knew that in Haiti the white man did not return triumphant.

"We ought to be grateful that any one of us is alive," Chesnut said, "but nobody is afraid of their own negroes. [They] are horrid brutes—savages, monsters—but I find everyone like myself, ready to trust their own yard." That awareness of her own contradictions seems characteristic—it's what makes her such a provocative witness. The anger is new to her, though, and grows directly out of an incident that was suppressed in the first, 1905 edition of her diary. Servants were supposed to be loyal, and her bowdlerizing editor did not print Chesnut's account of the news she got in September 1861. One of her cousins, an old woman named Betsey Witherspoon, had been murdered by her slaves; they wanted to avoid a threatened punishment and deftly smothered her as she slept on her South Carolina plantation. The story haunted Chesnut and fascinated her—she set down everything she learned about it, the motive and the process of detection, the punishment too. Never before had she "thought of being afraid of negroes. I had never injured any of them. Why should they want to hurt me?" But she no longer recognized the world she had taken for granted, and while there wasn't an immediate link between the war and her cousin's death, anyone reading the diary will find it impossible not to connect the two. If slavery is so bad, she asked herself that July, "why don't they all march over the border. . . . [T]hese creatures . . . are to me inscrutable in their ways and past finding out." Every slave was a spy for the other side and yet without becoming the individual slave owner's enemy; every black face seemed to her marked by a fixed duplicitous grin. A year after her cousin's death she picked up a book about India's Sepoy Rebellion of 1857—what the English called the Mutiny—and in reading wondered how long it would be before her own slaves would "rise and burn and murder us all." Meanwhile she continued to trust her husband's valet with gold and jewels, and teased him about running off to the Yankees.

———·•·———

WHAT DID "THEY" THINK of the war? Chesnut never found an answer to that quandary, and indeed some version of it sat on the mind of white America as a whole; in this at least, North and South were as one. More than seventy years later Du Bois would put that question again in his *Black Reconstruction in America*, a book that appeared even as Faulkner himself worked on both *The Unvanquished* and *Absalom, Absalom!* "What did the war mean to the Negroes," Du Bois asked, "and what did the Negroes mean to the war?" Some earlier historians had argued that the slaves waited passively, faithfully working as before until freedom was "thrust" upon them; others that they had all immediately run off to join the Yankees. For Du Bois that was far too simple, as Chesnut's own questions might indeed suggest; and simple above all because it had not at first been clear that the war would lead to liberation. Few Union officers were abolitionists, many of them claimed to respect the rights of private property, and in the war's opening months some of them returned runaway slaves to their owners. And so, in Du Bois's words, "What the Negro did was to wait. . . . There was no use in seeking refuge in an army which was not an army of freedom, and no sense" in revolt so long as it looked like a punitive Confederacy might win. Then the balance shifted, and slaves who had begun the war by serving their masters now began to serve both the emancipating army and themselves.

One of the war's ironies is that the most prejudiced of the Union's great captains is also remembered as a liberator. William Tecumseh Sherman had no quarrel with slavery as such and thought that black people were in every way inferior to white. Grant came to believe in abolition; Sherman merely accepted it. It was the best way to beat the South, and his Special Field Orders No. 15, which in 1865 offered "forty acres and a mule" to black families along the South Carolina and Georgia coast, wasn't motivated by a spirit of justice. Instead, it helped his quickly moving army shake off the thousands of freed people who marched after it, and denied resources to those who had made war on the Union. In the summer of 1862 Sherman took command of

the Federal forces in Memphis, where among other things he had to decide
what to do with the many hundreds of Looshes who had come into his lines.
That August he received a letter from a West Point classmate named Thomas
Hunton, a Delta planter and secessionist. Some men had run away from his
place fifty miles to the west of Oxford, and he wanted Sherman's help in getting them back; he even offered to come to Memphis himself, so long as he
didn't have to take an oath of allegiance to the United States. Sherman could
make the most bitter sarcasm masquerade as fellow-feeling, and replied that
for an old friend he would give up his "last Cent, my last shirt and pants." But
as a present enemy, "I will do you all the harm I can." The Constitution might
well protect property in slaves, but a Rebel who wanted to put a new compact in its place had no right to the protection of the old one. He would find
Hunton's men—and tell them that they could go or stay, just as they chose,
for as their "master has seceded from his Parent Government . . . [so] you have
seceded from him." Meanwhile the Union army would put all male runaways
to work, and pay them.

A complicated history lay behind that letter, and we must keep it in mind
to understand the world that Faulkner's Loosh and Philadelphia walk into
once they leave the plantation. In the summer of 1861 a congressional resolution held that the war's sole purpose was the restoration of the Union as it
was; Washington would not interfere with "the rights or established institutions of those States" in rebellion. Some of the men who voted for that
resolution believed in it; others saw their vote in strategic terms, a way to
placate the four slave states that remained, Kentucky in particular. But that
resolution was outmoded before it passed and there would be—could be—no
restoration of the status quo ante. The story has often been told, and magnificently so in Adam Goodheart's *1861: The Civil War Awakening*. A month
after the fall of Fort Sumter, three Virginians who had been put to work con-
structing a Confederate battery at the mouth of the James River stole a boat
and rowed across a narrow strait to a Union fort. Most Federal commanders
would still have returned them under the Fugitive Slave Act, but Benjamin
Butler was grateful for the intelligence they brought and refused to surrender
them when a Confederate officer appeared to demand their return. In civilian life Butler was the canniest of Yankee lawyers, and he now found a for-

mula that allowed him to keep them safe. He took the Rebels at their word. Slaves were property—and in wartime an officer has the right to seize whatever enemy property may be used against the enemy. Slave labor was one of the Confederates' principal military resources; why shouldn't the Union take it from them? "Contraband of war," Butler called the men in the rowboat, as if they were a cargo of shoes, and the word stuck. A few days later fifty people made their way to the fort, whole families among them; and then hundreds more, the start of an unending procession.

It would be that way throughout the South, and over time the contrabands would present the western armies in particular with a significant problem in human welfare. But the government's policy had yet to catch up with its actions. Lincoln squashed two early attempts by his generals to free the slaves in their districts. He was, however, willing to accept Butler's fait accompli, and a few months later the justification his fellow-lawyer had supplied would shape the Confiscation Act of 1861. Anything that might serve as a Confederate resource was now subject to seizure as a "military necessity." That law passed just a few weeks after Congress had resolved to leave slavery alone; the government could no longer claim to control events but was instead controlled by them. The next year a second act extended the principle, holding that all slaves of belligerent masters were now forfeit, whether they were being used in the war effort or not. Sherman told his old friend Hunton that he hadn't yet seen the new law, but he really didn't have to; he already knew that "we ought to take your effective slaves . . . to use their labor & deprive you of it."

By that time Lincoln was readying the Emancipation Proclamation. He too feared that any move toward abolition would undercut the Union's position in the slaveholding states that remained loyal, but he was under increasing pressure from within his own party, and in the summer of 1862 he decided that he must at last do something to put slavery "in the course of ultimate extinction." He told his cabinet of his decision that July and released a preliminary version in September, after the Union turned back Lee's invasion of Maryland at Antietam. He signed the final version on January 1, 1863. It was a carefully phrased and strictly limited document that extended freedom as a "war measure" just in those states then in rebellion. Cynics have said in the years since that it emancipated only those slaves in areas over which the Federal government had no control; that its writ did not apply in border states like Maryland and Missouri, in occupied New Orleans, or indeed in Confederate Tennessee, where the president believed that Unionist sentiment remained strong. But few people at the time had any doubts of its importance. The purpose and the meaning of the war had changed. The Confederate Congress called the Proclamation "an outrage on the rights of private property, and an invitation to an atrocious servile war"; the *Times* of London had Haiti on its mind and accused Lincoln of exciting "the negroes of the Southern plantations to murder the families of their masters." A local committee in Liberty County, Georgia, suggested killing any runaway slave who got caught, and in the North the most famous runaway of all found that he could at last applaud the president's "peculiar, cautious . . . slothful deliberation."

Black men with property had the ballot in New York State, but Frederick Douglass had not voted for Lincoln, whom he thought no friend to abolition; the best thing about his election was that the South hated it. Douglass had cast his own vote for Gerrit Smith of the tiny Radical Abolition Party and in the war's first years he became the most brilliant and vehement of Washington's domestic critics. In particular Douglass attacked the Federal refusal to enlist black troops. Many white soldiers were not yet ready to fight for slavery's end. They shared Congress's belief in the Union as it was, and they wanted only to put it all back together again: a white man's job, in which the Negro could have no part, for any man with a rifle had to be seen as an equal. Douglass thought, in contrast, that reunification would *require* abolition, lest the conflict start all over again. But it would first require victory, and victory meant that the government had to use whatever tools it could find; "this is no time to fight only with your white hand, and allow your black to remain tied." Douglass saw that from the beginning; by 1863 Lincoln agreed with him, and not only about emancipation. For the Proclamation also stated that "the people so declared to be free . . . will be received into the armed service of the United States." The navy had always had black sailors, though they were usually assigned to a ship's worst jobs; still, its crews were at least nominally integrated. The army, refusing to go so far, raised regiments of black soldiers led by white officers; eventually there were almost 180,000 of them.

Douglass himself helped recruit more than a hundred men for the most famous of the war's black units, the Fifty-Fourth Massachusetts, two of his sons included; they each survived the war, and Lewis Douglass served as the regiment's sergeant major. The Fifty-Fourth became celebrated for many reasons, but its fame began with its doomed and yet well-publicized assault on Fort Wagner near Charleston in July 1863, during which its colonel and many of its soldiers were killed. The battle persuaded the North that black soldiers could fight as well as white ones if they were only given the chance, and the regiment has had a significant afterlife. Thirty years later one of the greatest of all Civil War monuments was dedicated to its memory on the edge of the Boston Common, a bas-relief in bronze by Augustus Saint-Gaudens, the most important American sculptor of the period. The Fifty-Fourth was not, however, the first black regiment to see combat. The First South Carolina Volunteers took part in raids along the Sea Islands in the opening months of 1863, and later that year black troops from Louisiana played a significant role in the Vicksburg campaign. Units from New Orleans, formed in part from the city's *gens de couleur libres*, fought in the siege of Port Hudson on the Mississippi, while a Confederate attack on Grant's swampy base of supply at Milliken's Bend was beaten off with the help of some barely trained companies of freedmen. At the end of the year, the secretary of war, Edwin M. Stanton, wrote that many people had "believed, or pretended to believe ... that freed slaves ... would lack courage, and could not be subjected to military discipline." Those claims now looked foolish. "The slave has proved his manhood," and the chance to offer that proof was indeed one of the things that Douglass himself urged as a reason for joining up. "Enlist and disprove the slander. . . . Enlist and you make this your country."

Even the Confederate commander at Milliken's Bend praised the courage of the black troops he faced. But not all Southerners could see them that way. Kate Stone was born near Jackson, Mississippi, in 1841 and grew up on a Louisiana plantation called Brokenburn thirty miles to the northwest of Vicksburg, where her widowed mother owned more than a thousand acres and 150 slaves. Stone kept a diary throughout the war, first published in 1955, in which she recorded both her reaction to the war's daily news, with its moments of exhilaration and despair, and the details of an increasingly difficult daily life. Many of Stone's opinions were common to other girls of her class. She firmly believed in the justice of the Confederate cause and did not at first credit the report of Lee's surrender in 1865. She also admitted, however, that she couldn't blame any slaves who chose to follow the Yankees, and in 1900 she wrote that with age she found herself trying to imagine what it had been like to be always and forever under someone else's power. The effort made her despair—made her ask how a slave owner could possibly enter heaven: "Always I felt the moral guilt of it." Stone never regretted emancipation, and yet as a young woman she refused to accept the story of the Confederate repulse at nearby Milliken's Bend. Southern troops had been "whipped by a mongrel crew of white and black Yankees. . . . It is said that the Negro regiments fought there like mad demons, but we cannot believe that. We know from long experience they are cowards."

As a diarist Stone lacks both Chesnut's wit and her access to the Confederacy's most powerful people; the value of her work lies instead in its account of a slowly eroding sense of order. Some nearby plantations have been burned and others spared; it all depends on "the officer in charge. . . . If a good-natured enemy, he takes what he wants and leaves the buildings standing. Most of them are malicious." A Yankee soldier demands that she swap her horse for his "pack of animated bones" and holds a pistol to her head when she refuses. She jots down prices, notes what supplies they can still get—molasses, calico—and keeps track of their foodstuffs; plenty of corn and potatoes yet. When New Orleans falls her family joins neighbors in setting fire to the last year's crop of baled cotton, lest the Federals take it. It smolders for days, even after each four-hundred-pound bundle is slashed open and its packed fibers raked and loosened; "Mamma has $20,000 worth burning on the gin ridge now." And meanwhile speculators from the North have moved on to some of the abandoned plantations. They pay their laborers up to $7 a month, but don't feed or clothe them.

A few of her neighbors take the oath of allegiance, hoping to protect their land, and in March 1863 they hear artillery along the river and the sound of a steamboat whistle; Grant "must be landing troops." A few months later

Stone's family left Brokenburn and went to Texas, along with the only two enslaved people they could persuade to accompany them. The process was known as "refugeeing," and for many planters it was a way to keep their human property away from the emancipating Union army, moving as much of their operation as they could out of the war's path. Her own family had a more immediate motive. Walking up one day to a friend's house, she sensed something that troubled her and was told that a group of "Yankees and armed Negroes" had just left and were likely to return; their leader was a once-trusted slave who had vowed to kill his master. Stone and her companions shut themselves inside but almost immediately "a big black wretch, with the most insolent swagger" broke in, waving a pistol and threatening to shoot their neighbor's baby boy. Then he came up close to Stone herself, "standing on the hem of my dress while he looked me slowly over . . . I felt I would die should he touch me." But he turned away, even as other men were ransacking the house, and indeed it was hours before they were finally gone. The threat or at least the fear of rape seems real, and some of the students with whom I have read these pages find them terrifying: an experience so mind-consumingly immediate that Stone herself is too petrified even to think of what Mary Chesnut calls the "St. Domingo stories."

That, however, is the specter those hours would have evoked for a Confederate reader, and two days later Stone's family left home "at the sacrifice of everything we owned." Yet there's a difference. Kate Stone was not raped and the baby not shot; the freed slaves kept some white men at gunpoint on the gallery outside but never fired. The house was looted but no lives were taken, and indeed the records of black-on-white violence during the war and its aftermath are remarkably thin. Certainly it was far less common than the murder of black men during Reconstruction or the rape of black women by their white masters. Louisiana was not Haiti; neither was Mississippi. The servile insurrection the white South feared never happened, however much, in the years to come, some old Confederates would act as if it had.

———————

THOMAS SUTPEN HAD A kind of overseer on his land while he was away with his regiment, a poor, malaria-ridden white named Wash Jones. Before the war his job had required little more than laughing at the planter's jokes and fetching a bucket of spring water for his whiskey, and after the fighting began it didn't even call for that. Jones had been allowed to share the liquor but not to enter the house, and his own tumbledown shack was in worse shape than any cabin in the quarters. When the war started he appointed himself to the overseer's post, claiming he'd been asked to look "after Kernel's place." The slaves only laughed at him, and all he did in reply was wave an impotent stick and utter threats that they all knew to ignore. Still, it was as good a way as any of avoiding a musket ball, and soon Jones was able to drop the stick. There was no one left to oversee. Sutpen's slaves went off with the first Yankee troops to pass through Jefferson, and Yoknapatawpha's history says nothing more about them.

Young Bayard Sartoris in *The Unvanquished* will see Loosh again, once the war is over. But for now the character has vanished, announcing as he leaves the burning Sartoris plantation that "God's own angel proclamated me free and gonter general me to Jordan." But where is Jordan, and how does one get there? Rivers provide barriers to cross and places in which to be washed clean. Joshua had led the Israelites over the Jordan into the promised land, its waters had been the first baptismal font, and the biblical river figures in any number of spirituals. Its rolling current held the irresistible force of Christian faith, and its very name marked the border between servitude and freedom; crossing it would lead to some blessed home on the other side, however fraught the journey. But Jordan was also the flowing columns of the Union army itself, an army on the move and with physical rivers of its own to cross.

The three Virginians who in 1861 rowed over to Benjamin Butler's fort had needed a destination; reaching the army made them "contrabands" as opposed to runaways. It gave them a new if ambiguous legal status, and though some commanders still turned black people away, an ever-increasing number of those people greeted the Federal army as a liberating force, even before abolition found its place in the Union's war aims. Many took an active part in their own emancipation, though few went so far as those on one Lafayette County plantation, who responded to the news of Lincoln's Proclamation by driving off their overseers; they divided up the tools and the land and began to work it for themselves. Others resisted their masters' attempts

to move them to "safety" in Texas or the Alabama black belt. They refused
to be refugeed and ran away instead, becoming refugees in our own sense of
the term. Still others saw those masters run away themselves, and by the fall
of 1862, when Grant's troops began to move through Mississippi, one thing
seemed clear. Freedom lay wherever the Union army was. The Emancipation
Proclamation only increased that certainty. Not everyone could reach the
Federal lines and Lincoln's order might not be enforceable in all the territory
it claimed to cover, but as far as the Union was concerned those running from
slavery were no longer slaves.

The Unvanquished's third episode, "Raid," begins with a six-day journey by wagon from the ruins of the Sartoris plantation to a place called
Hawkhurst in Alabama, the home of Bayard's cousin Drusilla. Grandmother
Millard has decided she must try to recover Loosh and Philadelphia, along
with some mules and the silver the Yankees have taken; Hawkhurst lies near
the spot where the units that swept through Jefferson are now camped. The
burned-out houses on the way show that the Federals have passed, but neither Bayard nor Ringo can at first make sense of the dust clouds they see in
the distance, not until Bayard wakes one night to what sounds like "about
fifty of them; we could hear the feet hurrying, and a . . . kind of gasping mur-
muring chant and the feet whispering fast in the deep dust" of the road. The
moving men and women remain invisible in the dark, but at least he now
knows where the dust comes from, and when they camp out the next night
he's woken three times by similar troops of marching black people, the last
of them at dawn and sounding "like they were running, like they had to run
to keep ahead of daylight." A bit later Bayard and his companions find an
exhausted woman with a baby in the road; she hasn't been able to keep up
with her group, and Granny puts her in the wagon until they reach her band,
hiding in the woods and waiting for the safety of the night. And still Bayard
does not know where these people are going, or why.

Hawkhurst has been burned as well, its "four chimneys standing gaunt
and blackened in the sun," but it still offers rest, and stories to share of each
other's suffering. Moreover, Drusilla knows all about those wanderers. She
too rises in the night to listen and to watch, so many people passing in the
road that she

couldn't count them: men and women carrying children who couldn't walk and carrying old men and women who should have been at home waiting to die. They were singing, walking along the road singing, not even looking to either side; the dust didn't even settle for two days because all that night they still passed. . . . Going to Jordan, they told me. Going to cross Jordan . . .

They are themselves a river, she adds; only they have now gotten dammed up by an actual one, by the stream to which they have followed the Federals, their path blazed by one burning plantation after another. Those newly freed people are bent on crossing to the other side of that broad unnamed river—except the soldiers won't let them. The Union troops may stand to them for freedom, but they also have imperatives of their own, and the Yankees have put a line of cavalry along the bank "to hold them back while they build the bridge to cross the infantry and artillery." The men and women sing and the soldiers push them back even as the pressure of new arrivals builds up behind them. All they want is to get down to the water; and yet the army has already set explosives and plans to blow that bridge once its men are across, a way to cut off any Confederate pursuit.

Or perhaps a pursuit by the freed people themselves. "Negroes coming in by wagon loads," Grant had cabled to Washington in November 1862. "What will I do with them?" But he didn't wait for instructions; instead he ordered a regimental chaplain named John Eaton to establish a system of relief. Eaton was a Dartmouth graduate who in civilian life had been superintendent of the Toledo schools, and he wrote in his 1907 memoirs that many of the army's new followers were in desperate circumstances, "in every stage of disease or decrepitude, often nearly naked, with flesh torn by the terrible experiences of their escapes." They were filled with terror and hope alike, they believed that their own interests were identical with those of the invading forces, and there were so many of them their arrival "was like the oncoming of cities." They needed food and shelter and especially doctors, but Eaton's job wasn't purely humanitarian; the contrabands' very presence threatened an army in which deaths from disease always outnumbered those in battle. He met the emergency by establishing a series of camps that effectively protected and quarantined the contrabands at once. Today we would call them refugee camps, and they would be served by an array of well-established organizations and procedures. Nothing like that existed in 1862. The contrabands numbered in the tens of thousands, the victims not only of the unending work of the fields but also of war's increasing privation; men and women who saw themselves as the Israelites of old, and in flight from Pharaoh's vengeance. No private charity could meet that need, and no army, as the historian Chandra Manning has argued, had ever tried to do the work that now fell to the Federal troops.

None of the camps Eaton set up in Tennessee or Mississippi were especially healthy. Infection spread freely, mortality rates were high, and food at times ran short; while in some cases, he admitted, "the slaves . . . met prejudices against their color more bitter than any they had left behind." But it was better than being on the road, where many people starved, and the settlements were garrisoned for safety from marauding Confederates, even as they also gave the Federals the freedom to move without their trailing columns. If Loosh and Philadelphia were lucky they would have gotten to the camp in Corinth, the rail junction in Mississippi's northeast corner. It was large, with between three and four thousand people, fairly administered, and well-supplied with clean water. The people at Corinth built houses along with a school and a church, and planted hundreds of acres of fresh vegetables for both themselves and the market. Loosh probably wouldn't have stayed there, though, not after the start of 1863. The government put many men and women back to work in the cotton fields of abandoned plantations, and the camps also provided recruits for the United States Colored Troops. A Loosh in real life might soon have found himself with a musket. He probably wanted it.

But armies rarely stand still. The war moved elsewhere, and by January 1864 the Union no longer needed its base in Corinth. Most of the contrabands went by rail to new camps near Memphis, and the Rebels came back to re-enslave those black people who remained. The Federals marched on, with more runaways in their wake, forever in search of a future, and Eaton's work needing to be done all over again as they entered Alabama and then Georgia. Faulkner doesn't give us a date for the action of "Raid," nor does he define its setting with any precision, but Bayard has gone fourteen and so let us call it the spring of 1864, with the Union army beginning to roll toward Atlanta. After a night at Hawkhurst Bayard takes to the road again, with Granny and Ringo in the wagon, Drusilla mounted beside them, and a cloud of dust in the road ahead. "We never did overtake them," he says, "just as you do not overtake a tide. You just keep moving, then suddenly you know that the set is about you, beneath you, overtaking you," a force that gathers you in and pushes you on. How does a boy who hasn't yet seen the ocean know about tides? But the description is so evocative that one hardly stops to ask. Men and women step out of the woods behind them, alongside, in front, and soon they are themselves a part of that crowd, the wagon "enclosed by a mass of heads and shoulders . . . [and] breasting slowly and terrifically through them" as the wave carries them on to the river.

Then the cart seems to lift clear of the ground, just as the tail of the Federal column steps off the bridge on the other side. The people push forward, and some of them fall beneath Bayard's wheels. Everything is confusion, and the river looks like rose-tinted glass. He will remember "the horses' and mules' heads all mixed up among the bayonets, and the barrels of cannon tilted up," and in the confusion he hears the high voices of women calling "Hallelujah" as the troopers try to keep the massed bodies away from the mined span. They beat them back with the flats of their scabbarded swords, and an officer tells the hysterical Granny to turn aside. Not that she can. The crowd is too dense, and then the cavalry breaks, with horses and men going down under the crush of people even as the sky fills with the explosion's sudden glare and "a clap of wind" hits out. The riverbank itself seems to crumble, the wagon rides downward "on another river of faces," and the water fills with screams.

Faulkner did something unusual here. He often drew on the historical record but usually that record was a local one, an event from somewhere in the territory between Oxford and Memphis, if not from Lafayette County itself. This scene, in contrast, has its origin in an event that took place five hundred miles away, during Sherman's march from Atlanta to the sea. In the fall of 1864 the general's sixty thousand men famously cut themselves loose from their lines of supply. They moved fast and without much of a baggage train, ammunition aside; too fast and too light to feed the many thousands of freed people who trailed after them, or to stop and build camps to house them. Every one of his generals saw them as an encumbrance, a hindrance to the army's free movement. But they differed in their willingness to accept it. One especially reluctant officer was a corps commander from Indiana with the unfortunate name of Jefferson Davis; though it suited him, for this Union leader was as untroubled by slavery as the Confederate president himself. Davis had about thirteen thousand soldiers on his books, and they were all white, as was Sherman's entire army; but he also had several thousand contrabands following after him. The men he used as pioneers, doing the heavy work of building roads and fortifications. He wanted, however, to lose the women and children, the old and the sick, and on December 9 he got his chance at a stream called Ebenezer Creek, some twenty miles north of Savannah.

The novelist's description in *The Unvanquished* is far from a documentary account of what happened next, but still it seems clear to me that Faulkner took the idea for "Raid" from this moment in Georgia. At that time of year the creek was in fact an icy river, 160 feet wide and ten deep. Davis had the equipment he needed to make a pontoon bridge, and by now his troops could both set it up and dismantle it quickly. The contrabands were ordered to wait until the army had crossed—but as soon as the last soldier was over the general had the pontoons pulled in and the bridge destroyed. He would later plead both a shortage of rations and his fear of the Rebel pursuit. The one excused his desire to cut free, the other his decision to do it here, and indeed some units of Confederate cavalry had already caught up with him and begun to fire as the bridge came to pieces. Perhaps the people Davis abandoned would have panicked in any case, but the approaching whistle of the enemy swords drove hundreds of them into the freezing water, with those on the riverbank itself pushed in by the pressure of the crowd behind them: a desperate attempt by people who could not swim to reach the other side. Many of them drowned, and a Union colonel named Charles Kerr wrote that "from what we learned afterwards of those who remained on the land, their fate at the hands of [the] troopers was scarcely to be preferred." Sherman excused his subordinate's decision on the grounds of military necessity and defended him against the Northern newspapers, where Davis's action was widely reported and criticized; and in truth the atrocity resulted from the actions of both sides. But in Kerr's words "there was no necessity about it" at all. Davis's troops had a duty to protect the civilians who followed them, and the general's actions were "unjustifiable and perfidious."

Ebenezer Creek figures very briefly in Sherman's own memoirs, as if he knew it wouldn't stand much scrutiny, but we are unlikely to learn just how Faulkner heard about it. He liked, of course, to claim that he never did any research at all. It fit the brag on the map he drew of Yoknapatawpha County: William Faulkner, Sole Owner and Proprietor. But one can read widely without doing what a scholar might call research, and we have to assume that over the years Faulkner opened memoirs and biographies, bad novels and regimental histories. He listened too, and the incident may have appealed to him—might have been widely spoken of in the South—as an example of Yankee hypocrisy, an instance of racism at odds with the North's claims to virtue. The real question, for our purposes, lies in the differences between the historical facts and what *The Unvanquished* makes of them. "Raid" says nothing of an immediate Rebel pursuit, and the contrabands' actions there seem motivated instead by a religious yearning in which freedom and salvation appear as one. At the same time their movements appear more heedless than those of the actual people at Ebenezer Creek, not panicked so much as automatic and unthinking, herdlike. So for that matter do those of the Union army itself; Faulkner's story offers no reason at all for that army's decision to hold the contrabands back. Meanwhile, young Bayard's wagon is borne along on the human tide itself, and powerless. Then the earth drops away and he finds himself in the river, the wagon atilt and the horses drowning, yet somehow remaining upright until a Yankee patrol can haul the white folks out.

The sequence that Faulkner begins with the sound of those feet in the dust is exhilarating, mysterious, disturbing, and finally indeed sublime. None of the black people Bayard sees on this journey acquires a name or even a face, and Ringo is if anything even more distant from them than his white friend. Nevertheless, they embody a force that this teenaged narrator knows he doesn't understand and with which he must reckon. "Raid" ends with a bit of comic business, trivial in comparison to what's passed. Granny has hoped to find Loosh and Philadelphia, but instead a Union officer gives her a chit authorizing her to take a 110 mules "captured loose near Philadelphia in

Mississippi," along with an equal number of contrabands. It's a conventional army snafu that tweaks away the story's complications with the kind of smile that the *Post*'s readers required, leaving them satisfied that in the struggle between the Blue and the Gray there had been well-intentioned people on both sides.

Bayard's grandmother can sell the mules, but the only thing she can do with the people is to tell them to go home, warning them against "straggling off" again; certainly the ruined Sartoris plantation can't feed them. We never learn their fate. They simply disappear from Faulkner's pages—and yet the more one reads in the literature of the war the less possible it seems to forget them. "I been in the storm so long," the old song goes, and the historian Leon Litwack has taken those words for the title of his Pulitzer Prize–winning account of slavery's end. How free is free? Nobody yet quite knows, and nobody knows where home is either. But that storm certainly doesn't end with emancipation, and the men and women following Bayard's wagon now live in a maelstrom, its current whipping fast, uncertain and ever-changing. Few of them would want their old lives back, but freedom is a hard school, and in John Eaton's words, "the law, to the Negro, took any form of caprice." Some people will be lost in that freedom, forever cut off from family and friends; some will be lost to it.

In his memoirs Eaton writes that he wants to provide "some definite and reliable notion of . . . a task which is all but forgotten by the present genera-tion." He offers deeply admiring portraits of both Grant and Lincoln, but the book's heart lies in its minute account of a job that needed to be done, a job that "represented an important phase in the National policy, and one closely associated with the principles of the Union cause." By the time he wrote, the white South had functionally replaced the Civil War amendments to the Constitution with Jim Crow; and the white North accepted it, as if civil rights were no longer even worth an argument. Reunion seemed to require amnesia, and accounts of the conflict instead looked to constitutional ques-tions on the one hand, and military ones on the other.

Yet the role of black soldiers, the story of the contrabands, or indeed of those people who simply stayed put in a land that, as the armies swept back and forth, was neither quite slave nor quite free—those who lived through the war felt that these were among its major issues. They were, in the end, what the struggle was about, and today these questions of social history seem utterly compelling once more. It was very different in Faulkner's time, when few scholars were willing to view slavery itself as the fighting's motive force. There were exceptions. Some works of state and local history took up those questions, and Eaton himself must have been among the first to cite Du Bois's newly published *Souls of Black Folk*. Yet the major historians of the American South, such as Phillips, preferred to write of the antebellum world, and the critics of Reconstruction were hardly interested in the lived experience of black people. That would begin to change in the years of Faulkner's maturity, but his account of Loosh's self-emancipation doesn't fit the historiography of his own day, Du Bois aside, so much as it anticipates that of ours. Bayard's understanding may be strictly limited, but he does at least acknowledge the chaos around him and knows he cannot fight its tide. Another way to put that is to say that Faulkner couldn't keep from remembering what other people wanted to forget.

And Loosh? We need to speculate a bit—to pretend for a moment that these characters are actual people—for Faulkner has very little more to tell us about him. After the fighting stopped he and Philadelphia might have gone north to Saint Louis or south to New Orleans. Maybe they farmed on shares for a while in another county, or perhaps they simply found their way back to Jefferson, where they still had family. Whatever happened, by the mid-1870s Loosh was at work on the Sartoris place once again. After disappearing from *The Unvanquished* in the book's second chapter, he returns for just a few sentences in its last one, "An Odor of Verbena." There Faulkner describes him as tending to the horses, just as he had before the war, and I imagine that the book's first readers would have taken his reappearance as a matter of course. The most rebellious of former slaves has gone back to his old master and been forgiven. Even after emancipation nothing much has changed: the county's old families are its old families still, and life goes on as before. But that's not enough for us now, and in reading I want to know just what has made Loosh return, what has driven him back. What might his experience have been in what the historian Douglas Egerton has called "the wars of Reconstruction"? The novelist himself says nothing about those missing years, about the events that have sent this once-determined man back to the land and service of those who had held him in bondage. We can only imagine them—no, we *need* to imagine them. We will need, when we move into Faulkner's account of the postwar period, to listen to the silence and read for what his work leaves unsaid.

NINE

The Stillness

Historical fiction always relies on our knowledge of what lies off the page. Walter Scott invented the genre with *Waverly* (1815) and assumed his readers already understood many of the dynastic, constitutional, and religious questions that defined the relations between England and Scotland from the seventeenth century on. Tolstoy in *War and Peace* expected his audience to know not only what happened to Napoleon after his 1812 retreat from Moscow, but also about the Decembrist uprising of 1825, when the tsarist government squashed any hopes of a liberalized future. These novelists give us the past by locating their characters on the edge of great historical events; they make them serve as witnesses. Faulkner does it differently, does it backward. History in his work stands as but a border or a fringe to his characters' individual lives, their psychic lives above all. It may be determinative, and yet it also remains oddly incidental: not dramatized so much as invoked. Nevertheless, we need to know that history, to know the facts his characters take for granted, and this seems especially true with his glancing, allusive account of the Civil War's last year. Faulkner's work touches on almost every question posed by the war's concluding stages. But he spreads his account of those final months over many different novels and stories, and it must be carefully pieced together.

He writes in *Absalom, Absalom!*, for example, that Thomas Sutpen came back to Yoknapatawpha just once during the course of the war. He returned for a flickering visit of only a day in the fall of 1864 and left his regiment out east, the same soldiers he had led at Gettysburg. But what would he have been doing in the year and more since leaving Pennsylvania in defeat? Faulkner offers no details, and so we have to assume that his troops shared the experience of the rest of the actual Army of Northern Virginia; that they were among the soldiers who in the spring of 1864 fought and died during the forty days of attrition known as the Overland Campaign.

That March, Grant had taken command of the Union armies in their entirety. His strategy required continuous action on all fronts: a great coordinated pincer movement with Sherman moving in the west toward Atlanta even as he himself operated against Lee in Virginia. In May he brought the Army of the Potomac over the Rapidan River, fifty miles to the south of Washington, and met the Confederate forces in an area of scrub forest known simply as the Wilderness. They fought for two days, with the trees aflame around them, and the Yankees taking seventeen thousand casualties to the Rebels' eleven thousand; higher in raw numbers on the Federal side, but with Lee losing a greater percentage of his command. Then they disengaged, each side trying to outflank the other, and fought for two weeks more at the nearby Spotsylvania Court House, and disengaged, and fought, and disengaged again, and again, with Lee winning a series of narrow but costly tactical victories even as the Union edged south, ever closer to Richmond. In June the campaign became a siege, with the Confederates corked up in the fortifications around Petersburg, an industrial city of about twenty thousand inhabitants just below the Confederate capital. Grant too built fortifications and redoubts, drawing on his experience at Vicksburg, but this siege would last until the following April and beggar its predecessor in scale.

Still, there came a moment when each side realized that nothing would change for a long time: a lull, with the battle furious but its progress arrested, and we can imagine that that's when Sutpen got away for a bit. A narrow path remained open to the west and he took it, bringing a curiously loaded wagon from Virginia down through the Tennessee mountains and on into Mississippi. He spent a few hours in the Jefferson office of the one-armed General Compson and then drove out to Sutpen's Hundred, where, as Faulkner writes, his two daughters awaited. He nodded to his black daughter, Clytie, his firstborn, whose mother was a nameless slave; he kissed Judith, the white one, whose marriage to Charles Bon he had forbidden on the very eve of the war. Then he unshipped his load and drank a cup of coffee and was gone.

The wagon held two tombstones, "bombastic and inert" blocks of Italian marble that he had somehow smuggled through the Federal blockade. One was for his wife Ellen, the daughter of the Jefferson shopkeeper Goodhue Coldfield. She had died the year before, and the Tuscan stonecutters had chiseled in her dates; the other was for Sutpen himself. Those monuments had traveled for months in his regimental wagon train, with his soldiers cursing their weight "through bog and morass." They were shoeless and starving, his men, their eyes desperate and burning with "undefeat," but they had humor enough to give each rock a name: Colonel and Mrs. Colonel. Sutpen set his Missus in the earth; she had never had more than a shadowy presence, and the stone now defined her fully. Then he propped his own slab in the front hall and vanished back to the war; and perhaps his white daughter, her wedding foreclosed, wished that his tombstone as well was now fixed in the ground outside.

Judith Sutpen did, however, have a death in her family that year: her grandfather Coldfield. He was Jefferson's one conscientious objector, a figure of chilly rectitude who at the start of the war had shut up his general store after refusing to sell to soldiers. The town wasn't safe for such a man, and so he had vanished, climbing up into his attic and nailing the door shut behind him. For three years his younger daughter, Rosa, hoisted up a nightly basket of food, but one evening no hand drew it in, and she got a neighbor to break the door down. They found several days of uneaten provisions by the bed on which his body lay, as if he had simply decided to starve himself out. He found his release. Rosa never did, never freed herself from the impotent fury that would become the single note of her life, and during the long years that followed her only outlet was a manuscript portfolio in which she wrote heroic verse "about the very men from whom her father was hiding." By 1885, *Absalom, Absalom!* tells us, Rosa Coldfield had composed a thousand poetic tributes to Confederate valor, "ode eulogy and epitaph . . . in which the lost cause's unregenerate vanquished were name by name embalmed." But the first of them coincided with her father's decision to wall himself up, as though she were putting both the poems and that cause in his place.

I need to pause over those poems, for that army in verse raises a historical issue to which I'll return throughout this chapter. Some of Rosa's lines found print in the newspaper of Faulkner's imaginary county, but he gives us no samples of her work and no warrant for thinking it either better or worse than the formulaic stanzas, many of them by women, that filled the papers of other Southern towns. At the start of the war most of those poems spoke of triumph. So in "Manassas" the Mississippi-born Catherine A. W. Warfield announces that

> *Long shall Northmen rue the day*
> *When they met our stern array,*
> *And shrunk from battle's wild affray*
> *At Manassas!*

Later there came an overriding sense of loss, as in the 1863 attempt of the Charleston poet Caroline A. Ball attempt to imagine the feelings of love and sacrifice with which a mother puts away her dead son's uniform:

> *Fold it up carefully, lay it aside;*
> *Tenderly touch it, look on it with pride;*
> *For dear to our hearts must it be evermore,*
> *The jacket of gray our loved soldier-boy wore.*

The rhymes make me wince—Ball chimes *gray* with *fray*, *lay*, *day*, and *pay*—and the insistence on godly purpose in much of the period's poetry, both North and South, is now hard to accept. Each side hoped the Christian belief in salvation might make the war meaningful, but the North, as the historian Charles Reagan Wilson has argued, had victory with which to console itself for its losses. The South, in contrast, needed to make defeat itself seem sacred.

It did so through a rhetoric that turned loss into a form of nobility and memory itself into a promise of the life to come. Wilson calls it a "civil religion"—the house of worship known as the Lost Cause. It began to take shape even before the war was over, and the title of his *Baptized in Blood* gives some sense of its creed. In the decades to come its faith would be manifested in many ways: in the textbooks Southern schoolchildren read and in the monuments in front of every county courthouse; in the local chapters of the Daughters of the Confederacy; and in the cult of this general or that, the "marble man" Robert E. Lee above all, cults that included a display of relics to rival those of a Catholic saint. The faith lived in sermons and stained glass, memoirs and works of history, in fiction and poetry and finally in film. And it lived too in the belief that the North was a godless waste, and white Southerners a uniquely virtuous nation. Those who believed in the Lost Cause saw themselves as a chosen people, who had accepted the most chastening of defeats, and they appealed to that cause in the name of a divinely ordered white supremacy.

With time that religion became the special province of Southern white women, ready symbol of the homes and the virtues for which the war had supposedly been fought. They wrote most of the poems and decorated the churches, they outlived their men and folded those uniforms away. Faulkner himself spoke ironically of the old women who had never surrendered and would "walk out of *Gone with the Wind* as soon as Sherman's name was mentioned," and yet he admired them too. Those widows and daughters had twitched the canvas off every local monument; the job of memorialization had been theirs before it was his. But Faulkner's women have other jobs as well, even during the war itself. The Charleston-born poet Henry Timrod wrote in 1863 that the South had two armies, one in the field and

> *The other, with a narrower scope,*
> *Yet led by not less grand a hope . . .*

That army worked with the needle and loom, it sat by the bed of the wounded and nerved "the son's, the husband's hand." Timrod's words speak to the conventional Victorian image of women in wartime, to a belief in each gender's separate sphere. Faulkner himself gives voice to it; and he also repudiates it.

In the early days of the war, as we saw in *The Unvanquished,* Grandmother Millard expected that enemy officers would, as gentlemen, respect the sanctity and privacy of her home. But the longer the fighting lasts, the more her relation to it changes. In my last chapter I left her holding an order that allowed her to requisition 110 mules from the Union army; now let's see how she uses it. One night Ringo brings home a few quires of Federal letterhead, and after that it's just a matter of copying out the old order and making sure to "sign the right general's name to it." By the end they have requisitioned almost 250 mules from the Federals, which they promptly rebrand and sell back for good United States dollars. Many Southern planters sold cotton across the lines to Yankee speculators, but private gain is the furthest thing from Granny's mind. On Sundays she goes into a Jefferson church and stands before a congregation of plain people from "back into the hills where they lived in dirt-floored cabins," people who have come to hear the sermons of an unordained minister, a gut-shot former private from Sartoris's old regiment. Such a preacher would once have spoken about the victory God would bring, but by this point in the war all Brother Fortinbride can do is insist that "defeat with God is not defeat." When he finishes, Granny asks everyone to pray for her and then takes out a ledger as one by one her people approach.

To some of them she gives mules, the animals that couldn't be rebranded and sold. Others get cash, but they need to tell her how they spent what "they had received before." Sometimes she takes a mule away and gives it to a family that will use it better, or she catches a man out in a lie; always she tries to find a balance, however precarious, between what people need and what they deserve. Granny weighs and judges, and certainly her benevolence comes freighted with paternalism. But it would be too simple to see her actions as a mere exercise in charity, Lady Bountiful in her village. What Rosa Millard has done, rather, is to organize a system of poor relief.

The historian Stephanie McCurry has argued that the Civil War required the state to expand its functions while also making them impossible to fulfill; to recognize the need for a rudimentary network of social services even when it could not provide one. Her *Confederate Reckoning* weighs the costs that the war imposed on noncombatants and shows that much of the South's internal dissent was both organized by women and meant to address their needs. Those who appealed for public assistance often did so as soldiers' wives and widows, who by definition had a claim upon society as a whole, a claim that in itself produced an ever-expanding sense of their relations to civic life. Poor women protested the Twenty Negro Law; hungry ones led the bread riots that hit Richmond and other Southern cities in the spring of 1863.

Yoknapatawpha doesn't know that kind of dissent, and the historiography of Faulkner's own era underplayed such quarrels in order to stress what, in another context, was termed the Solid South. Nevertheless, the war has so drained and destroyed the land that the county's people can no longer feed themselves, not without help, help that neither the state nor the established churches now have the resources to provide. Granny fills the gap. Her thievery allows her to offer the support that the region's authorities cannot, and yet to do so she has had to step away from the world of home, from Timrod's second army. The assurance with which she manages it may depend on her class, her position as a plantation mistress: someone used to giving orders and having them obeyed. Nevertheless, the war has made her into someone other than the woman who accepted a Union colonel's protection as she hid Bayard and Ringo behind her skirts.

Another character in *The Unvanquished* does even more to undermine the divisions Timrod defines. Drusilla Hawke had showed her young cousin Bayard the crowds of black people walking through the night, walking toward Jordan. But before that she had lost her fiancé at Shiloh and thereby became the "bride-widow of a lost cause." That's how her mother puts it, anyway, as the war ends: *a* lost cause but not yet *The* Lost Cause, as if Faulkner has caught the moment before that way of thinking hardened into proverb. Drusilla has other plans, however, and won't accept the passivity that convention requires. She rides "astride like a man," and when the Yankees try to take the horse her dead sweetheart had given her she puts a pistol to the animal's ear. Touch him and he dies, she says, for she would rather kill the beast herself than surrender it to her enemy. So it's no surprise when she turns to Bayard and wonders if "Uncle John ... [would] let me come there and ride with his troop ... maybe I can learn to shoot."

Each Civil War army had women in its ranks—women who dressed and passed as men, though the masquerade was sometimes an open one. On a train from Chattanooga the British military observer Arthur Fremantle had "a goodish-looking woman ... pointed out" to him as having fought in several major battles. The whole regiment knew of her sex, "but no notice had been taken of it," and the soldiers who served with her told him she was far from unique. Current estimates, as McCurry notes, put the number of women in the Confederate army at about 250. But the figure is doubtless low, for it depends on those who were either detected or later acknowledged their actions. Some of them accompanied husbands or lovers or brothers into a locally raised regiment, others joined to escape an abusive home, and some female soldiers had been living as men for years before the war came. Medical examinations for new recruits were often cursory. Doctors saw what they expected to see; and once enrolled, women were usually discovered only if wounded. Their presence was commonly winked at by enlisted men, who probably enjoyed putting one over on their officers, and a few women even became officers themselves. Mary Ann Pitman, from western Tennessee, used a male disguise to help raise a cavalry company and was then elected its lieutenant. She fought at Shiloh and afterward served under Forrest, who knew her identity; at times she returned to women's clothing in order to work as a spy. Confederate women were, in fact, more likely than Federals to stay in the ranks after their sex was known, and some Southern towns even organized groups of women for local defense.

Drusilla soon disappears from home, and it's almost a year before the news comes that she's with Colonel Sartoris's troop in the Carolinas. The war has long since moved on from Mississippi and is now approaching its end. Sherman has completed his devastating march from Atlanta to the sea and turned north from Savannah to work even more destruction on the Confederacy's South Carolina birthplace. There are few large battles now, but skirmishing seems continuous, an unending rattle of fire around the edge of the moving armies, and with the Southern cavalry giving no quarter to those they catch straggling. That is the Colonel's grim business in the war's closing phase, and Drusilla is with him, riding "like a man," her blond hair cut close and wearing the sweat-stained clothes of a private. Where she differs from most female soldiers is in her very openness; the entire troop knows of her sex. Drusilla serves so openly, in fact, that her own mother assumes, incorrectly, that she has become the Colonel's mistress, "a lost woman and a shame to her father's memory": an assumption that leaves her outraged, for her only purpose has been "to hurt Yankees."

Faulkner doesn't show her in combat but he makes it easy for us to imagine her there, bent over the sights of her rifle and squeezing it off at any Federal in range. Yet what's most interesting about Drusilla isn't the simple fact of her fighting—it's the justification she offers for it. She goes to war in the Confederate cause but she also delights in the idea of war itself, war as an escape from the dull stupidity of everyday life. Before it all began "you lived in the same house your father was born in ... and you fell in love with your acceptable young man," you wore your mother's wedding dress and settled down forever and then died. The war has changed that—there's nothing to "worry" about anymore because the house has been burned and the young man killed. Now she lives in a perpetual present, free of the past and femininity alike, free of the entire world of predictable habit; lives at the very peak of experience, riding hard and alive and exalted by the flame of an excitement that seems to burn forever. Or so she says, denying that she ever wanted what she cannot now have, even as the febrility of her voice suggests how much damage the war has done. But a peak implies a descent, and after the fighting is over Drusilla will indeed dwindle into John Sartoris's second wife.

———

IN 1861 JEFFERSON'S YOUNG men had stood in the square and hoped that they were brave; by the winter of 1865 they knew that they were and also knew that bravery was not enough. The previous fall a Union army had burned its way through Virginia's Shenandoah Valley, destroying the crops and livestock on which the South depended. Another army still lay encamped around Petersburg, its trenches squeezing ever closer, with the Confederates starved not only of food but also of new recruits with which to replace the dead. Sherman had taken Savannah; Charleston fell in February and left the South without a port. "Generals as plenty as blackberries," Mary Chesnut wrote in January, but "none in command." This one is sick, that one wounded; some of her friends claim the South can be saved if only the prickly Joseph Johnston is put in command, others that it can never be saved if he is. Everything is Jefferson Davis's fault, unless it's the fault of everyone else. Chesnut spent the closing days of the war in a land of hunger and fear, and all around she could hear the recriminations grow. *If, if, if only* ... Southerners like Chesnut expect reprisals—the Yankees will swing a noose—and while they wait they must also "look out for bands of marauders, black and white, lawless disbanded soldiery from both armies."

Those bands are among the morbid symptoms of a fading world, of what Faulkner called "the deep South dead"; and so, to the ladies of Jefferson, is Drusilla's career as a soldier. A New South might struggle to be born from its ruins, and yet the ghosts of the old order linger on through the interregnum, and to Faulkner those symptoms each carry a story. The simple fiction of purposeful dedication around which the white South had gathered in 1861 has now splintered and burst, and he finds more narrative possibilities in the chaos and flux of the war's end than he did in its beginning. There was a young woman in Jefferson named Cecelia Farmer, whom Faulkner describes in *Requiem for a Nun* as a dreamy child, with "narrow workless hands." She didn't cook or clean; she did nothing at all but sit musing each day in her father's window, who stirred herself only on the day when John Sartoris mustered in his regiment. Then she got up, not to watch or cheer, but simply to take her grandmother's chip of a diamond and scratch away at the glass. *Cecelia Farmer*, she wrote, *April 16th 1861*. Having marked her presence she sat down again, and she was still sitting there three years later, when the war came to Jefferson for the last time.

In the summer of 1864 there was a sharp little fight a few miles to the north, along a creek on the edge of the Sartoris plantation, and then the Southerners fell back through the town with a burst of gunfire and "the rush and scurry of a handful of horsemen." The girl looked up at the sound to see a young Confederate lieutenant, "battle-grimed and fleeing and undefeated," and for a few seconds he saw her as well. A year later the war was over and he came back and with barely a word took her away to an Alabama farm. But in between Jefferson had been set aflame, lit up almost as soon as that lieutenant had fired his last shot at the Yankee pursuit, with its courthouse a blackened pile of tumbled brick. And so, for that matter, was Oxford itself: the town was almost entirely burned in August 1864, its destruction ordered in a fit of pique by the Union general Andrew Jackson Smith.

The place would be rebuilt, both of them; but by April 1865 Jefferson had already gotten so used to defeat that the "knell of Appomattox made no sound." What got Smith to burn the actual town was his inability to dispose of—to capture, defeat, or destroy—the charismatic Rebel cavalry commander Nathan Bedford Forrest. In the spring of 1864 Sherman began his sweep toward Atlanta. But he had a huge and hostile country at his back, and an army in Georgia could be stopped by a raid on its lines of supply in Middle Tennessee. Sherman was especially worried about Forrest, whose riders appeared where they were least expected and could do the most damage. Forrest led from the front, kept count of the men he had personally killed, and had consistently beaten larger Union forces, as he did that June at Brice's Crossroads, some sixty miles to the east of Oxford. There he took apart a Union detachment of eight thousand soldiers, more than twice his size, and all Sherman could do in reply was to send an even larger expedition in pursuit. Still, the Yankees had troops to spare—and so long as they made Forrest fight in Mississippi, he couldn't attack their supply trains above Chattanooga.

In mid-August Forrest had his men dug in on Hurricane Creek to the north of Oxford, but after a week of intermittent fighting, he realized that he wouldn't be able to win in the field. Instead he disengaged: he marshaled two thousand men on Oxford's courthouse square and then took them on a long looping ride over muddy roads and rain-swollen rivers to Memphis. The Federals had held that waterfront city for two years, but it was lightly garrisoned and Forrest planned to take it; he knew he couldn't keep it but the raid would scare his enemy, and any pursuit would stretch them out. The attack on August 21 was a complete surprise. His men charged in at three in the morning, and Confederate folklore holds that Forrest himself rode his horse through the lobby of the city's best hotel, hoping to capture a Union general. The account is disputed, but what matters is that people accepted it, that it fit the legend of his daring and skill. Nothing was beyond him, and though his men stayed in Memphis for only a day, they retreated so skillfully that the Union forces were convinced he remained a threat long after he was gone. Forrest's raid had achieved its purpose. Though so, paradoxically, had Sherman, who had kept him away from any place of strategic importance; and ten days later the Federals had taken Atlanta. As for Oxford—well, Smith had just moved into town when he heard about Forrest's exploit, and that was when he burned it.

Forrest is the one Rebel general who stands for Faulkner as more than a name. The novelist mentions him in half-a-dozen books, seeing him as a kind of trickster, forever sowing confusion and counting coup on a clumsy enemy; and he even sends one of his own characters along on that ride to Memphis. In *Go Down, Moses*, the sixty-year-old private Theophilus McCaslin is said to have ridden into the city under Forrest's command and "up Main street and (the tale told) into the lobby of the Gayoso Hotel where the Yankee officers sat in the leather chairs spitting into the tall bright cuspidors and then out again, scot-free." *The tale told.* The attack becomes a legend, something shared out over a bottle of whiskey, and Faulkner's own family tradition held that at one point the Old Colonel brought his Partisan Rangers into Forrest's command. The record doesn't bear that out but the novelist himself may have believed it, confusing his great-grandfather with another William Faulkner—this one from Kentucky and spelling his name with a *u*—who did ride with Forrest.

Over the years the tally of those who said they belonged to Forrest's brigades seemed to grow, like the numbers of those at Woodstock, men who claimed, in a hollow present, that they had once lived at the pitch of excitement and courage. That was a part of Forrest's myth, and it reached a new height in Faulkner's day on the strength of Andrew Nelson Lytle's *Bedford Forrest and His Critter Company* (1931)—"critter company" being a nickname for the general's often bedraggled troopers. Lytle himself was a classmate of Robert Penn Warren's at Vanderbilt, and like him a contributor to *I'll Take My Stand*, the 1930 volume of essays by "Twelve Southerners" that pitted the white South's agrarian tradition against the encroachments of industrial modernity. His own fiction and essays made him an apologist for a distinctive part of that tradition, one that celebrated the region's plainspoken yeomen farmers rather than the courtliness of plantation life. But he spent far more of his own life in academia than he did on the farm, teaching at the University of Florida and then at Tennessee's University of the South, where for many years he edited the *Sewanee Review*.

Lytle's contribution to the South's civil religion carries a thesis. He argues that the North feared Forrest far more than the South valued him, and that the South didn't value him because he wasn't a Virginia gentleman but had started life as the son of a blacksmith: a man whose own fortune came not from the land but from the buying and selling of slaves. Forrest was a millionaire before he was forty, but owning slaves was one thing, and dealing in them another. Even Memphis thought it a disreputable trade. He was physically fearless and always ready to tell his superiors how little he thought of them; after the squandered Confederate victory at Chickamauga he accused his commanding general of cowardice and offered to make the insult good. Forrest's personal legend fitted snugly into the larger mythology of the Lost Cause. For Lytle implies that the South could have won if only it had known how to use his talents. Suppose he had been given an army of his own and the freedom to take it behind Sherman's lines? Forrest thus stands as another instance of the war's what-ifs, of how—as at Gettysburg—it might have all gone differently. The corollary of that argument is that the North's victory wasn't the result of its own efforts; in this view, even Grant's Vicksburg campaign depends above all on Southern mistakes.

Faulkner's account of Forrest is not so worshipful, and yet he nowhere alludes to the two things with which he is most associated today. One is his leadership of the Ku Klux Klan. Forrest joined soon after it was formed in 1866 and the next year planned and supervised the campaign of terror with which it tried to keep Southern black men from voting in local elections. The other is his April 1864 capture of Fort Pillow, north of Memphis on the Mississippi. The Union garrison included several hundred black troops, many of whom were killed after the fort was taken. Historians argued for a century about whether the Federals had in fact surrendered before they were shot or if some of them were still firing; about whether Forrest himself ordered the massacre, condoned it, or simply lost control of his troops. The *Century*'s "Battles and Leaders" series merely presents the opposing views of each side, quoting from letters and official reports and making no attempt to determine the truth. But more recent research has settled the question. A letter home by a Confederate sergeant, written immediately afterward but not fully published until 1982, tells of soldiers shot as they tried to surrender, with the general himself ordering the "butchery" to continue. Forrest's own report noted that the blood of the Union dead stained the river to a distance of two hundred yards, and he lamented the twenty lost from his own command. Lytle writes only that "there was some work of private vengeance" after the Union flag came down, produced in part by "the insults of former slaves," an insult that lay in the very fact of their bearing arms at all.

The novelist could not have known that sergeant's letter, but he certainly knew about the battle itself and the bitter arguments that followed. In some parts of the South, Forrest remains celebrated; as of 2019, Tennessee still marks an official Nathan Bedford Forrest Day, proclaimed each year by its governor. But even in the 1930s the general's reputation was at best equivocal, and the novelist could if he wanted have ignored him entirely. So it's hard to stomach the 1943 story in which Faulkner gave Forrest himself a speaking role, describing him as "a big, dusty man with ... eyes like a sleepy owl" who says " 'fit' for fought ... and 'drug' for dragged." The tale revives the characters of *The Unvanquished* and has a cumbersome, Twain-like title: "My Grandmother Millard and General Bedford Forrest and the Battle of Harrykin Creek." It is at once broad and slight, a tall tale in which the Confederate army's progress is halted by a lovesick junior officer, and it turns on the fact that Backhouse, the lieutenant's family name, is also a synonym for "outhouse." Faulkner allows himself a reference to Forrest's earlier traffic in "human meat," but as a character the general seems quaintly humorous and the story ends with a wedding and a barbecue. In his greatest books—in *Light in August* or *Absalom, Absalom!*—Faulkner put any Lost Cause sentiments into the mouths or minds of one character or another, while allowing the novel as a whole to remain skeptical. He would not, I think, have permitted himself to present so callow a version of the Southern past if he had taken this story at all seriously. Yet that is precisely what makes the tale so troubling and so damaging. This is how Faulkner chose to relax, as if the Lost Cause were a pair of old slippers, something comfortable for home. But then many people had forgotten their history by 1943, and this picture of a man whom we would now call a war criminal found a ready national audience in the *Saturday Evening Post*.

One of the few interesting things about the story is that Faulkner backdates its action from 1864, the date of the actual fighting on Hurricane Creek, to 1862. He could not have ended such a comedy with the burning of Jefferson, but that wasn't his only reason to shift its moment. For *The Unvanquished* had already imagined a different fate for young Bayard's Grandmother Millard. Scarlett O'Hara in *Gone with the Wind* kills a Yankee thief at the end of the war, but as Mary Chesnut's words about those marauding bands suggest, an actual Scarlett would have been in as much danger from Confederate deserters. There were thousands of them on the roads in the war's last months, many simply trying to get home and others who saw no point in dying for a polity that was itself on the verge of death. Some of them, however, meant to make a profit out of the skills the war had taught them.

In the mule business Bayard's grandmother has had the help of a talkative, self-pitying man called Ab Snopes, a master at whining his way into what he calls "cash money." He's the first of his name to appear in Yoknapatawpha, the feckless ancestor of the unlikely swarm that will settle over the county in the next century. Granny uses him to run the mules through the Union lines, and he looks so patently dishonest that the Federal commissaries paradoxically trust him, seeing him as a disloyal Confederate, a smuggler out for himself alone. But by late 1864 the last Yankee regiment has gone and with it any trace of authority and order. In its place is a gang of Southern deserters, draft-dodgers, and renegades known as Grumby's Independents, a band that lives by raiding any house where they know the men are gone, stealing food and "frightening white women and torturing negroes to find where money or silver was hidden." They are more feared than the Union army ever was, and among their spoils are four fine horses worth up to two thousand dollars.

So Ab Snopes says—stolen horses, horses that Rosa Millard could sell. All she needs to do is to forge one last requisition, this time signed by a Confederate general. Against her better judgment she agrees, and with Bayard and Ringo behind her rides off to a meeting at an old abandoned farm building. But she won't let her grandson come in with her: no Southerner will harm a woman, she says, but Bayard is now grown enough to look threatening. She walks on alone "into the wet twilight and never come[s] out again," and when the two boys finally go after her it is too late. For Grumby has seen her ruse, and the air now smells of gunpowder, with the "little sticks" of her dead body lying collapsed on the floor.

That's the end of *The Unvanquished*'s fourth chapter, one that I still read with a sense of open-mouthed shock. Faulkner's touch had been so light, but the prospect of peace seems to darken the book's tone, as though with the war ending the real blood could begin. So now Bayard and Ringo ride over a wintry Hobbesian landscape in search of revenge, and armed with but a single pistol between them. Their pursuit of Grumby will last for months. Some days they seem just an hour behind; on others they lose his track entirely. They find the burned-out houses of his other victims, and once Ringo comes close enough to get shot at. Eventually the bandit tries to throw them off by giving them Ab Snopes, "tied hand and foot and hitched to a sapling," and maintaining all the while that none of it has been his fault. Ringo uses three pairs of knotted suspenders to give him the kind of beating a master would a slave; anyone reading will appreciate the irony, and no one will question its justice. Then one afternoon as they ride along a tree-shrouded lane, Bayard's mule shies at a "thing hanging over the middle of the road from a limb." It takes him a second to realize what it is, to see the bare toes of the black man lynched in the path before him, with a note pinned to his body to warn them off the chase. Dusk falls, the man's head tilts to one side "like he was thinking about something quiet," and this casual killing, this moment of understated horror, reads as something out of the movies. Only not the movies of Faulkner's own period—it seems, rather, to anticipate the spaghetti Westerns, the parched amoral wasteland, of Sergio Leone.

Then it is the spring of 1865, the soldiers are coming home, and Grumby's band wants to pull out for Texas. Yet the man himself has become such a liability that his remaining "Independents" decide to let the boys have him. They hand the murderer over at a meeting along a river bottom and keep their pistols on him as they ride off, but Grumby is still armed when he turns toward the boys and Bayard sees "two bright orange splashes" of gunfire against the gray of the man's coat. One of Faulkner's underappreciated gifts is his ability to describe physical action, an ability that depends on both his precise visual imagination and the quickened cadence of his sentences. The pistols flame, and then Bayard feels Grumby upon him, smelling of horse sweat; feels his arm almost pulled from its socket. Release comes when Ringo jumps on the outlaw's back and gets bucked off as if he were riding a steer. The man begins to run—but now Bayard's arm can move, his own gun is out, and "I could see Grumby's back . . . and the pistol both at the same time and the pistol was level and steady as a rock."

FAULKNER SET HIS MOST suggestive accounts of the war's end hundreds of miles away from Yoknapatawpha itself. "Mountain Victory" (1932), one of his finest short stories, takes place in the hills of eastern Tennessee and describes the attempt of a Confederate major named Saucier Weddel to return to his Mississippi home. His right sleeve is empty, and his horse lacks a saddle, but the horse is a thoroughbred, and so is he; his face may be gaunt but its expression seems arrogant still. Weddel's body servant, Jubal, boasts to the poor whites with whom they spend a night that they come from a place named "Countymaison," a plantation the size of a county. The major himself calls it "Contalmaison" and explains his own dark skin by saying that his father is of mixed French and Choctaw ancestry, a chief who holds a remnant of the tribe's land as his own. And such a man did in fact exist. His name was Greenwood LeFlore, and he owned four hundred slaves on a great demesne in the middle of the state.

The major has, however, picked exactly the wrong house at which to stop. Every state in the Confederacy had areas of resistance to Richmond's central authority, usually populated by small farmers who owned little besides their land and saw the conflict as a slaveholders' war, fought to preserve an institution from which they got no benefit whatever. In Mississippi the best-known was the "Free State" of Jones County, a swampy district in the forested lowlands of the state's southeast. Most such places, however, were in the upland hills, and among them the peaks and hollows of eastern Tennessee were an extreme case. Unionist sentiment ran so high in that part of Appalachia that early in the war the region had talked of seceding from secession, as had the counties that became West Virginia; its young men were as apt to join the Federal forces as they were the Confederacy's.

To an outsider the loyalties of any individual household remain unreadable, and Faulkner's Weddel has no idea that he's chosen a Unionist farm as his shelter for the night. Indeed the family's oldest son, Vatch, has served with the Yankee army, and that night, after several glasses of colorless, explosive whiskey, he takes a vicious pleasure in describing his battlefield murder of a wounded Southern officer who had asked him for water. He hates Weddel's uniform, and he also hates the mixed blood that makes him see the major as a "nigra." And Weddel is in turn appalled by this family's hilltop isolation, its suspicion of all outsiders, and quickly realizes that he shouldn't risk a night in this treacherous land. Jubal is soon too drunk to sit a horse, however, and Weddel won't leave him behind, not with people who detest and fear black folk with a violence he has never seen in the Deep South itself. It's dawn before they ride off, and he knows that Vatch will be waiting in the woods to send a bullet after him. Yet whose victory is it? Vatch will indeed kill his enemy, but Weddel has stayed true to an idealized code of behavior: the officer has sacrificed himself for his men, the master has protected his servant. He rides through the woods, wondering when the farm boy will shoot, and realizes to his surprise that he has not yet "lost the privilege of being afraid." He wants to live, after four years of battle he can begin to see a future—and in consequence he dies happy.

Weddel's voice in this story carries a sardonic grandiloquence, and four years later Faulkner gave that voice to Charles Bon in *Absalom, Absalom!*, setting his words in italics. In the winter of 1865 Bon sits in camp over an elegant sheet of French notepaper, salvaged from a ruined plantation house in the Carolinas, and writes a letter to Judith Sutpen in Mississippi, using the best Yankee stove polish for ink. He writes without "date or salutation or signature" to tell her that "*We have waited long enough*," and adds that he won't insult her by saying that "*I have waited long enough*." They have each waited, hoping perhaps that death would find one of them or maybe catch up with Thomas Sutpen himself; waited for anything that might change the terms of their canceled engagement. As he dips his pen Bon hears the sounds of battle in the distance, but to mention them seems "*redundancy. . . . Because sometimes I think it has never stopped.*" They still live in the blast and echo of what began four years ago, by which he does not mean the war alone. His own voice, he admits, might seem to come from the grave, and certainly he writes from a world in which thinking or remembering or hoping appears irrelevant. Nevertheless "*I now believe that you and I are, strangely enough, included among those who are doomed to live.*"

The regiment in which Bon serves along with Judith's brother Henry belongs to what Faulkner calls the Army of the West, one whose main business in the war's last year has been "*to walk backward slow and stubborn and to endure musketry and shelling.*" Their military situation is hopeless, and Faulkner expects that his readers will know why without his needing to define it: an expectation that at this historical distance seems misplaced. Under the leadership of Joseph Johnston, that army had in the summer of 1864 fallen back before Sherman as he moved south from Chattanooga to Atlanta, fighting when they had to and delaying the Union forces whenever they could, in what Shelby Foote called a "red clay minuet." Stall the inevitable for long enough and maybe it isn't inevitable at all: if the Union casualties continue to climb, if Grant stays stuck at Petersburg and Sherman before Atlanta, then the North might get so impatient that it will vote Lincoln out of office, and the Confederacy can then negotiate with his successor. That's how the Southern thinking went, anyway, but thinking—hoping—isn't doing. Sherman took Atlanta at the start of September, and Lincoln's reelection was assured. The Yankee general then rested his men for two months, and when he left the city in November he also left it in ashes, marching his army toward Savannah and the sea, moving on a front some fifty miles wide and moving, moreover, without any lines of supply. He took only a few weeks' worth of rations; once those were exhausted, his men had to live off the land.

Savannah surrendered without a fight, and in the New Year Sherman's army went north into the Carolinas. By now all the Confederacy could do was to slow him down, hoping to delay a meeting with Grant around Richmond. So in *Absalom, Absalom!* the Rebel army in which Charles Bon is a junior officer lies to the north of the Union forces, its ragged men "*curiously*" turned to the south, where they can see the "*flicker and gleam of the Federal bivouac fires myriad and faint and encircling half the horizon.*" Each side puts out pickets, and their lines are so close that the two armies sometimes talk to one another, their voices "*not loud yet carrying*" through the night:

—*Hey Reb.*
—*Yah.*
—*Where you fellers going?*
—*Richmond.*
—*So are we. Why not wait for us?*
—*We air.*

Are and *air*. Each army wants the same thing, albeit in its own way; they might as well be traveling together, and this terse layered exchange tells us everything we need to know about their situation at the war's end. The Yankees move north and Joseph Johnston's Rebels try to stop them, knowing they will fail, but knowing too that if they can link up with Lee they will, as Bon thinks, *"at least have the privilege of surrender."*

But the great drama of Sherman's campaigns in 1864–65 doesn't lie in the battles themselves. It rests instead in the *"gutted mansion"* in which Bon found his notepaper; in the way the Union brought the war to the South's civilians. Georgia had an easy time in the conflict's first years. It saw little fighting, and though it suffered from the Union blockade, its land remained productive and food plentiful. That would change. Many older Americans got their first image of the siege of Atlanta from *Gone with the Wind*, either from Margaret Mitchell's novel itself or the 1939 film. I did myself, around 1970. The old single-screen theater in my hometown brought the movie in for a few days each fall, and I remember sitting through it on a middle-school afternoon, remember the famous long take that follows Scarlett into the blood-soaked open-air hospital at the city's rail depot, the camera slowly pulling back to rest on a breeze-blown Confederate flag; a flag we are meant to see with sympathy. It has been many years since I could either watch that film or read the novel with anything approaching pleasure. Neither is separable from the racial politics of the world in which Mitchell grew up and in which she always believed. Neither has any distance at all on either the Confederacy itself or the busy work of memory called the Lost Cause; the occasional praise Mitchell receives today for having created a "strong" female protagonist is entirely misguided. We can find a far richer account of this moment in the family letters collected in *The Children of Pride*.

Charles Jones Sr. had died in 1863 and left his wife alone on the family's plantations along the Georgia coast; their two sons were in the army and their one daughter, Mary, had moved with her minister husband, Robert Mallard, to an Atlanta parsonage. The letters Mary sent her mother in the spring and summer of 1864 show us a world that looks startled to find itself coming apart. In March she receives her first refugees, a family from Alabama with a story of a Union officer who claimed, as he killed their cattle and burned their clothes, that he was simply following orders. The price of food climbs, and crime with it, with flour barrels now liable to break-ins. Butter goes to ten dollars a pound, and her mother offers to send up a cow; the railroads still accept such private commissions. Even at the start of May, Mary's letters remain full of domestic detail, an aunt's rheumatism and the making of diapers; no one yet "seems to apprehend any danger for this place." Then the fighting starts. By May 15 the Confederates have retreated from defensive positions at both Dalton and Resaca, off to the city's northwest; and in June Mary confesses that it "would be a great relief to us could we be assured" that the Rebel army did not mean to fall back once more.

That too is the real war, the war of those who wait and wonder what's to come. What makes these letters so vivid and suspensefully alive is that the writer doesn't know what we do, doesn't know how either the war or her own life will turn out. Mary Mallard writes aquiver, in hope and fear, her mind a switching yard of contingencies, and her words—unlike Mitchell's or indeed Faulkner's—remain untouched by teleology. Fiction may show us things about the war's deep structure that no documents of the period can, its causes and consequences, its ironies too. But all novels are shaped by a sense of their own endings. Their plots point toward some conclusion, and to catch the war's unfolding action we need to read what was written at and for the moment.

One of Mary's aunts arrives from Marietta, twenty miles to the north; she had been told that the Yankees would never get so far right up to the moment when they did. Now Mary begins to worry, and the historical situation becomes inseparable from the cares of daily life. She hopes for victory, but if a siege looks likely she plans to take her "servants" back to the coast, keeping that property at least out of the Union's hands. Still, she anticipates "heavy losses in furniture and everything else," and weighs the cost of moving her household goods against their possible destruction. Atlanta's mayor calls for a day of fasting and prayer, and yet the mails continue to run; at the start of July Mary even thinks of inviting her mother for a visit, writing that "we do not feel there is any immediate danger." But just a few weeks later the city's hospitals receive an order to evacuate, and the Mallards know they must leave.

They escape the siege. That doesn't mean they've escaped the war, and in December Mary Mallard would have a far more direct encounter with the Union army. Her husband hoped that once Atlanta fell he might be allowed to go back to his church, but in the end there was no church to go to—no congregation anyway, though the building itself escaped destruction. Early in September Sherman ordered the expulsion of the city's entire civilian population, and the letter in which he explained his decision stands in its bitterness among the greatest of American sermons, a jeremiad at once clear-eyed and self-serving. "War is cruelty," he wrote to Atlanta's mayor, "and you cannot refine it: and those who brought war into our Country deserve all the curses and maledictions a people can pour out." Any Confederates who now "deprecate its horrors" should have thought a bit harder before they went into rebellion, and the general's sentences seem all sulphur, as though he both hates and glories in what he believes he must do. "I want peace," Sherman told the mayor, "and believe it can now only be reached through union and war, and I will ever conduct war partly with a view to perfect and early success." By that he meant fire: the flames that consume morale along with cities and supplies. Let the people at home feel the struggle's hard hand—let Georgia howl—and their men will abandon the field.

Sherman destroyed Atlanta's railroads and factories before leaving the city, and as he began his march through the middle of the state he ordered his men to "forage liberally on the country," while forbidding them to enter private houses. But he seldom punished those who exceeded their orders, and the soldiers Mary Mallard encountered that December showed no intention of obeying them at all. She had moved from Atlanta to her mother's plantation thirty miles to the south of Savannah, and at twenty-nine was in her ninth month of pregnancy. In their journals both mother and daughter described the almost daily home invasions of one Union detachment after another. They began on December 15, when a "Kentucky Irishman" searched the house for arms, while also demanding whiskey and jewelry. The next day another band raided the storerooms, "yelling, cursing, quarreling," rifling the sideboard and breaking the crockery. One group loaded the family's carriage with chickens and drove off, and Mrs. Jones caught a man at the sugar in the smokehouse; he seemed "a little ashamed . . . but did not return" it. Others robbed the Jones's slaves, taking potatoes or hams from their cabins, blankets and even spoons. And they may have done more besides. Mary writes with a Victorian discretion, and so we have to imagine the actions of the Yankee soldiers whose behavior was "so outrageous . . . that the Negro men were obliged to stay at their houses for the protection of their wives."

On December 20 another Northerner took the chain from the well and told her that she had no right even to water. The house itself was spared, and Mrs. Jones certainly overstates their troubles in asking, after a life of cushioned plenty, if the "annals . . . of warfare afford any" comparable record of brutality; the worst is not, so long as we can speak it. Still, Mary felt harrowed by the very protraction of the experience. She could never tell when a fresh band of Sherman's "bummers" might appear, and on January 4 she went into labor. Her mother sent one of their slaves riding off for the doctor, having managed to hide a pony, already saddled, "for this very purpose." The birth was a difficult one. Mrs. Jones's account suggests that the baby needed to be turned, and all the while the laboring woman could hear the "wild halloos" of the marauding Yankees beneath her window, their curses sounding in her ears as she lay "amid her agony of body." At one point they even pushed their way inside, simply to show that they could. War cannot be refined. Sherman's policy was a necessary one, and the behavior of Lee's troops in Pennsylvania was no better, with every black man they encountered seized and sent south into slavery. Moments like this nevertheless became part of the white South's memory, in a way that explains why Sherman's name remained anathema into Faulkner's day and after: a memory that underlies the intransigence with which families like Mary Mallard's clung to the memory of their lost cause.

Mrs. Jones told the doctor that if he had to make a choice in this dangerous birth, he must save the mother and not the child. Both Mary and her newborn daughter lived, however, and the Union's next visit, when three horsemen asked about the yellow hospital flag on the porch, was the last. Then Sherman swung north, a hammer striking toward the anvil of Grant around Richmond. The end came before the two could meet, though, and Sherman's troops were still in North Carolina when on April 2, 1865, the Army of the Potomac forced Lee from the Petersburg trenches. Union troops entered the Confederate capital the next day, and the war in Virginia became a race to the west. Lee still cherished delusions of victory. He thought that if his men could outsprint the Yankees they might turn south and join up with Joseph Johnston's forces; together, he dreamed, they could beat the Federal armies one at a time. But Grant blocked their way, and soon a second Union army sat across the roads to the west and the north as well. The Confederates were now encircled. They had taken heavy casualties, they had gone without food for days, and their numbers had melted as they marched, with many soldiers dropping from the ranks and heading home. On April 8, at a tiny rail depot called Appomattox Station, a cavalry division led by George Armstrong Custer captured the waiting rations that the Confederates had counted on to sustain them, and the next morning Lee had to face the truth at last.

Two days before, on the seventh, Grant had invited Lee's capitulation, hoping to prevent any further "effusion" of blood. But the corps commander James Longstreet had said "not yet," and Lee agreed with him; the South still counted on receiving its provisions, and the Union circle was not quite closed. Even on the morning of the ninth—Palm Sunday—not everyone in the Rebel army was ready to give up. The young artillery chief Edward Porter Alexander told Lee that his men were "proud of your name & record & the record of this army. We want to leave it to our children," and begged that the army be allowed to disperse rather than suffer the ignominy of surrender. Most would simply go home, he said, but others might continue the fight as guerrillas. Lee's reply made Alexander feel ashamed of himself. Any soldiers who did so "would have no rations and they would be under no discipline. . . . They would have to plunder & rob to procure subsistence. The country would be full of lawless bands": hundreds of real-life versions of what Faulkner called Grumby's Independents. The Union, Lee added, would have no choice but to send its cavalry after them, a counterinsurgency that would ravage the land for years to come. Young men might view it differently, he knew, but for him the only dignity lay in seeing General Grant and taking "the consequences of my actions."

The meeting that day between Grant and Lee in the little village of Appomattox Court House is one of the best-known moments in all of American history; so well-known that in *A Stillness at Appomattox* Bruce Catton doesn't even describe it. Rather than compete with the account in Grant's memoirs, he ends his own great book at the moment when the Union commander, a "brown-bearded little man in a mud-spattered uniform," got word that his opponent was waiting for him. Lee had changed into a new dress uniform, sash and epaulets and all. Grant's baggage was lost on the road; he wore his customary private's shirt and had nothing clean for a moment he knew would become myth. The difference in their costume has been taken to mark the difference between the two men and that between the war's two sides as well. Lee left no memoirs, and we don't know what he thought. Grant wrote that he himself was rather surprisingly "depressed," and his words at this sudden release of tension recall his account of the surrender at Vicksburg. "I felt like anything rather than rejoicing at the downfall of a foe who had fought so long and so valiantly, and suffered so much for a cause, though that cause was, I believe, one of the worst for which a people ever fought."

Grant's terms were in essence as follows: all rifles and artillery were to be surrendered, and the Confederates would each sign a parole stating that they would not take up arms against the Federal government. They could then return home, "not to be disturbed by United States authority" so long as they observed the law. No prison camps; no arrests. Officers kept their sidearms, and anyone "who claimed to own a horse or mule" could take the animal home to help with the crops. All this was both generous and kind, and I always read this part of Grant's memoirs with moist eyes. But that charity worked, as the historian Elizabeth Varon has argued, to obscure a full awareness of what was and wasn't surrendered. The Army of Northern Virginia yielded as the army of one country might to that of another, with its men treated, in Varon's words, "as defeated enemies rather than criminals." Its leaders were not held as traitors, and most Rebels were soon voting in American elections once more, unpunished, as if in legal terms their actions had no consequences. Perhaps it couldn't have been otherwise. "The massive scale of the rebellion vitiated the case for retribution"—where to start, where to stop?—and hanging Bobby Lee might well have sent his men back into the field once more.

But if Lee, or Davis, or Forrest were *not* to be hanged, then who among the South's leaders could be? Lee's apparently stoic posture in defeat contributed over the years to the legend that almost immediately grew up around him, that of an always-dignified and disinterested man, who claimed to hate slavery and acted on the basis of principle alone. That legend survives in the schools that still bear his name, and in the Virginia holiday that marks his birth, but it has been chipped and battered in recent decades by our growing awareness of just how firmly he believed in slavery as an institution and how fully he supported its survival. He was fifty-eight when the war ended and suffering from angina; he had his eye on history itself and though his sense of resignation was real he also knew that it would play well. So did his decision to refuse the business opportunities he was offered after the war, some of them from the North. Instead he became president of Washington College, a tiny struggling place in the Shenandoah Valley. When he died in 1870 its enrollment had grown from fifty to four hundred, and it is now known as Washington and Lee University.

Lee's example cast a glow. Or a shadow. His aides and generals wrote memoirs that sought to protect him from any criticism, and in their pages he appeared to bring the whole Confederacy within the penumbra of his rectitude. He became the South, and that hagiographic process continued into Faulkner's day with the work of the Pulitzer Prize–winning biographer, Douglas Southall Freeman. But there were other things that fed the myth of the Lost Cause, and one of them, paradoxically, was the very generosity of the conditions Grant laid down for surrender. For the South took those terms, as Varon argues, to mean that the war had been a fight between two honorable opponents, a historical fiction that conduced to the advantage of Confederate memory. The struggle may have ended in reconciliation, but the South had been a separate nation indeed. Lee himself had said as much in his farewell to his troops, speaking of their "constancy and devotion to [their] country," the sacrifice that endeared them to their fellows. And he also told them that "after four years of arduous service, marked by unsurpassed courage and fortitude, the Army of Northern Virginia has been compelled to yield." He didn't say that they had lost, that they were conquered or defeated. They hadn't even surrendered. Instead, he used a more gracious and reassuring word, one that suggests an element of choice. They had yielded merely, compelled to do so by the North's "overwhelming numbers and resources."

As if to say: it wasn't a fair fight. Maybe Lee needed to offer that balm to his beaten and exhausted men, but his words also suggested that in a struggle between equal powers the South would have triumphed, and the Confederacy's apologists have played with that possibility ever since. Man for man, the South was better, they argued, and the North didn't win in the field. It won instead in the factories, it won with the torch, and with its boatloads of immigrant recruits. It won by making the trains run on time, by starving civilians and letting its own men be butchered. Of course, no modern army wins simply by slugging it out face-to-face. Victory depends, at least in part, on shredding an enemy's infrastructure and destroying its ability to make war in the first place. Grant understood that, and yet it's little wonder that in an 1878 interview he took pains to borrow Lee's own word, and insisted that "we never overwhelmed the south . . . what we won . . . we won by hard fighting." The Confederacy had yielded. But it remained, in Faulkner's terms, unvanquished.

That March Joe Johnston's army in North Carolina got some reinforcements. Or so the novelist says—a few scant regiments that Lee sent down from Virginia, Thomas Sutpen's among them. Charles Bon saw him in camp but Sutpen gave no sign of recognizing the man who wanted to marry his daughter, the man for whom his own son had abjured his family and his birthright. Then one night an *"orderly came along the bivouac line"* and told Henry Sutpen that their regiment's commander wanted him. But when the young man steps inside the colonel's tent he finds that it isn't his own colonel he's going to see. He needs a minute to recognize the *"jutting nose [and] shaggy droop of iron-riddled hair,"* but then he is folded in his father's embrace, the body's reflex pulling them together. Afterward they face each other across a candle, each dressed in "leaf-faded gray," and the older man begins to speak. Only this time he tells Henry what he had not deigned to tell

him before. He tells him just why they cannot allow Charles Bon to marry
Judith Sutpen.

When Henry leaves the tent he's already thinking of what he must do, of
what Bon's actions might force him to do, as if the leveled pistol were already
in his hand. He knows that his friend has sent that letter in stove-polish ink;
knows that Judith expects his arrival and their marriage. And when the two
men meet Bon realizes what has happened—and recognizes what he and
Henry will each now do. Their war is over, one war anyway, and a different,
quieter struggle begins or maybe resumes. It would be easy enough for Bon to
slip off, but instead the two saddle up, as they had done that long-ago Christmas in Yoknapatawpha, and ride away together. Side by side they go, their
horses matching steps and neither of them ever either falling behind or getting ahead, riding for seven hundred miles and more over the ruined land,
"dodging Yankee patrols all the way back to Mississippi" and on up to the
gates of Sutpen's Hundred.

PART THREE

Dark House

TEN

The Shooting at the Gates

. . . *a nd on up to the gates of Sutpen's Hundred*, where with one shot Henry will kill his best friend along with his sister Judith's future and his own. But why? Nobody in Jefferson really knows, though they have talked about it for almost half a century. Quentin Compson will hear Rosa Coldfield's version of the story, when he is summoned to her house in September 1909, at the start of *Absalom, Absalom!* He will hear his father's version too and then offer his own in his Harvard dormitory room that January, trying to "tell about the South" as he talks to his Canadian roommate, Shreve McCannon. He too will ride through those gates, and he will bring us with him, reader and character going at midnight to Thomas Sutpen's darkened mansion and working together to uncover the past. Only not yet. I need to take us through another gate first: to step back for a moment into the chronicle of Faulkner's own life and career, and define just where he was when he began his most demanding and majestic novel.

The house he called Rowan Oak sits on Old Taylor Road, fifteen minutes' walk from Oxford's square. Its entrance is unmarked, a winding, unpaved drive cutting into the woods and then past a gate of its own; the structure itself lies far back through the trees, invisible from the road. The drive swells a bit to allow for parking, but the trees make it seem cool even in summer, and on my own visits I've always walked, coming slowly down the side streets from the center of town, waving to each passing vehicle as the local custom dictates, and then stopping for a moment when the drive reaches a brick walkway. Old brick, filmed with moss, and the path itself running straight between two rows of cedars to the house at its end: a building that looks more imposing than it actually is, painted white and with its outsized Greek Revival portico framed by the trees themselves. It was built in 1848 and survived the town's burning, but when Faulkner himself bought it in 1930 its gardens had been turned into cornfields and the house itself was near ruin. Its timbers and roof had rotted, and it was without indoor plumbing, not even a tap; at first he and his wife, Estelle, had to carry their water in buckets from the well.

Faulkner got the place from an older couple named Will and Sallie Bryant; they had inherited it, never lived there, and gave him the easiest of terms. He paid $6,000 for the building along with four acres: no money down, a mortgage of $75 a month, and the option to buy more land when he could. The novelist was a good carpenter. He did much of the necessary restoration himself, and over the years he and Estelle turned a near-wreck into a comfortable home. Comfortable—but not grand. No visitor remembers much about its architecture, that portico aside; not as they might the brick Gothic fantasy of Mark Twain's house in Hartford or the Frenchified elegance of The Mount, Edith Wharton's place in the Berkshires. What sticks with me instead is Faulkner's small wooden desk, with his portable Underwood typewriter sitting in an open case, and then his study, on whose walls he blocked out his 1954 novel, *A Fable*. Its plot was giving him trouble, and he took a pen to the plaster, wrapping a summary of the book's day-by-day events around two sides of the room.

He had finished five novels by the time he moved in but they had earned almost nothing, and what made him feel he could afford a house at all was the fact that he had begun to place his short stories in national magazines. The $200 that *Scribner's* paid for "Dry September" (1931) matched his advance for *The Sound and the Fury* itself. Rowan Oak nevertheless misrepresented his position. However broken down, its antebellum origins and columned portico suggested that he was a more respectable and established figure than he actually was: established both as a writer and within the local community. "I don't read Billy's books much," his Uncle John once said, and added with something like contempt that "I guess he makes money at it—writing those dirty books for Yankees." John Falkner was a tough, almost viperish lawyer, and a lot of people in Mississippi agreed with him. As a young woman in the

1930s, the novelist Elizabeth Spencer heard of Faulkner "as someone to be ashamed of," and for many years the consensus held that he was indeed only after the Northern dollar. That reputation goes back to the early days of Yoknapatawpha, and there was just enough truth in it to stick.

Estelle's divorce from Cornell Franklin became final in the spring of 1929, but Faulkner was broke and though *The Sound and the Fury* was in press he knew he could not count on its sales. So he had quickly drafted the most sensationally lurid story he could imagine, hoping that a quick hit would give them enough to get married on. *Sanctuary* (1931) told of bootlegging, brothels, lynching, and rape; it had a courtroom revelation that still makes one gasp, and ends with a grimly comic hanging. Faulkner's publisher, Harrison Smith, thought that the novel would land them both in jail, but he released it after some revision, and the book did indeed find readers. Its sales topped seven thousand copies in the first two months, more than three times those of *The Sound and the Fury*, and it reappeared almost immediately in the Modern Library. And there was a movie deal too, which only added to the local belief that the novelist worked for export. Nor did his other work do anything to ease the town's discomfort. *The Sound and the Fury* dealt with madness and incest; *Light in August* (1932) with racial passing. In this Faulkner stands as an unusual instance of a situation familiar to many writers from minority groups: the belief, among those on the cultural periphery, that metropolitan success inevitably comes at the cost of spilling secrets, of telling things about one's own people that are best held close, locked within the community itself. Richard Wright and Ralph Ellison were each charged with that betrayal, and so was Philip Roth; V. S. Naipaul made himself hated by refusing to present his English audience with positive images of Trinidadian life. Faulkner belonged to a regionally dominant group that nevertheless saw itself as marginalized within the national culture as a whole, and insofar as his publishers were all in New York he did of course write for Yankees. But even they had a hard time with what he gave them to read.

Not that there was much money, not until the Nobel Prize; John Falkner was wrong about that. Or rather there wasn't much money from the books— their earnings came instead in the form of prestige, a prestige that Faulkner capitalized upon in two ways. One of them was indeed through the sale of short fiction. In 1930 the *Saturday Evening Post* paid $750 for "Red Leaves," the first of his tales about Yoknapatawpha's Indians, and a few years later he asked $1,500 for "Ambuscade," the opening story in what became *The Unvanquished* (1938), while settling in the end for $1,000. The *Post* sat at the top of the scale, however, and Faulkner usually had to take less; in 1940 he hoped that *Harper's* would give him $400 for "Pantaloon in Black." His other source of income was Hollywood. Some of it came through the sale of film rights; he cleared $19,000 on *The Unvanquished*, though no movie was ever made, and used it to buy a farm outside of Oxford. More often, though, he found work as a screenwriter, preferring a studio paycheck to the occasional pieces on which other writers depended and for which he was temperamentally unsuited. Faulkner would not, however, have been invited to California without the reputation his books had earned, and so his finances rested upon a paradox. He made money *because* he was a novelist, not *as* a novelist.

Faulkner first went to Hollywood in 1932, on contract to MGM at $500 a week. He planned to stay for just six weeks, but he quickly discovered an ability to improvise dialogue on set that made him an efficient doctor for other people's scripts. Very little of what he wrote made it to the screen, but he had five months of work, and that set a pattern he would often repeat in the next twenty years, taking a short contract and then remaining for much longer than he'd planned. He got on especially well with Howard Hawks and in the 1940s received screenwriting credit on two of the director's best movies, *To Have and Have Not* and *The Big Sleep*, each of them starring Humphrey Bogart and Lauren Bacall. But he always claimed that he went west for the money and the money alone. One question, then, is why he wanted it, or needed it. For in 1930 Mississippi's annual per capita income was just $173, and by the standards of his cash-poor, Depression-era home state Faulkner's earnings from writing alone would seem much more than enough.

Some of that need grew from simple extravagance. Estelle's first husband had been a notably successful lawyer. She had always had money, and Faulkner himself had expensive tastes, spending freely whenever he could and failing to cut back when he couldn't. He lived well on his trips to see his publishers in New York, bought more land, and returned to his World War I dreams by taking flying lessons and even buying a plane of his own. But much of his spending can be explained by a sense of obligation: obligations that numbered not only his own immediate family, Estelle's two children from her first marriage included, but also his widowed mother, with a household of her own, and other relatives too. By 1935 those pressures were especially acute, and at the end of the year Hawks reeled him back to Hollywood with the promise of $1,000 a week. He would stay on the payroll until the following December.

Faulkner's work during his first weeks in Hollywood wasn't limited to screenwriting, however, and in the mornings before he reported to the studio he sat down to the almost-finished manuscript he had brought along from home. The materials out of which he built *Absalom, Absalom!* had been with him a long time, incidents and characters and even modes of narration that had freckled the pages of his unpublished stories since the start of the decade. He already had Thomas Sutpen's name and character, and his children too; he had the New Orleans suitor, Charles Bon. But none of it cohered until he wrote a story about a poor white named Wash Jones and the Confederate officer he worships, a story filled with the fading echo of galloping hooves and men caught in their own "impotent and furious undefeat." Sutpen's family situation is radically simplified in "Wash" (1934) but he has the same cold arrogance as the character in the novel Faulkner almost immediately began to write, and he meets the same fate. Today the tale seems a mere sketch for *Absalom, Absalom!* itself, and yet the piece did its work. Faulkner sold it to *Harper's* and it paid a few bills. But it also spilled his ideas loose, jarred his material into form. It helped him find a novel for the people who waited in his mind.

He wanted to call it *Dark House*—a title he had already used for the early drafts of *Light in August* and couldn't quite let go. And indeed it would work for either book, each set around a crumbling mansion, a place of both psychic and physical violence: houses that carry the past. He announced the project in a February 1934 letter to Harrison Smith, telling him that the book's central "anecdote which occurred during and right after the civil war" would be narrated almost fifty years later by *The Sound and the Fury*'s Quentin Compson. Of course Quentin had killed himself in that novel, at the end of his freshman year at Harvard, drowning himself in anguish at his inability to stop time, to go back to the days before he knew of his sister Caddy's promiscuity. The new book would be set a few months earlier, but in returning to the character Faulkner would seem to make him speak from beyond the grave. And to speak, moreover, of a situation that recalls his own, that of a brother who wants to place a curb or prohibition on his sister's sexuality.

The novelist planned to use two time frames, one in the boy's present and the other set back in the shadowy undimmed past, and though it was a historical novel he expected Quentin's own "bitterness which he has projected on the South" to hold any costume drama at bay. He wanted, that is, "to keep the hoop skirts and plug hats out"; even as two states over in Georgia Margaret Mitchell was trying to put in just as many as she could. Faulkner thought he might finish the book in the fall of 1934, but as always he needed money; or perhaps that was just a way of stalling, of buying the time that the novel itself needed. For he had no sooner told Smith his plans than he began to write the stories that became *The Unvanquished*; with the Civil War already on his mind he thought he could produce them quickly, and hoped the *Post* might pay as much as $10,000 for a series of six. As for *Absalom, Absalom!*, he told Smith in August of that year that he already had "a mass of stuff," but it hadn't yet ripened, even leaving aside his desire to "make a nickel every so often." There would be more stories before it was done, and even another novel, a book about boozy New Orleans stunt pilots named *Pylon* (1935). But in January 1936 Faulkner called a studio friend into his office at Warner Bros., handed him a manuscript, and told him that he thought it was "the best novel yet written by an American." Judgments will differ, but for me *Absalom, Absalom!* is matched only by *Moby-Dick* and *The Golden Bowl*: books whose difficulties all push the outer limits of what their moment could say, and that push our own limits still.

———•—•———

TELL ABOUT THE SOUTH. That's what Quentin Compson hears over and over again as a Harvard freshman in the fall of 1909, the Yankee accents asking him what it's like down there, as if puzzled that the South exists at all. It was a common enough question for those who found themselves up north in the century's first decades, maybe one that Faulkner himself had heard in the early 1920s when he worked in Elizabeth Prall's Manhattan bookshop. The answer Quentin gives will take the form of a story, one the boy has been telling in pieces to his roommate Shreve since the very start of the school year. The tale he finishes at last on a wintry iron night is not, however, directed at the North alone. It serves instead to tell the white South about itself, and to tell Quentin about the world that has made him: a story about the things his people have always known but would rather not speak of and that they cannot for that very reason ever stop thinking about. And it is in a way a ghost story, one from a vanished world that yet refuses to stay quiet, "the deep South dead since 1865," yet still peopled with outraged insistent voices that make the living themselves into nothing more than shadows.

My earlier chapters have already given us the central spine of *Absalom, Absalom!*'s narrative: how in 1833 Thomas Sutpen first appeared in Jefferson, a deadly looking stranger who without any apparent resources secured the deed to one hundred square miles of Yoknapatawpha County's best land. He built a plantation, working it with French-speaking slaves smuggled in from the Caribbean; got married, had children, grew rich. At Christmas in 1859 his son Henry brought home a college friend named Charles Bon, of New Orleans, and soon the news spread that Bon was engaged to Sutpen's daughter Judith. The next year Sutpen forbade the marriage, and Henry abjured both father and fortune and went off with his friend. Then the war came, and four years later, at the end of the fighting, the two young men rode back to Sutpen's Hundred together. There Judith waited with a wedding dress—and there Henry shot Bon dead, and vanished.

But *Absalom, Absalom!* offers us something more than Sutpen's story, and to understand it we need to wrestle with its form, with the novel's sense of how we try and largely fail to make sense of the past. That's the difficulty Quentin faces—and the difficulty that this extraordinarily disorienting novel presents to its readers. Faulkner begins with a moment from which I quoted in my first chapter. Quentin sits on a "weary dead September afternoon" with Miss Rosa Coldfield, listening to a story that grammar itself cannot contain, to her tale of the way Sutpen destroyed her family: first by marrying her older sister Ellen, and then, after Ellen had died and the war was over, by offering to marry her as well. She speaks in the hopes that Quentin might someday tell that story to others, and as he listens her voice seems to vanish into the very telling itself. So he doesn't hear but rather watches as Sutpen emerges from a "thunderclap . . . faint sulphur-reek still in hair clothes and beard," followed by his band of slaves and captive French architect, and begins like Milton's Satan to tear a world from "soundless Nothing." Yet the details emerge almost parenthetically, allusions or asides in the torrent of Miss Rosa's emotion. That's how we first hear, in the novel's opening pages, of "the son who widowed the daughter who had not yet been a bride," but nothing is explained to us because nothing needs yet to be explained to Quentin himself. These are stories he already half-knows, about people he's heard of his whole life.

Rosa Coldfield speaks; and then the novel's second chapter gives us the same tale again, only now in a distanced third person, a chronicle of what Jefferson made of Sutpen, who at first owned little more than his horse and pistols. But already this most recursive of novels has offered a moment of prolepsis. It anticipates what it comes to remember by telling us that five months later Quentin's father will send a letter up to snowbound Cambridge and prompt the boy's own version of the story Miss Rosa began. We will, however, be fifty pages in before Faulkner comes back to that unmarried widow, fifty pages before we hear the name of Charles Bon, and by then the narrative voice will have switched once more.

The old woman asks Quentin to drive her out that night to the empty husk of Sutpen's great house, twelve miles from town and a place she hasn't seen for more than forty years. So we sit with him on the veranda of his family's home as he waits for dark, listening as his father goes over the whole history once more. Mr. Compson first mentions Bon as a supporting player in Rosa Coldfield's life, and on our initial reading we will have almost no idea of whom that new name belongs to. That puzzlement is the book in miniature—that sense of bewildered confusion suggests what the experience of reading *Absalom, Absalom!* is like. Understanding does come. Sometimes it takes just a few sentences, more often a few pages or even chapters, and when it does that understanding will carry a sense of the uncanny. *I knew that*, we say to ourselves; *at least I think I did, I guess I've heard something about it anyway.* We read in half-knowledge, as if nothing has been told to us for the first time, and yet nothing ever in its entirety, and it seems impossible to remember just where and when we've come upon any particular fact about these people. But *fact* is the wrong word—any particular judgment or description rather, any particular sentence.

There will be other voices before we are finished, voice embedded within voice. We need to know the whole of *Absalom, Absalom!* before we can know any one of its parts, need to read it a second or fourth or seventh time, and yet that initial floundering remains an essential part of its meaning. Each of its first four chapters is longer than its predecessors—twenty pages in the Library of America edition, then twenty-three, twenty-five, thirty-seven. And each covers much the same ground, for *"maybe happen is never once,"* as Quentin later thinks, *"but like ripples maybe on water after the pebble sinks, the ripples moving on, spreading . . ."* Events might not repeat themselves but their telling certainly does, and each time the circle of implications grows larger, deeper, spreading and penetrating at once, soaking down within as our own understanding grows, becoming ever more involved as the novel's different speakers sift its world of motives. Faulkner's fifth chapter is almost entirely in Miss Rosa's voice and printed in italics, a furious thirty-three-page amplification of what she's told Quentin in the book's opening moments. Then the pieces grow bigger once more—thirty-six pages, sixty-one, fifty-four—before the novel closes with a bare sixteen of accelerated apocalypse. But in these later chapters *Absalom, Absalom!* doesn't settle for recapitulation, and by the end we will know much more than its first ones could tell us. We have watched as Quentin and Shreve posit an explanation, from the bitter heart of our nation's founding sin, of just why Henry Sutpen murdered his best friend; of why, in the words of the poor white overseer Wash Jones, he "done shot that durn French feller. Kilt him dead as a beef."

Faulkner offers three successive rationales for that shooting, and I will take them in turn, showing how one replaces another. Each defines a particular sexual transgression, and each, in the Sutpens' world, seems larger and more persuasive than its predecessor, even as the evidence for them grows steadily weaker. At one point Quentin's narration depends on things that he only *imagines* Sutpen told his grandfather, old General Compson: things the

General never mentioned to Quentin's own father, but that the boy has somehow learned. And by the end we're reduced to the guesswork of a late-night dormitory conversation. Over the years Faulkner's critics have put a lot of effort into sorting out whatever narratological warrant there is for those different explanations, asking what we can know for sure, worrying at the novel's epistemology and defining its anomalies. Few scenes or moments beyond the book's opening pages are presented to us directly, without the intervening scrim of one character's perspective or another. Instead they are remembered, argued or speculated about, talked over, meditated upon, reminding us in the process that no fictional incident is separable from the circumstances of its narration. No reader can disregard such questions—and yet the more often I pick up this novel, the less they seem to matter. What counts instead is the entirety of the story it tells, with all its flaws and holes, conjectures and revisions. What counts is Quentin's belief that Sutpen's story is the best way he has to tell about the South.

Jefferson has come to think that Charles Bon, the man for whom Henry Sutpen "repudiated blood birthright and material security . . . was at least an intending bigamist even if not an out and out blackguard." That's the first explanation, the first reason we're given for the shooting. That's what Mr. Compson tells Quentin, and then hedges. Judith Sutpen found a photograph on Bon's dead body of another woman and a child. Did her father know about it? Is that why he opposed her marriage? Sutpen might have learned about that other woman on the mysterious trip he took to New Orleans in the summer of 1860, and yet why would Henry have repudiated his father that Christmas only to stop the marriage himself at the war's end? Was the other woman really a threat to the family honor—was she even enough, Mr. Compson asks, to prevent the marriage? For the photograph wasn't that of a wife. Instead it showed Bon's light-skinned, mixed-race mistress and their son: the kind of mistress that many men with money acquired in New Orleans, the product of a sexual economy that Faulkner leaves unnamed but that in other accounts of the antebellum world was known as *plaçage*.

One of the city's most distinctive features lay in its population of *gens de couleur libres*, free people of color, most of them descended from white Francophone fathers and enslaved mothers. Men and women of mixed race existed throughout the South, and so did small communities of free people, but they were rarely defined or accepted as a separate social category. In New Orleans they were, with a recognized if limited place in the city's culture, a third term in America's usual binary of black and white, slave and free. Some of them were rich, and some were acknowledged by their white cousins; some even fought, at first, for the Confederacy. What visitors to the city usually noticed, however, was a particular group among them, their heads turning, in the words of Frederick Law Olmsted, to follow "the graceful and elegant carriage . . . the taste and skill . . . beauty . . . charm or accomplishment" of the city's young mixed-race women. Free—but with their lives governed by the hierarchies of the slave society in which they lived. Olmsted's inevitably simplistic traveler's account defines marriage with a black man as undesirable for such a woman, and with a white one as unthinkable. Sexual liaisons were not, however, and some of the women he saw therefore entered or were *placed* in arrangements such as Bon's; placed, in theory, with an eye to financial security. And some men maintained those establishments after their marriage to a white woman; a second family even if, as in Bon's case, it came first.

Plaçage figures in many of the local color stories that came out of New Orleans in the postwar decades, those of Kate Chopin and George Washington Cable among others. Their accounts, like Olmsted's, stick some glamour onto an often seamy transaction, but Cable in particular provides his characters with a sense of individuality, and his account of the practice in tales like "Madame Delphine" has a pith and a social specificity that Faulkner's version lacks. *Absalom, Absalom!* puts its description of *plaçage* into the mouth of Quentin's father, and though he claims merely to describe it his characteristically heightened language serves to sanction it as well. Bon's magnolia-faced mistress, Mr. Compson says, has been made for the pleasure of man alone. She has been "culled and chosen and raised more carefully than any white girl, any nun, than any blooded mare even," and Faulkner himself here seems to share that fantasy. The novelist never allows her to become more than her beauty, and her racially determined sexual function remains indistinguishable from her narrative one. She is a figure created for use.

Mr. Compson sees her but faintly—a character derived not from the hard facts of antebellum life so much as from *La Dame aux Camélias* and other French romances of the demimonde. The more he thinks about her, however, the more he realizes that what he, what Jefferson, has always believed about Charles Bon's shooting simply won't stand. Henry Sutpen could not have been shocked by the sex in itself; no slave owner's son was shocked by the existence of a black mistress. What must have startled the Mississippian into violence, he says, was the fact that in New Orleans such relations were sealed by custom with a form of ritual, a few ceremonious words mumbled by a crone. But nobody in Bon's world would see that liaison "as a valid objection to marriage with a white woman," and even in provincial Mississippi it would be "drawing honor a little fine" to imagine that such a business could prohibit a marriage, let alone lead to murder. It's unbelievable, Mr. Compson says; it's "incredible. It just does not explain." Though maybe, he adds, maybe that's the point. There *is* no explanation, not one that we can grasp. No certainty is possible, we can never know enough, and all we have of the ever-elusive past are

a few old mouth-to-mouth tales; we exhume from old trunks and boxes and drawers letters without salutations or signature, in which men and women who once lived and breathed are now merely initials or nicknames out of some now incomprehensible affection which sound to us like Sanskrit or Chocktaw; we see dimly people, the people in whose living blood and seed we ourselves lay dormant and waiting, in this shadowy attenuation of time possessing now heroic proportions, performing their acts of simple passion and simple violence, impervious to time and inexplicable—Yes, Judith, Bon, Henry, Sutpen: all of them. They are there, yet something is missing.

Though what? We make inferences and cast hypotheses, we draw our conclusions on the basis of always inadequate evidence, old stories and letters, a skeleton imagined from a few surviving finger-bones. We glimpse that past but we do not know it. We don't even know what's missing; can never fully define the space or shape of its absence. We may learn a bit about Charles Bon's life in New Orleans, we see the woman and the child somewhere off in the shadows, but it's not enough to tell us why, after riding side by side through a ruined land, Henry spurred ahead of his friend and pulled the trigger at the gates to his father's house.

Rosa Coldfield was in Jefferson when Bon was shot. She went out to see Judith as soon as she got the news, but she wasn't allowed into the upstairs room to which his body was brought, and tells Quentin that "I never saw him. I never even saw him dead. I heard an echo, but not the shot; I saw a closed door but did not enter it." The past remains impenetrable, and all we have of its living blood is that echo of another life and time. Mr. Compson can go no further in trying to understand Bon's death. His son will, and precisely because he doesn't care about Bon so much as about Henry, about the brother willing to kill over the question of his sister's sexual honor. The Quentin that Faulkner imagined in *The Sound and the Fury*—the Quentin of spring 1910, who exists both before and after this one—would have liked to be such a brother. We'll meet that Quentin in a later chapter. For now it's enough to say that he finds himself arrested by the thought of Judith, standing in her bedroom and holding her wedding dress up before her, wondering how long it will be before her fiancé comes home from the war. Then the door crashes open and her wild-eyed brother stands in its frame and tells her what he's done, the two of them oddly "alike as if the difference in sex had merely sharpened the common blood to a terrific, an almost unbearable, similarity."

Absalom, Absalom! offers its second explanation for Bon's death in terms of that tableau, and in doing so it imagines a second and greater form of transgression. That explanation will be utterly implausible and entirely compelling, but for Faulkner to offer it, and for us to understand it, we need to go back to Thomas Sutpen's earliest days. I have written already of the demon's Appalachian childhood and also shown him firing into the Haitian night. What Faulkner uses to link those episodes is a moment on the Tidewater plantation where Sutpen spent his adolescence. His father had a kind of job there, yet it barely paid and the boy knew his family wasn't as well-clothed as the slaves of the planter, a man who spent his days in a hammock, and with a body-servant to hand him his whiskey. One day young Sutpen was sent to the big house with a message and went up to the front door, curious about what the place might look like inside. But a black butler blocked his path before he could say his piece, and told the boy never again to approach that way; people like him needed to go around back to the servant's entrance, the slave's entrance. The incident enraged him. "Sprung from a people whose houses didn't have back doors," he had never before encountered a social barrier between one white man and another, and for a moment he thought about shooting the planter who maintained it or beating in the butler's "balloon face." Then he realized that what he really wanted was to be on the other side of that division, a man with a hammock of his own. For that he would need money and slaves, land and a house, children and "incidentally of course, a wife"; and so he went to the West Indies, where he had heard that poor boys might grow rich.

This is an immensely simplified version of the story Sutpen tells Quentin's grandfather, a story that the Compson family has passed on like an heirloom. He went to the Caribbean—he formed a plan, an ambition, a design. He wanted to found a family, and for a while Sutpen thought that he had, with the planter's daughter who had passed him the muskets that he shot out into the night. But though they married and had a child, he found that she could not be "adjunctive or incremental to the design which I had in mind." He repudiated his first wife—he was the bigamist, not Bon—and after providing for her went out to another place where a white man could make money quickly, to a Mississippi newly cleared of its native peoples. It was almost thirty years before he had to think about the family he had abandoned, and he must have thought he was safe when he looked down his dinner table and saw his own face in that of Henry's best friend.

Charles Bon of New Orleans: the son of a vengeful mother, a woman rich, perfumed, and pampered, who after many years has learned exactly where Sutpen has gone and how much he is now worth. She sees an opportunity for punishment in the fact that the monster has a daughter of just the right age; the lawyer who advises her sees a chance for profit. So they send the young man up to an obscure country college called the University of Mississippi, where he meets Henry Sutpen and finds himself thinking that the other young man has "*my brow my skull my jaw my hands*." He understands the game, Bon does, understands it without being told; he admires Judith, and after a while admits that he does indeed "*want to go to bed with who might be my sister.*" But he wants something else as well. He wants Sutpen to recognize him: not to acknowledge him publicly but simply to let Bon know that he knows; to look him in the face and register his human presence. It is, in a way, what Sutpen himself had wanted at the door to that Tidewater mansion, but that recognition is no more likely now than it was then, and in its absence Bon will act with the same ruthless determination as his father. He will marry his half-sister, unless their brother Henry can stop him.

Bigamy; incest. The latter stands as a far more likely explanation for Bon's death, shot by a younger man who has already said he wants to be just like him, a man who in killing him can also kill his own desire. "He has known all the time that he is yours and your sister's brother," Sutpen tells Henry at Christmas, in that brief season between Lincoln's election and the war. Or so Quentin and Shreve imagine, in the winter of 1910, the two boys in Cambridge thinking their way back into the lives of the two at Oxford. They imagine Henry's response, his refusal to believe his father even as he knows it's true; imagine the young men riding off into the winter, both hoping that the coming war will settle the question for them. And yet this too does not explain. It leaves the question of Sutpen's first marriage unanswered, the question, as Bon puts it, of "whatever it was" about his island bride that he could not finally stomach.

Absalom, Absalom! gives us no real reason to accept the story that Quentin and Shreve now tell, in the book's penultimate chapter, no genuine basis for believing that the third explanation of Bon's shooting is anything more than the product of midnight in a freezing dormitory. Even the incest has seemed unlikely—for if that's the reason, why would Mr. Compson have first said that the trouble between the two brothers began with the woman in New Orleans? Quentin maintains that his father simply didn't know better. He didn't know the truth about anything until the boy himself got back from his drive out to Sutpen's Hundred with Rosa Coldfield. So the student tells Shreve a story that his father told him and that he first told his father; and Shreve in turn will tell a bit of it back to him, as though truth were a closed circle. We shouldn't believe any of it; we believe all of it. As the novel draws toward its close, Shreve reminds his roommate of how on that wistaria-scented September night he had helped Miss Rosa break into the old house, searching for something she both hoped and feared to find. Then he stops talking, and as we read it is as if time and space have snapped and the two boys are no longer even in Cambridge. For somehow they are "both in Carolina and the time was forty-six years ago . . . both of them were Henry Sutpen and both of them were Bon," and smelling the smoke of the bivouac fires as the word comes for Henry to go to his colonel's tent.

His father waits for him there, with a single candle to light their faces. It is the last time they will ever see each other, and the Colonel begins by repeating what he had said on that long-ago Christmas. *He cannot marry her*, and the italics in which Faulkner presents their dialogue suggest that the words aren't so much spoken here as remembered. Though remembered by whom? The young soldier can no longer even be bothered to tell his father that he's lying, not after four years of war. Nothing matters except the fact that they have survived, and brother or not, he refuses to stand in Charles Bon's way. And so the old man must now surrender his cover story and confess what he's kept hidden for more than thirty years. Sutpen has always spoken with an audidact's grandiloquence, but he makes this confession in the barest and plainest of terms, a simple statement of fact. It is not just the incest. His first wife's father had told him, in Haiti, that *her mother had been a Spanish woman. I believed him; it was not until after he was born that I found out his mother was part negro.* That was why his first wife and child could form no part of his design. Then Henry stumbles from the tent, having said nothing at all to his father. Nevertheless, he knows what he will do if Bon rides west. Will have to do; for the heir of Sutpen's Hundred there can be no choice.

So it's the miscegenation, not the incest, which you cant bear. That's what Bon says to Henry in the dawn, after a night of talk, and then adds that their father could have stopped him at any time, that all he wanted was a nod or a word. Now it is too late. Now he must think of himself and of what he wants, and who will stop him? Henry—weak, hero-worshipping Henry? Bon watches the younger man, a cold smile on his face, and then hands him a pistol. *Do it now.* But Henry can't, not yet, not here; he trembles and seems to suffocate as he insists that Bon is his brother. *No I'm not*, says the man from New Orleans. *I'm the nigger that's going to sleep with your sister.*

THAT IS THE SHOCK of *Absalom, Absalom!*—that in its world, in the white world of a Mississippi plantation, what is called "miscegenation" outweighs incest in the scale of sexual sins. Bon's words show that he understands his society's racial codes and prohibitions. Nevertheless, he seems so frankly incredulous at the idea that he rubs Henry's face in it, using a term that belongs far more to his brother's language than it does to his own. Doubly incredulous, in fact, disbelieving in both that scale and the thought that its terms might apply to him. I'll turn in a moment to the questions that wait upon his strangely laden words, but I need first to touch upon one unresolvable issue.

Faulkner's use of Caribbean history rests upon an anachronism, and no scholar has given an entirely satisfactory explanation of Sutpen's time there. Slavery in Haiti was finally abolished in 1804, when the forces of the newly independent country turned back a French invasion, and its white population was either killed or fled. How then could Sutpen have helped, around 1830, to put down what appears to be a slave rebellion on that island? His experience as an overseer might be plausible on Martinique or Guadeloupe, where Napoleon had reintroduced that bondage, but the name of neither island carried the emotional charge that Haiti did. Neither provoked the same terror in the slaveholding American South; neither could stand, in the twentieth century, for what that South had most feared. John T. Matthews has suggested that Sutpen's employers may have been a family of mixed-race, light-skinned *jaunes*—yellow as opposed to *noir* or black—who wouldn't "think to mention their black ancestry since anyone of French descent left in Haiti after 1804 would also have to be of color." *Jaunes* did in fact hold much of the island's wealth and faced frequent revolts from what remained a semifeudal *noir* workforce; they even at times employed white overseers, bringing them in from the mainland or the Caribbean's other islands. Could Sutpen have worked for such a family, and worked for them without having talked to other overseers or known anything at all about the island's history? That supposition makes him improbably ignorant rather than duped; it begs as many questions as it answers. Nor does Faulkner himself suggest such an explanation, and I think instead that he decided to cheat in reconstructing Sutpen's dreamlike account of his early life. It wouldn't have been the only time he shaved the truth.

But go back to Bon's words. What exactly does his epithet mean? And what, for that matter, is "miscegenation"? The latter word was a Civil War neologism that first appeared in a fraudulent pamphlet, published in December 1863, purporting to announce a Republican plan for the reconstructed nation. It was in fact written by a proslavery journalist posing as an abolitionist: a bit of fake news intended to discredit Lincoln's party in advance of the 1864 election. The pamphlet claimed that in a restored Union black men and white women would be free to indulge their hidden passion for each other. It circulated widely among the troops on both sides, and many white soldiers both believed its rumors and read it with horror. We can imagine that Bon and Henry were among those who picked up that publication, but everything about it is forgotten now except for the word itself, which quickly replaced the period's own accustomed term for racial mixing. That was the oddly quaint "amalgamation," and Lincoln himself had been accused of favoring that practice during his 1858 debates with Stephen Douglas. Many things can be amalgamated, though. "Miscegenation" had no other meaning or reference, and that clarity ensured its survival.

Its meaning is, in fact, a good bit clearer and simpler than that of the other and far older word that Bon uses. "Who him, calling us niggers?" That's what Sutpen's slaves say in "Wash" of its poor white title character, telling him that the Colonel wouldn't let any of them live in such a tumbledown shack as his. They use the term as a synonym for servitude, a mark of subordination and at times of contempt whose significance in black speech may depend upon but is not limited to race. And in speaking among themselves many of Faulkner's other black characters will use it in that way as well; Dilsey Gibson in *The Sound and the Fury* applies it to her grandson as she summarizes the mistakes he's made. But whites used the word after the war to insist upon black people's continued subordination, even after slavery's end, and Bon himself gives it the conventional meaning it had in Faulkner's own day: a pejorative designating anyone with any degree of African ancestry, and the way in which Henry must now see him.

Whether he ever sees himself in those terms is a question the novel simply doesn't explore. Certainly he can't be understood as having *passed* for white; the term implies a consciousness or intentionality that he lacks. Nor is it even certain that he would have been counted as black in the culture the novel describes. The one-drop rule of the early twentieth century had no absolute hold on the antebellum world and indeed would not congeal for some years thereafter. According to the Mississippi Code of 1880, persons with less than "one-fourth of Negro blood" were legally white. In Louisiana the figure was one-eighth, and a court decision in South Carolina held that in any doubtful case one's "reputation [and] reception into society" would be determinative. That judgment suggests that race stands above all as a social category: in Charleston, and despite some notional admixture of "blood," the Charles Bon who exercises all the privileges of the white man, even to the keeping of a mistress in *plaçage*, would if he were real be white.

Yet the white South could abide those of indeterminate race only so long as its own position was guaranteed by the existence of slavery. Abolition paradoxically hardened the color line. Some light-skinned men and women did, admittedly, slip or "pass" into the white world—moved north or west, and kept their family ties a secret. To them that line seemed porous: deceptively so, for they needed to be all white in order not to be all black. The end of Reconstruction led to a series of laws and court orders that tried to legislate racial ambiguity out of existence, with *Plessy v. Ferguson* standing as the definitive case among them. That 1896 Supreme Court decision grew out of a New Orleans test case in which an apparently Caucasian man, with one black great-grandparent, was denied a seat in the white car of Louisiana's newly segregated railroad. Homer Plessy had bought a ticket and then informed on himself, hoping to be arrested as part of a carefully planned challenge to the new law: a gamble lost.

Black and white became by the end of the nineteenth century as absolute a division as slave and free had once been; but "let flesh touch with flesh," as Faulkner himself writes, "and watch the fall of all the eggshell shibboleth of caste and color too." Bon's dangerously taunting words—*I'm the nigger that's going to sleep with your sister*—are scarcely credible in the world of 1865, unfathomable as a spoken sentence. Indeed they are unlikely to have been said at any time by a black man to a white one. But they *are* a statement of what the white South in Faulkner's period claimed to fear, a fear kept bubbling as a means of social control by movies like *The Birth of a Nation* (1915) and in the stem-winding campaign speeches of Dixiecrat politicians like Mississippi's own James K. Vardaman. Bon's statement doesn't threaten Judith Sutpen's sexual purity so much as the color line itself. Her virginity provides an emblem for white supremacy: insist on the one, with a rope in your hand, and you can maintain the other.

Faulkner said little about race in his early books—or rather he said a great deal about the speech and behavior, the manners and mores, that governed the relations of black and white. Almost all the black characters in his first novels are servants, men and women filling a conventional role, and yet they are as clearly individuated as the white figures in whose houses they work, from Dilsey and her grandson Luster to the terrified washerwoman Nancy in "That Evening Sun." But the only passage in that early work to consider race as an idea—as an issue or problem in American life—is set, paradoxically, in Boston. W. E. B. Du Bois said in 1923 that a "black man is a person who must ride 'Jim Crow' in Georgia," but though Boston has its own history of racism its public transportation was not segregated, and in *The Sound and the Fury* Quentin steps aboard a streetcar and finds that its single vacant seat is beside a well-dressed black man. He sits down and thinks that one of the things he's learned up north is to take everyone, "black or white . . . for what they think they are, then leave them alone. That was when I realised that a nigger is not a person so much as a form of behavior; a sort of obverse reflection of the white people he lives among."

Quentin's thought isn't fully realized, and it's hard to tell whether its groping quality belongs to the character or to the novelist himself. Nevertheless, its implications are enormous—implications that virtually no other white writer of Faulkner's day was prepared to suggest. Du Bois's words suggest that race is above all a social construction rather than a fact of nature. And Quentin here stands on the verge of learning the same thing. White and black each take their definition from the other; at times they may even mimic each other. For race isn't a person—an essence or an identity. It is instead a "form of behavior," a mask, a role, a performance. Most people have those roles assigned by the world around them, and yet what if you could choose?

Faulkner's greatest books never have a single concern, but his investigation of the performance of race would become an ever-larger part of his work through the 1930s and beyond. It figures of course in *Absalom, Absalom!* and later in *Go Down, Moses*, but his richest account of it comes in the character of Joe Christmas in *Light in August*. Raised in an orphanage for white children—left at its door on Christmas Day—he nevertheless grows up believing, without evidence, that he has some trace of black ancestry. The other children brand him with it. They call him "nigger" on the playground, and as an adult, with his skin "a level dead parchment color," he reveals what he takes to be the truth about himself whenever he's looking for a quarrel. He fights black men who see him as white, and white men who call him black; at one point he beats a prostitute who doesn't think it makes a difference. Christmas first appears in Yoknapatawpha after fifteen years of wandering. He works in a sawmill by day, sells bootleg whiskey by night, and sleeps, secretly, with a white woman named Joanna Burden: a Northerner who has settled in Jefferson precisely because her abolitionist ancestors were murdered there. She in turn will be slaughtered by Christmas himself, her throat cut, and he will be hunted through the town's streets and then shot, castrated too; not all lynchings need a rope. He is killed for her murder and for having slept with a white woman. But he is killed above all for his racial indeterminacy: because he refuses to act as if he is either white or black in a world where people have to be the one or the other.

Some of Faulkner's light-skinned characters are told to head north and pass; offered money to go in search of an easier life. None of them do, and one of those who refuses is Bon's pale and delicate son, Charles Etienne. Though it's more accurate to say instead that he decides to pass for black. Colonel Sutpen is dead by the time the boy comes to live at Sutpen's Hundred, and the old man never knows that he has a male heir on the place, an heir of precisely the type he wanted to avoid. Somehow the boy learns of his ancestry, and like Christmas begins to pick fights with any black man who insists that he's white. He marries a black woman and has a son, a "saddle-colored" man whom Quentin knows as Jim Bond, and who at the end of the novel will be the only person left on Sutpen's ground. We could say that Charles Etienne accepts the racial definitions of the postwar South, that he lets his one drop of color determine his life. But there's a better way to put it. He chooses, rather, to become what his father was killed for; to become what the Sutpens' world believed his father to be.

That choice insists on his freedom to be whoever he claims to be, and Charles Etienne stands with Christmas and Bon himself as a limit case, men in whom race is a matter of consciousness alone. Each functions as an extreme version of a recognizable type in American fiction. In 1933 the poet and Howard University professor Sterling A. Brown published an essay called "Negro Character as Seen by White Authors" that defined the various conventions through which white writers had depicted black people—"The Wretched Freeman," "The Brute Negro," and so on. Only one of his categories, however, has lasted as a term of analysis: that which Brown calls the "tragic mulatto." He traces the type back through Harriet Beecher Stowe and forward to the popular fiction of his own day, though without mentioning Faulkner himself; and he might have added that such figures also appear in the work of African-American writers like Charles W. Chesnutt and Nella Larsen. Most of these characters are women, caught between two worlds and made to suffer because of it; caught sexually, with white lovers whom they cannot marry. So it is, in fact, with Bon's own mistress, a woman made tragic by one who becomes tragic himself.

Faulkner breaks the convention by using male figures to embody the type. Race for Charles Bon is an abstraction for which he must pay with his life, and none of the writers Brown looks at offers anything so entirely liminal. But Bon isn't Thomas Sutpen's only black child. The wagon in which he brought his first slaves to Yoknapatawpha had a woman inside, maybe two. We don't know how often Sutpen raped them, how often they bore his assault. He himself would have had different terms for it, euphemisms that underlined their status as property: he would have said he "used" or "had" or "visited" them. But those words too contain the note of coercion, and none of them imply consent. Faulkner doesn't tell us what the relations were between Sutpen's victims and the black men he had brought from the islands with them; he doesn't tell us how many children they bore, or who their fathers were. All we know is that the first of them was Sutpen's own, the girl he named Clytemnestra, Clytie, his first American child. She lived in the house, always, a companion to his white daughter; each other's only friend in the years after one of their brothers had killed the other. Later still, after Judith died of the yellow fever, Clytie would live on in a cabin behind Sutpen's crumbling mansion, the effective mistress of what had always been her home.

Did she have brothers and sisters at work on her father's land? Undoubtedly. Olmsted writes in *The Cotton Kingdom* that one Louisianan told him that there wasn't "an old plantation in which the grandchildren of the owner are not whipped in the field by his overseer." Mary Chesnut thought, as we have seen, that the men of her world lived surrounded by "concubines" and with their wives pretending not to notice; but she also saw those enslaved women as prostitutes and blamed them. It wasn't entirely the white man's fault, she suggested, not when temptation lay so near, and Olmsted's own informant thought of leaving the South itself as a way to keep his sons chaste. Yet though many white Southerners spoke of those practices and even claimed to regret them, few would admit to understanding the structures of power behind them. Few acknowledged that such relations, for those women, were not and could not be freely chosen. The abolitionists knew that, and so did the enslaved themselves. Writers like Harriet Jacobs make that clear, and after the war the legacy of that "amalgamation" would become a major theme in African-American fiction. The best example is Charles Chesnutt's *The Marrow of Tradition*, which begins with two half sisters, their relation unacknowledged but known to all, women who look so much alike that "folks sometimes takes 'em fer one ernudder."

Plantation owners could speak of such things; the popular genre called plantation fiction did not. Mixed-race people simply don't figure in the nostalgic form codified after the war by Thomas Nelson Page, whether in the essays of *The Old South* or the stories he gathered for *In Ole Virginia*. Instead he offers a world of fondly loyal servants and proud wise masters, a world that lives on in the sweet memory of what's been lost, of moonlight, magnolia, and dead heroes. Stark Young does allow his characters a reference to *plaçage*—that exotic custom of the French city down the river. Still, nothing

like that ever happens around his Natchez, nor indeed at Tara and the surrounding plantations in Margaret Mitchell's Georgia. But Faulkner himself
is unblinking, and he makes Mr. Compson tell Quentin of a habitual practice in the world of their ancestors. A planter's son rides up, after a morning's
hunting perhaps, and looks out over the sweating fields; he calls the overseer
and tells him to "send me Juno or Missylena or Chlory and then rides on
into the trees and dismounts and waits." Sometimes it's a housemaid, neat
and clean; and in some cases, Mr. Compson says, a white girl might owe her
virginity to the sexual availability of a black one. The bluntness with which
Absalom, Absalom! depicts the planter's sexual abuse of his slaves has no
precedent in the literature of the white South. Mr. Compson himself takes
the practice for granted—something out of a vanished time—and doesn't
mention the violence or coercion, the fear. But he doesn't need to for us to
know that it's there, in one of the most casually and deliberately chilling lines
Faulkner ever wrote.

What do the Compsons—the Sutpens and the Falkners, the Lees and
the Chesnuts—what do they owe to those they held in bondage, and to their
children after them? What work of repair? Forty acres and a mule, General
Sherman had famously said of the soil along the Georgia coast, only to have
the federal government renege on his pledge and return that rich land to its
former owners. Freedom, citizenship, and suffrage, equal rights before the
law: so claimed the new amendments to the Constitution, amendments that
after the 1876 end of Reconstruction had almost no force at all in the states of
the former Confederacy. For many white Americans the letter of the law was
enough, indeed much more than enough, and even some of slavery's opponents feared that any material support from the government might produce a
habit of dependence. The freedmen would get no share of the wealth they had
helped produce; those with nothing were told instead that they must learn
self-reliance and make their own way.

Not everyone agreed, though, and in 1884 George Washington Cable
wrote in the *Century* magazine that the whole nation faced "a moral responsibility . . . never to lose sight of the results of African-American slavery until
they cease to work mischief and injustice." Cable reminded his readers that
he wrote as a Southerner and the son of a slaveholder—just the kind of man

who might be expected to wink at that injustice. But he also wrote as a citizen dismayed by the federal government's abandonment of Reconstruction and consequent decision to leave all such questions to the states. "The Freedman's Case in Equity" argued that his home region could recover from the Civil War only by engaging with the issues that caused it. Southerners needed to stop pretending that the bitterness left by the fighting itself was the reason for the South's resistance to the extension of civil rights; they needed to abandon the "vicious evasions" with which they fought any attempt to build a just society. Only in theory did a freedman enjoy the Constitution's guarantees, for he lived under a system of rank oppression that "in daily practice heaps upon him in every public place the most odious distinctions. . . . It spurns his ambition [and] tramples upon his languishing self-respect." The war didn't cause that. Such feelings, Cable wrote, had been grinding away long before Sumter, motivated by the belief that there was "a disqualifying moral taint in every drop of Negro blood." The white South insisted on that taint, as though that belief were the only way in which the region could live with the misery on which it fed.

Cable mixed boldness and caution, a fastidious man forced to take up questions he would rather have left alone. He would go only so far, and in a second essay, "The Silent South," he tried to distinguish between political and social equality. The South blurred those things—it feared the "social intermingling" of the races and therefore suppressed all questions of civil rights themselves. Cable thought, in contrast, that an equality of citizens said nothing about the dinner table or the marriage bed; "national harmony" needn't entail an amalgamation that he believed neither race wanted. Today that distinction between civic and social relations seems impossibly strained, legally untenable and false, a crust thrown not only to the white world but to his own upbringing as well. Yet Cable probed more deeply in his fiction, the stories of *Old Creole Days* (1879) in particular. The interracial liaisons and half-hidden family histories that he describes in those tales have been shaped by a slave society, and in that moral economy he imagines them as inevitably tragic. Nevertheless, he also sees them as an inescapable fact of American life and insists that the refusal to acknowledge them inevitably produces a "racial confusion" and hysteria of its own.

Absalom, Absalom! turns, finally, on the failure to admit what everyone knows—to admit, in public, the consequences of what is whispered on every plantation and in every town. Just who is related to whom? Who gets to be in the family? Who can share in its wealth or claim a voice in governing its affairs? The scholar Barbara Ladd has written that Sutpen's refusal to recognize Bon as his son is what has created "the dual threats of incest and miscegenation." Neither threat would be possible if only Henry and Judith had been able to call him brother from the start. We can push that a little further, though, for an odd strain in antebellum thought held that amalgamation was in itself a form of incest. The idea, which seems nonsensical, rests upon the tortured claim that they are equally against nature. But remember Olmsted's Louisiana informant, with his story of the planter's grandsons at work in the fields, grandsons who would themselves have had sisters. *Send me Juno.*

Henry does say "brother" in the end, when Bon hands him a pistol and tells him to use it. What he cannot say is "brother-in-law," and it matters here that Bon's blackness remains invisible. The tincture of the skin may fade with the generations, but Henry's whole world—Faulkner's whole world—believes that one can be black without looking it or knowing it. The "taint" endures in the blood, and if even Bon is not white enough, then what hope can this country hold for a man like Loosh or Ringo? The two soldiers ride together toward their father's gates, the children of a house divided. Only it's a new division, now that the war is over, no longer that of slave state or free, North or South. White or black, two absolute and opposing qualities—that's what counts in the late spring of 1865 and after too, even if the pair of them can, for the moment, ride side by side, as brothers should. The fate of something more than their family will depend on whether the one will let the other ride through those gates beside him; on whether or not they can enter their house together. I am sorry to say that we know that question's answer.

"KILT HIM DEAD AS a beef." That's what Sutpen's overseer Wash Jones says when he carries the news of Bon's murder in to Jefferson, and that news is all we get. We hear the echo, not the shot, and Faulkner never shows us the moment itself. He works toward it and then away from it: works toward it repeatedly, skirts around and lets his speakers evoke it as they tell the story over. But he never shows us the men themselves, never allows us to see Bon's unsurprised look as Henry's pistol takes aim, or to smell the gunpowder's flash. That remains an ellipsis, a skipped beat, like the presence or defining absence in his work of the Civil War itself, and Henry Sutpen's own future life will remain another such absence. He disappears after the shooting, and no one in Yoknapatawpha County seems to know where he's gone. Maybe Texas, or Mexico? California? And that disappearance will determine the shape of his sisters' continuing life, of the long busy empty days they endure on that ever-less-productive plantation.

Thomas Sutpen himself returns in January 1866—returns to discover that one of his sons has killed the other. He sets immediately to work, hoping both to restore his land and to make another son to whom he might leave it. Even at sixty he would find women in Jefferson to court, young war widows among them, but for convenience's sake he turns his eye first on Rosa Cold-field and then on Wash's teenage granddaughter Milly. As a boy, we remember, Sutpen had been sent around to the back of a big house in the Virginia Tidewater, told off by a butler who barred the front door against him. The slave's entrance, the servant's entrance: on into Faulkner's time no black man in Mississippi would approach a white man's home from the front. The boy's baffled rage stands as the originating moment of his design, his plan to found a family, and he has never forgotten that the man who owned that butler had another slave to hand him his whiskey while he swung in his hammock. Sutpen will go him one better—he'll keep a white man for that. That's what Wash does. He reminds Sutpen of who he was and of how far he's come. He fetches the spring water and holds the jug while his master lounges, and in the years before the Civil War Wash would no more dare to come up to the front door of the big house than would one of Sutpen's slaves. But during the war he begins to use that front door, and Wash now stands as a mark of how far the old man has fallen; fallen so far that he is now trying to seduce his servant's granddaughter with candy and ribbons. In 1869 Milly gives birth to Sutpen's child, but when the planter learns that it's a "mare," a girl, he simply walks away. Girls are of no use to him. Wash has counted on "Kernel" to marry Milly and make the situation "right." Now he has had enough, and he holds a scythe in his hands.

Sutpen's death seems almost an afterthought. He has lived too long in the echo of Henry's shot, and after killing his master Wash ties the loose ends, using a butcher knife on the girl and her baby before facing the posse that awaits him. But *Absalom, Absalom!* is as full of loose ends as history itself, and it will be up to Quentin to knot the longest of its strings. The book begins in Rosa Coldfield's house on a dusty September afternoon, and it ends with Quentin's account, in his Harvard dormitory, of the ride they took out to Sutpen's Hundred that same late summer night: the boy driving in the dark, smelling her "fusty camphor-reeking shawl" in the buggy beside him and imagining that he can hear the galloping ghostly hooves of Sutpen's own horse. Rosa believes—guesses, knows with the certainty of her lifelong anger—Rosa thinks that Clytie is hiding something in that old enormous house, something or someone that she has kept and guarded for years. The white woman wants to know what it is, and so when they arrive Quentin steps through a glassless window and climbs the stairs to the room in which Charles Bon's body once lay.

Home is where they have to take you in. So Robert Frost made the husband say in "The Death of the Hired Man," only to have the speaker's wife reply that it's the place "you somehow haven't to deserve." What Quentin finds in that upstairs chamber will shock him. It will leave him feeling as if he needs to bathe, though Faulkner, typically, will not describe it directly. The novelist waits until he gets the boy back to Jefferson, when in his father's house Quentin will see himself walking down that corridor once more, in memory's repetition, walking toward an age-yellowed face upon a pillow, a man with "wasted hands" crossed upon his breast as though he were already a corpse, and yet still with a voice:

> *And you are—?*
> *Henry Sutpen.*
> *And you have been here—?*
> *Four years.*
> *And you came home—?*

To die. Yes.
To die?
Yes. To die.
And you have been here—?
Four years.
And you are—?
Henry Sutpen.

To die. Yes. To die? Yes. To die. Those words, at the center of these twelve riddling lines, make something close to a palindrome, and the passage as a whole approaches one as well. They are the same going and coming, forward and back, they look at themselves as if in a mirror, with Henry's statements enclosing Quentin's questions like an envelope or a pair of parentheses. What these sentences don't give us, however, is anything like an explanation, and in reading them I can't help but wonder if the two of them said anything else. How does Quentin know what he knows? Did Henry tell him about the "miscegenation," offering some longer but unrecorded story from which Quentin might learn the Sutpens' family secrets? Some tale of which these few lines of dialogue are but the ghostly residue? Or is this all, and enough— has Quentin understood without the words, without needing them because that story is one he's always somehow known? The words of a palindrome look at themselves. Quentin walks down that hallway, drawn by the faint light at its end, as Bon rode toward the gates of Sutpen's Hundred, and when he enters that room what he finds is himself: the remembered body of the man who wanted to sleep with his sister, and the body as well of the man who killed him. And he is each of them, Henry and Bon, doubled and one, the other who is also the self. So he looks upon his own deathbed, and no one who has read *The Sound and the Fury* will come away from this scene unchilled.

But Quentin finds something more than himself in that room. A palindrome repeats itself, it circles around and bites its own tail, and that's what he offers when he's asked to tell about the South: a story marked by an endless recursion to what has already been done and said, the recursion that for a boy of Quentin's generation is the course or curse of his region's history. "You cant

understand it," he tells Shreve. "You would have to be born there," and yet he
hesitates when the Canadian asks if he understands it himself. "I dont know,"
he says, and then adds that of course he does; pauses and again says that he
does not know. His words make us wonder what this story does in fact mean:
a tale of pride and ambition, greed and folly, of those who have to live with
the consequences of what can never be undone. That summary seems easy
enough, and yet in trying to understand the burden of what Quentin tells
us I find myself asking just what Henry Sutpen is running from. Why has he
needed to leave Sutpen's Hundred at all?

It's true that he has killed what Yoknapatawpha County believes to be a
white man, a fellow soldier and an officer too. But he does have a story to tell,
an explanation for his actions that comes backed by his father's authority.
Henry Sutpen wanted to protect his sister's racial and sexual purity, and no
court in his Mississippi would find him guilty, if only he could make them
believe his tale. He isn't running from any legal consequences. He isn't even
running from Judith. He runs from his father and from what his father has
made him do. He knows that in killing the "nigger" he has also killed his
brother, that he has allowed a few drops of his brother's blood to make him
shed the rest, and so he runs from the code or law that has made him draw his
pistol. He runs from the South, and he runs from himself, with no choice but
to flee a world in which he has had no choice. He runs from history itself, and
what Quentin really means when he says that he doesn't know if he understands his own story is that he too would have acted in exactly the same way.
Would have wanted to, anyway: to pull that trigger, and then start from himself in horror. But the past is never past. Time offers no escape, and at the end
of forty years all Henry Sutpen has been able to do is go home, back to the
dark house of his childhood.

There Clytie has kept and sheltered him, fed and hidden and protected
him, remembering always that he is her brother. But three months after her
visit with Quentin, Rosa Coldfield will head back out to Sutpen's Hundred
once more. This time she brings an ambulance, planning to take Henry back
to a doctor in town—and when she starts up the drive Clytie burns the house
down, setting fire to the "monstrous tinder-dry rotten shell" of Sutpen's
Hundred and immolating both herself and her brother in the flames. Only

Jim Bond remains, Bon's grandson and another loose end, and in their room at Harvard Shreve will point to him as the note of all our futures. The Canadian can say that, a voice neither Yankee nor Southern, and able to anticipate an America of indistinguishable black and white in a way that Quentin cannot. Shreve has a final question, though, and as he weighs his roommate's awful tale he asks Quentin to tell him "just one thing more. Why do you hate the South?" And the boy's answer will come too quickly. "I dont hate it." Then he finds himself panting in the winter air, and the book's last words are a jackhammer in his mind. *I dont hate it . . . I dont. I dont! I dont hate it! I dont hate it!* Faulkner later wrote that Quentin didn't speak for him here, that "he not I was brooding over a situation." I have never quite believed him.

ELEVEN

A Legacy

Faulkner liked titles with a pedigree, and he found them everywhere. He took them from the Old Testament and the *Odyssey*, from Shakespeare and even the Gettysburg Address, borrowing from Lincoln's last sentence in "Shall Not Perish," a 1943 story about a Mississippi soldier in World War II. He also, however, drew upon the African-American vernacular tradition at a time when few white writers found it a source of inspiration, and indeed when some members of the black middle class were suspicious of it themselves. One of his finest stories, "That Evening Sun," takes its name from W. C. Handy's "Saint Louis Blues," which Faulkner would have heard in its 1925 recording by Bessie Smith. And then there is *Go Down, Moses*.

The title of Faulkner's 1942 novel comes from a song popularized in the 1870s by the Fisk Jubilee Singers, a Nashville choir from one of the nation's first colleges for African-American students. No one knows the song's exact origin. Its first recorded use was among the contrabands working at Virginia's Fort Monroe in the early days of the Civil War, but Harriet Tubman—herself known as Moses—is said to have used it in the 1850s, a bit of code through which to communicate on the Underground Railroad. Faulkner himself never quotes from it directly. Instead he shows a black family gathered in mourning at the end of the novel, and their threnody evokes a young man who has been sold "to Pharaoh and now he dead." But that's not a line from the song itself, and the novelist feels no need to cite its chorus, whose words nevertheless lie at the heart of this book: *Let my people go.* For he expects that even his white readers will know those words already, an essential cultural reference, in the same way that they recognize his titles from Shakespeare or the Bible.

Go Down, Moses describes the relationships, over several generations, between the black and white descendants of a Yoknapatawpha planter named Carothers McCaslin, the two sides of a family linked by blood and divided by history. Faulkner dedicated the novel to the memory of Caroline Barr, who lived in a cabin behind Rowan Oak until her death in 1940 at the age of one hundred. He gave the eulogy at her funeral, which he held at his own house rather than at her church, and he paid for her tombstone, which he had engraved with her name and dates, and these added words: "Mammy. Her white children bless her." Her family deeply resented his arrogation of grief's privilege, the way that even in death he insisted on her filling that conventional and subordinate role. But the novel itself offers something more complicated, and remains always uneasy about the values of the world it comes from even though it does always escape them.

Two characters dominate that book, two men born after the Civil War who almost never appear on the same page: not brothers, but cousins, and old Carothers's last surviving grandsons. One is a fearless, intransigent black farmer named Lucas Beauchamp, who wants people to know he belongs to one of the county's oldest white families. He lives forever on the verge of provoking white rage, and Faulkner would use him again a few years later in *Intruder in the Dust*, where he is falsely accused of murder. The other is Carothers's nearest white descendant, Isaac McCaslin, the legal heir to the family's land. But Ike will refuse that inheritance. He will not enter the moral and monetary economy of theft and bondage from which his family's fortune grew. Ike knows that there would be no inheritance at all without the labor of the enslaved, and through him Faulkner suggests that he too understands that our country's history rests upon a crime. Neither Ike's tale nor Lucas's has much to say about the war itself. They do, however, say a great deal about what that war was over, and about what happened *when* it was over. *Go Down, Moses* is a novel about Reconstruction—which means that it's also about the white South's resistance to Reconstruction. Yet it's not Faulkner's only attempt to think about the postwar period, and Charles Bon wasn't the only man in Yoknapatawpha to get shot when that war was done. For in this apocryphal county the resistance to that new birth of freedom all starts with murder.

Thomas Sutpen said when the fighting was over that the South would come right so long as each man took care of his own land, and yet for John Sartoris in *The Unvanquished* that wasn't enough. As soon as he got back to Yoknapatawpha, Sartoris put his crops in, rebuilt the plantation house the Yankees had burned, and married his cousin Drusilla Hawke, who in the struggle's last months had ridden alongside him. But a reborn county needed a link to the world outside, and so the Colonel started a railroad, putting into it every cent he could borrow and staying just "two cross-ties ahead" of insolvency until the work was done and the first whistle blew. He saw himself as raising up the whole region by its bootstraps, and maybe that's what he thought he was doing when he shot two Yankees who were trying to get black people to vote.

Faulkner told that particular story in three different novels. He gave it a few sentences in *Flags in the Dust* (1929), with Old Man Falls recalling a pair of unnamed "cyarpet baggers," but *Light in August* (1932) offers another and much fuller version, dating the incident to 1874 and giving the dead a name. One is a fierce old New England abolitionist named Calvin Burden; the other is his grandson and namesake, a boy just out of his teens. Burden believes that African skin bears the stain of the white man's sin, that black people have been marked through no fault of their own with the wrath of God himself. But with freedom "they'll bleach out," and during Reconstruction he brings his family to Jefferson in the service of the Freedmen's Bureau, keeping a loaded pistol beside him as he asks each new voter to make his mark. Calvin Burden is very nearly as violent a man as John Sartoris himself. He too has killed, and Faulkner supplies the New Englander with four generations of family history: his stern Unitarian father; his son Nathaniel, who needs to bury both Calvins in secret, for fear that the townsfolk will mutilate their corpses; and then in the twentieth century his granddaughter, Joanna, whom Faulkner describes in *Light in August* as having stayed on in Mississippi to be near her dead. Around 1930 she will take Joe Christmas as a lover and offer him her family's story, explaining why she lives in the midst of the people who hate her.

That's one way to tell it, and if we're looking for fiction that bears some relation to history itself it's probably the best; the Freedmen's Bureau was defunct by the mid-1870s, but the Fifteenth Amendment had given black men the right to vote and the white South's reaction made violence at the polls common. The most dramatic version, though, belongs to *The Unvanquished*, a section called "Skirmish at Sartoris" that first appeared in *Scribner's Magazine* for April 1935. It's a skillfully made piece of magazine fiction, with its major action mirrored by a subplot, and yet it's also one of the most disturbing things Faulkner ever wrote: repellent in the politics it appears to endorse, and with its tone jarringly at odds with its material. The title doesn't refer to the Burdens' murder but rather to a face-off in the summer of 1865 between Colonel Sartoris's discharged soldiers and the assembled ladies of Jefferson, each group looking at the other as if "waiting for a bugle to sound the charge." And Sartoris himself stands between them, along with that fierce young soldier, his cousin Drusilla. The ladies want the Colonel to make an honest woman of her; Drusilla finds their concerns absurd and insists she and Sartoris were too busy chasing Yankees to think about sex. Nevertheless, she allows herself to be thrust into a dress, and the couple rides off to church.

Only they never get there. For it's Election Day, and though the only contest is for town marshal, the Burdens are pushing the candidacy of Cash Benbow, the newly freed and illiterate coachman of the county's judge. Faulkner is stretching his history here. Local elections were indeed held in the immediate aftermath of the war, but black candidates were not at first on the ticket and in Mississippi no freed people managed to vote until 1867. Nor will they here. When Sartoris gets to town, he sees a bunch of strange white men "herding" a crowd of black people to the polls, and other men, "Jefferson men," running toward them with pistols. He puts his troop between them and then walks into the hotel where the Burdens sit with the ballot box. The Yankees fire first, and then Sartoris votes twice, with the derringer hidden up his sleeve.

We never actually see the Burdens—their deaths happen off the page, the echo not the shot—and in the comedy of the sexual skirmish it's all too easy to forget about them. Sartoris emerges to cheers, looks hard to see if anyone will dare to question him, and then moves the election out to his own plantation. The wedding has to wait until the end of the story, when the Rebel yell sounds for both the Colonel's marriage and his actions alike, as though the two were indistinguishable: the white South's new beginning. By the 1930s most of America's white population believed that the Confederacy had been led by gallant men of principle. They accepted the myth of the Lost Cause; they admired Robert E. Lee and saw the Civil War as a quarrel over states' rights. Southern-slanted histories sold well across the country, and so of course would *Gone with the Wind*. In his high-spirited bravado, John Sartoris is stamped from the same tin as Rhett Butler. But "Skirmish at Sartoris" is a sickening tale, sickening especially when read on its own, as its first audience would have done in *Scribner's*. Like the rest of *The Unvanquished*, it is narrated by the Colonel's son Bayard, whom the earlier chapters have taught us to trust. Yet nothing he says in this one serves to challenge his father's action, and his picture of black voters as inevitably ignorant and corruptible simply parrots the view of Reconstruction that was current in Faulkner's childhood and for some decades thereafter. Any administration that rested on black votes was by definition unrepresentative, and white rule was believed essential to good government. Sartoris sees himself as preserving public order—order threatened by the mere fact of black men voting, rather than by those who will kill to stop it. "We were promised Federal troops," he says, as if their presence would keep his peace. In their absence he decides to become the law himself, and he is often gone at night, with other men to help "with what he was doing"—with some unspecified action that he won't allow his son to know about.

Later Bayard will have a name for it. He recognizes, at the end of the book, that the Colonel has "organised the night riders to keep the carpet baggers from organising the negroes into an insurrection." John Sartoris is the leader of the local Klan, and though Bayard doesn't stop loving him he will reject his father's ways. *The Unvanquished* concludes with a chapter called "An Odor of Verbena." It is 1873 and Bayard is a law student at the University of Mississippi when his best friend and former slave Ringo brings word that the Colonel has been shot in the street by John Redmond, a business partner he has insulted. Faulkner's own great-grandfather was killed in just that way, though there's no evidence that he himself was a night rider. The two young men head back to Jefferson together through the "hot thick dusty darkness," their horses pacing the miles, and as Bayard tries to work out what he must

brother—and the man who now heads the Sartoris family, marked by "that white skin you walks around in." They will have no future together. Or perhaps I should say that they have had no past: that in his earlier *Flags in the Dust*, Faulkner had not dared to imagine the companionship of two old men, of an aged white banker and his black friend. Their intimacy belongs only to childhood, to a time that can, however briefly, sustain the illusion of an undifferentiated equality. It cannot extend to an adult life in the Redeemed South that is coming up around them, in which the gains of Reconstruction will be canceled by Jim Crow. In that world Ringo could live only as Bayard's client, only as what Zora Neale Hurston would later call a "pet Negro." And Faulkner simply didn't want to see him that way. He didn't want to show us what Ringo might be at thirty or forty and with a family of his own; what he might become if he ever left the Sartoris land, and how diminished he would be if he didn't. He couldn't imagine an adult life for him. Or rather he chose not to, having first imagined that intrepid intelligent adolescent. He never took the character further, and after finishing *The Unvanquished* he didn't go back to the adult Bayard either, not as anything more than a passing reference; never returned to a life in which he would have to explain an absence.

Yet before putting Ringo aside, Faulkner did allow him to define the future course of Southern history. "Do you know what I aint?" he says to Bayard as the war ends. "I aint a nigger anymore. I done been abolished. . . . They aint no more niggers, in Jefferson nor nowhere else." And whatever the white world around him might say, in one sense at least he's right. To the degree that that word denotes servitude, Ringo has indeed been abolished, emancipated out of existence. His legal status as but three-fifths of a person has been changed, wiped off the books, and nobody knows what will take its place, what new status the country will afford him. "They're free now," says a planter named Hubert Beauchamp in *Go Down, Moses*, as he tries to keep his sister from hustling his black mistress away. "They're folks too just like we are," and those words, however self-serving, point to a truth that Yoknapatawpha's white world hopes to deny. Folks, full persons, the old definition abolished and the old word too. Except that Ringo knows it isn't so. Slavery may have been abolished but he hasn't been, nor has blackness, nor whiteness. Bottom rail on top? He'd call anyone who believes that a fool, and yet his voice also contains a touch of amusement, as if enjoying a paradox. I am not what you think, he seems to say; I am not what white people will continue to call me and everyone else who looks like me. Ringo is so closely identified with the Sartorises as to find the idea of a black elected official absurd. But he also stands as the voice of double-consciousness, ever aware of the gap between the self and the definition imposed upon it.

Faulkner underlines that gap by emphasizing—exaggerating—the difference between Ringo's speech and Bayard's standard English; differences scarcely credible in two boys who have never been apart. No white writer would now employ that kind of phonetic spelling in depicting a character like Ringo. Few of them had any qualms about it in Faulkner's time, however, and indeed the middle-class readership of popular magazines like *Scribner's* and the *Saturday Evening Post* expected it; that difference underwrote their sense of their own relative privilege. In fact, Faulkner often catered to that readership by broadening the speech of his black characters for magazine publication. He was cynical about anything he saw as a potboiler, but the book versions were something else, and in revising the short stories that formed the basis for both *Go Down, Moses* and *The Unvanquished* he brought that speech closer to conventional orthography: "turnt" and "chawges" in the magazine, "turned" and "charges" in the book. Still, Ringo's racialized diction doesn't simply underline his blackness. His embodied voice reminds us, rather, of all that being black will mean in post–Civil War America, of everything that hasn't been abolished at all. For as he says to Bayard, "This War aint over. Hit just started good."

———

THOUGH WHAT WAR IS that? The attempt to rebuild the country—to make it a single polity once more—was already known as Reconstruction before the Civil War was over, as the Union army spread its control through Louisiana and Tennessee, in northern Virginia and along the coast of South Carolina. It had few fixed policies or principles, and everything about it remained in flux at the moment of Lincoln's assassination. How hard should the peace be—what punishment, if any, should be exacted on those whom many Americans saw as traitors? And what, exactly, would be the position of the freedmen in the reborn nation? Would they vote? Would they be given land? None of that was settled, and Ringo's words suggest indeed that the Civil War has had no clear end. Certainly John Sartoris himself sees Reconstruction as but a continuation of that war by other means. The South has been invaded by ballot boxes, and his own nighttime resistance stands as a guerrilla action in response.

But Ringo's words probably strike us more powerfully than they did Faulkner's original audience. To most readers in the 1930s, the conflict had long seemed a settled business. The white South kept its sense of grievance but foreign conflicts made it loyal once more; the distinctively American dilemma of the color line remained intractable, and yet its terms seemed fixed and permanent. Settled: and with everything about to change. We know more, now, about all that the fighting had left unfinished; know how much is unfinished still in the forever war over the place of black people in American society, and of slavery in American history. I'll focus here on two aspects of that struggle, those that bear most fully on Faulkner's treatment of the decades that followed Appomattox. One is what the historian Douglas Egerton has called "the wars of Reconstruction," the violence with which men like Sartoris responded to emancipation and that ended in former Confederates taking control of the South's state governments: governments "Redeemed" for white supremacy. The other is the war over those wars: a struggle of interpretation, a historians' strife in which for a time the South wholly triumphed, and that served to mask the truth about the Reconstruction era itself.

Slavery wasn't over when it was over. We have already met Louis Hughes, the onetime butler and author of *Thirty Years a Slave*. In June 1865, two months after the war's end, he made his fifth attempt to escape from his master's plantation one county to the west of Oxford. His McGehee owners paid little attention to the Emancipation Proclamation, and so long as there were no Union soldiers in the area conducted their business as before. Some runaways were shot as they tried to reach the Federal lines, and a Confederate soldier threatened to hang Hughes himself before word came that he was too valuable an investment. "The proclamation had long been issued—yet still they held us," and as the fighting came to a close the "reins" grew tighter and any communication between neighboring plantations was forbidden. Hughes had swum rivers and hidden in forests, but none of it worked, until one Sunday he simply walked off with a friend during the "servants' prayer meeting" and caught a wagon that took them to Memphis. Their wives remained in Mississippi, however, and though a Union officer assured them that they could go where they wished, they were at first afraid to try a rescue, lest their old owners "shoot the gizzards out of us." But Hughes did have money enough to hire a wagon and supply some sociable whiskey, and he soon found a few Yankee cavalrymen willing to provide an escort back to Mississippi. They claimed to be a foraging expedition, and as the soldiers requisitioned a load of fodder, Hughes and his friend got their wives on board. Almost a dozen other of the newly freed came with them; they reached Memphis on the fourth of July.

Hughes was lucky. He almost immediately went north, where both he and his wife found the siblings who had been lost to them by sale; he learned to read in Chicago and eventually settled in Milwaukee. But the historical record shows that many freedmen continued to be held in something as close to slavery as possible. On the same day that Hughes got his wife to Memphis, a Union army chaplain named James A. Hawley submitted a report to the Freedmen's Bureau of a tour through Mississippi's northern counties. He wrote that while some planters had expelled their former slaves and sent them out on the roads to starve, others wanted them to remain. Emancipation need not mean the loss of their homes, so long as they continued to work *"as they always had done."* That form of words masked a continuing hostility to abolition. Few land owners offered any payment beyond food and clothing, and Hawley quickly learned that the phrase "was designed to cover both the matters of discipline and compensation" alike. Most planters refused to believe that the freed people had earned a share in the crops their labor produced, and some preferred to let those crops rot rather than pay to have them picked.

Hawley thought that many white Mississippians who took the "amnesty oath" were lying. By swearing loyalty to the United States they reacquired the civil rights the rebellion had cost them, but he believed they would use their votes to reduce "the people as nearly to Slavery" as they could. The Thirteenth

Amendment had abolished the institution, but the state's unreformed legislature refused to join in ratifying it and quickly passed a set of laws known colloquially as the Black Code. Such laws were issued throughout the South, but Mississippi's was the first and among the harshest. Under the paradoxical name of "An Act to Confer Civil Rights on Freedmen," it required black people to sign yearlong labor contracts. They were held liable both to arrest and the forfeit of their entire wages if they left even the most brutal employer before their term was out, and runaways were treated as fugitive slaves had been. Vagrancy was loosely defined and severely punished, with "beggars, jugglers . . . [and those who] misspend what they earn" all liable to a sentence of plantation labor. So were those who failed to pay their court fines, including penalties levied for "insulting gestures." In Oxford petty criminals were sometimes suspended by their thumbs on the square. Children whose parents could not support them were "apprenticed" to their old owners, and blacks were forbidden to own firearms, a provision that the Union general in command of the region refused to enforce.

The Federal government responded with a series of civil rights measures that overturned the Black Codes, beginning with the Fourteenth Amendment: "all persons born or naturalized in the United States" were now defined as citizens, and under the equal protection of the law. The Fifteenth Amendment guaranteed the right to vote, and after Ulysses S. Grant was elected president in 1868, Washington showed an increased willingness to enforce the war's verdict, at times through a military presence. Reconstruction got teeth, and even in Mississippi some black men soon owned their own farms. They voted and made money, and the state sent two black senators, Hiram Revels and Blanche K. Bruce, to Washington. But the white South had an answer for that in the form of domestic terrorism. The 1866 murder of one white woman in an outlying part of Lafayette County was met with the killing of twenty black people and more, and in 1868 a local chapter of the Ku Klux Klan was organized at a meeting said to have been attended by Nathan Bedford Forrest himself. One of the chapter's leaders was a newspaper editor; another the chair of the county's Democratic Party. Burned-out houses became common, school buildings too, and many black leaders were whipped near death; black militias formed throughout the region in response and only United States troops prevented an open battle. In 1871 members of the Klan went on trial in Oxford under a new Federal statute. They were defended by L. Q. C. Lamar, who a decade before had written the state's ordinance of secession. During the hearing he punched a United States marshal in the face and then stage-managed his clients' suspended sentences. Two years later Oxford and its surrounding area sent him to Congress.

But most white violence didn't need the Klan. Faulkner's John Sartoris kills his carpetbaggers "over a question of negro voting," and no issue provoked an actual old Confederate so much as that of black suffrage. In Louisiana the 1872 election was so marred by charges of corruption that each political party claimed the governorship. The confusion was replicated on the local level, and in March 1873 a black Republican named William Ward declared himself sheriff of Grant Parish in the center of the state, slipped into the courthouse in the parish seat of Colfax, and with his supporters began to fortify it. On Easter Sunday a group of up to three hundred whites rode into the village, many of them former soldiers, well-armed and with a cannon too. Both sides fired, but the whites set the courthouse aflame and then picked off its defenders as they fled. The killing continued even after Ward's group surrendered, with men made to beg for their lives and then shot, as if in repetition of the massacre Forrest had led at Fort Pillow in 1864. The few prisoners the whites took were murdered that night. Their killers were drunk by then, and when Federal marshals finally arrived from New Orleans they found some bodies burned and others with their faces battered by rifle butts. Nobody knows just how many black people died in what quickly became known as the Colfax Massacre, but fifty years later the town put up an obelisk to the three whites who "fell," as the inscription has it, "in the Colfax Riot Fighting for White Supremacy." The most reliable estimates of the dead range between 60 and 80, though in later years the whites of Grant Parish boasted that the figures ran upward of 150. No one was ever punished.

The word "riot" on the Colfax obelisk needs attention. It became the white South's favorite term for mob violence and mass killings, and was used as well to describe a series of attacks on black citizens in both Memphis and New Orleans in 1866. In each case those attacks were led by the city police, and black deaths outnumbered white by more than ten to one. The word was used again in 1898 to describe a carefully planned assault on the elected government of Wilmington, North Carolina, an assault that destroyed one of the South's last remaining pockets of black suffrage. But "riot" both spreads the blame and denies all responsibility. It suggests that such actions were spontaneous and uncontrolled, and it stands as a profoundly dishonest description of the white-led violence of the late nineteenth century. An actual riot will flash and flare, a spark dropped on dry ground; it depends on existing tensions but its precipitating incident can come from anywhere: a bump on the street, an accident of the moment. It is set off, it isn't planned, and though it may produce leaders it isn't led from the start, as Colfax was by the white claimant to the sheriff's office. Individual actors in Colfax or Wilmington may have *run* riot, beserkers who did things they had not planned, and yet what happened there was not a riot. It was a pogrom.

There was also a massacre in Ellenton, Mississippi, in the late summer of 1876, when the shooting started as an attempt to disrupt Republican canvassers. In fact, a program of violent voter suppression became known as the Mississippi Plan and played its role throughout the South in that year's disputed presidential election. No candidate gained a clear majority of the electoral vote, and eventually the Republicans agreed, in exchange for the presidency, to leave the white state governments of the South alone. Rutherford B. Hayes of Ohio took office, and Reconstruction was over. Northern opinion had grown tired of the expense and the strife; there were new lands and opportunities to the west. We shouldn't discount the extraordinary difficulty of what the United States tried to do during that postwar decade. The change of one political system for another, an economic system and a social one too: that has never been easy, as Eastern Europe's recent history has demonstrated. It was made impossible here by the fact that those interlocking systems each rested on the white refusal to see black people as fully human.

That difficulty cannot, however, exonerate the historians who in the generations to come would write that period's story. W. E. B. Du Bois ended his 1935 *Black Reconstruction in America* with a catalogue of what was commonly thought and believed about those years, drawing upon a collection of current textbooks and quoting from them liberally. Children were taught that "the Negroes were so ignorant that they could only . . . vote aye or no as they were told" by the carpetbaggers who claimed to look out for them. Some black people refused to work, the schoolbooks claimed, believing that "freedom meant only idleness," and many "were worse off than they had been before." Other volumes argued that the region had been amply punished already. Reconstruction added insult to injury, with "self-respecting Southerners chaf[ing] under the horrible regime" and suffering through a time of "extravagance, fraud and disgusting incompetence." In such a world, the white South believed, the Klan stood as a necessary means to address the section's own humiliation. That's what most people were told about Reconstruction in Faulkner's day, and not only in the South. It's what their textbooks taught them, and those books had in turn learned their lessons from some of the most highly regarded academic historians of their day.

The key figure here is the Columbia University historian William Archibald Dunning, who did not even have the excuse of being a Southerner. Born in New Jersey, he was a partisan Democrat in an age when that party stood for segregation, and he believed that the Reconstruction amendments had been both a mistake and an injustice. The South's rejection of the Fourteenth Amendment in particular was but "a dignified refusal by honorable men to be the instruments of their own humiliation and shame," and the Black Codes found their warrant in the "well-established traits and habits of the negro." Dunning loved the passive voice, and he rarely bothered with evidence. His *Reconstruction: Political and Economic* (1907) simply asserts and assumes, as though the truth went without saying; and the truth that mattered most was that of the white South's easily outraged feelings. But his real influence came not through his own published work but through that of his graduate students, who under his direction produced a series of state histories that determined both the popular and scholarly view of Reconstruction for the first half of the twentieth century.

The volume on Mississippi was written by James Wilford Garner, who later taught at the University of Illinois. Du Bois thought Garner had more "scientific poise" than the other products of the Dunning School, and *Reconstruction in Mississippi* (1901) does indeed offer a judicious account of the machinery of state government. It can be relied upon in its account of legislative expenditures and tax policy, judicial appointments and the establishment of a system of public education. New laws forbade "whipping or maiming as a punishment for crime," and Garner scrupulously records the actions of the Klan, including its threats to the white teachers of black schools. Still, "much of the responsibility for these so-called KuKlux disorders" must rest with a Congress that had taken political power from a "hitherto dominant class" and given it to their former slaves. And that's the point at which the cloak of impartiality slips and analysis turns to advocacy. Sharing any power is equivalent to losing all of it, and Garner stands too close to his subjects to catch the flaw in the argument. He sees the small things; the large ones go unsaid. Faulkner made up the shooting of Calvin Burden, and his attitude toward it is equivocal at best: it provides a bitter and determinative family memory for Joanna Burden in *Light in August*, and yet an exhilarating assertion of white manhood in "Skirmish at Sartoris." But he doesn't bury the lede, and his work faces a truth that the historians of his childhood ignored. The white South thought it was worth killing to stop black people from voting.

Garner found an extra degree of influence in working on exactly the kind of textbook Du Bois criticizes, helping Franklin L. Riley with the Reconstruction chapters of his 1900 *School History of Mississippi*. That's the book Faulkner would have used in school, and its treatment of the period is rather less restrained. The agents of the Freedmen's Bureau were "the worst class of adventurers ... [who] did much to disturb the harmony and good feeling which had hitherto existed between the races." The killings at Ellenton go unmentioned, but the book does describe an 1875 "riot" near Jackson, when trains of armed men came from around the state "to aid the white people, for it was believed that there was to be a general massacre." Though believed by whom, and on what evidence? Later that year a new era began with the election of a Democratic legislature; "in many instances the negroes did not go to the polls," and yet Riley never pauses to ask why.

Reconstruction failed not because of white resistance but because black people could not be made to understand the responsibilities of freedom. So the Dunning School argued, using the occasional statistic to put a scholarly gloss on what white Southerners said during Reconstruction itself. And yet neither Dunning nor Garner were negligible figures. They both taught at important northern universities and were both elected to the presidency of the American Political Science Association. They were no more negligible than the Southern politicians of their day, and however biased their work we cannot underestimate their influence on American thought. Indeed, that school's belief in "negro incapacity" provided the intellectual cornerstone for the entire edifice of Jim Crow and soon found itself compounded in Confederate historiography with the celebration of the Lost Cause and the romanticization of the Old South. Garner's work was contemporary with the Klan romances of Thomas Nelson Page and Thomas W. Dixon, and that historiography would later shape *Gone with the Wind* and even the tap and warble of the young Shirley Temple. Those later works kept their popularity into the 1960s and '70s, with their disturbingly anodyne depictions of slavery continuing to amuse an audience that saw it as mere background for Temple's disarming ringlets and Scarlett O'Hara's indomitable will. On those pages and in those images the Southland was "redeemed" from indignity, and the story of how it fought against "Negro rule" stood, in the words of the Mississippi historian Dunbar Rowland, among "the greatest triumphs of [its] honor and manhood." That was the air Faulkner breathed in childhood; a world in which his spot of native soil had been saved by noble failures like Colonel Sartoris or indeed his own great-grandfather. So the myth said, so memory told him, a story passed from mouth to page and ear. But that is not the same thing as history itself.

His own work would both rend and patch that myth, and then rend it again, always leaving the tear a little larger than the patch. Few historians and fewer novelists of his day saw the hobbling vainglorious past so clearly, and few of them made slavery so central to their accounts of the war. One who did was W. E. B. Du Bois himself. Faulkner probably never looked at *Black Reconstruction in America*, but its challenge to the accepted view of the American past coincides in time with his own work on both *Absalom, Absalom!* and *The Unvanquished*. Du Bois argued that Reconstruction began in the middle of the war itself, began with the first attempts to envision the time to come. Black people were not the passive recipients of freedom, as most of the historians who preceded him had suggested. Instead they had worked, like Faulkner's own character Loosh, to bring that freedom into being. They had taken it for themselves, as soldiers and as refugees, men and

women walking toward Jordan. Time and time again they got out in front of
Federal policy and forced the Union's hand, and Du Bois never doubts that
their experience lay at the heart of the war's story. The white America of his
time might find itself stirred by the tale of the Blue and the Gray, but "the
most dramatic episode in American history was the sudden move to free four
million black slaves in an effort to stop a great civil war, to end forty years of
bitter controversy, and to appease the moral sense of civilization." That's the
book's first sentence, and its claim is at once blunt and subtle; subtle because
it suggests that emancipation had other causes than justice alone, that it was a
consequence of the war and not its purpose. And of course that sentence has
its ironies. The Civil War ended one bitter controversy, but other arguments
would take its place.

The Massachusetts-born Du Bois was teaching at Atlanta University
when he finished *Black Reconstruction*, as he had been more than thirty years
before when he published *The Souls of Black Folk*; in between he had helped
found the NAACP and spent many years editing its monthly magazine, *The
Crisis*. Much of his argument depended on a tightly grained social analysis of
a kind that lay beyond the Dunning School's capabilities. Dunning's followers lampooned the activities and indeed the existence of black lawmakers; Du
Bois drew on the work of the pioneering African-American historian John
R. Lynch to tell us exactly who they had been, the numbers of teachers and
ministers among them, and how far they were from Faulkner's illiterate Cash
Benbow. The Dunning School ridiculed the idea, first proposed by General
Sherman, that black families should be given forty acres and a mule; anyone
who believed that must think that freedom was a land of milk and honey.
Du Bois traced the growth in the number of black farmers and showed how
successfully they worked their land. He has figures for everything: the number of marriage licenses issued in Mississippi for both blacks and whites, of
churches built, and schools too. And he demolishes any idea of what Garner
had called an era of "negro domination." Only twelve of the state's seventy-
two counties ever had black sheriffs, and white candidates who supported
civil rights had few problems getting elected in black majority districts.

For Du Bois the collapse of Reconstruction was in no sense simple, but
one crucial factor was the absence of any coherent system of land reform, of

parceling out the South's enormous acreage of cotton and corn. Many planters had lost their land. They were cash-poor when the fighting was done and
couldn't pay their taxes or cover the debts once secured by their property in
slaves. A great deal of land should have been available, enough indeed to give
each black family that famous forty-acre freehold, but the banks took much
of it and speculators some more; the people who worked the soil got very
little. Land had to be paid for. The North felt a "deep repugnance" for any
government policy that expropriated private property, even that of Rebels,
and the South wanted "to keep the bulk of Negroes as landless laborers." Du
Bois writes that many whites ridiculed the black desire for ownership, and yet
that desire shouldn't surprise us in the least. Land is property, land is power,
land endures. Those who own it have a literal stake in the country, that classic requirement for citizenship and suffrage. Black landowners scared white
America, and the more acres a farmer held, the more likely he was to find the
Klan at his door. But it was easy to disenfranchise anyone working in another
man's field, and to Du Bois black people were politically vulnerable to the
precise degree that they were without property.

"Back Toward Slavery." So he calls his penultimate chapter—so he defines
Reconstruction's end. Southern legislatures never tired of finding new ways
to keep black people in something close to servitude. Among the most inven-
tive was the system of convict lease, which obtained throughout the South
and in which prisoners' labor was sold to private industry: the chain gangs of
American legend. They cut roads and chopped cotton, they died in the dark
of the Alabama coal mines, and their work was priced so cheaply as to make
a black man's life worth far less, in cash terms, than it had been under slavery. Faulkner's fictional John Sartoris builds his railroad with what appears
to be free labor. William Falkner, the Old Colonel, built his own with con-
victs leased by the year for fifty dollars each. The state got all the profit from
the sale of prisoners and none of the expense of housing or feeding them; no
wonder that the rates of conviction soared, and almost every black family
lived in the fear of the law. Reconstruction didn't fail because of corruption
or incompetence. It failed because most of white America did not want it to
succeed. Du Bois didn't find much of an audience at first, and even now some
textbooks haven't caught up to his reading of the past. But this black Yankee

scholar stands as a necessary voice and an essential companion to the picture of the postwar era that Faulkner would offer in *Go Down, Moses*.

———+·+———

A NEW SOUTH CHIPPED away at emancipation's promise, and for many freed people in the nineteenth century's last decades an independent life proved ever more difficult to sustain. Some became sharecroppers, held in place and peonage by debt, the money they owed a landowner for food and supplies. And others returned as if forced to their earlier lives, to the relative safety of the land where they were known, like Loosh in *The Unvanquished*. Early in that book, as we have seen, he goes off with a detachment of Union soldiers, but by 1873 he is once more at work in the Sartoris stables, exactly where he'd been when the Yankees first arrived. We're told nothing about the years between, and yet any reader of Faulkner gets used to filling an absence, to sketching the shape that defines it. We brush back on what we're told and read for what goes unsaid, and Loosh's case isn't the only one in which Faulkner's work invites us to step within the unwritten lives of its black characters, to think our way inside a postwar experience that never quite gets on the page.

It's 1886, and in *Go Down, Moses* a black man enters the commissary store on the McCaslin plantation outside of Jefferson. He wears good ministerial broadcloth, a better coat than young Ike McCaslin is used to seeing on anyone, black or white, and he walks and speaks with a white man's confidence. Faulkner doesn't give him a name and presents him instead through his errand: he wants to marry Fonsiba Beauchamp, Lucas's older sister, and take her away to Arkansas, a girl who's grown up on the land where some of her relatives were slaves and others the white people who owned them. He's come not to ask permission but simply to announce that fact to the white man who stands as the head of her family, Ike's older cousin Cass Edmonds, and their brief conversation is at once underplayed and extraordinarily charged. Cass speaks:

"You dont say Sir, do you?"
"To my elders, yes."

"I see. You are from the North."

"Yes. Since a child."

"Then your father was a slave."

"Yes. Once."

"Then how do you own a farm in Arkansas?"

"I have a grant. It was my father's. From the United States. For military service."

"I see. . . . The Yankee army."

"The United States army."

The incident takes just a handful of pages and plays little role in the novel's scheme as a whole. Still, I've always found a curious resonance here, and as they stand in the commissary the two men speak for a moment as if equally matched, a moment of strangled possibility, a world that might have been. This man will acknowledge Cass's authority only insofar as Cass in turn recognizes his responsibility for Fonsiba herself: his responsibility not as the plantation's master but as her cousin. The visitor admits that Cass is an honorable man "according to [his] lights and upbringing," but the white man isn't used to seeing that upbringing in relative terms, as but one set of manners among many. He isn't used to black men who correct him or who won't say "Sir." And of course they are not equally matched, for Cass has the power to order him off the family's land.

The man will take Fonsiba with him, but he is no farmer, and five months later, when Ike sees his cousin once more, she seems like no one he has ever known. He makes a slow interminable December journey west, with a thousand dollars concealed in a money belt, Fonsiba's share of an inheritance left by their white relatives to her and her siblings, and finds her crouching on the floor of a log cabin, on a farm with no barn or stable or stock. Her coffee-colored face looks dead, thinned by hunger; her eyes watch him without following, and her voice is without tone. Meanwhile her husband rocks himself in the house's one chair, his own voice still sonorous, and wearing a pair of spectacles that the visitor can see have lost their lenses; and as he talks, all Ike can think of is the man's "boundless folly and the baseless hope." Fonsiba's husband knows nothing about how to prepare the soil or to store up for the winter ahead. He speaks of what he might do in the spring, yet really he expects the land itself to provide, like Canaan, and meanwhile there is his father's army pension.

But we can read another story here too, even if it isn't the one that Ike himself sees, and setting aside the fact that by 1886 no one would have had the illusions of this soldier's son. We can see the scenes that Faulkner didn't write and perhaps did not even imagine. By now that voice and those spectacles are all this man has left of the person he once was, before he came south to the promise of a new land. For imagine the greetings he would have received in the Redeemed Arkansas of the 1880s: a black landowner and a stranger, a man with an educated voice and manner, a Yankee proud of his father's military service. Imagine his treatment in the nearest town, the nighttime knock at his door, the torches in his yard. The days when he might have counted on or at least hoped for help from the Federal government are long past. Will anyone dare aid him or offer advice about how to work his land? The other black men in the neighborhood are afraid to, their wives are afraid to know his, and so the couple remains friendless and alone, without even the degrading protection that subservience can bring. Their clay chimney melts in the rain but they are lucky that the house still stands—lucky, maybe, to be alive at all.

Faulkner didn't write any of that. He knew it all, of that I'm sure, and yet this is one moment when his honesty failed him. He saw the antebellum planter's sexual violence and greed; he had a clear vision of the white hysteria of his own day. But this is where he chose to patch the white South's myth about Reconstruction, where he saw black failure without also seeing the reasons for it. Young McCaslin draws exactly the wrong lesson here, and at this point in the book the novelist is too close to his character to know it. Ike believes that slavery has cast a blight upon the land. He will build his future upon that belief, but this scene suggests to him only the folly of an emancipation undirected by the white South. Faulkner's interest lies, admittedly, in defining Ike's relationship to his family's past, rather than his cousin's to the South's present. Nevertheless, he has missed a chance here, and I can only wonder how much more powerful this book might have been if he had taken it.

Go Down, Moses is never quite the novel one wants it to be, and yet despite its blind spots it does always return to the central question of our post–Civil War history. What will slavery's past mean for the South's, for the nation's, future? In his 1888 essay "The South as a Field for Fiction," the Union soldier, lawyer, and novelist Albion Tourgee argued that the long history of "bondage has left an ineradicable impress on master and slave alike," and suggested that the color line had become even more "portentous" after emancipation than it was before. Faulkner uses the black and white progeny of the semi-mythical Carothers McCaslin to define that impress: a family chronicle that covers a century, a history in which Carothers himself never actually appears and yet no one can escape his ghost. The old man dies in 1837 and the novel itself opens in 1859 with his white sons in possession, bachelors approaching sixty and known throughout the county as Uncles Buck and Buddy; Cass is their great-nephew, their dead sister's grandson, and Ike is Buck's late-life son. Buck had earlier appeared in *The Unvanquished*, helping Bayard track his grandmother's killer, and there is another way in which this book recalls that one. For it too was put together out of a series of magazine stories, fragments of Yoknapatawpha life that Faulkner then pieced into a whole. He was never short of material, but for many years his work in Hollywood left him little time for the sustained composition that a novel like *Absalom, Absalom!* required. The books that followed it were loosely built and episodic, and he would not again write a single story at novel length until 1948 with *Intruder in the Dust*.

The first bits of *Go Down, Moses* to appear were about hunting, tales that focused on the characters' relations to an ever-vanishing wilderness: a side of the novel given new currency by our own understanding of the natural world's fragility. But that concern is inseparable from Faulkner's interest in the nature of inheritance itself, and no matter how deeply the novel goes into the big woods, it always returns to the McCaslin lands to the north of Jefferson, lands now worked by sharecroppers, "laborers still held in thrall '65 or no." It is 1883 and at sixteen Ike spends a day in the plantation's commissary store, a square galleried place in the middle of his family's fields, full of the "old smells of cheese and salt meat and kerosene and harness." Its shelves are loaded with overalls and patent medicines, and barrels of flour sit beside the desk on which his cousin Cass records in a ledger the "slow outward trickle . . . which returned each fall as cotton," debiting the croppers' accounts for the food and supplies that they have no choice but to buy from him. But there are other ledgers in the commissary too, older ones, their pages yellowed and spines cracked, and written in the half-legible and half-literate hands of Ike's father and uncle. It's not the first time Ike has read those volumes, but it is the first time he can begin to understand them, and what he discovers there is the buried history of his family's past, a chronicle in faded ink of "injustice and a little at least of its amelioration": a restitution to which he will try, however ineffectually, to add.

In those ledgers Ike sees the record of the plantation's gains and losses, of the birth and purchase and death of slaves, and of Carothers's death as well. He reads of *Fibby Roskus Wife . . . Dide and burd 1 Aug 1849*; of her son Thucydus who was freed after the old man's death and eventually set up as a blacksmith in Jefferson. He reads too of Thucydus's wife Eunice, bought in New Orleans for $650 in 1807 and *Drowned in Crick Christmas Day 1832*. Those words are in his father's hand, and then his Uncle Buddy answers it, corrects it, as if they were talking to each other. *June 21 1833. Drownd herself.* Not simply drowned—drowned herself. But why, and how does Buddy know? So Ike wonders as he leans above the age-stained leaf, and then he turns the page to find the records of people he himself remembers, their details as spare as ever but now thickened, quickened, by the inferences he begins to draw. What he finds isn't just the tale of slavery's "general and condoned injustice" but also an account of something peculiar within his own family, "the specific tragedy which had not been condoned and could never be amortized."

Tomasina called Tomy Daughter of Thucydus @ Eunice Born 1810 did in Child bed June 1833. Her son is called Terrel, a name that Buck and Buddy misspell as Turl, Tomy's Turl. No father is listed. None needs to be. Everyone on the McCaslin place knows that Tomy's Turl was Carothers's last child, but Ike can remember him as a man who was supposed to be black but was instead not quite white, and knows that he must have had some white ancestry "before his father gave him the rest of it," something that came from his enslaved mother. And now Ike can see it, see Tomy's mother Eunice walking into that icy water after learning her daughter was pregnant with her master's child. He can see it, and can see as well the one fact those ledgers don't record, the fact his uncle and father would guess six months after Eunice's death, when they could look at the newborn's face. Her master's child, and her father's too. Tomasina was herself their sister, and her son their brother. Amalgamation here is incest indeed, rape and incest both. That is what slavery allows, that absolute mastery over what the law says is one's own. Buck and Buddy know what their father has done, and when he dies they move out of his "tremendously conceived" but unfinished plantation house and into a cabin that they build themselves. They won't allow their two dozen slaves to work on it except as neighbors might, raising the logs too large for them to handle alone, and when it's done they move the enslaved into the big house itself. But Ike will go further.

One of the few works of Southern history that we know Faulkner read is a volume by John Spencer Bassett called *The Southern Plantation Overseer* (1925). We know that because in the spring of 1940 he wrote a letter of his own apologizing for his tardiness in returning it; he'd borrowed it from Will Bryant, the man from whom he had bought Rowan Oak. The book collects the business letters written by the different men who worked as overseers on the Mississippi plantation of James K. Polk from the 1830s on. Polk was an absentee owner, busy in Congress and then as the ruthlessly expansionist president behind the Mexican-American War. But he was hardly an inattentive one, and he wanted regular reports on the state of the cotton crop and the production of pork, and on the health of the "hands" as well; so a John Garner wrote to him in 1839 that "the balance of the negros ar well." Some letters note the punishments meted out to fugitives, but few of Polk's runaways went north. More often they stayed in the area, temporary truants who hid out in the neighborhood in order to visit their wives on other plantations. And in fact Faulkner was reading Bassett as he worked on what became the first part of *Go Down, Moses*: a tale set in 1859 that he called "Was," in which Tomy's Turl sets off to see his sweetheart in the next county.

Faulkner's great-grandfather, the Old Colonel, probably seized the sexual opportunities that slavery gave him, but there's no evidence that his own predations matched those of Carothers McCaslin, and *Go Down, Moses* goes far beyond the particulars of any individual case. The book is steeped in the documentary records of the antebellum South, in the letters and ledgers that were a necessary part of any plantation's business. Yet what matters more than any research or indeed any bit of family history is the use to which Faulkner put it all, and here he had a special daring. He set his account of Ike's coming into knowledge in the middle of a long story called "The Bear," a tale about the annual hunting expeditions that the boy and his cousin Cass make into the bottomland along the Tallahatchie River. Each year they go into the woods, into land once owned by Thomas Sutpen, hoping to track and kill an enormous bear that has been eating corn and bagging shoats on the area's farms for time out of mind. Each year the party is bigger—men and boys, white and black—and each year they fail, no matter how many bullets they put into Old Ben's hide. But with every season Ike grows more expert in the woods, at one with its beasts and its trees, and what he learns there prepares him to act when he comes into his inheritance. No one can own the land. That's what he comes to believe. Not Carothers, or Sutpen, or Major de Spain, the Jefferson banker who claims it now; not even Ikkemotubbe, the Chickasaw chief from whom Sutpen bought it for money. No piece of that land has ever been theirs "to relinquish or sell," sell it though they did. For anything owned can be sold. That's the definition of ownership, any bit of property over which you have dominion, anything that can be alienated from the self. Yet at the moment you believe that it is yours to sell, that you have such power over a piece of land or another person, at that moment you deny your kinship with the rest of the created world. You violate your oneness with it and stand estranged, and only those who own nothing can truly own anything at all.

People belong to the land rather than the land to them. The earth will allow us to live on it only so long as we use it well, and here Faulkner anticipates such later environmentalists as Aldo Leopold, who in *Sand County Almanac* (1949) would write that we must see the land not "as a commodity belonging to us ... [but] as a community to which we belong." That is what Ike learns in the forest, and on his twenty-first birthday, in a sixty-page parenthesis that breaks the action of "The Bear," he will renounce and relinquish the land that every law of inheritance says is his own. He will refuse possession. For the idea of ownership itself is an outrage upon the earth, and an insult, he thinks, to God's own handiwork. Even the best of masters comes stained with sin, and too many are like old Carothers, so many that God himself has called *Stop!* and sent a great civil war to end it. So Ike tells his cousin Cass, as they stand once again in the commissary store. Servitude has cursed their soil, and he must do what he can to lift it, must atone and abstain, renounce and refuse what his father left him, owning little but his clothes and a set of carpenter's tools: the tools of the man he calls the Naza-rene, on whom he hopes to model his life. And Cass answers, reasonably, that nevertheless the land *is* owned and someone must hold and work it.

Which isn't good enough. "I'm trying," Ike says, "to explain to the head of my family something which I have got to do which I dont quite under-stand myself," something he has to do in order to live with himself at all. That explanation seems both theologically coherent and historically confused. Quentin Compson wonders why God let the South lose, but Ike has an answer. It was a mark of his special favor. He allowed the Confederacy to lose so that its people might have a chance to work out their salvation, to cleanse their "lightless gutted and empty land" of the sin they had put upon it. The South must redeem itself, though not precisely in the way intended by the politicians of the 1880s, and men like Ike and Cass must work in their gen-erations to wipe out what their forefathers had done. Cass remains incredu-lous, and yet Ike insists that God has never turned his face away from their devastated land. For how else but by his favor, he asks, could they have gone on fighting until that fighting itself had removed the cause of the conflict and lifted slavery's curse. But he believes that it is also a part of God's plan for the white South to discharge its debt through stewardship, that it must continue to care for and lead his people and bring them, someday, to Jordan. Debits and credits. Each day Cass takes down those ledgers and notes the flow of meat and meal, shoes and straw hats, of cotton picked and ginned. Another century will not be enough to discharge what the McCaslins owe, and mean-while those who actually make that cotton remain bound for life to the land their sweat has moistened.

The South must work out its own salvation, in its own time. That was a common sentiment in Faulkner's day among those white Southerners who passed for moderates, as he did, and he would argue the same point in his essays and speeches of the 1950s, after he had become a public figure. A better version of that belief would suggest, as this novel also does, that the white South had a special responsibility to face itself. It needed to ask Ike's questions—a need that stands in itself as the particular burden of the region's history. Though not only that region. Much of what Faulkner writes in "The Bear" seems to me troubling, bound by its moment, and Ike's own account of Reconstruction is the stuff of cliché, of Yankee "rapine and pillage," carpetbaggers and corruption. Yet much of it also brings me to tears: the ledgers themselves, with their sparse misspelled notations of tragedy and crime; then the boy's groping attempt to understand just what those ledgers mean to him and for him, what they will cost him; and finally his decision to accept that cost. Faulkner gets the big things right. He knows what the Civil War was about, and knows too that Ike himself remains bound to the precise degree that in Egypt land his black cousins must demand to be let go.

But there is another great work from which this novel seems to draw, even if Faulkner no more quotes from it directly than he does from that spiritual. Both North and South read the same Bible, as a man in Washington once said. They "pray to the same God; and each invokes His aid against the other." And perhaps that God has sent this war as the sorrow and punishment due to those, to all of those, by whom the offense of American slavery came into the land. It is an offense so great that the war might with justice continue "until all the wealth piled by the bondman's two hundred and fifty years of unrequited toil shall be sunk, and until every drop of blood drawn by the lash, shall be paid by another drawn with the sword." Retribution, restitution: a stain that must become its own solvent, a debt that must needs be requited. Faulkner was no more an orthodox Christian than Abraham Lincoln himself, and yet they were each steeped in the Bible's language. Each knew how to use its cadences and imagery. Isaac McCaslin hates slavery even as he believes in the South's cause and separate destiny. But I think the language of Lincoln's Second Inaugural would give him the shock and the shiver of recognition.

Still, that version of the Southern past—that understanding of the land, of what it means to own something—is not the whole of *Go Down, Moses*. Ike may believe that he's saved himself, and yet his example changes nothing. His cousin Cass still holds the land, and so will his son, and his son's son: good landlords, fair within the limits of their lights and upbringing, and each generation a little softer than the one before; yet landlords all the same. But there are other heirs too, whose lives, as Du Bois would remind us, remain subject to very different moral imperatives. Old Carothers left a thousand dollars in his will to Tomasina's son Terrel, the son called Tomy's Turl because he could not be called McCaslin. Buck and Buddy have added another thousand for each of Terrel's children: for Fonsiba, and for James, who went North and disappeared, and finally for Lucas. As an old man, Lucas Beauchamp will look like nothing so much as a Confederate soldier in the faded tintypes of the period: a man so fiercely stubborn that he seems to his white cousins more like old Carothers than Carothers himself. He will also have something of the white man's belief in possession, and on the day that *he* turns twenty-one he will demand his inheritance and become one of the few black men in Jefferson to keep his own bank account.

Faulkner set the novel's second section, "The Fire and the Hearth," around 1940 and filled it with Lucas's memories of his relations with his white cousins. Now in his sixties, he has more money than he will ever be able to spend, and he has farmed the same acres on the McCaslin place for forty years, "plowing and planting and working it when and how he saw fit," and sometimes choosing not to work at all; ignoring all advice, as befits "the oldest living McCaslin descendant still living on the hereditary land." The one thing Lucas doesn't have is title to the acreage Cass allotted him long ago, and yet somehow it doesn't matter. His land is his own, "though he neither owned it nor wanted to nor even needed to," doesn't need to because no McCaslin now alive is tough enough to take it from him. Lucas gets what he wants from the commissary and never pays a bill; "he approved of his fields and liked to work them, taking a solid pride in having good tools to use and using them well." Nevertheless, he remembers a time when he stood over a sleeping white man with an open razor in his hand and wondered whether or not to use that tool as well.

The man is his cousin Zack Edmonds, Cass's son, his almost-brother. They have hunted and fished together since boyhood, but Zack's wife dies in childbirth and Lucas's Molly moves into his house to care for the infant, and who knows what else beside. Slavery may be gone but white men are white men still, and old Carothers's blood runs in this one too. So Lucas steals into the man's house one day at dawn, wondering whether he has something to avenge—and then the moment passes. Zack isn't his ancestor, Lucas's suspicions are unfounded, and the black man lets the white one live; lets himself live too, for he knows what the consequences of using that razor would be. "A nation can never bury its past," as Albion Tourgee wrote, and Faulkner himself would famously insist that the past is never dead, it isn't even past. All the wrongs of Yoknapatawpha's history survive in Lucas's mind, they shape his thoughts and actions, and Faulkner's sympathies are entirely with him. Lucas's pride in possession reminds us that Ike's scruples and conscience, his decision to relinquish his inheritance, are in themselves a luxury, that his choice is but the product of that white skin he walks around in. Du Bois's account of Reconstruction suggests that no black farmer would make that choice, and when he brought Lucas back for *Intruder in the Dust* Faulkner altered his condition and gave him the land in law as well as fact.

TWELVE

A New South

In 1886 the Atlanta journalist Henry Grady gave a speech in New York that announced the birth of what he called the "New South." Not the old one of "slavery and secession," but a region emerging out of ruin and ready to take its full and proper place in the Union, forward-thinking and industrious; a South that cherished its past but admired Abraham Lincoln and determined in "conscience and common sense" to do right by the "Negro." That South had raised a beautiful city from out of Atlanta's ashes, it welcomed Northern capital and emigrants alike, and it saw abolition as a blessing. The Old South had relied too much on "on slavery and agriculture, unconscious that these could neither give nor maintain healthy growth." Grady's generation claimed to know better. Their ancestors may have acted within their rights, but still the Confederacy's fall was a fortunate one, and the region now stood on the verge of a "perfect democracy." The newspaperman had a keen sense of his audience. He told practiced, well-timed jokes, some of them at his own expense, and he showed the Yankees to whom he spoke yet another place to make money. He was a booster, a Chamber of Commerce in the making, and hoped to put the late unpleasantness behind him. Of course conscience could go only so far. The North shouldn't worry about the South's black citizen; "those among whom his lot is cast" would know what to do with him.

Grady's vision became a byword in the years to come. Birmingham's steel mills and the textile towns of North Carolina, the port of Mobile and the boom of his own Atlanta: that was the South he saw, a region given birth by the war itself. And Faulkner would offer a fictional account of that vision in the person of a character he called Cassius de Spain. Major de Spain is said to have ridden with Bedford Forrest, and though he must have had land and slaves before the war, his real career started afterward. He did a term as Yoknapatawpha's sheriff, but he also ran a bank, and a decade later he had become one of the county's biggest landowners, catching hold of the property that less fortunate men could not keep. Among his spoils, as Faulkner tells us in *Go Down, Moses*, was the bottomland along the Tallahatchie River that had once belonged to Thomas Sutpen: a rich tangle of virgin forest, a woodland "bigger and older than any recorded document" where the men from Jefferson go to hunt each fall. Faulkner depicts the major as both a hard man and a cultivated one, whose polished manners will let you pretend for a moment that you're equals; a man equally at home in his hunter's muddy corduroy or a banker's glazed white shirt. But it's the white shirt that matters, and late in *Go Down, Moses* de Spain sells the timber rights to his hunting ground to a Memphis lumber company. Where the unaxed forest had once seemed to stretch forever there will soon be a "planing-mill . . . which would cover two or three acres" along with miles of new steel rails and high-piled cross ties, the smell of creosote and the eternal whirr of the saw. The land will be clear-cut, nothing left but stumps: no longer a wilderness but a wasteland, despoiled so that the South can build itself afresh.

Many of those who were rich in the Old South stayed that way in the New; they simply found other ways to make money. But Faulkner's New South was not Henry Grady's. Mississippi remained agricultural, a state without a great industrial city, indeed without any real cities at all; in 1920 even Jackson, the state capital, had fewer than 25,000 people. The novelist sees the role that an entrepreneurial figure like de Spain might play in the society that emerged from the Civil War, a role rather like that of his own great-grandfather. His own New South would take a different form, however, and have a different relation to the old one as well. It would depend on radically different social types, and we can best approach it by looking not at Major de Spain but at one of his tenant farmers instead.

"Barn Burning" tells the story of a boy called Colonel Sartoris Snopes, whose father has taken one of the major's farms on shares. The man himself isn't given a first name here, but we're told enough to identify him, and he appears as Ab Snopes in both *The Unvanquished* and *The Hamlet*. Ab talks

with Faulkner from the start, and he had already used its various members in one work after another. The first piece of fiction he ever wrote about his apocryphal county, the unfinished "Father Abraham" (1926), had told of a scam perpetrated by Ab's other son, Flem. He sells his neighbors a string of spotted horses, while managing to disclaim responsibility when they prove useless and unbreakable; and a much longer version of that early tale would form the climactic sequence of *The Hamlet* itself. Faulkner made one Snopes cousin into a crooked state senator in *Sanctuary*, and another into a hairy-handed embezzler in *Flags in the Dust*; a third runs Jefferson's dirty picture show.

Flem's own chicanery drives a series of comic magazine stories, and his name captures him perfectly: blandly shrewd, a man seemingly without emotion, and forever chewing tobacco with the "steady, curious, sidewise motion of cows." Ab himself plays a major role in *The Unvanquished*, talking Bayard Sartoris's grandmother, Rosa Millard, into the meeting with the bandit Grumby that gets her killed. After that, it takes cheek to name a child after Colonel Sartoris, but then the Snopes family stands in Faulkner's imagination for everything that is fraudulent in American life. Some of its members are vicious, others merely feckless, but they each and all stand as a weevil-like and ever-spreading infestation upon the land. And Faulkner loved them. He loved the head-shaking incredulity and befuddled outrage they produce in Yoknapatawpha's other citizens; loved the narrative possibilities in their double-dealing, the fictional energy they carried, the skill with which any given Snopes can seem to pick his own pocket while actually picking yours.

Faulkner thought of the largely comic *Hamlet* as the first volume of a trilogy, and he planned to write the other books immediately. He wanted to show how, after moving to Jefferson, Flem Snopes rises to take over the Sartoris bank and even to buy de Spain's great house. Yet the material lay so readily available within him that he paradoxically kept putting it off in favor of anything more immediately pressing. He didn't return to the Snopes country until the end of the 1950s, and both *The Town* and *The Mansion* suffer from that delay, his powers diminished by age and alcohol and exhaustion. Those books find a set of darker possibilities in the family, and yet the Snopeses' spider-like venality seems finally too transparent to be dangerous. Robert Penn Warren's *All the King's Men* provides a good contrast. That 1946 novel won the Pulitzer Prize, and three years later a film version took the Academy Award, with Broderick Crawford earning an Oscar of his own for his portrait of Willie Stark, a populist Louisiana governor for whom people will crawl. He is both demagogue and savior, seductive and threatening, a man his constituents fear even as he pulls them toward him, just as they were pulled by the charisma of Huey Long, the Depression-era politician whom Warren took as his model. And the reader both believes in that fear and feels a bit of it too.

Nobody ever quite does that with Flem Snopes, but Faulkner's early critics still found something mythic in the family, a "universal conflict" in the opposition of Sartorises and Snopeses, between the old order of the plantation and the new land of commerce. The former act with what George Marion O'Donnell described in 1939 as a sense of social and ethical responsibility; the latter operate without considering "the legitimacy of [their] means." The old families of Jefferson embody a tradition under siege by modernity; they no longer know what to believe, and suffer in their decline from the "psychological effects of the Snopes world" upon them. That analysis is indeed present in Faulkner's work, a minor strain that sounds in Sarty's very name, but as a piece of moral calculus there's not much to be said for it. Warren indeed suggested that the good grooming of the planter class hid a corruption fully as deep as anything the Snopeses might offer. Certainly the family can't be taken to define any meaningful opposition between the different phases of Southern history, and in some ways Major de Spain himself seems a more representative figure. He's a man who looks to the past and the future at once, who loses his human capital but nevertheless becomes a great and destructive investor in the South's natural resources.

No, the Snopeses are but a sideshow, a set of human curiosities, and their distracting presence masks something to which the novelist gives a far greater imaginative weight. He does have a great deal to say about the difference between the Old South and the New, and about how the Civil War helped turn the one into the other. But his imagination of that process is more complicated than it seems, and to understand it we need to look closely at the world of Frenchman's Bend. Only not at the Snopeses—rather at the people who were already there when Ab first slouched in.

———•+•———

THEIR NAMES WERE ARMSTID and Tull and Quick, Winterbottom, McCarron, and Bundren, families that rolled into the country from the northeast, coming down slowly from the Tennessee mountains and beyond. They got a little further inland and a little further south with each decade, moving in wagons and on foot, and holding prayer books that most of them could not read. They might start a farm and leave it, and then start another where the land was a little easier; they came to Mississippi with no slaves and not much more property than they could carry, and in the Old South they lived in the margins of the big plantations. Such people could be found all over the region; the ones I've named came to a stop about twenty miles away from Jefferson, down in the county's southeast corner. They got some land and built small houses which they left unpainted, dogtrot cabins with another box of a room added every few years, as needed; they grew a bit of cotton and a little corn, they made whiskey and looked after their own. Probably most of them fought for the Confederacy, though few went so far as Pappy MacCallum in *Flags in the Dust*, who named his seven sons after Confederate commanders; and probably too some of them tried to sit it out, reluctant to fight in a rich man's war.

And there was a rich man in that neighborhood. He was called Louis Grenier, but by 1890, when *The Hamlet* opens, he was remembered only as the Frenchman, though you could still find his name, written in a fading hand, in the land records in the county courthouse. At the Bend itself he was barely even a memory, and his enormous house had begun to fall back into the "cane-and-cypress jungle" from which it emerged. Grenier laid out stables and slave quarters, he put in brick terraces and gardens and made his people straighten the Yoknapatawpha River to keep it from flooding his cotton. He built a monument to his own magnificence. Then he vanished into the war, and the cultural sway that such men once held seemed to vanish with him, leaving behind only a touch of legend and the land itself: fields and acres that were then parceled out "into small shiftless mortgaged farms." Mortgaged, most of them, not to a Jefferson bank but to another man in the neighborhood. He was rich too, a different kind of rich, and his name was Will Varner.

Faulkner begins *The Hamlet* with a thick description of social change, of a history that within a generation after the Civil War's end has produced a new but seemingly stable rural world; a "savage Arcadia," in the words of the critic Cleanth Brooks, that seems to have been there always. I call it "thick," and yet the writing is relaxed and colloquial, pages that work through a list-like accumulation of detail. The large planters have gone, and Will Varner is instead a "farmer, a usurer, [and] a veterinarian," a man with falsely innocent blue eyes, who might stuff a ballot box and yet looks like a Sunday School teacher. At sixty he owns the only store in Frenchman's Bend, along with the blacksmith shop and the cotton gin too. But he leaves his oldest son to run the business while he himself rides from farm to farm around the county, a man "at once active and lazy; he did nothing at all . . . and spent all his time at it." Varner owns most of the district's good land and holds the paper on the rest, and among the things he owns is Grenier's ruined mansion. It's the only thing he's ever bought that he couldn't sell, and he likes to sit over a pipe on its weed-choked lawn, wondering "what it must have felt like to be the fool that would need all this." His neighbors claim the spot just gives him some privacy to plan out his next foreclosure; nevertheless, they always ask his advice and usually take it. They do what he wants, and believe it's "bad luck for a man . . . to do his trading or gin his cotton or grind his meal" anywhere but at one or another of his concerns.

Varner has no interest in living like a great planter even though he could probably afford to. He rides an "old fat white horse," not a high-blooded stallion, and lacks Grenier's or Sutpen's desire to set himself apart; his interests and habits are the same as those of everyone around him. That only makes him more powerful—and yet how did he get that position in the first place? The historian Gavin Wright has argued that economic power in the Old South depended above all on the control of labor, the control and ownership of slaves. Land was plentiful and not worth much without the labor to work it, and that proved ever more true the further west one went, the further out into cotton country. The war changed that, and within a few years the South's economic base shifted from the ownership of labor to the ownership of land. Many plantations tried at first to run as before, with the freedmen working in gangs and under the close supervision of an overseer. But that looked too much like slavery. People resisted, they wanted to work for them-selves, they wanted at least the appearance of autonomy, and what quickly emerged was a system in which each family took over an allotted bit of land in return for a share of the crop; so it is on the McCaslin plantation to the north of Jefferson. However, not all landholdings remained intact. Credit was tight in the postwar South, and money scarce. Some planters lost their capital in losing their slaves and couldn't pay either their debts or their taxes. Some tried to sell out and found no buyers, others lost title to the banks and saw their property chopped into farm-sized pieces; and what happened to rich men happened far more often to poor ones. The first sharecroppers were black, and yet it wasn't long before there were white ones too, many of whom had once run their own land.

But even those who held on to their farms needed cash or credit. A bank might therefore advance money against a crop, enough to cover the family's supplies, and at harvest take a piece of it in return; it might also take the land itself in a year when prices fell or the yield was bad. A storekeeper could do the same thing, supplying credit in exchange for a lien on the crop, and watching patiently as each year a few of his customers got ever more deeply in debt. That's how Varner gets his power. Everybody in Frenchman's Bend is on his books, buying supplies in "six-bit dollars," seventy-five cents' worth of goods for every dollar they spend. His businesses produce enough to let him buy any farm in the area on which the banks foreclose; but sometimes he does it all on his own, exercising his lien and as likely as not renting the place back for its old owner to work on shares. Probably he doesn't do it as often as he could. Will Varner has known these people a long time, and can afford to be forgiving. The land won't go anywhere, and meanwhile he's got cheese and tobacco and harness to sell. He is merry and shrewd, and likable; but he had better like you as well.

Time in Frenchman's Bend is elastic. *As I Lay Dying* is set in the 1920s, but Varner isn't any older there than he was in *The Hamlet*, with its action set back in the 1890s; and as he stands by Addie Bundren's deathbed he will describe his son Jody, who had turned thirty before the turn of the century, as having been born in 1888. Elastic—or maybe nonexistent. New people come in to the Bend and others die; Flem Snopes takes over the store, marries Varner's daughter, and moves on to Jefferson. But that rural settlement itself endures without change, as though history had stopped. In the opening pages of *Light in August*, Henry Armstid and his neighbor Winterbottom squat in the shade and watch as a young white woman walks down the road beside them. She is pregnant and a stranger, and they can tell from her gait that she's used to walking, she's been on the road a long time. After she passes they wonder who she is and "where she got that belly"; and then, having no answers, they go back to talking about farm equipment. Eventually Armstid climbs into his wagon and sets his mules going, a "slow and mile consuming clatter" that soon catches up to the woman. Her name, she tells him, is Lena Grove and she hopes to reach Varner's store by dark and Jefferson a few days later; but Armstid insists that she rest for the night at his place and let his wife take care of her.

Yet though he overtakes her as she walks in the "pinewiney" August heat, his wagon "does not seem to progress. It seems to hang suspended in the middle distance forever and forever," all motion slowed. Its wheels crack and pop with each turn, and their sound precedes its sight, a ghost moving ahead of itself as time and distance collapse into one. The next day Lena boards another wagon that will take her into town, and this one too moves through "the sunny loneliness of the enormous land as if it were outside of, beyond all time and all haste." *Light in August* is set around 1930, at the time of its own composition, and that second wagon will travel on into a world of telephones and electric light. But you wouldn't know it from the book's opening chapter, which could take place at any time in the previous half-century and more. Jefferson itself has drawn level with the rest of the country and now has gas stations and picture shows; Armstid's world remains stuck in time. To Quentin Compson the deep South may have died in 1865, but there has never been the money to make anything new, and the country folk in Faulkner's work live in his day as they did in his grandfather's. Varner never ages, and the future seems arrested, as if the war has fixed it in place.

This isn't Henry Grady's New South, but it *is* Faulkner's, and in their apparent stasis those wagons stand as its emblem. This place belongs to its plain people. They have moved as if by right into a land from which the great plantations have disappeared; have taken it over, both on the ground and in our minds as well. They embody this world as Sartoris did the time before the Civil War; they have become its representative men, the overalled image, in our cultural imaginary, of what it means to be a white Southerner in that war's long aftermath. Sometimes that figure takes the shape of the sharecroppers that James Agee wrote about and Walker Evans photographed in *Let Us Now Praise Famous Men* (1941). Sometimes he is an independent farmer, a yeoman: an English term adapted to very different American ways. Armstid himself is of variable age and temperament, a character who works the land around the Bend and shows up whenever Faulkner needs him: choleric and half-insane in *The Hamlet*, but a good neighbor both here and in *As I Lay Dying*. There are other people like him in the novelist's world—Vernon Tull, Odum Bookwright, a dozen names and more. Some of them do better than the rest: some are in debt and others are what is called forehanded; Tull has even paid off his mortgage. Most of them own their own land, and on Saturdays their wagons line the square in town. And back at the Bend the Old Frenchman's Place continues to crumble. By 1930, when the county's roads are already filled with Ford automobiles, that house will seem more isolated than ever, its wreckage lost in the most tangled of forests, and a perfect hideout for the bootleggers of *Sanctuary*. Nobody appears to own it anymore, and even its legend has blown off.

Quentin can touch the past at will, it echoes deep within. Men like Armstid and Tull, Varner too, seem in contrast to pay it no heed at all, even though the social structure of their neighborhood is itself a product of that past, and of the recent past at that. They live as if outside of history's flow, untroubled and eternally in their place, and with these characters Faulkner approaches a line of argument about Southern culture that was contemporaneous with his own great work. The novelist had mixed with a literary world in 1920s New Orleans, but once he returned to Oxford he kept his distance from other writers. In the 1930s Faulkner said what he had to in his fiction. He didn't write reviews or deal in the politics of taste, and to everyone's embarrassment he drank his way through the one writer's conference he went to, a 1931 gathering of other Southerners in Charlottesville. Among those attending were the poets Allen Tate and John Crowe Ransom, who the year before, as I noted in my preface, had published a book of essays in collaboration with a group of other writers clustered around Nashville's Vanderbilt University. It was called *I'll Take My Stand*.

They described themselves as "Agrarians," and their work made no apology for the Southern past or indeed for slavery itself, "a feature" that Ransom described as "monstrous enough in theory, but, more often than not, humane in practice." Instead, they pit a mythified Southern culture against what they saw as modernity's dominant mode of life, defining an opposition between a precapitalist agricultural community on the one hand and a mechanical, market-driven society on the other. None of the Nashville writers called for their home region to secede. That was a settled question, and yet they believed that the South did offer the chance of a distinctive way of being, a separate line of historical development. Grady's rapacious New South was to them a foreign growth, and the preindustrial past a lost opportunity. Those who worked the soil remained identified with a particular spot of ground in a way that city folks could never be, and the Agrarians saw the subsistence farmer as the culture's typical figure. Andrew Nelson Lytle—Forrest's biographer, and one of the group's younger members—described such farmers in his own contribution to the volume as yeomen who "had hardly anything to do with the capitalists and their merchandise." Such men had been self-sufficient before the war. Even in 1930 they did their best to remain so, and Lytle provides an idealized image of a Tennessee farm family that has stayed put into the fourth generation. They work their two hundred acres, churn their own butter, and make their own soap, and at midday they eat in such an unhurried fashion that an office worker would grow nervous. No "fancy tin-can salads . . . litter the table," but there is always plenty of pot-likker.

The Nashville Agrarians spoke for a modernism that resisted the struggles of modernity itself. With their own poetry influenced by Eliot and Yeats, they dreamed of a vanished wholeness, a lost organic world. Faulkner remained aloof. They were among his first and greatest admirers but he stayed away from them, and their picture of the agricultural world is entirely without the extremity of his own: without the violence, or the sex, or the hatred, without the hunger and the bitter poverty; without the weather, and the laughter too. And their vision of the South lacks one thing more, one thing on which much though not all of the Yoknapatawpha cycle depends.

Ransom writes that "abolition alone could not have effected any great revolution in society," and the South that he and his fellows envision is in essence a South without black people. If abolition brought no change, then African-Americans are not an integral part of the culture; they can be simply written out, their presence suppressed in an appeal for tradition and stability. One of the group's leaders, Donald Davidson, doesn't even mention slavery in evoking the Civil War, a war he claimed was fought "for principles clearly defined, in the light of history, as presenting fundamentally the cause of agrarianism and against industrialism."

This is the point at which the Agrarians' thinking most nearly touches that small slice of Faulkner's creation called Frenchman's Bend. Their picture of the white farmer has little in common with his own. The presence or absence of black people is a more complicated question. *I'll Take My Stand* provides a classic instance of a phenomenon Toni Morrison identifies in *Playing in the Dark*, in which an "Africanist" presence is deliberately pushed to the margins of American culture, a process that then allows that culture to be "positioned as white." African-Americans might be physically present but they carried no weight in the world that Ransom and his colleagues imagined: their very existence stood as an ideological blind spot, a fact of Southern life that the Agrarians worked hard to ignore. It's very different in Faulkner, and not only in a book like *Go Down, Moses*. He won't allow himself to ignore that presence, and yet neither *The Hamlet* nor *As I Lay Dying*, the two novels he set around Frenchman's Bend, contain a single named black character. Still, that absence isn't precisely a lacuna, a hole in his thinking. It points instead to a set of social and political facts; to the quite literal business of pushing that Africanist presence physically aside.

Once again we need to ask what Faulkner *isn't* writing here. We need to read for the unspoken, for the stories that peep around the edges of the ones he's chosen to tell. We need, as with that soldier's son in *Go Down, Moses*, to envision the history that the novelist suggests but does not define; and once again, we may wish that he had written more. Louis Grenier had many slaves, but by the time of *The Hamlet* there is "not one negro landowner in the entire section. Strange negroes would absolutely refuse to pass through it after dark," as though that entire stretch of the country were a sundown town. Varner keeps a black cook, but we aren't told of any black tenant farmers or sharecroppers. We have to imagine the process by which the Bend's freedmen have vanished—some perhaps searching for family elsewhere, but others foreclosed upon, driven off, or worse. A black farmer might be sent to the state prison on the most trivial of charges, maybe an unpaid bill; his house might be burned, he might meet a rope, or get shot in his fields; his wife and his daughters could be raped without any hope of legal redress, and his own death to follow if he lifted a hand in vengeance. Many whites had lost their farms and had to rent from somebody else. They couldn't accept their new social equality with black men who were also farming on shares, still less with a landowner who had been born a slave. How would Ab Snopes treat such a man? How would the seemingly mild-mannered Varner? The Klan was gone, but groups known as "whitecaps" used the same tactics to "bulldoze" black farmers off the land; sometimes they also went after the merchants who supplied then. Those attacks ran strong in the late 1870s, and again at the start of the '90s, exactly when *The Hamlet* is set; and the section of Lafayette County on which Faulkner modeled Frenchman's Bend had long been a byword for violence of all kinds.

The novelist gestures toward that history; he allows us to glimpse a past that he never quite describes, in which the district's black population was in some sense harried beyond the margins of his narrative. But he doesn't dramatize it, and of course the more one knows already, the more one will see in that sentence about "negro landowner[s]." Both Frenchman's Bend and the society described in *I'll Take My Stand* have rid themselves of the South's black citizens: the one, as it were, in fact, and the other in ideology. Or maybe we can say that in Faulkner the ideology belongs in the first place to his characters rather than to the novelist himself. Different books can, admittedly, fill different agendas in an oeuvre so large and varied as his, and a full depiction of that history's brutality would have undermined the folk humor with which he describes Will Varner and his people—even assuming that he could have presented it fairly. Still, it's easy to imagine another novel, from another point of view, a book whose story might run alongside *The Hamlet*; another one of Faulkner's missed chances, or perhaps an opportunity for someone else. Was there ever a black landowner at Frenchman's Bend? The odds are good—but just when did he disappear, and how, and who got his farm? His absence leaves us with a racially purged countryside in which the Southerner is always white and where the Old South might therefore have never been, a place on which it seems to have left no traces. Yet this particular New South is in every way dependent on the Old: on its erstwhile existence, and its destruction too.

———•———

FAULKNER FIRST GAVE A name to his imagined land in *As I Lay Dying*, the short and perfect novel that he claimed to have written in six weeks during the fall of 1929, and in which the telling moves from one to another of fifteen separate first-person narrators. The Bundren family is on the road in the July heat, trying to reach Jefferson from their farm near Frenchman's Bend. Their wagon carries the coffined stinking corpse of the family matriarch, ready for burial in town, but the roads have washed out and they need to go around to the south and through another county to find a way. Buzzards trail their wagon, drawn by the smell of rotting flesh; the family's teenage daughter is pregnant, one of the adult sons is mad, and another has a broken leg that his siblings have set in cement. "They came from some place out in Yoknapatawpha," a pharmacist in the next county says, as if that were explanation enough. The father whines about not letting himself be beholden even as he gets his neighbors to do his work, and he will remarry as soon as his dead wife, Addie, has some dirt over her.

They come from Yoknapatawpha, and yet the book has always sat a bit to the side of Faulkner's other work. It doesn't take up the same issues, not directly; doesn't worry at the questions of race or remembrance, doesn't seem as if it wants to "tell about the South." The Bundrens are among his most memorable characters: the father, Anse, always "mumbling his mouth," trying to rule his children and yet literally toothless; Darl, who finds himself cursed by his ability to imagine the inner lives of other people, to see what he cannot see; Cash, the stoic carpenter, who knows "it aint none of us pure crazy and aint none of us pure sane until the balance of us talks him that-a-way." Yet with the exception of a one-sentence reference in a later story, "Uncle Willy," the family has no presence at all in the rest of Faulkner's work.

Some of the novel's narrators do appear elsewhere, the ones who comment on the Bundrens' actions—Vernon Tull and the country doctor Peabody, even the Jefferson soda jerk MacGowan. It would have been easy to use the Bundrens again, to imagine the luckless Anse spitting off the gallery at Varner's store, but Faulkner seems instead to have conceived them in isolation. They stand alone, proud and often angry, sometimes hating and yet forever dependent on each other in the face of the world around them. It's perhaps no accident that a family so closed in upon itself never reappeared in his work, never mixed their tale with the lives of others; and no accident, either, that the book Faulkner wrote about them would be the tightest and most self-contained of all the Yoknapatawpha novels.

Anse owns his own farm and can afford to hire another hand for the harvest, but every nickel counts and there is nothing in his world of the yeoman's ordered plenty that Andrew Lytle described in *I'll Take My Stand*. He cajoles and lies and steals from his children, but there's one promise he is determined to keep. Addie has asked him to bring her body for burial to Jefferson, and he'll do it simply because it will get him to town, where he can buy some false teeth. The Bundrens make the same journey that Lena Grove does, rolling from a stilled world of cedar buckets and cornshuck mattresses into modernity itself; and something very odd will happen in the process. Halfway through their trip they come to a river in flood, and as he prepares to drive the wagon through Darl looks over to the other bank and thinks that the space, the stream, between them has become "time: an irrevocable quality. It is as though time, no longer running straight before us in a diminishing line, now runs parallel between us like a looping string." The Bundrens will manage to cross that flow, but when they do time itself will seem to snap.

The river goes forever and irreversibly on, but the Bundrens cross at right angles. They slice across its stream, no longer moving *with* time but against it, inside it. Time wraps its current around them, it smothers and envelops them, and as it does the dead begin to speak. Nothing in all of Faulkner is more startling—terrifying—than the sudden presence on his page of Addie Bundren's voice. She has died many chapters before, and yet the past she embodies seems frighteningly alive and entirely present: alive because it is already dead, because it cannot be changed. Addie speaks in full knowledge of her own ending, telling us that living is terrible and language itself a lie, that "words dont ever fit even what they are trying to say at . . . [and] sin and love and fear are just sounds that people who never sinned nor loved nor feared have for what they never had." She speaks, and what she says shows us the events and forces that have shaped the Bundrens' lives: forces that the rest of them cannot begin to understand, not even Darl with his second sight. Addie knows why they are making this ruinous journey, why one sibling hates another. The dead past knows; the living do not. They cannot see the way that the past has determined and foreclosed their futures, and in that, at least, *As I Lay Dying* is not so different as it seems from the rest of Yoknapatawpha.

The swollen river lives, its current thick and malign, its yellow surface dimpled by the water's swirl, whitened by the hillocks of its waves. Darl and Cash guide their wagon through and have begun to feel success when a log suddenly shoots up, "rocketed . . . from the bottom," and bearded with foam as though it were an old man or a goat. Then it hits, the log rears and surges and strikes; the wagon tips, the mules lose their footing and drown. Time is a river, and now it spews up an obstacle: unavoidable and incomprehensible, a blow with which they must learn to live.

THIRTEEN

The Saddest Words

Basil Ransom had fought for Mississippi and come out of the war crippled only by debt. He had his health but his family had lost their land, and so after struggling for some years, and trained in the law, he left home and went north, to New York. We have no record of the date, nor does Henry James say much about the kind of practice that the hero of *The Bostonians* tried and largely failed to find. But there were other Dixie lawyers at work in the city, some of them specializing in the claims of Southern clients against Northern interests, and as for the year, it couldn't have been much before 1874. That was when a great exercise in Victorian Gothic went up in Cambridge, a place called Memorial Hall that stands as a "buttressed, cloistered, turreted" monument to the Union cause and the Harvard men who died for it. I say the "Union cause"—and yet that understates the building's claim.

The character himself visits Memorial Hall about halfway through James's novel. Basil has come to Boston on some scant piece of business and called on a red-haired feminist named Verena Tarrant, whose opinions he abhors. But physically she draws him, and he's begun to fall in love; in love, even though she lives, on unspecified terms, with his Yankee cousin Olive Chancellor. Now they walk through Cambridge's narrow wooded streets, and Verena, looking for something to show him, recalls a place to which it might "be indelicate to take a Mississippian." He is willing, however, so long as there's nothing in it specifically against his native state, and as for the Latin inscription that claims the dead were brave, "Well, so they were.... I must be brave enough to face them. It isn't the first time." Memorial Hall is divided into three, with a theater on one side and a "vast refectory" on the other, its wooden paneling polished to a rich dark honey. Those make the building useful, but its real business is transacted in the hall or nave that lies between them, a pewless high-arched aisle, pierced at either end by a rose window. Its walls bear a set of marble tablets, and on them, in "proud, sad clearness" are cut the names of Harvard's Civil War dead, or most of them, listing them first by their class year and then by the battle and date of their death.

James writes that the hall speaks of duty and honor and sacrifice, "simple" ideas that make the visitor read each name with "tenderness." What the novelist doesn't tell us is the particular meaning he found in the place himself. Harvard sent far fewer of its alumni to the war than did, say, the University of Virginia. But two of his cousins are listed there, and so is Robert Gould Shaw, the colonel of the Fifty-Fourth Massachusetts, in which his brother Wilky was a junior officer. Wilky's best friend is present as well, Cabot Russell, who fell with Shaw at Fort Wagner, where the young James was also wounded. The plaques for the class of 1860 note twelve names, more than 10 percent of its number; eleven men on that wall died at Gettysburg, including a Paul Revere, the silversmith's grandson. And to Basil the place seems the very reverse of a "challenge [or] taunt. . . . He was capable of being a generous foeman, and he forgot, now, the whole question of sides and parties," remembering only that he too had been a soldier. That is what, to him, the building commemorates, arching "over friends as well as enemies, the victims of defeat as well as the sons of triumph."

The Bostonians was serialized in the *Century,* appearing in thirteen issues from February 1885 on. It was the period's greatest magazine, and its table of contents offers in itself a history of American literature: James's novel ran concurrently with excerpts from a work-in-progress called *Huckleberry Finn,* and with William Dean Howells's *Rise of Silas Lapham* thrown in for good measure. The *Century* published George Washington Cable's "Freedman's Case in Equity," but it also printed Henry Grady's sharply critical reply, along with Thomas Nelson Page's "Meh Lady," in which the white writer used the voice of an elderly freedman to offer a nostalgic defense of the Old South. The magazine's editor, Richard Watson Gilder, had fought for the Union. He wanted, however, to heal the division between the different halves of white America, and many of his pages were devoted to a series I've already mentioned, "Battles and Leaders of the Civil War." That set of first-person memoirs claimed to look at the conflict from a strictly military point of view: to stand outside all questions of "sides or parties," analyzing neither the war's causes nor its consequences. Basil's note of reconciliation is very much that of the magazine itself, and his visit to Memorial Hall appeared in the same issue as Grant's account of the siege of Vicksburg; James provides no details of the lawyer's own military life, but it's tempting to think that he might have been within those walls. Now he stands in Cambridge, conscious of death, and for many men like him, as Drew Gilpin Faust has written, that soldier's sense of "shared suffering" would override all differences and establish "sacrifice and its memorialization as the ground on which North and South would ultimately reunite."

Yet that sense of a common loss emerged only after the end of Reconstruction. It was not the spirit in which Memorial Hall was built. Other colleges in the North eventually commemorated their dead on both sides of the war. Harvard did not. Death seemed still too fresh in 1874, victory too, and so a dedicatory carving upon the wall tells us that the building marks "the patriotism of . . . [those] who served in the Army and Navy of the United States during the war for the preservation of the Union." It was built for the Union dead, the nation's loyal citizens, and like Lincoln's words at Gettysburg, it was meant for those dead only. Most Harvard students of the day did, it's true, still come from Massachusetts, but not all, and a classmate of Henry Adams named William Henry Fitzhugh Lee became a cavalry commander in his father's army. He survived; many other Harvard Confederates did not. They have no place here. That went without saying at the time, but then the "Battles and Leaders" series did its work, and around the turn of the twentieth century there were calls for a second monument, one that might honor all the dead. The university paid them no heed.

Memorial Hall is a space of triumph, and frank about it. This war was successful, its sacrifice was not in vain, and even today the visitor thinks not just of death but of victory too. I am a New Englander, and I like the building's note of aggression, its solemn call to attention. I believe there was a right side to that war, and that neither the Confederacy nor its soldiers have a claim upon the polity they sought to ruin. But I am not consistent. Whenever I reread *The Bostonians* I am stirred by Basil's openhearted emotion, and when

I step inside Memorial Hall I also remember that during the academic year of 1909–10 an equally fictional Mississippian would have had to enter that building three times a day, at least if he wanted to eat. There are, however, other doors to the dining hall, and Quentin Compson wouldn't necessarily have had to walk past that line of memorial tablets. Though maybe sometimes he did, this young Southerner who would die in the North, as those other students had in the South. What would he have made of them? Would he have been brave enough to face them, as Basil had, this boy who already saw himself as a ghost, an afterthought?

Once in Oxford I sat at a lunch counter over a sandwich, and when he heard my voice the man on the next stool asked where I was from. I told him, and he laughed out another question: did anything good *ever* come out of Massachusetts? I smiled too and said that back home some people might flip that question around. Henry James never went to Mississippi, and Faulkner hadn't been to Cambridge when he set Quentin down there; he knew just enough to know that the Charles had a bridge or two. But each novelist recognized one big thing. They saw that each of those states provided an emblem for its section as a whole, that they stood as the most extreme version of a regional consciousness: one the heart of Yankeedom, of abolition and Union, and the other the South of the South. "Mississippi or Massachusetts," Quentin thinks when he returns to his dormitory room on the night of June 2, 1910. "I was. I am not. Massachusetts or Mississippi." He cleans a spot of blood off his shirt and changes into the right clothes for suicide; he brushes his teeth and remembers to take a hat for the walk down to the river.

"EVER TRIED. EVER FAILED. No matter. Try again. Fail again. Fail better." Samuel Beckett's words in his 1983 *Worstword Ho* echo the anecdote Faulkner liked to tell about the writing of *The Sound and the Fury*. The novel started as a short story called "Twilight," and though he didn't record the date on which he began, it was probably close to the one scrawled next to that title on the manuscript's opening page: April 7, 1928, Easter Saturday, and the day on which the first of the novel's four sections is set. The story concerns four children whose parents have sent them outside one evening to play, hoping to keep them from realizing that their paternal grandmother has just died. But the second Compson child is curious, the only girl, called Caddy for Candace. They've been splashing in a creek, and her drawers under her short dress have gotten muddy and wet. Now she climbs a pear tree next to the house, looking in at an upstairs window and hoping to see what's happening, while her brothers stare up at her from below. That moment will fix them forever. Caddy remains adventurous and soiled, generous, impulsive, and ruled by a desire that will end with her expulsion from the family. Her older brother Quentin lags behind, afraid to follow and yet wanting to; then Jason, querulous and aggrieved, who threatens to tell on her. The youngest, Benjy, watches without being able to speak. He is the "idiot" in the lines from *Macbeth* from which Faulkner takes his title, whose tale is "full of sound and fury"; and we will first see Caddy through his eyes.

That image, Faulkner said, was "the only thing in literature which would ever move me very much," that glimpse of her muddy drawers in the dusk, but the manuscript shows that even in his opening pages he had moved beyond that kernel of narrative. The grandmother's death takes place thirty years before the date on the book's first page; and we begin with Benjy, who cannot distinguish between past and present. His first-person narration slips from moment to moment, back from 1928 into childhood, then to some nearer date, back again, and forward into what isn't yet the present, each period encased within another and his movement between them triggered by association or repetition. He watches as a pair of golfers plays across what was once the Compsons' land, and bellows when one of them calls for his caddy, a sound that can only mean his missing sister. Benjy provides the bobbled lens through which we first approach this family history: Caddy's pregnancy by one man and her short-lived marriage to another; their father's fatal alcoholism; Quentin's suicide; and then Caddy's own daughter, whom she names after her dead brother and is forever forbidden to see. Faulkner later said that he had tried to tell all this through Benjy alone. It didn't work and so he started over, this time with a section in Quentin's voice and set in 1910 on the last day of his life. Try again, fail again, and he moved the narration back to Good Friday in 1928 and gave it over to Jason. But he still wasn't satisfied, and before giving up he let "Faulkner try it" with a final section set on Easter itself and written in the third person; a section that used Dilsey Gibson, the family's black housekeeper, to reframe our understanding of the Compsons themselves.

Faulkner believed in failure. He put Thomas Wolfe first among his contemporaries, for he thought that the now little-read author of *Look Homeward, Angel* (1929) had dared the most, had taken the biggest chances. Wolfe failed—but the attempt had been too big to succeed. Faulkner felt the same way about *Moby-Dick*, and maybe he believed in failure because he had to, because it was what he knew best when he started to work on "Twilight." *Flags in the Dust* had been rejected, the book on which he had staked his future. He thought that a door had swung silently shut between himself and any thought of a public, and in that isolation, he later recalled, he had said to himself "Now I can write. Now I can just write." He set to work without allowing himself to think about where he was going, and he wrote his way through each inadequate section without any sense of strain or trouble, indeed with what he remembered as ecstasy. Faulkner was always a good mythmaker, and the tall tale he made from the writing carries all the satisfaction of success: a gambler's account of drawing on hand after hand to an inside straight. But it shouldn't obscure a larger truth: *The Sound and the Fury* is *about* failure.

It made his reputation. Some reviewers couldn't abide the novel's difficult oddity, and its sales were low; he himself called it "the damndest book I ever read," as if he'd had nothing to do with it. But as the years passed Faulkner became known as the author of *The Sound and the Fury* above all, and so he remains. The novel depicted the relation between time and consciousness with a depth that no American has ever matched, not even James; an account of the inner life rivaled but not surpassed by Joyce and Woolf and Proust. And the demands of representing that life were greater than anything his peers had tried, with each character a limit case: the idiot, the suicide, and even Jason's hundred pages of apparently lucid hatred. That makes the book sound like a stunt, and yet its technical achievement is inseparable from its emotional force. None of the book's three first-person sections depends on its narrator's present day, but rather on what he has already experienced, the past he cannot escape; and in each case that past is defined in terms of the sibling whose voice we don't hear. Caddy is both missing and not, an absent presence to which her brothers cannot accommodate themselves: what she has done, what her actions have cost them. She is the past that determines their present, and none of them will ever get over her.

"To be traumatized," as the cultural theorist Cathy Caruth has written, "is precisely to be possessed by an image or event," an experience one cannot master, a door one cannot pass, "the unwitting reenactment of an event that one cannot simply leave behind." Trauma lies in our delayed response to something we couldn't comprehend at the moment it happened, the violence that our minds could not encompass and that returns to us in the form of flashbacks or nightmares. It is an unwilled memory, a repetition or recurrence that forces us to relive our pasts and presses when we least want it to; a fateful sense of doomed reiteration, a "wound of the mind," in Caruth's terms, and one "that cries out," that wants to speak its pain, and never just once. Those who suffer it have no choice but to circle around their own experience, trying but not quite daring to look. We draw close, we turn away, we try again, try to approach the place where we least want to be and yet must, drawn by its fascination and horror. Faulkner tells the Compsons' story four times, hoping that each will be the last, and he later told it again in the 1946 Appendix he wrote for *The Portable Faulkner*, each version drawing his readers ever more deeply within. And the brothers themselves always return to Caddy's memory, sniffing at it, unable to let it alone. For Benjy she was comfort, and the moment when he found her entangled with a boy is the loss of it. To Jason she contains the future he hasn't had. Her marriage represented his one chance to leave Jefferson, and when that marriage failed so did he. But for my purposes Quentin is the one who matters here.

On the last day of his life most of what happens to Quentin happens in memory. Most of what counts, anyway; leave aside the epiphenomena of the present. He knows what he will do that night, and he buys two flatirons to weight his way in the river; he goes over to Boston for breakfast at the Parker House and sits next to a black man on the streetcar, amazed at how easy it seems. Later he finds that he can't shake a little girl who follows him out of a bakery. But what's really determinative is the life that lies behind him, the past in which he couldn't stop Caddy from doing what she wants, being who she is. What matters is failure. He rides in an open automobile through the Boston suburbs, not listening to the other passengers' chatter, and then the day slips gears and he stands by the creek where they had played as children. Caddy lies in the water, her skirt soaked and flopping against her as she climbs out; then she sits with "her face tilted back in the gray light the smell of honeysuckle." Push it in, she tells him, push harder, I want you to, and he asks her to touch it, to put out her hand and guide his way, her hand upon the knife he holds at her throat. And she is willing—willing to die, as she says she did when other men touched her, died without knowing whether she loved them or not.

Have you ever done that, she asks, telling him not to cry; he asks her how many there have been and she can only say *too many*. Neurologists have recently identified a disorder called hyperthymesia, in which a memory presents itself, unbidden, with a totality of sensory detail, as if its every sound and image were unspooling in the mind. Those afflicted with it can see their own past as if it were a film, a continuous show, reruns of unforgettable reruns. Such memories seem more real than one's very present, and in his National Book Award–winning *Redeployment* Phil Klay makes an Iraq War veteran describe his own PTSD as a condition in which "the day remembers itself for me." So Quentin's conversations with both Caddy and their father will return throughout this June day, vivid and crippling, an earlier life of which he is never quite free. Morning and evening they arrive, a few lines of talk, her face in the dark, the whiskey in his father's voice; arrive in nothing like a recognizable sequence, a fractured collage of consciousness, a swamp and not a stream.

He can't push it in—can't kill her, in his misery at her willingly outraged honor, kill her and "then I can do mine," turn the knife upon himself. Instead he tells their father that he's pushed the other thing in, and he suffers from Mr. Compson's refusal to credit his claim of incest. Quentin wants the act's stigma but not the act itself, and under pressure he admits that he never suggested it to her because "I was afraid she might and then it wouldnt have done any good." Yet someone else's belief that they had, their father's belief—that would have cut them off from "the loud world so that it would have had to flee us of necessity." It would put them in a hell beyond all others, alone, walled off *amid the pointing and the horror* and in that isolation it would be all as if it had never been, canceled by a *clean flame the two of us more than dead*. His claim and the world's condemnation would wipe out both the men she's slept with and his failure to avenge her, but in this, as in so much else, his father is at once disappointing and wise, and tells Quentin that he seems "too serious to give me any cause for alarm." Of course it's Mr. Compson himself who should take action and hold Caddy's seducer to account. That's what the son of a Confederate general ought to do, and yet as that son he's come to believe that no principle is worth a struggle and no struggle worth beginning.

Two moments in which Quentin seems to lose his present call for particular attention. After he fails with the knife he hunts through town for a man named Dalton Ames, whose shirts he has taken for army khaki until he realizes that they are of "heavy Chinese silk or finest flannel." A dandy, and potent, a man who looks like bronze. He isn't the seventeen-year-old Caddy's first lover but he is the one who's gotten her pregnant, and when Quentin meets him on a bridge outside of Jefferson, the boy orders the man to leave town. "I say you must go not my father not anybody I say it," and if he doesn't, "Ill kill you." Ames is both amused and concerned. He tells Quentin not to take it so hard, hoping to avoid any trouble, but when the boy tries to hit him he stops the blow and emprisons both wrists in one hand while the other flicks under his coat. "Look here." He holds the pistol loosely, drops a bit of bark into the quickly flowing water, and watches it bob away. Without seeming to aim, he shatters the chip and then shatters its broken pieces, reloads, and hands the gun over; "youll need it from what you said." Again Quentin tries to hit him, only to find his hands caught once more; he faints, and when he revives Ames offers the boy his horse as a way to get home.

Only then does Quentin realize that he's holding a wet and bloodstained rag, that his eye smarts and his face feels cold. He isn't in Mississippi at all, but rather is in Massachusetts still, and without realizing it has picked and lost a fight with another Harvard student who's been talking too casually about women; has entered a fugue in which the present seems to vanish, the fight triggered by his memory, the memory by the fight. And that present has vanished for us as well. We stand for a dozen pages in memory's hall, reading without quite knowing where Quentin physically is, and only Faulkner's broken syntax—the unpunctuated and lowercase lines of dialogue spilling down the page—reminds us that we live here within the character's mind:

> he let me go I leaned against the rail
> do you feel all right
> let me alone Im all right
> can you make it home all right
> go on let me alone

The day remembers itself for him, Dalton Ames blowing down the barrel of his gun, Caddy holding his hand against her throat so he can feel the "surge of blood there it surged in strong accelerating beats." Then he snaps to, and his roommate Shreve tells him he'll have a shiner. Most first-time readers are shocked by this moment, shocked not by the ease with which Faulkner drops into the past but by the abruptness with which he makes us leave it. Only when it's over do we realize how far these pages have taken us, and I can't reread them without thinking of Ambrose Bierce's "Occurrence at Owl Creek Bridge," a story Faulkner must have had in mind as he wrote. There a Confederate spy stands with a noose around his neck—and when the drop comes the cord breaks, he plunges deep into the stream, dodges the Union bullets, swims on, and makes his way home. Yet all that happens in his consciousness alone, an entire future in the half-second before the rope pulls tight. That isn't Quentin's fate, not exactly; nevertheless, he too stands upon a bridge, and he won't need a rope to help him off another one.

It's after he meets Dalton Ames that Quentin tries to convince his father of the incest. His last hope, and in Cambridge their conversation replays itself when he returns to his dormitory to prepare for the night. I've already quoted some of its lines, and Mr. Compson is the first of Faulkner's grandiloquent speakers, drunk on something more than whiskey, an unstopped rhetoric that Quentin can barely manage to interrupt. Your anguish, his father says, grows out of a purely "temporary state." That's what virginity is, both Caddy's and his own; it's something meant to end, to lose and move on from; and so is pain itself. The boy will have none of it:

... and i temporary and he you cannot bear to think that someday it will no longer hurt you like this ... and i temporary and he it is hard believing to think that a love or a sorrow is a bond purchased without design and which matures willynilly and is recalled without warning to be replaced by whatever issue the gods happen to be floating at the time no you will not do that until you come to believe that even she was not quite worth despair perhaps and i i will never do that nobody knows what i know ... and he every man is the arbiter of his own virtues but let no man prescribe for another mans wellbeing and i temporary and he was the saddest word of all there is nothing else in the world its not despair until time its not even time until it was.

Was. Something that *was* lies in the past, fixed and unchanging, over and done with; concluded and therefore temporary indeed. *Is* in contrast is ongoing and permanent, *is* for Quentin is trauma, the ever-present family history that defines him. The only thing worse than the pain it brings would be the idea that he might get over it, that it might no longer hurt and that even his sister was not worth despair. *Was* allows survival, and yet to discard that trauma, to believe one might outlive it—that discounts its importance, dismisses the very wound that has come to constitute the self. Nobody knows what I know, and Quentin would rather die than imagine "that someday it will no longer hurt," that someday the honor of their cursed name might no longer matter. And Mr. Compson recognizes that. *Was* is the saddest word: the past he cannot mend, that he no longer cares enough about to fight with. *Was*, for him, is despair; and so is time itself.

But Quentin will find a different word. The full memory of this talk returns to him only at the very end of the evening, the very end of his life, and yet it's been at the edge of his mind all day. That morning he stood along the river, watching a friend pull a scull, and with the stiff envelope of his suicide note crackling through his coat. For a second there he imagines himself in the future, a college senior with the privilege of not wearing a hat, but then his father's word comes back to him, one spoken in Mississippi the summer before. *Was.* That's what he soon will be, but here that time-laden syllable floats on the page without explanation. Quentin has already had that conversation; we haven't. For us it lies fifty pages on, and we can't know what that word means to him, not yet. So his next thought seems especially cryptic. "Again. Sadder than was. Again. Saddest of all. Again." We won't understand that claim until it becomes literally true, until that exchange with his father runs through his head once more. Play; repeat: the past on its endless loop in his mind. He will hear his father's words again, remember Caddy again, sadder than was, saddest of all.

WHY, THOUGH, DOES THIS novel even need a section set in the North? The Cambridge location increases Quentin's sense of isolation, cut off from the past that consumes him. He would not have found himself so solitary, so alone in his emotional plight, at a place like the University of Virginia, even though there's nothing in his wrangle with the past that he couldn't have felt there. A better question might ask what the Massachusetts setting allows, and the short answer is that it gave Faulkner a ready-made place and character when he found, in the mid-1930s, that he wanted to tell about the South. *The Sound and the Fury* invokes a sense of regional difference, and yet its most powerful moments take Mississippi for granted. They don't interrogate it; *Absalom, Absalom!* does. The second novel depends upon that difference, and it casts a retrospective shadow. Scholars have tried to distinguish the Quentin of one book from that of the other, to take each novel on its own terms, but nobody can ever really separate them. The later book is shaped by the suicide that Quentin hasn't yet begun to plan, and his meeting with Henry Sutpen draws half its power from what we know of his future. Yet *Absalom, Absalom!* also changes the way we read its predecessor. It privileges Quentin's narration over his brothers' and makes him more central to our experience of the novel than he might otherwise be. More: it bends a book about the workings of consciousness into one about the South, and it does so by letting us listen to the historical resonance that lies under its breath, to hear what *The Sound and the Fury* only half-says. Or to put it another way: what do Quentin's troubles have to tell us about the war?

The literary historian Eric Sundquist has argued that Faulkner's abiding subject is "the inchoate . . . grief and unfulfilled desire to which his characters are forever subject." That anguish, however, is never purely personal, and there's a deep congruity between the movements of Faulkner's mind, with its sense of an inescapable family trauma, and the history and culture of his region—so deep that it hardly seems possible to distinguish between them. The Reverend Hightower in *Light in August* believes that his life "had already ceased before it began," that he himself is but "a single instant of darkness in which a horse galloped and a gun crashed" and his Confederate grandfather fell into the Jefferson dust. But happen is never once, and at the end of *Absalom, Absalom!* Quentin tells Shreve that he is already "older at twenty than a lot of people who have died." As if to say, it is time to go; time because he has failed, because he still stands on that bridge with Dalton Ames.

It is time because the past goes on forever, because he can't see his own pain as temporary and doesn't even want to. It is time because, as Gavin Stevens says in *Intruder in the Dust*, there remains a place in the mind of every Southern boy "when it's still not yet two oclock" and Pickett hasn't yet left the woods opposite Cemetery Ridge: a place in which Caddy is still a virgin and Quentin has not yet been unable to act. That's what he wants—the past for which he and every other Southern white boy have arrived too late, one that is *not yet*, that has yet to become *was*. Not before, and certainly not after, but rather a moment in which it all still *is*, and in which he can stay forever. Someday all this will no longer hurt him, Mr. Compson says; and the boy's suicide suggests that he thinks his father is right, that what he can't accept is the idea of outliving his own pain.

Quentin begins that morning in Cambridge by breaking his grandfather's watch, crushing its glass and snapping off its hands. But the tick remains. Time stops even as it creeps irrevocably on, and the richest account of his struggle remains John Irwin's classic *Doubling and Incest / Repetition and Revenge* (1975). For Irwin all sons are condemned to a sense of belatedness simply because they *are* sons, because they've had fathers who themselves are "struggling in the grip of Father Time." That repetition precludes any sense of one's own generative power; it condemns each son to a life in which, as Mr. Compson says, all "tragedy is second-hand," a catastrophe that has already happened. That much is true anywhere, and Irwin rarely appeals to history or biography as such. But he does allow that in a newly settled country the Civil War had shut off the "virgin space and the time of origins, so that the antebellum South became in the minds of postwar Southerners [a] debilitating 'golden age' " that made the present look impotent by comparison. That past seems so fully and painfully lost precisely because it's the only one this place has known. The stopped clock always points toward two, not yet and was; there is always a bridge on which to fail once more. Quentin lives in an afterlife, and what he has to tell us about the South is that it all happens over and over again, "ripples maybe on water after the pebble sinks." The irony is that Faulkner needs what's newest about *The Sound and the Fury* to make that repetition seem so vivid. "Stream of consciousness" is a weak phrase for what he does with Quentin's inner life, in which his thoughts may now run smoothly and now pool; their flow split and dammed, arrested or even reversed. Yet without that body of radically contemporary technique, Faulkner could not have made us feel that the past is never past.

So it happened, as Robert Penn Warren has written, that "in the moment of death the Confederacy entered upon its immortality." Loss created an enduring "mystique of prideful 'difference,' identity, and defensiveness" that made the South into a single and coherent region in a way that slavery alone never could. Nor was that a matter of consciousness alone. The states that had remained in the Union went on changing, modernizing, industrializing, growing: a region defined not by what had happened, but by what was going to. The North could afford to forget the war, but in the South its scars endured on something more than the bodies of its soldiers, endured in the decrepitude of its buildings and the absence of any money for renewal. In that South the Confederacy stood as a fixed point, and the war became the still and violent center of time itself.

There are many ways to understand this, but to me the most useful lies in pushing our sense of trauma beyond the bounds of the individual psyche, as indeed Freud's *Moses and Monotheism* suggests we must. Insofar as different people share a sense of history, a past recalled in common, so too they may share the same wounds. But Freud also suggests that the traumatic event remains unrepresentable: the event, as opposed to its memory. We've already seen that Faulkner likes to work up to and then away from the moment of climax, that he almost never presents it directly but prefers to write around a gap instead. We hear Henry Sutpen's conversation with Quentin not at the time of speaking but rather as it echoes in the boy's mind. Nor do we ever actually see Caddy Compson; we know only her remembered presence, only the pain of her loss. And so it is with the Civil War itself, a struggle that in Faulkner's work is everywhere felt and nowhere fully presented, not even in *The Unvanquished*. We walk around its edges; we don't come close to what Tolstoy called "the reality of war, the actual killing." Though as it happens there is a lot of killing in Yoknapatawpha, a lot of murder. But it almost always happens offstage, deaths that we walk toward and away from, and often presented through the eyes of those who find the body and need to talk about it. The past cries out for Quentin and Hightower and perhaps for their creator too, a trauma induced by a loss they have never not known; their voices are marked by the compulsion to repeat, a part of the pleasure principle that endures even in pleasure's absence. *Again.*

Yet this raises a question. *The Sound and the Fury* ends with a scene on Jefferson's square, where the statue of a "Confederate soldier gazed with empty eyes beneath his marble hand in wind and weather." Monuments remind us that we must always remember, memorials that we should never forget, but what does such a statue ask us to remember, and what does that memory require we forget? In Faulkner's day the white South littered its public spaces with the mementoes of its own ruined cause, it deployed a sense of its own suffering and mastered the rhetoric of victimhood and hatred alike. And indeed its people were victims—victims of what they had done to themselves. They were also perpetrators, and their insistence on their own sense of loss effectively denied the greater trauma with which their land was stained: the trauma that Lincoln described as 250 years of bloody and unrequited toil. But I would go further. That denial wasn't limited to the South. It belonged to much of white America, the country in which the Blue and the Gray became one; and meanwhile the marble man stood—stands—sentry in the courthouse square, in silent triumph over the resubdued black body. Indeed the book's famous last page makes that literally true: the teenage servant Luster tries to take the Compson carriage to the statue's left rather than the accustomed right, making Benjy bellow in fear at the violation of routine, and gets a beating in return.

Nevertheless the past will speak, the suppressed return. One night in the summer of 2002 I was walking with my wife and daughter down a residential street in the northern German city of Hamburg. We had lived there before but now there was something subtly new in the sidewalk before us, a bright metallic gleam in the streetlight, and when we bent to look we saw that it was a brass plate the size and shape of the cobblestone it had replaced. It was engraved with a name and some dates, and in front of the next house we saw two more, then another down the block. All the surnames were Jewish, but though the birth dates varied everyone had died in 1942 or 1943 at places whose names we knew too well. Over the next few weeks we saw many more of them, and especially in our own neighborhood near the university. *Stolpersteine*: so we learned they are called, stumble stones, and they mark the last German address at which the person they name had lived freely. Not all of them list a death in the camps; some note a suicide, and others an escape to Switzerland or America instead. But they all remember a particular person at a particular place, not an abstract mass of victims, and by now Hamburg has more than 4,000 of them, with many thousands more installed throughout Germany and indeed the whole of Europe. Local groups, schoolchildren, and sometimes the current householder do the necessary research to find out who had once lived at a given address, and the artist who conceived of the project, Gunter Demnig, then makes the stone by hand, the brass attached to a concrete cube. The first of them was placed in Cologne in 1992, and though most remember the Nazis' Jewish victims they may be made for any of the persecuted.

Germany has many memorials to the Holocaust, mute witnesses to an absence, and they are quite often cerebral, installations for which the visitor usually needs some explanation, a bit of text to tell you what you're seeing. Such places avoid the blunt legibility of a statue or catafalque. You need to work at what they say, to puzzle over them, as if halting at an impasse of meaning rather than moving directly from the image to some expected or accustomed emotion. The genius of Demnig's work is that its burden seems immediately clear and yet you stumble anyway, pause, and think. That brassy

glow stops you short, that name and a date: a site you've come upon casually, without looking for it, and that then forces itself upon you. Not everybody likes stubbing their toes that way, and some towns have preferred more
obtrusive and yet less omnipresent memorials. But the *Stolpersteine* provide
the best vehicle I know for the process of what in German is called *Vergangenheitsbewältigung*, the process of working through or overcoming through
the past. It's a term for which there is no single English equivalent, though
perhaps that's not surprising. The German itself is both a compound and a
relative neologism, a fusion of the noun for "past"—*Vergangenheit*—with the
word that denotes the idea of coping or mastering, and always with a sense of
struggle. It is what one does, must do, with a difficult and recalcitrant history,
a history for which one's people bear responsibility; a struggle that may last
for generations and that extends even to those individuals who carry no personal share of the burden.

The term became common in the aftermath of World War II as a way to
reckon with what had been done in Germany's name. The largely ineffective
process called Denazification was just the start, and the Nuremberg Trials
only touched the very top. And in the decades since, that process has taken
many forms and had many ramifications. Some parts of it were quickly recognized as necessary, and in the 1950s the West German government agreed
to pay reparations both to Israel and to individual German Jewish survivors. A checkbook is never enough, however, and one obstacle lay in what in
1967 the psychoanalysts Alexander and Margarete Mitscherlich called "the
inability to mourn." Their argument is complex and in many ways counter-
intuitive, but at its heart lies the claim that many Germans approached the
recent past as if stunned, numbed into a sense of moral indifference in a way
that allowed them to blame everything on the Nazi leadership. Often they
drew a distinction between the Nazi Party and ordinary Germans, between
the SS and the regular army, or Wehrmacht. *I didn't know, it wasn't me, he
was good at the start.*

Yet one needed to accept one's own involvement before laying the past to
rest, and recognizing that complicity required that one first be able to mourn
what had been lost, even an emotional investment in Hitler himself; to let it
wring one out in exhaustion and tears. Only then could one begin to face the

past in all its fullness, and that is what the country itself began to do in the 1960s. Novels like Gunter Grass's *The Tin Drum* (1959) played a role, with its picture of the nation's complicity in crime, a complicity that Grass himself knew more about than he was willing to admit, hiding his teenage member-ship in the SS until near the end of his life. So did work like the Mitscher-lichs' own, and then the student movements of the period as well, that revolt against the parents. New trials reached down below the Nazi command, and concentration camp guards went into the dock. Many of those trials resulted in acquittals, but even then they required an attempt to master the enormity of the past; even a failed prosecution revealed the inadequacy of any ordinary terms of judgment. Historians showed that the Wehrmacht had committed atrocities of its own. More people had known about the camps than good Germans would once have been willing to believe, but each access of knowl-edge had to fight its way to acceptance, debated in books and newspapers, around dinner tables, in seminars and churches and in barrooms too.

That work is ever-ongoing and unfinished, indeed unfinishable, and some people on the country's right have always resisted it. Nevertheless, the process of *Vergangenheitsbewältigung* has become in itself a central part of German national identity, and for many non-Germans the seriousness of that engage-ment with the past stands as a model to emulate. It did, true, take a genera-tion fully to begin. In the white South it took a century: a century in which the region remained frozen in place, furious, immobile, and "static in *quo*." Of course it is profoundly anachronistic to lament the inability of the Con-federacy's immediate survivors to overcome the past, to note their failure to engage in anything like that process. The very concept depends upon a psy-choanalytic language that did not then exist. What did exist was a religious vocabulary that might have gotten them to the same place, a vocabulary of justice and atonement, if only the Southern churches had not long before made their peace with slavery. The Confederate states squabbled endlessly, and large segments of its population had opposed secession. Yet there was lit-tle disagreement about that bondage itself, and in some ways the continuing prejudice against black people was more universally shared, if less immedi-ately lethal, than German antisemitism. Many Germans felt sorry for them-selves when the shooting was over, but few of them insisted, as Edward A.

Pollard did in *The Lost Cause* (1866), that they had been perfectly within their rights. They quickly recognized that military defeat was a defeat for their ideas as well. The white South did not. Secession might be a practical impossibility, but they had merely bowed, in Lee's words, to "superior numbers and resources"; their soldiers had lost and yet their principles remained unvanquished.

In Germany the Allies imposed and enforced a new order. They did it with troops, a military presence whose weight no country in 1865 could have imagined. They did it with money; suppose Sherman's casual suggestion of forty acres and a mule had been funded on the scale of the Marshall Plan? Moreover they had, on both sides of the Berlin Wall, a significant history of German dissent to draw on, of freed political prisoners and returning exiles. The South had no such body. And one thing more offered the grimmest of help in Germany's reconstruction. The Third Reich had done its work so thoroughly, and so few of its returning exiles were Jewish, that there was no one left on whom a diehard could focus a lingering *ressentiment*. The white South, in contrast, had in its former slaves an ever-present reminder of defeat. It had someone to hate, and to fear. No analogy is perfect, but I have never in Germany seen anything like a conventional memorial to World War II—only a block of stone marked with the dates 1939–1945 or a book in a country church, open to a page that listed the dead of the parish. Yet no carved or cast figure of Erwin Rommel, still less of Hermann Goering, looms above a German city as Robert E. Lee and Stonewall Jackson do over Virginia's capital. Not that the statues of Richmond's Monument Avenue were really meant to honor their nominal subjects. They went up around the turn of the twentieth century as a way to remind us all of who was once more in charge, a celebration of the white South's renewed political power; and other bits of stone, like South Carolina's state memorial at Gettysburg, were in fact erected during the *1960s* in resistance to the movement for civil rights. Every now and then you hear somebody say that he flies a battle flag or values such statuary as a sign of "heritage," a way to honor his ancestors. But the Confederacy didn't last nearly so long as Jim Crow, and one wants to ask which ancestors, which heritage.

The South's own work in confronting its past eventually took public form in Selma and Birmingham, at a Greensboro lunch counter and at Jimmy Carter's church in Plains, Georgia. It happened with a glossy novel called *Roots*, it happens at the ballot box, and at Montgomery's National Memorial for Peace and Justice, which tries to record every lynching of a black person. It is happening now in Faulkner's Oxford, where at the University of Mississippi a series of skeptical contextualizing plaques have been placed next to the school's Confederate monuments, with other tablets to document the labor of the slaves once owned by the university itself. But some of that work had to happen in print before it could happen in public, and maybe fiction ran just a bit ahead of its time. For at their best and in spite of their flaws, Faulkner's own books are themselves *Stolpersteine*. Ike McCaslin trips over what he reads in his family's ledgers, a history "that could never be amortized"; Bayard Sartoris rejects his father's gun. Quentin Compson tells us of a land that he does not think he hates, and perhaps *The Sound and the Fury* stands as the greatest of the novelist's attempts at *Vergangenheitsbewältigung*: the greatest, because the most intractable, the most marked by a sense of its own failure. Mastering the past is precisely what Quentin cannot do, no matter how much he struggles and fights, can't because the past for him is not even past, because he still lives in the moment of loss. It simply goes on happening, and yet the novelist's account of that very impossibility provides in itself an instance of that never-finished process. Fail again; fail better.

Faulkner knew that in his great-grandfather's day he too would have served the Confederacy. He also knew that its cause was, in Grant's words, "one of the worst for which a people ever fought," and he believed that the principle on which that cause was built was evil. His work lies in the space between, and at times the contradiction must have been unbearable; at times it must have approached a psychic war within. Warren wrote that when he began to read Faulkner he found, as did "almost all the book-reading Southerners I knew," that the Mississippian had captured some truth about his own home and identity "that had been lying speechless in [my] experience." Some of it was the landscape, or the voices, the wagons and mules and houses, even the way his people stood or squatted. Some of it was the pain.

But Warren also brings me up short. Born in 1905, he marked Sumter's centennial with a book-length essay called *The Legacy of the Civil War* (1961), a legacy that he saw everywhere in American life, from our banking system to the manufacture of ready-made clothing. One thing stands above all, however. The war may have "abolished slavery . . . [but] it did little or nothing to abolish racism," and in that tension lies its meaning. Or rather its meanings—meanings contained in the very different psychological costs it imposed on either side. The white South embraced what Warren calls the "Great Alibi," in which a reference to the conflict served to justify its every failing. Poverty, lynching, laziness: the war excused them all, as if turning the region's defects, its inability to mourn, into virtues. That belief allowed that South to evade its reckoning with what Lincoln called the offense of American slavery; it stands as one reason why it did not do the work of *Vergangenheitsbewältigung*. Of course, the Yankees had a corresponding myth of their own, one that Warren found "equally corrosive." Southerners felt trapped by history but Northerners believed themselves redeemed by it. They forgot how many Yankee fortunes depended on slave-grown cotton and saw the war as having filled the region's "Treasury of Virtue." Victory underlined the section's sense of its own righteousness. It made the North into the "bright surgical instrument in the hand of God, or History," and left it free to enjoy its own prejudices. Yet Warren knew, as Lincoln did, that the offense behind the war was not the South's alone. It was national or communal instead, the guilt and the responsibility communal too, and that troubled past is even now, especially now, not even past.

Whenever I stand inside Harvard's Memorial Hall, I feel just a little bit smug, as though I were drawing on that still undepleted treasury. My side *was* right, but the building wants to persuade us that victory *proves* it was right, made it right, and the place seems all too effective in doing so. Repellent; and in recoiling from my own Yankee reflexes, I sometimes think that the *Century* magazine's belief in reconciliation was no bad thing. In 1884 Henry James's friend Oliver Wendell Holmes Jr. gave a Memorial Day address to a veterans' group in New Hampshire. The future justice had served with the Army of the Potomac from the start of the war through the summer of 1864 and missed Gettysburg only because he had just received the last of his three wounds, at Chancellorsville. "The soldiers who were doing their best to kill one another," he said, "felt less of personal hostility . . . than some of those who were not imperiled by their mutual endeavors." Holmes wanted the Union to win, he believed that slavery should die, and he knew that the men on the other side wanted to kill him. He did his best to kill them instead and yet believed as he pulled the trigger that he could regard every "soldier's death with feelings not different in kind, whether he fell toward them or by their side." These are so close to the sentiments James gives his own Basil Ransom in *The Bostonians* that I suspect the novelist had read the speech and had it in mind as he wrote: sentiments that make any Northern sanctimony into something like fool's gold.

Holmes believed that his own generation had been set apart by the knowledge of war, that their hearts "were touched with fire," a spirit that united the men of both sides. Yet a soldier's appeal to experience is not in itself a historical judgment. In Richmond I drive west down Monument Avenue, away from the center of town and out through a set of traffic circles. The first of them holds the statue of a mounted J. E. B. Stuart, and then a block further on there's a much grander equestrian sculpture of Lee, sixty feet high from the foot of its stone base to the top of his bronzed head. Jefferson Davis is further down the road, a tall man standing before the kind of column that usually marks a victory, and then Stonewall Jackson seems almost an afterthought, sitting his horse in the middle of an intersection. The memorial to Lee was the first to go up, in 1890. It stood outside what were then the city limits, and for its first few years the land from which it rose was still a field of tobacco. As late as 1907 James described the avenue as suburban, one whose building lots were not yet filled in and whose only function seemed that of bringing the visitor out to Lee's effigy. The statue itself struck him as rather finely made, cast as it was in "far-away uninterested Paris," and yet it also looked bereft, a work that spoke not of a lost cause but of "one that could never have been gained." The monuments to Stuart and Davis were placed two years later, and that to Jackson in 1919. By then loss had become intransigence, and the street was lined with the city's finest houses.

And by then the meaning of the Civil War itself had begun to appear settled, as fixed in place as those statues themselves. It no longer does, and the questions of race and region and remembrance that the thought of that war provokes lie again at the heart of our national life and quarrels. I will always second-guess myself, but I think that Memorial Hall is a legitimate exercise of public memory. It crows a bit in marking the victory of the United States, but those tablets set like gravestones into a cathedral wall make it finally into a place of mourning. Its act of commemoration is just and right. The Confederate statues on Monument Avenue do not have that same legitimacy. They once spoke to the tyranny of Virginia's majority opinion, but they serve no valid purpose and their presence remains a great wrong. They were installed in celebration of a pernicious cause, and their very existence is now and was always intended as an insult to a large portion of Virginia's citizens; and this country's willingness not simply to tolerate but to celebrate those who tried to destroy it says something very peculiar about our national life. There may be political or practical questions about the removal of Confederate monuments. There are no moral ones.

Neither *The Sound and the Fury* nor *Absalom, Absalom!* mentions Memorial Hall, but the first of them does provide a curious relic of the war in the form of a minor character called Deacon, a black man who has met every train at the start of school for the last forty years. "He could pick out a Southerner with one glance," the story goes, "and once he had heard you speak, he could name your state." Deacon runs errands and helps with the luggage; he lives on tips and has been in and out of Quentin's room all year. Sometimes he appears in a costume of patches, dressed like Uncle Tom and talking like Uncle Remus; at other times he wears a Brooks Brothers suit and speaks as one gentleman to another, "his manner ... [moving] northward as his raiment improved." He switches codes, plays the fool when it suits him, and has made a comfortable profit off generations of students. The details of his biography are never clear, though, and Quentin doesn't even know where he comes from. Forty years takes us back to 1870, when the memory of the fighting was new. Is Deacon a Southerner? Was he born a slave? The man likes parades and ceremonies, he marches in as many as he can, and Quentin has seen him just a few days before, stepping out for Decoration Day in the uniform of the Grand Army of the Republic. The G.A.R. was a fraternal organization whose members had all served in the Union's forces. Its posts were integrated and during Reconstruction it fought for black voting rights; later for military pensions. Nothing here can be certain—many of Deacon's clothes are other people's cast-offs, and Quentin probably assumes that the uniform is too. Still, I like to think that it was Deacon's from the start; that whether born in Mississippi or Massachusetts itself, he might once have been a soldier.

Yet no matter its source, a man with Deacon's sense of occasion would surely have been on Boston Common in May 1897 for the unveiling of Augustus Saint-Gaudens's bronze relief in honor of the Fifty-Fourth Massachusetts. New England's most stirring work of Civil War memory sits at the very top of Beacon Hill, across the street from the State House. Many things make it powerful, and among them is the perfect fusion between the artist's skill and the ethical imperatives of his subject. Colonel Shaw rides alongside his regiment, positioned on the sculpture's outside edge, and with row after row of soldiers marching four abreast. Every face remains distinct, every individuality recognized. Some arms swing free, molded in the round rather than in simple relief, and so do the legs of Shaw's horse, his sword too. Nothing here is abstract: canteens and shoes, the seam of a trouser leg or the stripes on a bearded sergeant's arm, the bedrolls creased by the straps that hold them on to each soldier's pack. I count twenty-six rifles with their barrels in the air, and then two drummer boys as well, at the head of the column, their sticks caught in mid-beat. No other work of Civil War art can match the perfection of this statuary's detail, not at Gettysburg or Shiloh, not in any cemetery or city square of North or South, and yet that alone is not the source of its power. That isn't why it brings a viewer to tears. Saint-Gaudens shows these men at the start of the journey that would lead to their defeat near Charleston, with each hoof-beat and every soldier's step carrying them closer to glory. His work implies a story, it has the narrative force of the greatest history paintings, and that force reminds us why the Civil War was necessary.

The bronze was intended as a memorial to Shaw himself rather than to his regiment, and it's true that as its mounted commander, his figure is the first we see. But the faces of his soldiers are modeled with equal care; he takes his place among them, as he did in their mass grave at Fort Wagner, and time has renamed the work in our minds, making the individual monument into a collective one. Its dedication was a great ceremony, with speeches by the governor and the mayor, though not by any of its surviving soldiers. Booker T. Washington was asked to talk instead, and then the Harvard philosopher William James, brother of Henry, and also of Wilky, the Fifty-Fourth's adjutant, who never fully recovered from his wounds and died in 1883. Neither man's address was held at the time to be of much consequence, and they have rarely been reprinted. But already James notes that this memorial is not for Shaw alone, and that the care with which Saint-Gaudens has depicted a group of ordinary soldiers rather than some great captain makes it exceptional. Except, of course, that they were not ordinary soldiers. They were the "first Northern Negro regiment" and as such they embodied the meaning of the war itself: a war that has "but one meaning in the eye of history." It destroyed the "social plague" of slavery and reminded us that there are "Americans of all colors and conditions."

That is why, James says, Massachusetts has chosen to honor a regiment that lost its fight, and in describing both the monument and the troops' own march he seems to echo "The Battle Hymn of the Republic." But then Saint-Gaudens's work is itself a version of that great hymn: it gives us that swift sword in bronze, it evokes the watch-fires of a soldiers' camp, and the "burnished rows of steel" are there in the slanted muskets that rise above each man's shoulder. Let us die to make men free—so Julia Ward Howe wrote in 1862, and that is the resolution the sculptor has placed in each man's eyes. They did not make this war, their faces say, but they have accepted it, and they will not call retreat.

FOURTEEN

The Human Heart Against Itself

Old Bayard Sartoris died one December morning in 1919 while out for a ride in his grandson's car. Young Bayard had been a fighter pilot. He could only ever drive fast, and swerved around a stalled Ford in a "sickening, unhurried rush" before hastening into a downhill curve. The Yoknapatawpha country roads had frozen in the night, but the warming sun changed them into a skidding mix of mud and clay; the car missed the turn and slewed down a bank through a grove of scrub cedar, with the young man's arm shooting out to keep his grandfather from going through the windshield. The old man's heart had been bad for a while, and he was dead before they reached the bottom. Nobody in Jefferson ever saw young Bayard again. He wrote from Mexico City, and then Rio and San Francisco, before finding the death that, like Quentin, he had always wanted. Not on a bridge. He killed himself instead at a military airfield in Ohio, testing a plane he knew should never have been flown.

Old Man Falls survived for a time, and maybe the Sartorises even kept on giving him tobacco; only now it probably came from the dead banker's aunt. Virginia Du Pre had been born a Sartoris, the Colonel's younger sister, a Civil War widow who came out to Yoknapatawpha in 1869. Nobody in Jefferson seems to have known much about her husband, a presumably gallant officer who fell early on, but everybody knew she had once danced with J. E. B. Stuart. And everybody knew the story "Miss Jenny" told about her brother Bayard, Stuart's aide-de-camp, who had gotten himself killed one April morning in Virginia, galloping into a Union camp on a quest for a jar of anchovies. With age—her age—the story grew ever richer, until his foolish prank mellowed into the focal point of history itself. But when in 1930 she too died, at ninety, the war's living memory died with her, its flags turned to dust at last.

The plantation myth was fading—*Gone with the Wind* would give it new life—and now there was room for another one, a myth that came out of Faulkner's own books as much as it did from anywhere. Southern Gothic, the Richmond novelist Ellen Glasgow called it, and it would shape three generations of American literature, an imaginary that showed the present-day South as a grotesque and benighted land of collapsing creeper-covered mansions, of incest and violence, the morally and the physically misshapen. That description is hardly an adequate account of Faulkner's own work, though it might cover some of the books that grew out of him, like the back-country nightmare of James Dickey's *Deliverance* (1970). But it *is* the way in which the early Yoknapatawpha books were first read. It's why his neighbors distrusted novels like *Sanctuary* and *Light in August*, why they were appalled by the buzzard-haunted wagon of *As I Lay Dying*, and even by *The Sound and the Fury*. The impotent gunsel Popeye in *Sanctuary* rapes a Mississippi belle with a corncob and then puts her to work in a Memphis whorehouse. *Light in August* turns on the *Liebestod* of Joe Christmas and Joanna Burden, the bootlegger who might be black and the granddaughter of an abolitionist, with him pulling a razor as she snaps a pistol. Quentin Compson's fear of his sister's sexuality was bad enough on its own, but *The Sound and the Fury* added in his two brothers, the "idiot" Benjy and the venomous Jason. "Once a bitch always a bitch, what I say." Those are Jason's first words, on Good Friday 1928, and he sustains that note throughout his narrative, a representative man of the Jazz Age South.

These figures made Faulkner's reputation. But his work offers another and far more important story about the region as well. "Get me a nigger," the county sheriff says when Joanna's body is discovered in *Light in August*: get any black man from any little cabin around. He'll know something about this murder, even if a deputy's belt has to help him remember; the violence is as casual as the slap of that word itself. "The problem of the Twentieth Century is the problem of the color-line": so Du Bois wrote in the first paragraph of *The Souls of Black Folks*. Much can and must be said about Faulk-

ner's limitations, and yet no white writer in our literature thought longer and
harder about that problem, the one that the Civil War's aftermath had set
in place. That reckoning begins in *Flags in the Dust* and continues in every
book that follows, those I've named here and of course *Absalom, Absalom!*
and *Go Down, Moses* too; and then afterward with *Intruder in the Dust* and
on to the last installment of his lifelong serial, the posthumously published
Reivers (1962). The world those books show us, the world the war made, is
fixed and determined by that endlessly crossed and immovable line. Jim
Crow, we say, but that's too simple, and Faulkner's friend James Silver found
a better name for it. He taught history at the University of Mississippi and
was a regular guest at Rowan Oak, where anyone who wanted to be invited
back knew better than to ask about his host's fiction. In 1964 Silver published
an unlikely bestseller about the university's court-ordered desegregation and
then moved, after almost thirty years in Oxford, to a new job at Notre Dame.
Mississippi: The Closed Society: that's what he called it, a self-contained system, a shut box in which there was virtually no room for people of any race
to step outside the terms in which white supremacy had defined them. The
closed society lived in the unwritten law that made "strange negroes ... absolutely refuse to pass through" Frenchman's Bend after dark; it lived in that
sheriff's voice.

It lived even in those who we think should know better. Faulkner set the
penultimate chapter of *Go Down, Moses* in 1940. Ike McCaslin is over seventy in "Delta Autumn," and it's more than fifty years since he relinquished
his land, turning in horror from what the family ledgers had told him. He
owns as little as possible and works as a carpenter, but that decision has shred-
ded his marriage and left him "uncle to half a county and father to no one."
He still hunts, but the big woods near Jefferson are gone now, and he must
drive for hours to reach good ground, out into the twists and swamps of the
Delta. The trip tires him, though, and on the first morning in camp the old
man stays in bed long after his companions have gone into the forest. Then
he hears the *put-put* of an approaching boat, "the lap and plop of water," and
a young woman enters his tent, wearing a man's raingear, and with a baby
in her arms. She calls him Uncle Isaac, and though she sounds "almost like
a Northerner," he thinks, at first, that she's using the name in the same way

that a lot of people in Yoknapatawpha do, a mark of informal respect. But she speaks as well of Uncle Lucas, Lucas Beauchamp, and when Ike looks at her more closely he realizes that she is what the one-drop rule calls black. He is Uncle Isaac indeed, and she knows the whole history of the black half of his family, from whom she is descended; of the cousins who left Yoknapatawpha in the earliest days of the Great Migration.

And he is doubly related to the baby she holds, whose father is his white cousin Roth Edmonds, the present owner of the McCaslin land. Roth has known the woman for a year and knows too that she's black, but he isn't aware of their common ancestry; for what good, as she says, "would that have done?" They have spent just a few weeks together, much of it in New Mexico where they could share the same apartment; but now she plans to go north, and Roth has left an envelope for her, with money. That's all she expects— but the reader expects something more from Ike himself, something other than the reactions Faulkner gives him. Because Ike McCaslin has changed. He has become a windy old man, and he is appalled by this new crossing of the color line. "Get out of here," he screeches. "Go back North.... That's the only salvation for you—for a while yet, maybe a long while yet. We will have to wait." He thinks she wants revenge, revenge on the past itself, and tells her to take it elsewhere. A black man would be happy to marry a woman who is almost white, even one with a baby already: that's what he says. Then she looks at him from beneath her hat and speaks a judgment upon his world: "Old man ... have you lived so long and forgotten so much that you dont remember anything you ever knew or felt or even heard about love?"

We will have to wait. Ike has lived in Mississippi too long. He can no longer open its door and step outside, as he did, once, when young. Though even then, even in giving up the land, he was more concerned with his own salvation than he was with the people around him. In his Nobel Prize address Faulkner said that the only thing worth writing about was the story of "the human heart in conflict with itself," and I want to believe that Ike recognizes his failure here, even as my own head spins in trying to fit this old man onto the young one hunched over those ledgers. He gives the woman a hunting horn, wrapped in buckskin and bound with silver; General Compson had willed it to him, and he wants the baby to have it, the youngest McCaslin, whatever his last name might be. That gesture marks the pulsing conflict within him—a private acknowledgment of what cannot be said in public. But for how long must we wait?

———————

FAULKNER WAS ELECTED TO the National Institute of Arts and Letters in 1939, and the book he published that year put him on the cover of *Time*. *The Wild Palms* told two stories in alternating chapters, and with only the faintest of connections between them. One narrative was an operatic storm, a love story that ended with a botched abortion and its protagonist on his way to the Mississippi state penitentiary at Parchman. The other was a grim comedy set during the great flood of 1927, when that same prison's inmates were put to work on the levees. The reviewers were even more baffled than usual, but the magazine cover helped and *The Wild Palms* sold better than any of its predecessors, the deliberately tawdry *Sanctuary* included. His next books weren't so lucky, and after *Go Down, Moses* in 1942 Faulkner seemed to fall silent. He had written eleven novels and two volumes of short stories in the thirteen years that began with *Sartoris* in 1929, he produced more great fiction faster than any other American writer, but it wasn't enough, not to keep him solvent. He had cashed in a life insurance policy to help his friend Phil Stone out of a jam; he was in debt to his publishers and owed years of back taxes. And so in July 1942 he went out to California once more. In the 1930s Twentieth Century-Fox had paid him $1,000 a week, but the best he could do now was $300 at Warner Bros. Faulkner would remain under contract until 1946 and didn't finish another novel until 1948.

He missed the books he wanted to write, his family too, and in Los Angeles he was never not drinking; he collapsed in both 1943 and 1944, and the second time had to be hospitalized. Sometimes he took a leave without pay and returned to Oxford; in 1945 he simply skipped town, heading east without the studio's permission and spending the fall in Mississippi. But he couldn't afford to quit, and the paradox is that his unhappiest years in Hollywood were also his most successful. Most of Faulkner's movie work went uncredited, revisions to other writers' scripts or scenes added after shooting had begun, along with several unproduced screenplays of his own. In the

mid-1940s, however, the other talent at Warner Bros. included his favorite
director, Howard Hawks, and a veteran actor named Humphrey Bogart
who had just become a star. Hawks was also a friend of Ernest Hemingway's
and bet the more popular novelist that he could make a good film out of his
worst novel. He won his wager by putting Faulkner to work on *To Have and
Have Not*, with Bogart and the young Lauren Bacall, and the same group
then made an even better movie out of Raymond Chandler's *The Big Sleep*.
Faulkner had his name on each of them, and he wrote parts as well of a third
great film, Michael Curtiz's version of James M. Cain's *Mildred Pierce*. I
don't think it's an accident that his best work for the movies came in the form
of adaptations. Warner Bros. always had an eye for American fiction, and
Faulkner's own novels were as marked by violence and crime as Chandler's or
Cain's. He listened to other writers' characters as easily as he did to his own,
he described physical action at least as well as Hemingway, and no modernist
in any language could match his skillful plotting, the precision with which he
mixed revelation and delay. In film that's called suspense.

But he was getting up at four in the morning for a few hours' work before
going to the studio, and early in 1946 his publishers at Random House persuaded Warner Bros. to release him. They wanted a new novel—and yet an
observer might well have wondered why. Few of his books had done well com-
mercially. Some had had a second impression but in America at least there
was no continued demand, and by the time he left Hollywood the only one of
his major novels still available was the Modern Library edition of *Sanctuary*.
It's easy to overstate the degree of Faulkner's mid-'40s obscurity. Books *did* go
out of print. There wasn't yet much of a paperback industry to keep a writer's
backlist in stock, nor were there many college courses in American literature,
let alone in contemporary fiction. Faulkner's work had never gone unnoticed
and younger writers in particular read him; other Hollywood novelists were
tongue-tied in his presence, and Jack Warner boasted that he had America's
best writer on his payroll, for cheap. But there'd been nothing new for a while
now, and at the moment his standing on what the critic and editor Malcolm
Cowley called the "literary stock exchange" was decidedly low. Another book
might change that; and it did.

Only it wasn't a new novel. Cowley had memorably depicted the expatriate life of his own lost generation in *Exile's Return* (1934); he had discovered the short story writer John Cheever and would later publish Jack Kerouac. His greatest skill, however, lay in the revival and reshaping of literary reputation. In 1944 he put together a volume for Viking called *The Portable Hemingway* that made the writer look far more difficult, troubled, and original than his simple declarative sentences might suggest. Now he proposed to do the same thing for Faulkner, and after some hesitation Viking's front office agreed. The novelist himself took his time about it, letting months pass before answering Cowley's first letters of inquiry. But he then entered fully into the project, commenting on a draft of the book's introduction, offering suggestions about its contents, and finally writing a new piece to go along with Cowley's selection from *The Sound and the Fury*. "Compson: 1699–1945" provided a family history that tells us why Quentin has always seen himself as the end of their line, and showed too what happens to his siblings after the novel's ending. "I should have done this when I wrote the book," Faulkner said. "Then the whole thing would have fallen into pattern.... I think this is all right, it took me about a week to get Hollywood out of my lungs, but I am still writing all right."

Some of the prose in the Compson appendix is overwrought; some critics have persuasively argued that it imposes itself upon the actual novel, distorting its characters in the process; and even today the standard Vintage paperback edition of the book doesn't include it. Yet by now that appendix stands as an essential part of the world he made. For it *is* a world—that's what Cowley showed. The editor mixed short stories with excerpts from the novels in order to define Faulkner's continuity of purpose, the way one book echoed off another; he revealed the inner structure and coherence of Yoknapatawpha's history. Some of his ideas were already in play, arguments first made by other critics, but Cowley codified them, and almost everyone who has written about Faulkner since has found a starting place in his work. And he was, moreover, an expert puller of reputation's wires. Cowley made sure that the right critics got advance copies and wrote about the volume in the right places. One of them was the Kentucky-born novelist Caroline Gordon, who was married to the Agrarian poet Allen Tate. She produced a long cover story for the *New York Times Book Review* that in essence made Cowley's point, showing how each of

Faulkner's books "seems to reveal more than it states explicitly and to have a subject bigger than itself." Edmund Wilson wrote about it for *The New Yorker*, Robert Penn Warren for the *New Republic*. And then things happened fast.

The Portable Faulkner appeared in April 1946, and in October the Modern Library released an omnibus edition of *The Sound and the Fury* and *As I Lay Dying*. At the beginning of 1948 Faulkner went back to an old idea for a mystery novel, took just three months to write it, and sold the movie rights for $50,000 before its September publication; *Intruder in the Dust* was shot in Oxford the next year and remains the best film made from his work. It also appeared, along with *Sanctuary*, in a line of paperbacks from a new publisher called Signet, priced at twenty-five cents and made to fit drugstore racks. At the same time Faulkner began to arrange his short fiction for a volume of collected stories, grouping them by their setting in places like "The Village" or "The Wilderness." He used only those he hadn't already slotted into a novel, but there were still more than nine hundred pages of them. The book came out in the summer of 1950 and went on to win the National Book Award in fiction: a nice honor if it had come earlier, and yet one that by then seemed small. For that November Faulkner got an early-morning phone call from a Swedish reporter. There had been an announcement in Stockholm; and by the end of the year his books would have millions of copies in print.

There are two stories here. One depends on the change in his American reputation, the rising fortune that began with the *Portable*. The other concerns Faulkner's reception in Europe and especially France, where his work had been admired since the 1933 translation of *Sanctuary*. They are not the same story, and the Nobel Prize owed much more to the latter, though afterward they became the same story, with his American fame bolstered and sustained by his international success. Faulkner's French translator was a man named Maurice-Edgar Coindreau, who taught at Princeton and brought twentieth-century American fiction into his native language, working as well with Hemingway and John Steinbeck, and later on with both Vladimir Nabokov and Flannery O'Connor. He wrote the first French essay on Faulkner, a 1931 account for *La Nouvelle Revue Française*; the journal was the house organ of Gallimard, the most distinguished of Parisian publishers, and over the years that firm would release the novelist's entire body of work. Gallimard commissioned Andre Malraux to write a preface to *Sanctuary*; *As I Lay Dying—Tandis que j'agonise—*was released in 1934 with an introduction by the poet Valery Larbaud. Coindreau worked steadily through the American's oeuvre, bringing out versions of *Light in August* in 1935 and *The Sound and the Fury* in 1938. And the last of those—*Le bruit et la fureur*—prompted a now-classic essay by Jean-Paul Sartre.

He too was a Gallimard author, though he wasn't yet the Sartre of history when that essay appeared, once more in *La Nouvelle Revue Française*. He still had his future to make, just one of the many young French intellectuals who admired the slightly older Southerner. But he had become that Sartre by 1945, when he told Cowley that *"Pour les jeunes en France, Faulkner c'est un dieu,"* and the next year he singled him out in an article for the *Atlantic* on the reception of American fiction in France. There were many reasons for Sartre's admiration, or indeed for that of Albert Camus. The moral isolation of characters like Quentin Compson and Darl Bundren provided an analogue for the existential despair of their own protagonists, and Sartre's 1939 essay also matched Faulkner's treatment of time and consciousness to Proust's. That mattered. Faulkner's French readers quickly found the right terms of comparison. American reviewers linked his work to such contemporaries as Sherwood Anderson and Thomas Wolfe, or to a series of now-forgotten Southern writers. But Malraux mentioned Balzac and Dostoevsky, and Larbaud saw *As I Lay Dying* as both a piece of exotica and a Homeric journey. Other French critics put Faulkner alongside Kafka and Woolf: a sense of the world stage that no American would as yet risk offering, and one that made him seem ready for what Yeats had called the bounty of Sweden.

The tale of Faulkner's international reception continues, and a generation later another Nobel laureate, Gabriel García Márquez, would cite him as an inspiration, someone who proved that great art could come from a cultural backwater. But that's not my interest here. Faulkner at first refused to attend the Nobel ceremony, claiming he was too busy on the farm he owned outside of Oxford. He didn't even have a passport, but family pressure finally put him on a plane, and the speech he gave in Stockholm made him into an export item. He spoke there of the "old universal truths . . . [of] love and honor and pity and pride and compassion and sacrifice," truths that endured even in a nuclear age. The State Department took note and later sent him to Japan and Brazil, trips on which he functioned as a kind of Cold Warrior, affirming his humanist faith that in the face of an inimical world "man" would not merely endure but prevail. Faulkner had almost always declined requests for interviews, including those that would have helped his sales when he needed it most. Now he became a public figure. He spoke at West Point, wrote about the Kentucky Derby for *Sports Illustrated*, and was also, inevitably, asked to comment on the nascent civil rights movement in the country at large and his home state in particular. And what he said in reply suggested that he had now turned into one of his own characters: that he too was infected with the same gradualism that he had looked at so skeptically in Isaac McCaslin.

———·+·———

ALMOST ALL FAULKNER'S NONFICTION dates from the 1950s, but his essays and public letters of the period are best approached by returning to the fiction itself, and in particular to *Go Down, Moses* and *Intruder in the Dust*. Du Bois had described African-American life as taking place behind a veil, a permeable tissue that nevertheless clouded the view from either side. It allowed black people to maintain a separate place, gauzed-off from white society and half-seen by it at best; at the same time it could be so all-enveloping as to block one's vision of the world outside. Faulkner knew this language, and in *Light in August* he described Joe Christmas, who Jefferson believes is white, as hiding "behind the veil, the screen, of his negro's job at the mill." Christmas shovels sawdust as a way to cloak his actual job of selling bootleg whiskey: an illegality that both excuses his menial post and masks the other and denser barrier behind which he really lives. But the novelist himself wanted a way to step within that netting. We have seen that early in his career he worked hard at rendering black speech, catching his characters at moments when they assume no white person is listening. In his fiction of the 1940s he went further, and made that attempt to go behind into a drama of its own.

The brief concluding title section of *Go Down, Moses* begins in a Chicago prison, with a numbers runner sentenced to death for killing a cop. He is

Lucas Beauchamp's grandson, and the chapter turns on his family's attempt to bring his body home. Lucas's wife Molly goes to see Gavin Stevens, the talkative lawyer whom Faulkner often used as a mouthpiece, and the attorney organizes a collection, with the businessmen around the square chipping in to pay the corpse's freight, trying to help a family from their community. That's how Gavin would put it, anyway, and yet the reader sees something else, sees that the white town's benevolence depends on its assumption of a fixed racial hierarchy, a paternalism underwritten by an act of seeming generosity. Gavin brings the news of the body's coming to the house where Molly Beauchamp is staying, and he sits for a moment in a circle of mourners. "Sold my Benjamin," Molly chants; "Sold him in Egypt." And her aged brother Hamp responds to her call, "Sold him in Egypt . . . Sold him to Pharaoh." The low-voiced music goes around the room, "strophe and antistrophe," *sold him in Egypt/ and now he dead*; and in the mourners' words we hear, unspoken, the spiritual from which Faulkner takes his title. Then Gavin gets up, realizing that he shouldn't have come. He has intruded upon their grief, peering into the private world of the men and women with whom he has always lived and yet knows, now, that he does not know.

Intruder in the Dust tells a more complicated story, and there it's a white boy named Chick Mallison, Gavin's nephew, who tries to part that veil. One day he falls into a frozen stream. Lucas Beauchamp pulls him out and then treats him with a mixture of amusement and contempt: treats him, that is, as a worldly man does a callow youth, and not as black or white. That baffles and enrages the boy—Chick can't accept that this man doesn't fit the town's accustomed terms, that he cannot so easily be placed or known. Lucas shows him that he can no longer take his world for granted, and in consequence Chick will begin to recognize the black Jefferson that lives alongside his own, always present but never quite seen. Then Lucas gets framed for murder, and both Chick and his uncle are drawn into an attempt to clear him. That attempt prompts a sequence in which Gavin lays out his beliefs on the course of Southern history: the sequence from which, at the start of this book, I took Faulkner's account of Pickett's Charge, of the vainglorious moment when it was "not yet two oclock" on the third day at Gettysburg and the Confederacy's loss was not yet sealed. The lawyer claims that white Southerners make up a single homogeneous people, rooted in the land and sharing the same values, and determined to defend not "our politics or beliefs or even our way of life, but simply our homogeneity" against the diluting force of modernity itself. That defense, he claims, will eventually allow the South to assert its final privilege: the privilege of setting men like Lucas "free ourselves: which we will have to do for the reason that nobody else can since going on a century ago the North tried it and have been admitting for seventy-five years now that they failed. So it will have to be us," forgetting that "us" lay behind those long years of failure. No federal law can ensure civil rights, Gavin says. Only we can do that, "but it wont be next Tuesday." Or as Ike McCaslin says, they will have to wait, wait for a future that they have the comfort of knowing they will never see.

Gavin's argument recalls the work of the Nashville Agrarians, and it was common enough at the end of the 1940s, even among those who, like Faulkner, positioned themselves as moderates. Whites must take the lead in creating social change, and in doing so they would also manage to save or free themselves from the past. Indeed, that salvation stood as the endpoint and the purpose of making it possible for "Lucas Beauchamp . . . [to] send his children to the same school" that a white family does. To some degree Faulkner's plotting undercuts Gavin's claim, for Lucas uses Chick to organize his own liberation from within the jail itself. But it isn't enough. Gavin's speech is what one remembers, and it's so overblown as to damage the book as a whole. Faulkner often presented the lawyer ironically; here he only feints that way, and the character's words would haunt his public statements in the decade to come.

"We make out of the quarrel with others, rhetoric, but of the quarrel with ourselves, poetry." So Yeats said, and that is what Faulkner did in his own great books: he fought it out within his own heart in novel after novel. *Why do you hate the South*, Shreve asks, and Quentin insists that he doesn't, insists so much that no reader can believe him. But the poet's claim needs amendment. For sometimes you fight with others as a way to avoid that fight with the self, and grow aggressive in defending the ground that you aren't really sure should be defended at all. And that is what Faulkner did in his years of public fame. There are exceptions. The best of them is a magazine article from 1954, called simply "Mississippi," in which he plumbs his own attitudes, loving the place "even while hating some of it." Loving it "despite"; the world would be too easy if one only loved "because." That's the quarrel within, but the quarrel with others weighs upon *Intruder in the Dust*, and it disfigures the rhetoric with which he stumbled through the early days of the civil rights movement. He hits out—and it's not always clear at whom.

"Mississippi" appeared in April 1954, just before the first of the three events that cracked the violent uneasy stability of Faulkner's South, three events within a span of eighteen months. First came the May 1954 Supreme Court decision in *Brown v. Board of Education* that mandated the integration—however much delayed in practice—of the nation's schools. The second was the August 1955 murder of the Chicago schoolboy Emmett Till, for supposedly whistling at a white woman while on a family visit to Money, Mississippi, about eighty miles to the south of Oxford. And the last of them was the start that December of the Montgomery, Alabama, bus boycott, which began the process of making public accommodations equally available to all, from transportation to lavatories and water fountains. The novelist Elizabeth Spencer went to Italy on a fellowship in 1953; she returned two years later, just after Till's killing, and found that the Mississippi she'd written about seemed gone. The closed society now felt itself threatened and had stopped pretending to smile; it had grown angry, with its racism more open than ever before and more virulently expressed. Oxford had been proud of the film version of *Intruder in the Dust*, in which many townspeople appeared as extras. It was an optimistic movie, with a mild uplifting conclusion in which Gavin looked toward a future of racial equality, albeit one so distant that it did not yet challenge the present. That was in 1949. It would not have received that kind of local support just a few years later, when the future looked as though it might arrive; indeed, I wonder if it would have been possible to make the film in Mississippi at all.

Emmett Till's killers were quickly acquitted by a local jury and then felt free to sell their story to *Look* magazine; the wonder, in that white-ruled world, is that they ever even faced trial. Almost immediately after Till's body was recovered from the Tallahatchie River, Faulkner wrote a letter to the *New York Herald Tribune* in which he said that a society so desperate as to murder children didn't "deserve to survive, and probably won't." But the next year he wondered how the descendants of men who had fought at Shiloh and "had the courage and endurance to resist . . . Reconstruction" could have fallen so low as to be afraid of a teenager. Faulkner feels the proper horror at Till's death—and yet can't admit that the resistance to Reconstruction had depended on exactly that kind of violence. Indeed, he cannot even ask just what white Mississippi was resisting, and why. Here the Nobel laureate showed the same historical ignorance as the rest of his society; here he had never grown beyond the narrow textbooks and cracker-barrel memories that Du Bois's *Black Reconstruction* had so expertly flayed.

Faulkner's other comments on the civil rights movement showed a similar incoherence. He thought it foolish to maintain two separate school systems, "neither of which are good enough for anybody," and wrote that it was the "white man's shame" that his society refused economic and social equality to their black neighbors. He also asked, however, if ninety years of systematic oppression might have made African-Americans unfit for equality, and wondered if some interim stage of remediation would be necessary. At times he equated the NAACP and Mississippi's new Citizens' Councils. That was the euphemistic name for the white supremacist pressure group that formed in immediate reaction to the decision in *Brown*. It had branches in many of the state's cities and towns, and was known colloquially as the "uptown Klan." The Citizens' Councils met openly, without hoods or rituals. Their members included many clergymen and business leaders, and their legacy survives today in the network of "segregation academies" they organized as an alternative to the public schools. Faulkner persuaded himself that the NAACP was equally extreme; one was black and the other white and so there must be some equivalence between them. He wanted to stay in the middle, to speak on behalf of both civil rights *and* Southern "heritage," and he thought that his fellow moderates would be run over in the quarrel between "Northern radicals who believe we don't do enough . . . [and] our own Southern reactionaries who are convinced that anything we do is already too much." But the "radicals" did not send hate mail to the "Weeping Willie Faulkner" who had written in tepid support of *Brown*.

The headlines made him sweat, and he got used to late-night phone calls, with voices on the other end threatening to kill him; even moderation was too much for most white Mississippians to stomach. Friends told him to carry a pistol. Instead, he drank. He noted that sales of guns and ammunition were rising and worried that Autherine Lucy, the first black student at the University of Alabama, would be shot down on campus; the school soon suspended her for what it called her own protection. "Go slow now," he said in an article for *Life*. That's what he wanted to tell "the NAACP and all the organizations who would compel immediate and unconditional integration." Wait a bit longer and change will come of itself; move with something less, far less, than all deliberate speed and people like me will come along with you. Faulkner wasn't alone in this; such gradualism was the policy of the Eisenhower administration itself. Still, the novelist went a bit further— and a bit slower—than even the federal government in his belief that white Southerners should lead the way. They should set the pace, granting that change out of their own benevolence, but only when they themselves were utterly and entirely ready for it. *Brown* may have been necessary, and yet he thought it merely ratified what had been decided in 1863. If back then his people "had given Negroes proper schools there would have been no need for the Court's decision." That would have been a victory, but "in 1954 it was a tragedy." Yet in what sense, and for whom? About that William Faulkner had nothing to say.

Then at the end of February 1956 he sat down in the Manhattan office of Random House for an interview with London's *Sunday Times*, and snapped. Faulkner admitted that the white South was wrong about the civil rights movement. Its reactions were overblown and its rhetoric overcharged. But it could only be pushed so far—temperatures now ran as high as in 1860 and he believed that mass violence was imminent. The North needed to take the pressure off. Otherwise the federal government would have to send in troops, and "if it came to fighting I'd fight for Mississippi against the United States even if it meant going out into the street and shooting Negroes." Faulkner later issued a carefully hedged statement that suggested he'd been misquoted: the statements attributed to him were ones "no sober man would make, nor, it seems to me, any sane man believe." The reporter had gotten it right, however, and of course the novelist had not been sober.

He woke up the morning after in an apartment he didn't recognize and spent the next two days in a stupor.

Faulkner knew what he had said. He knew how shameful his words had been. He spoke in fear and he spoke in fever, the fever of whiskey and in fear not only of the white South but of himself too; of how much he still had in common with the world from which he'd come. He would go on speaking, but more often now in private, and later that year held a few meetings with other Oxford residents at Rowan Oak in which they talked about ways to face down the Citizens' Councils. In public he grew more cautious. That spring Du Bois challenged him to a debate on civil rights and suggested they meet on the steps of the Tallahatchie County courthouse, where Emmett Till's killers had been tried and acquitted. Faulkner declined and wrote in a telegram that there was no debatable point between them. All they disagreed about was the pace and the timing of change. They both believed that the challenger's position was "right morally legally and ethically," but if Du Bois did not also recognize that the novelist's call for patience was "right practically," then they would each waste their breath. Nobody imagines that Faulkner would have done well in such a debate. Du Bois wasn't only the more right of the two, he also had half a century's experience of political life and sharp polemic; he knew how to stick a point, to dart an argument that never missed. Faulkner's response to their shared moment wasn't enough, not anymore, and his statements about civil rights prompted one of the young James Baldwin's wisest and most urgent essays. "Go slow" wasn't at all about saving black people from white violence. The time for which Faulkner begged was merely "the time in which the Southerner will come to terms with himself"; a time that lay in some imagined future, a salvation forever yet to come. For Baldwin there was no such future, and "the time is always now."

How should Faulkner's readers think about these moments and words, about the public role he assumed in the 1950s, when his major books were all behind him? There is never a clear line between the work and the life, and many people now judge the tale by its teller, they see the book's best self in terms of the man at his worst. For some people the history I've detailed in the paragraphs above will be reason enough not to read him. Such decisions are personal and not perhaps subject to argument or exhortation. I have made a different one. I read him despite, and I read him for or because or on account of his difficulty. Not the formal difficulty of his work in itself, however compelling I still find it. The moral difficulty, rather, the drama and struggle and paradox and power of his attempt to work through our history, to wrestle or rescue it into meaning. But when I put it that way I see that his aesthetic and his ethical challenges are really the same, that his attempt to grapple with all the pain of the past is what pushes him toward that all-encompassing formal extremity, an attempt at which he will ever fail. Ever magnificently and disturbingly fail.

Faulkner the man shared many of the closed society's opinions and values, and he knew just enough to know that he should resist them. But when the novelist could inhabit a character—when he slipped inside another mind and put those opinions into a different voice—he was almost always able to stand outside them, to place and to judge them. His extraordinary ability to think his way within other people let him see his world more clearly. It made him better than he was; it made the books better than the man. In some ways the sheer confusion of his public statements in the 1950s simply confirms what those books had already told us. For what strikes me about those statements is their whipsaw of contradiction, the desire to have his world both ways and all ways, and without ever needing to decide. To suspend choice, as though each position were a character and what mattered to the novelist was the quarrel between them. They speak to us of a riven soul; of a battle in which the right side doesn't always win and he fights others as a way of fighting himself; of the civil war within him. The human heart against itself: it was always his best subject.

He remained prolific to the end, finishing three books in his last five years, and began to spend half his time in Virginia, where his daughter Jill had married a Charlottesville lawyer and he lectured at the state university. None of that matters very much—the last scenes of an eventful eventless life, in which everything truly important happened between the pen and the page. Faulkner himself was skeptical of biography. He knew that one would be written and chose a Virginia English professor named Joseph Blotner for the job. But he didn't think that the story of his life could say anything meaningful about his work, and told Malcolm Cowley that wished the actual facts of that life might be "abolished and voided from history, leaving it markless, no refuse save the printed books." He claimed to wish that he hadn't even signed his work, that it had all been published anonymously, and hoped that a single sentence might serve as both obituary and epitaph: "He made the books and he died." The end took the form of a heart attack on July 6, 1962, at a private hospital called Wright's Sanitarium in Byhalia, Mississippi, half-way down the road between Oxford and Memphis. The place specialized in alcoholics, helping them through the pains of withdrawal, and Faulkner had been there before.

A few months later the violence that he had predicted would follow the integration of Alabama's flagship university came to his own hometown. A series of legal cases ended with the Supreme Court's order that the University of Mississippi admit an Air Force veteran named James Meredith, and though the school itself was ready to comply, the rest of the closed society was not. Its governor saw the issue as a test of Washington's relation with the separate states, and the Justice Department of Attorney General Robert F. Kennedy agreed with him. It *was* a test. Did federal law apply in an increasingly restive South? It took ten days of lawyers' arguments and physical standoffs to get Meredith on campus and enrolled for the fall term. His safety was supposed to be guaranteed by hundreds of United States marshals, but the state pulled its own police presence back and up to three thousand white rioters gathered at the start of the semester, a mob drawn from all across the South.

They burned cars and tried to break through to the university's administration building, where Meredith was rumored to be; calls for his lynching echoed through the trees. The marshals stood for hours in a barrage of bricks and bottles and small arms fire, which they did not return. Then the National Guard came in, state forces under federal command, and later the United States Army, including an integrated battalion of military police, with fixed bayonets and prepared to shoot. They didn't have to, but the riot eventually spread to the square and took two full days to die down. The Battle of Oxford, some called it. Others described it as the Civil War's last fight, and for a while the town was once more occupied by federal troops, as it had been a century before. Most of the army's vehicles had their windows smashed, and more than 150 marshals were injured. Two people died, both of them white: a French journalist shot in the back at close range, and a bystander who got a bullet in the forehead as he stood near the university's monument to the Confederate cause. One of Faulkner's nephews was an officer in the Guard and had his arm broken by a chunk of thrown concrete. Another nephew, his brother, joined the rioters.

———•———

ONCE AGAIN THE WHITE South looked to be at war with America. Repetition, recurrence, a land willing to wreck and ruin itself "twice in less than a hundred years" over what Faulkner called "the Negro question"; a land where the past was forever undead. He sometimes suggested that any white American must curse the day in 1619 that the first slave ship appeared off Hampton Roads in Virginia. Baldwin knew, in contrast, that the long argument over the meaning of that question was precisely what defined the nation itself, that our country was founded on that unending in-house quarrel. Many white Americans try to hide from that truth, or to deny it, unwilling to recognize that question's centrality—indeed the centrality of slavery itself—in our nation's history. Even then it shapes our blindness, and Yoknapatawpha County is a case in point. Faulkner writes of failure and loss, of the inheritance that defines his region, and tries to be both adequate and just to the trauma felt by the different peoples, who are the same people, of his native South. But what really matters in his Mississippi isn't finally the lost war, the Lost Cause; nor is it the quarrel between the mythic grace of the Old South and the grasping hands of the New. What matters are all the wasted years since. What matters is the century between the Emancipation Proclamation and the Voting Rights Act of 1965. The legacy—the final meaning—of the Civil War lives on in the things undone, the work unfinished and the wounds unbound; it lives in the continued resistance to any attempt at amelioration. It lives in our quarrels; it lives today in the battle of the blue and the red. That's why it all comes back, why it isn't ever over, no more finished for us than it was for Quentin Compson or indeed for Faulkner himself. He told this story twice.

And I myself have just two things left to say, two things to tell. In *The*

Unvanquished Faulkner imagined a girl named Celia Cook, who looks out of her Oxford window to see Bedford Forrest riding down the street, and then uses a diamond to scratch her name on the glass in commemoration. She only exists in that book for a sentence, but Faulkner brought her back in *Requiem for a Nun*, this time calling her Celia Farmer and making her the daughter of the town's jailer. She cuts her name and the date—April 16, 1861—and with time her window becomes a part of Jefferson's memory. So, in the middle of the twentieth century, a visitor to Faulkner's apocryphal land might be brought to look at that bit of glass, as if at something remarkable, interrupting the current jailer's wife in her kitchen as she stirs a pot of peas, and gazing a little impatiently at "the cloudy pane bearing the faint scratches" until the window seems to move and that old dead April speaks: *"Listen, stranger: this was myself; this was I."* In 1949 Faulkner met a girl from Memphis named Joan Williams, a twenty-year-old Bard College undergraduate who wanted to write; he read her manuscripts, offered advice, and asked her to collaborate with him on *Requiem for a Nun*. She knew better than to accept, but for a few years she stood to him as a muse, and he wrote her some of his best letters. In 1953 he told her that he had finally gained "some perspective on all I have done. I mean the work apart from me, the work which I did, apart from what I am.... And now I realize for the first time what an amazing gift I had: uneducated in every formal sense, without even very literate, let alone literary, companions, yet to have made the things I made."

Faulkner writes here as if watching himself from a distance, a man astonished at his own doings. "What I am" stands separate from the books he made, and yet the letter also speaks to his total identification with that loved and hated postage stamp of ground. *This was I.* That's the first of those two things; the other comes out of *Go Down, Moses*. The book begins with a chapter called "Was" that Faulkner sets back in 1859, the tale of something not "participated in or even seen by" Ike McCaslin but rather by his older cousin Cass Edmonds. Cass is nine years old in that last year before Lincoln's election and shares a cabin with his uncles Buck and Buddy, while their slaves sleep in the plantation's unfinished big house. One morning they find that a man has gone missing, the man known as Tomy's Turl. He's run off—run off again, and in search of his future, a place he wants to reach. But he hasn't gone north and they know exactly where he's headed. Terrel is only trying to see his sweetheart, Tennie, on "Mr Hubert Beauchamp's place just over the edge of the next county," and Buck and Buddy and Cass want to chase him down, with dogs and horses, before he can get there. Not that they're angry or vengeful. Exasperated, rather, and a little fed up with their neighbor, who refuses either to buy Terrel or sell them Tennie, and so keep the peace by keeping the couple together. And Terrel knows in turn exactly what they are going to do, right down to the path they'll take in trying to cut him off at the Beauchamp gate. They all recognize their parts in this drama, and Faulkner presents the chase as if it were a game they play with some regularity, one with clear rules that they all understand.

It's a comic story, or seems to be, a fabliau that Chaucer himself might have enjoyed: a bit of make-believe about a runaway slave, with one bedroom mistaken for another, a dozen yapping dogs, and a climax that arrives in a pack of cards. The details of the single hand of poker that Uncle Buddy plays with Hubert Beauchamp will baffle almost everyone, but the stakes include Tennie, and at the end of the story she rides in a wagon to the McCaslin plantation, Terrel on a mule beside her. Before he folds his cards, however, Beauchamp lets the lamplight move up "Tomy's Turl's arms that were supposed to be black but were not quite white," the arms of the man he has earlier called a "damn white half-McCaslin." Those statements will puzzle any first-time reader; my students always ask about them, and I tell them to wait. Because what we're not supposed to know, not yet, not quite, is that the runaway and his owners are in fact half brothers. Buck and Buddy are chasing their own, and not just in terms of legal possession; all of them sons of the legendary Carothers McCaslin, the patriarch, the man who raped his own enslaved daughter.

Was. As in "Once upon a time there was," and this opening chapter is like a folktale indeed, a story of the way things used to be, long ago. But also "as it was in the beginning"—back at the start of things, and yet we all know the way that verse goes on, is now and forever will be. *Was*—the saddest word, as Mr. Compson says, past tense of "is." Yet is the past ever really past? It is, and is not. It *was*, and that's why it can't be changed or fixed, why it still has power and weight. That's why it hurts. *Was*—a determining force, on which we can

Maps

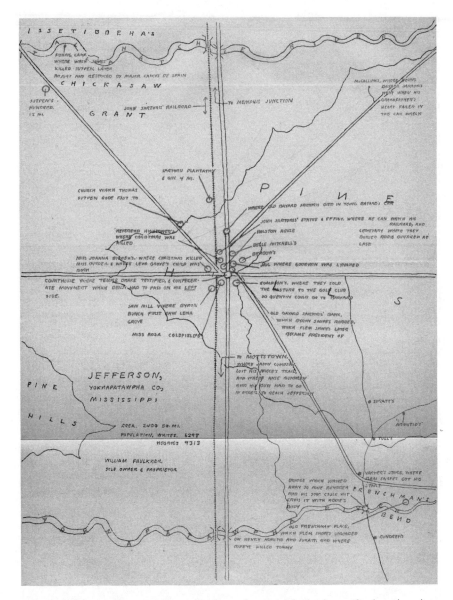

Map drawn by William Faulkner for the endpapers of *Absalom, Absalom!* (1936). Reprinted by permission.

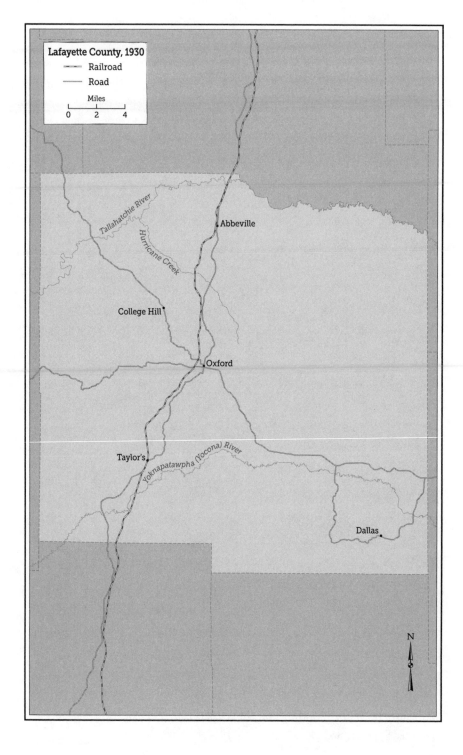

Lafayette County, 1930
Railroad
Road

Miles
0   2   4

Tallahatchie River

Hurricane Creek

Abbeville

College Hill

Oxford

Taylor's

Yoknapatawpha (Yocona) River

Dallas

N

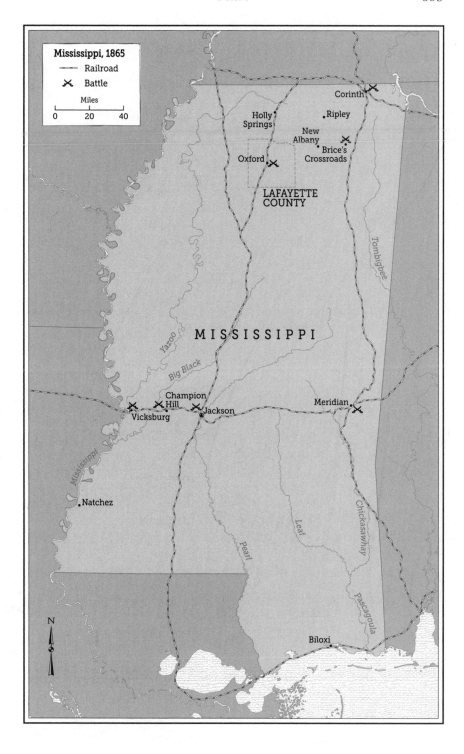

Mississippi, 1865

- Railroad
- ✕ Battle

Miles
0   20   40

Corinth ✕

Holly Springs • • Ripley

New Albany

Oxford ✕ • Brice's Crossroads

LAFAYETTE COUNTY

Tombigbee

MISSISSIPPI

Yazoo

Big Black

Champion Hill ✕
Vicksburg ✕ • Jackson   Meridian ✕

Mississippi

• Natchez

Pearl

Leaf

Chickasawhay

N

Biloxi

Pascagoula

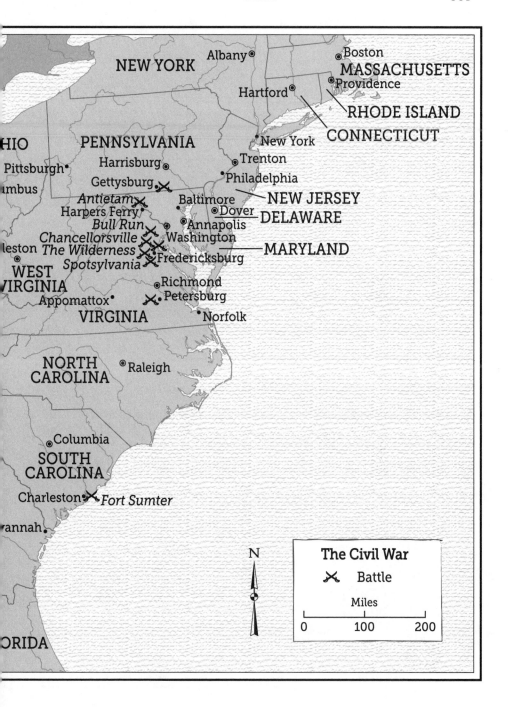

NEW YORK Albany⊙ ⊙Boston
MASSACHUSETTS
⊙Providence
Hartford⊙
RHODE ISLAND
CONNECTICUT
HIO PENNSYLVANIA ⊙New York
Pittsburgh• Harrisburg⊙ ⊙Trenton
mbus Gettysburg•✕ •Philadelphia
Antietam✕ Baltimore• NEW JERSEY
Harpers Ferry• ⊙Dover DELAWARE
Bull Run• ⊙ •Annapolis
Chancellorsville✕ Washington MARYLAND
leston *The Wilderness*✕ •Fredericksburg
Spotsylvania✕
WEST
VIRGINIA ⊙Richmond
Appomattox• ✕•Petersburg
VIRGINIA •Norfolk

NORTH
CAROLINA ⊙Raleigh

⊙Columbia
SOUTH
CAROLINA
Charleston•✕*Fort Sumter*
annah•

ORIDA

N

The Civil War

✕ Battle

Miles

0 100 200

William Faulkner:
A Chronology

Early Years

1897: Born William Cuthbert Falkner on September 25, in New Albany, Mississippi, first of the four sons of Maud Butler Falkner and Murry Cuthbert Falkner. Family roots are in Ripley, Mississippi, where in the 1880s his paternal great-grandfather, William Clark Falkner—landowner, novelist, and Confederate colonel—took control of the local railroad before being shot dead in the street by a former business partner.

1902: Family moves to Oxford, Mississippi, where his grandfather, John Falkner, is a locally prominent lawyer and politician. Father goes into business and opens a livery stable. Caroline Barr, born in slavery, hired to care for the Falkner children; thirty years later she will care for the novelist's own daughter as well.

1903: Meets and sometimes plays with Lida Estelle Oldham (b. 1896) whom in 1929 he will marry.

1909–15: Works in father's livery stable in his hours off from school. Starts to draw and write, and to read authors like Twain, Shakespeare, Conrad, Balzac, and Melville. Begins to fall in love with Estelle. Friendship with law student Phil Stone, who supplies him with new novels and magazines. Faulkner leaves high school without graduating and has already begun to drink.

1918: Estelle engaged to Cornell Franklin, a lawyer, but still talks of eloping with young "Falkner." Nevertheless, she weds Franklin, by whom she will have two children. Faulkner visits Phil Stone at Yale that spring and in July joins the Royal Air Force in Toronto. Enlists under the name "Faulkner." Discharged in December before finishing training.

Apprenticeship

1919–24: Writes poetry, publishes some of it, and briefly attends the University of Mississippi in his hometown. Called "Count No 'Count" by fellow students who find him pretentious. Visits New York and works briefly as a bookstore clerk, but returns home to take a job as postmaster at the university. Friendship with

Sherwood Anderson in New Orleans, where he writes for local magazines. First book: *The Marble Faun*, poems, published December 1924.

1925: Begins work on a novel *Mayday* (later *Soldiers' Pay*). In July sails to Europe on freighter; travels through Italy and Switzerland to Paris, then briefly to England. Returns in December.

1926: *Soldiers' Pay*. Set in Georgia, the novel describes the return from the war of a badly wounded pilot, but its real interest lies in the characters who opportunistically cluster around him, a young war widow and a demobilized soldier among them. Faulkner's parents are shocked at its sexual content. Begins work on the Yoknapatawpha cycle with the unfinished "Father Abraham," which contains the germ of his Snopes novels about the rise to local power of a family of poor white tenant farmers; and *Flags in the Dust*, the story of the Sartoris family from the Civil War to World War I, drawing upon an idealized version of his own family history. Estelle returns to Oxford, her marriage broken.

1927–28: *Mosquitoes*, a satiric novel about the New Orleans literary world, set aboard a pleasure boat cruising on Lake Pontchartrain; its thinly veiled portrait of Anderson strains their relationship. *Flags in the Dust* rejected by his publisher Horace Liveright, who sees it as too loosely structured. His career at an impasse, Faulkner writes *The Sound and the Fury*, using three different first-person narrators and breaking all rules of chronology and point of view to explore the disintegration of the once-proud Compson family. He later describes himself as having worked without plan or design in a state of never-recovered ecstasy. Estelle begins divorce proceedings.

THE GREAT PERIOD I

1929: Publishes both *Sartoris*, a revised and cut version of *Flags in the Dust*, and *The Sound and the Fury*. Marries Estelle. Works on early version of *Sanctuary*, which his new publisher, Harrison Smith, rejects as too scandalous to publish without fear of prosecution; the novel turns on the rape of a young woman with a corncob and also depicts bootleggers, a brothel, and a lynching. In the fall, writes *As I Lay Dying* while working as a nighttime supervisor at the University of Mississippi power plant.

1930: Purchases rundown antebellum Oxford house and names it Rowan Oak. *As I Lay Dying*, the darkly comic story of the poor-white Bundren family's attempt to move the corpse of the family matriarch across the Mississippi countryside, by wagon to her distant burial place in the full heat of summer. It employs fifteen different narrators, some of them members of the family and others the onlookers horrified by the spectacle.

1931: Revised but no less scandalous *Sanctuary* appears. *These 13*, a collection of stories, including such classics as "A Rose for Emily" and "That Evening Sun." The Faulkners' daughter Alabama is born in January, but dies after just nine days. Faulkner drinks heavily.

1932: *Light in August,* the longest of the Yoknapatawpha novels. Set in the county seat of Jefferson, it intertwines three different stories to illuminate the town's collective life, and stands as Faulkner's first serious interrogation of the idea of race. Faulkner goes to Hollywood under contract to Metro-Goldwyn-Mayer, and until 1951 will work intermittently in the movie industry as a screenwriter and script doctor. Father Murry Falkner dies.

1933: *A Green Bough,* poetry. Daughter Jill born in June. Faulkner takes flying lessons and earns his pilot's license in December.

1934: *Doctor Martino and Other Stories.* The volume includes "Wash," which contains the germ of the novel he begins that February; at first called *Dark House,* it will be published as *Absalom, Absalom!*

1935: *Pylon,* a novel about New Orleans stunt pilots. Brother Dean killed in plane crash. Faulkner assumes financial responsibility for Dean's widow and unborn child. In December he returns to Hollywood, where he will spend much of the next two years, and begins intermittent, fifteen-year relationship with Howard Hawks's secretary Meta Doherty Carpenter.

THE GREAT PERIOD II

1936: *Absalom, Absalom!* Now widely regarded as Faulkner's greatest work, an attempt to "tell about the South": first by chronicling the family history of the planter Thomas Sutpen from the beginning of the nineteenth century and on into the post–Civil War decades; and then by dramatizing Quentin Compson's struggle, at Harvard in the winter of 1910, to make a coherent historical narrative out of the fragmentary details about Sutpen's life that survive in Yoknapatawpha County's collective memory. Faulkner hospitalized with alcohol poisoning.

1938: *The Unvanquished,* a novel stitched from a series of heavily revised magazine stories (most of them first published in the *Saturday Evening Post*) about young Bayard Sartoris's experience during the Civil War and after. The book is sold to Hollywood, though never filmed, and Faulkner buys a farm with the proceeds.

1939: *The Wild Palms,* a book that tells two unrelated stories in alternating chapters: one about a doomed love affair that ends with a botched abortion, and the other about the great Mississippi flood of 1927. The book puts him on the cover of *Time.* Elected to the National Institute of Arts and Letters.

1940: *The Hamlet,* again drawing on earlier published material and returning to the characters and setting he had first invented in "Father Abraham." The first novel in the Snopes trilogy, the book depicts the communal life of a village called Frenchman's Bend and what his friend Phil Stone described as "the rise of the redneck" in the person of the sharecropper's son Flem Snopes. Caroline Barr dies; Faulkner gives the eulogy at her funeral and will dedicate *Go Down, Moses* to her.

1942–46: *Go Down, Moses and Other Stories*, a set of intersecting narratives about the moral costs of slavery, as seen in the lives of the black and white descendants of a planter named Carothers McCaslin. Badly in need of money, Faulkner spends much of World War II in Los Angeles, laboring under a punitive contract with Warner Bros. Nevertheless, this is his most successful period in Hollywood, and he works on such classic films as *The Big Sleep* and *Mildred Pierce* among others. Drinks heavily, and notes that all his books with the exception of *Sanctuary* have fallen out of print. Begins to work with the critic Malcolm Cowley on a selection from his work.

THE AGE OF ACCLAIM

1946: Cowley publishes *The Portable Faulkner*, including Faulkner's new appendix to *The Sound and the Fury*, "Compson: 1699–1945." The book makes clear both the scale and the interrelatedness of his achievement, and its reviews mark a permanent change in his critical and public stature. *The Sound and the Fury* and *As I Lay Dying* republished in a single volume by Modern Library.

1948: *Intruder in the Dust*, a mystery about a black man, Lucas Beauchamp, who gets framed for the murder of a white one. Sells film rights for $50,000. Elected to the American Academy of Arts and Letters.

1949: *Knight's Gambit*, a volume of detective stories. Movie of *Intruder in the Dust* released, with its premiere held in Oxford.

1950: In May, receives the Howells Medal for Fiction from the American Academy of Arts and Letters. *Collected Stories of William Faulkner* (National Book Award). November: Faulkner is announced as the winner of the Nobel Prize and reluctantly travels to Sweden for the prize ceremony.

1951: *Requiem for a Nun*, a closet drama about the death of a child that draws upon the characters from *Sanctuary*. Each act is preceded by a long prose narrative that uses characters from throughout his oeuvre to lay out the history of Yoknapatawpha County and its county seat, Jefferson.

THE OLD MASTER

1952–23: Hospitalized several times in Paris, Memphis, and New York for riding- and drinking-related injuries.

1954: *A Fable* (Pulitzer Prize and National Book Award), a heavily allegorical novel about an imagined mutiny of French troops during World War I, men sickened by the relentless slaughter of the trenches. Travels in Europe. Daughter Jill marries Paul D. Summers Jr., a West Point graduate and lawyer; they settle in Charlottesville, Virginia.

1955–56: *Big Woods*, a collection of hunting stories. Faulkner is deeply engaged by both the growing civil rights movement and the white backlash against it; tries, unsuccessfully, to steer a course between them, receiving hate mail from white supremacists even as he tells those in favor of integration to "go slow."

1957–59: *The Town*, second novel of the Snopes trilogy. Flem Snopes has now moved to Jefferson and taken over what was once the Sartoris family bank, an outsider who along with his many cousins slowly begins to dominate the town. Faulkner teaches at the University of Virginia and buys a house there to be near Jill and his new grandchildren. Enjoys fox-hunting but rides recklessly and is often hurt in falls. *The Mansion*, final Snopes novel.

1960: Mother Maud Butler Falkner dies. Faulkner divides his time between Oxford and Charlottesville.

1962: Gold Medal for Fiction from the National Institute of Arts and Letters. Hospitalized several times, his riding injuries exacerbated by his drinking. *The Reivers* (Pulitzer Prize), a comic novel about a horse theft, published in June; the book takes many of its characters from his other books and is both valedictory and atypically sweet. Faulkner dies of a heart attack on July 6 and is buried in Oxford.

William Faulkner:
A List of Major Works

**THE YOKNAPATAWPHA CYCLE—
NOVELS AND SIGNIFICANT STORIES**

"Father Abraham." 1926, unfinished. Published 1983

Flags in the Dust. Published in abridged form as *Sartoris*, 1929. Original version
  published 1973

The Sound and the Fury. 1929

As I Lay Dying. 1930

"A Rose for Emily." 1930

"Red Leaves." 1930

Sanctuary. 1931

"Dry September." 1931

"That Evening Sun." 1931

Light in August. 1932

"There Was a Queen." 1933

"Mountain Victory." 1934

Absalom, Absalom!. 1936

The Unvanquished. 1938

"Barn Burning." 1939

The Hamlet. 1940

Go Down, Moses. 1942

"My Grandmother Millard and General Bedford Forrest and the Battle of
  Harrykin Creek." 1943

Intruder in the Dust. 1948

Knight's Gambit (stories). 1949

Collected Stories. 1950

Requiem for a Nun. 1951

"Mississippi" (fictionalized autobiographical essay). 1954

The Town. 1957

The Mansion. 1959
The Reivers. 1962

OTHER NOVELS

Soldiers' Pay. 1926
Mosquitoes. 1927
Pylon. 1935
The Wild Palms. 1939. Now known by its original title as *If I Forget Thee,
    Jerusalem*
A Fable. 1954

Yoknapatawpha County: A Brief History of an Imaginary Place

Circa 1800: The land that would become known as Yoknapatawpha County had been occupied for centuries by the Chickasaw people when in 1798 the newly independent United States organized what was called the Mississippi Territory. At first that territory was just a strip of land in the southern parts of present-day Mississippi and Alabama; the rest of the region, up to the Tennessee border, was annexed in 1804. By then the first white settlers had filtered into the district: Louis Grenier, a planter of Huguenot origin; a medical doctor, Samuel Habersham, who established a trading post and later received an appointment from the federal government as agent to this part of the Chickasaw territory; and Habersham's groom, Alexander Holston, who opened a saloon in the settlement that began to take shape around that trading post. Initially those settlers depended on the sufferance of Ikkemotubbe, the Chickasaw chief, who as a young man had traveled to New Orleans and brought back the poison that he used to murder the relatives who stood between himself and the chieftancy.

1810–1830: The settlement called Habersham's was a village now, an enclave in the lands of the region's native people. One of its new inhabitants was a man named Jason Compson, who owned an exceptionally fast horse. He matched it in races against the horses of Ikkemotubbe's young men and then swapped it to the chief himself in exchange for a square mile in the center of what would one day be a town and a county; Compson's Mile, it was called. A few years later the settlement found that it had to build a jail and at the same time that it needed a name; so the town of Jefferson was born out of the combination of criminality and discipline. More settlers came, among them a North Carolinian named Lucius Quintus Carothers McCaslin, to whom Ikkemotubbe sold a large tract of land to the northeast of town. He brought with him twin sons, Amodeus and Theophilus, but no wife. In the middle of the twentieth century his white three-times great-grandson, Carothers Edmonds, would still run most of that land; his black grandson Lucas Beauchamp held the rest.

1830–1860: Jefferson had taken shape by the time of the last Chickasaw land cession in 1832, a town with houses and stores and churches, a bank and the Holston House hotel: a town with a county around it. The place seemed settled, no longer quite the frontier, and respectable enough to be offended by one of its new settlers, a man without apparent antecedents named Thomas Sutpen, who appeared from nowhere in 1833 and managed to talk or swindle Ikkemotubbe out of his last bit of territory, a stretch containing a hundred square miles of virgin bottom land. Sutpen broke and planted the land with French-speaking slaves from the Caribbean, and he brought with him a French architect too, a man who not only built the great plantation house at Sutpen's Hundred but also laid down a plan for the town itself, with four streets meeting in the center to form a square around a red brick courthouse. And meanwhile the county's other Frenchman, the Huguenot Grenier, built a monument to his own magnificence down in the county's southeast corner, straightening the course of the Yoknapatawpha River to keep it from flooding his fields.

Old Carothers McCaslin died, and his sons moved their slaves into his unfinished manor house, living themselves in a cabin that they insisted on building with their own hands—no one knew why. A new man appeared in Jefferson, a well-off Carolinian named John Sartoris, and met a better welcome than Sutpen. He had good manners and an old family behind him, bought land a few miles out of town, and quickly made himself into one of the county's leading men. The two planters would always be rivals. People admired Sartoris, but they needed Sutpen, needed his steamboat landing on the Tallahatchie River to get their cotton to market in the days before the railroad. Each of them had a son. Sartoris's was still a child, but in 1859 Sutpen's boy Henry went off to the new state university in Oxford and brought back a friend, a man from New Orleans named Charles Bon, who was soon said to be engaged to Sutpen's daughter. Then both young men vanished, at Christmas in 1860, and the news spread that Sutpen had forbidden the marriage and Henry had in consequence abjured his inheritance.

1861–1870: Mississippi seceded that January, the second state to do so, and in April John Sartoris organized a regiment of Confederate soldiers. He mustered them in on Jefferson's courthouse square and then took them off to Virginia, with Sutpen as his second-in-command. Colonel Jason Compson, the grandson of the settler with the fast horse, led another regiment, but it took a while for the war to reach down into Jefferson itself. Sartoris had a notable success at First Manassas, but a year later, after a second battle at that Virginia rail junction, his men voted him out of office, offended by his arrogant air of command. Sutpen took his place and led the regiment through Gettysburg and after, while Colonel Sartoris came home to organize a band of partisan cavalry, harrying the Union lines of supply.

In 1862 Grant put a storage depot in Jefferson, only to have his supplies burned in a Confederate raid. The town itself saw some fighting, a battle along Hurricane Creek, on the Sartoris land just outside of town, with the Confederate troops falling back through Jefferson's streets themselves. Sutpen's slaves left the plantation en masse as soon as the Union army appeared, following after the Federals into freedom. Sartoris's place was burned, and in 1864 the Yankees put the town itself to the flame, even as a band of Confederate deserters called Grumby's Independents terrorized the countryside. Then the war was over and then men came home. Henry Sutpen shot Charles Bon, his sister Judith's fiancé, at the gates of Sutpen's Hundred and then vanished. His father no longer had an heir, but he nevertheless set about trying to restore his own land, while Sartoris took the lead in trying to rebuild the town. He kept the new freedmen from voting in local elections and organized the night riders to keep whites firmly in control. He started to build a railroad too, a link from Jefferson to the outside world, raising as much money as he could and staying just two cross ties ahead of bankruptcy; and in the process he made enemies.

In 1869 Thomas Sutpen was killed with a scythe by a poor white named Wash Jones, whose fifteen-year-old granddaughter the old man had gotten pregnant.

1870–1890: Sutpen's land passed through the banks and some of it ended in the hands of Major Cassius de Spain, a planter, businessman, and Confederate veteran who had ridden with Bedford Forrest. In Jefferson John Sartoris used a derringer hidden in his sleeve to shoot two carpetbaggers, an old man named Burden and his grandson; and the Burden family would then, oddly, settle down in Jefferson itself, using a fortune made in the goldfields to further the cause of the freedmen. Sartoris's railroad began to roll, finished at last—and soon after the man himself was killed, shot down in the Jefferson square by a former business partner named John Redmond. The colonel's son Bayard refused to shoot Redmond in revenge, as the town expected; but he nevertheless drove him off and then established himself as one of the town's two bankers, with de Spain the other.

Each fall Major de Spain invited his Jefferson neighbors out to his hunting camp on Sutpen's old ground along the Tallahatchie River. There they lived for two weeks in the wilderness, telling stories and killing deer and hoping, always, to get a clear shot at the great bear known as Old Ben. Among them was young Isaac McCaslin, the son Theophilus had gotten in old age, and the rightful heir to all the McCaslin lands. But in 1888, on his twenty-first birthday, Isaac refused his inheritance, allowing his birthright to pass to a cousin: refusing it both because of what he had learned in the forest about the natural world and the impossibility of man's ever owning it; and because of the bitter family history that his reading in the old plantation ledgers had shown him. Other men in Yoknapatawpha were not so scrupulous, and at the end of the decade Major de Spain sold off the timber rights to his wilderness and had it clear-cut for profit.

1890–1910: Louis Grenier vanished with the war, and the great plantation he had built in the southern part of the county fell into ruin. He left behind only a myth of buried treasure, and even his name was forgotten by those who lived in the hamlet of what was now called Frenchman's Bend: a place of small hardscrabble farms, many of them run on shares and owned by a local usurer named Will Varner. Early in the decade a new tenant moved onto one of his farms, a man with a past named Ab Snopes. Ab was rumored to have been a horse thief during the war and a firebug after, with a reputation for burning the barns of the landlords with whom he disagreed. He brought with him a son named Flem, who soon became a clerk in Varner's store. Flem then began to settle one after another of an endless string of cousins into this business or that, always making sure that he got his cut. Snopeses would run the Bend's blacksmith shop and school, but by the turn of the century Flem himself had left the countryside behind and moved to Jefferson, married now to Varner's daughter Eula and eventually taking a job in the Sartoris bank.

The country folk were beginning to rise and the town's old families to fall. The first piece of Compson's Mile had been mortgaged soon after the war, and in 1909 the family sold most of its remaining land to the town's golf club: selling it, first, to pay for the wedding of the family's daughter Candace, pregnant by someone other than the man she was marrying; and second, to finance a Harvard education for the oldest son, Quentin. The boy would do his best to make sure that his parents got their money's worth. He would wait until almost the end of the school year to commit suicide, drowning himself in the Charles River in despair over both his sister's promiscuity and his own inability to stop time.

1910–circa 1930: By now there seemed to be more Snopeses than anyone could count. Flem was vice president of the bank and one of his cousins its embezzling teller. One ran the town's dirty picture show, another was a crooked state senator, Mink Snopes was in jail for murder, and there was even a Snopes wholesale grocer who appeared to be honest. They were all sharp dealers, who wanted a bigger field of action than Frenchman's Bend had allowed; so big, in fact, that the Bend itself now seemed depopulated, and the planter's ruined house had become a hideout for bootleggers.

Jefferson still had some people who remembered the Civil War. Old Bayard Sartoris went each day to his bank and liked reminiscing with his father's last surviving soldier. He died in 1919, out for a ride in the new car bought by his grandson and namesake, a World War I fighter pilot, and Flem Snopes then took over the bank, one family replacing another. The Compsons continued their slide, and after the family matriarch died the grand old mansion was chopped up into apartments; the Gibsons, the black family that had worked for them since the time of slavery, would outlast them. But the real excitement in town came from the lynching, in separate incidents, of two bootleggers. One was the white

man who ran his business out of the ruins of the Old Frenchman's Place, a reliable source of whiskey who was said to have raped a white girl. He was burned
alive on the Jefferson square. The other was possibly partly black, but no one
really knew, not even the man himself, who acted as if he were neither black
nor white. What people did know was that he had been sleeping with a white
woman, the crazy, shunned Joanna Burden, descendant of carpetbaggers, and
had taken his razor to her neck.

1930–1946: Jefferson continued to march into modernity, with electric lights, good
roads, a movie theater, and ever more automobiles on its roads. Ike McCaslin
still hunted, at close to eighty, but now had to drive for hours to reach the kind
of wilderness, out in the Delta, where good game could still be found. His cousin
Lucas Beauchamp was framed for the murder of a white man. He narrowly
avoided a lynching and orchestrated his own liberation from within his prison
cell, telling a white boy named Chick Mallison just how to find the information
that would clear him.

Flem Snopes grew rich. But his wife Eula committed suicide and was memo-
rialized in a new subdivision called Eula Acres, streets of tiny bungalows carved
out of what had once been the Compson Mile. In 1946 the banker was shot in his
own house by his cousin Mink, newly released from jail.

Acknowledgments

I HAD BEEN TEACHING Faulkner for many years in an introductory course on how to read fiction when Carol Bemis asked me to put together a Norton Critical Edition of *As I Lay Dying*. Her offer was both a dream and a challenge; I jumped at it even as it scared me, for however well I knew that particular novel I hadn't yet written about its author. So my first thanks go to her and her team at W. W. Norton for trusting me with it, and I'm happy that our relationship has continued beyond it. But I quickly realized that her commission called for something more than just a few months in the library, and I am grateful as well to Don Kartiganer, then the Howry Professor of Faulkner Studies at the University of Mississippi, for inviting me into his home, showing me around Oxford and Rowan Oak, sharing his stories, and asking me to come back to speak at the annual Faulkner and Yoknapatawpha Conference, held each July on the university's campus. His successor in that chair, Jay Watson, has been an equally superb host, a presence at once rigorous and warm.

My first reading for this project, before I knew it was a project, was done at the American Library in Paris during a sabbatical year in 2010–11. Smith College has, as always, been generous with travel grants and other research funds, and I am grateful to the Provost's Office for that material support. A Public Scholar Award from the National Endowment for the Humanities helped me get through much of this book's first draft.

Jill Kneerim, my agent, steered this book's initial, sketch-like proposal into shape and substance; Jim Shapiro offered a set of invaluable suggestions as that proposal neared its final form. *The Saddest Words* is the second book I've done with Bob Weil at Liveright, and I can only repeat what I said in my acknowledgments to the first of them: every page is stronger because of his work on it. Bob pushes me as no other editor and indeed no teacher ever has—pushes me to be clearer, larger, and more forceful. I am forever grateful to him and to the team at Norton/Liveright, Gabe Kachuck, Julia Druskin, and Peter Miller in particular.

Three very different scholars read the manuscript in its entirety: Christopher Benfey, John T. Matthews, and Elizabeth Varon. I am used to imposing on Chris, after almost thirty years of friendship. Jack and Liz are different, though, readers whom I approached out of my admiration for their work, in the one case at a conference and in the other through a blindly hopeful email. Jack pressed me into clarifying the stakes of this work, as I have tried to do in my preface. Liz saved me from many historical errors, reading these pages even as she saw her own *Armies of Deliverance: A New History of the Civil War* through the press. In addition, Russ Rymer and Tom Ferraro each read a draft of my Gettysburg chapter and told me not to stop.

The earliest version of this book's argument was developed for a lecture in the fall of 2013 sponsored by the English Department at Rutgers University. My thanks to Brad Evans for the invitation that got me thinking, and then to Robert S. Levine of the University of Maryland, where I gave a second version of that talk in his Local Americanist series. I offered a portion of Chapter Seven, under the title "Loosh," at the 2018 Faulkner and Yoknapatawpha Conference; it is scheduled to appear in a volume called *Faulkner and Slavery*, edited by Jay Watson, from the University Press of Mississippi. Kathleen McCartney, Smith's president, asked me to give the college's Sixty-First Annual Katherine Asher Engel Lecture during the 2018–19 academic year. I am deeply honored by her invitation; my talk was a shortened version of Chapter Thirteen titled "The Saddest Words: William Faulkner and the Problem of Memory."

SOME COLLEAGUES AT SMITH deserve special thanks. Rick Millington, Michael Thurston, Floyd Cheung, and Andrea Stone were encouraging whenever this erstwhile Victorianist felt like an interloper on their Americanist landscape; Liz Pryor shared some of her work-in-progress on the nineteenth-century valence of what we call the N-word. Rick accompanied me as well on a road trip to Gettysburg, where Peter Carmichael, the director of the Civil War Institute at Gettysburg College, showed us over the battlefield.

Many other people had the generosity to answer my questions, either in person or electronically. My gratitude to William L. Andrews, Nick Bromell, David Davis, Don Doyle, Sarah Gardner, T. Austin Graham, Minrose Gwin, Taylor Hagood, Dori Hale, Bob Jackson, Alice Kaplan, Nicholas Lemann, Peter Lurie, Jack Mayfield, Rick Moreland, Susan Scott Parrish, Carl Rollyson, the late David Sansing, Timothy Smith, Eric Sundquist, Melanie Benson Taylor, Philip Weinstein, Charles Reagan Wilson, and Brenda Wineapple. I am thankful for the help of my undergraduate research assistants Marie Wilken and Claire Morgan.

The Albert and Shirley Small Special Collections Library at the University of Virginia holds the greatest collection of Faulkner manuscripts and letters; I was happy during the days I spent there. Tracy Carr at the Mississippi Library Commission helped me track down some crucial records of the state's earlier history. At Smith I am grateful to Karen Kukil of the college's Mortimer Rare Books Room, and to Pam Skinner, Sika Berger, and Anne Houston at the Neilson Library's reference desk.

I have yet to entice Brigitte Buettner to join me on a trip to Mississippi. But she has throughout been the most searching of dinner-table companions, a passionate reader and talker and partner who always makes my ideas better than they were before we sat down. Our daughter Miriam has by now grown into a life of her own, past the point at which she has to listen to us each night. This book is for the two of them.

Notes and Sources

THE SCHOLARSHIP ON FAULKNER is enormous, but it's beggared by the quarrelsome, provocative, and ever-changing literature on the Civil War itself. I've learned from everything I've read but have kept my references to a minimum. These notes indicate the sources of my quotations and mark a few specific debts, but they aren't meant to summarize the terms of scholarly debate. Some readers may see that at times I work in close paraphrase of a Faulknerian text or even include the occasional ventriloquized phrase, an unmarked or buried quotation. I've given citations for some of these in the notes below, but not all. Similarly I have drawn biographical and historical facts throughout from the works by Blotner, Williamson, and Doyle listed below, but usually cite them only for particular quotations and not for each detail in my reconstruction of Faulkner's life and community.

All italics in quotations appear in the original.

ABBREVIATIONS FOR FREQUENTLY CITED SOURCES

I   William Faulkner, *Novels 1926–1929*. New York: Library of America, 2006.

II   William Faulkner, *Novels 1930–1935*. New York: Library of America, 1985.

III   William Faulkner, *Novels 1936–1940*. New York: Library of America, 1990.

IV   William Faulkner, *Novels 1942–1954*. New York: Library of America, 1994.

V   William Faulkner, *Novels 1957–1962*. New York: Library of America, 1999.

CS   William Faulkner, *Collected Stories*. New York: Random House, 1950.

SL   Joseph Blotner, ed. *Selected Letters of William Faulkner*. New York: Random House, 1977.

LG   James B. Meriwether and Michael Millgate, ed. *Lion in the Garden: Interviews with William Faulkner*. New York: Random House, 1968.

ESPL William Faulkner, *Essays, Speeches & Public Letters*, ed. James B. Meriwether. Updated Edition. New York: Random House, 2004.

B   Joseph Blotner, *Faulkner: A Biography*. 2 vols. New York: Random House, 1974.

W   Joel Williamson, *William Faulkner and Southern History*. New York: Oxford
      University Press, 1993.
D   Don H. Doyle, *Faulkner's County: The Historical Roots of Yoknapatawpha*.
      Chapel Hill: University of North Carolina Press, 2001.

PREFACE: A PARK BENCH IN PARIS

2   **"postage stamp"**: LG 255.
2   **"words dont ever"**: II 115.
2   **"My mother"**: II 54.
3   **"apocryphal"**: LG 255
3   **"gnawing like rats"**: Malcolm Cowley, *The Portable Faulkner* (1946: rpt. New
    York: Penguin, 1977), 389.
5   **"An Image of Africa"**: Chinua Achebe's essay can most readily be found in the
    Norton Critical Edition of *Heart of Darkness,* 4th ed., ed. Paul B. Armstrong
    (New York: W. W. Norton, 2006). The quotation from Conrad himself can be
    found on p. 7.
6   **"Africanist presence"**: See Toni Morrison, *Playing in the Dark: Whiteness and
    the Literary Imagination* (Cambridge, MA: Harvard University Press, 1992), 5.
    Crucial works of post-Brooks Faulkner criticism include John T. Matthews, *The
    Play of Faulkner's Language* (1982); Eric Sundquist, *Faulkner: The House Divided*
    (1983); Minrose Gwin, *The Feminine and Faulkner* (1990); and Philip Weinstein,
    Faulkner's Subject: A Cosmos No One Owns (1992). Weinstein's more recent and
    beautifully written *Becoming Faulkner* (2010) stands as the best brief introduc-
    tion to the writer.
6   **"the politicians"**: SL 176.
7   **"I sit and write there"**: SL 17.
7   **"gray light ... sad gloom"**: II 398.
10 **"For even when"**: James Baldwin, "Stranger in the Village," in *Collected Essays*
    (New York: Library of America, 1998), 129.

ONE: GETTYSBURG, AT NOT YET TWO

12 **At sunrise**: My reconstruction of the fighting at Gettysburg draws on many
    sources, only a few of which are cited directly here. I am especially indebted to
    the following: the documents collected in *The Civil War: The Third Year Told
    by Those Who Lived It*, ed. Brooks D. Simpson (New York: Library of America,
    2013); Allen C. Guelzo, *Gettysburg: The Last Invasion* (2013); Stephen W. Sears,
    Gettysburg (2003); Edwin P. Coddington, *The Gettysburg Campaign: A Study in
    Command* (1968); and the classic accounts by Shelby Foote and Bruce Catton.
15 **"I had not the ammunition ... good judgment"**: Edward Porter Alexander,
    Fighting for the Confederacy, ed. Gary W. Gallagher (Chapel Hill: University of
    North Carolina Press, 1989), 246, 254. Mostly written in 1899, this manuscript

served as the basis for Alexander's less personal *Military Memoirs* (1907), but remained itself unpublished for almost a century.

15 **"madness to send"**: Alexander, *Fighting for the Confederacy*, 258.

16 **"by the very ticking"**: Douglass Southall Freeman, *Lee's Lieutenants*, Vol. III, *Gettysburg to Appomattox* (New York: Scribner's, 1944), 148.

18 **"For every Southern boy"**: IV 430–31.

20 **"the golden dome"**: IV 431.

20 **"The past"**: IV 535.

21 **"frozen speed"**: Jean-Paul Sartre, "On *The Sound and the Fury*: Time in the Work of Faulkner," trans. Annette Michelson (1939: rpt. 2014 in the third Norton Critical Edition of the novel, ed. Michael Gorra), 318.

21 **"whatever must have"**: LG 220.

21 **"Something is"**: II 250.

22 **"Doomsday"**: LG 255.

24 **"This War aint over"**: III 454. Ringo's words have recently been used as the title for an important study of Civil War memory during the Depression; see Nina Silber, *This War Aint Over: Fighting the Civil War in New Deal America* (Chapel Hill: University of North Carolina Press, 2018).

24 **"aftereffects"**: Daniel Aaron, *The Unwritten War* (1973: rpt. Tuscaloosa: University of Alabama Press, 2003), 311.

24 **"summer . . . had rung"**: III 25.

24 **"minute fragile"**: I 1131–32.

24 **"From a little . . . abrupt"**: III 5–7.

25 **"the son who widowed"**: III 9.

26 **"Corner-stone"**: *The Civil War: The First Year Told by Those Who Lived It*, ed. Brooks D. Simpson, Stephen W. Sears, and Aaron Sheehan-Dean (New York: Library of America, 2011), 221.

26 **In 1927**: Charles and Mary Beard, *The Rise of American Civilization* (New York: Macmillan, 1927).

26 **"sectional differences"**: Avery Craven, *The Coming of the Civil War* (New York: Scribner's, 1942), 93. See also his *The Repressible Conflict* (Baton Rouge: Louisiana State University Press, 1939).

27 **"the deep . . . ghosts"**: III 6.

27 **"Tell . . . at all"**: III 145.

28 **"demon"**: III 6.

28 **"Maybe happen"**: III 216.

28 **"mystic chords"**: Abraham Lincoln, *Speeches and Writings, 1859–1865* (New York: Library of America, 1989), 224.

28 **"historical error . . . formations"**: Ernest Renan, "What Is a Nation." In English this 1882 essay is most readily available in Homi Bhabha, *Nation and Narration* (New York: Routledge, 1990), 11.

29   **stand as a binary**: This is the central argument of David Blight, *Race and Reunion: The Civil War in American Memory* (Cambridge, MA: Harvard University Press, 2001).

29   **"I heard an echo"**: III 124.

30   **"One ever"**: From *The Souls of Black Folk* in W. E. B. Du Bois, *Writings* (New York: Library of America, 1986), 364–65.

30   **"undefeated . . . mentioned"**: ESPL 15.

31   **"there was"**: Frederick Douglass, speech of May 30, 1878, in *The Frederick Douglass Papers*, 1st ser., vol. 4 (New Haven: Yale University Press, 1991), 480.

31   **"sacredness . . . righteous cause"**: Author's transcription of memorial inscriptions during a visit to Gettysburg, June 2015.

33   **"It is well"**: Quoted in Shelby Foote, *The Civil War: A Narrative* (New York: Random House, 1963), vol. 2, 37.

33   **"All this" . . . *now***: But Lee and Pickett are quoted by Arthur James Lyon Fremantle in his diary for July 1–4, 1863. In *The Civil War: The Third Year*, 302.

34   **"open-air . . . gave their lives"**: Garry Wills, *Lincoln at Gettysburg* (New York: Simon & Schuster, 1992), 38. The words of the Gettysburg Address themselves are too well-known and easily found to require citation, as are those of the president's Second Inaugural Address, quoted in Chapter 11.

35   **Lincoln's own cause** : For an important critique of Lincoln's decision to speak on behalf of the Union dead only, see Jonathan Lear, "Gettysburg Mourning," *Critical Inquiry* 45, no. 1 (Autumn 2018).

Two: Old Man Falls

41   **"odor . . . [and] spirit"**: I 543.

42   **"gallant . . . anyhow"**: I 733.

42   **"exactly like . . . fence"**: III 363–64.

42   **"in a dimension . . . boots"**: III 363–64.

43   **"imaginary men"**: John Singleton Mosby, *Mosby's Memoirs* (1917; rpt. Nashville: J. S. Sanders and Co., 1995), 115.

44   **"Be damned"**: I 733.

44   **James M. McPherson**: McPherson, *For Cause and Comrade* (Oxford: Oxford University Press, 1997); Chandra Manning, *What This Cruel War Was Over* (New York: Knopf, 2007).

44   **"set of"**: Manning 32.

44   **"to secure"**: Ibid. 43.

44   **"all of our"**: Ibid. 172.

45   **"My God"**: Quoted in Allen C. Guelzo, *Fateful Lightning: A New History of the Civil War and Reconstruction* (Oxford: Oxford University Press, 2012), 536.

45   **"the most dangerous set"**: Sherman makes this judgment in a letter to Henry W. Halleck; in *The Civil War: The Third Year*, 515.

46   **"spirit . . . convictions"**: I 550.

46 **South Carolina**: See its "Declaration of the Causes of Secession" in *The Civil War: The First Year*, 149

46 **"to interfere"**: See Lincoln's First Inaugural Address, Lincoln, *Speeches*, 210.

46 **"Our position ... schemes"**: Ibid. 183.

46 **"upon the ... passed"**: Ibid. 221–36.

47 **"degradation ... fanaticism"**: Quoted in Charles B. Dew, *Apostles of Disunion: Southern Secession Commissioners and the Causes of the Civil War* (Charlottesville: University of Virginia Press, 2001), 62–63.

48 *"the status"*: *The Civil War: The First Year* 92.

48 **"civil, social"**: Quoted in Dew, *Apostles of Disunion*, 89.

49 **"separate control"**: South Carolina's "Declaration" in *The Civil War: The First Year*, 153.

49 **"idle to talk"**: Robert E. Lee to George Washington Custis Lee, ibid. 200.

49 **"the American ... people"**: Jefferson Davis, "Inaugural Address," ibid. 201–6.

50 **"We are not"**: *Richmond Examiner*, August 2, 1864.

50 **"whatever extent"**: Jefferson Davis, *The Rise and Fall of the Confederate Government* (New York: Appleton, 1881), 66.

51 **"a holy cause"**: III 419.

51 **"in no way"**: Quoted in James M. McPherson, "Long-Legged Yankee Lies: The Southern Textbook Crusade," in Alice Fahs and Joan Waugh, eds., *The Memory of the Civil War in American Culture* (Chapel Hill: University of North Carolina Press, 2004), 68.

51 **"the Confederacy"**: Robert Penn Warren, *The Legacy of the Civil War* (New York: Random House, 1961), 15.

52 **"been compelled"**: Robert E. Lee, General Orders No. 9, *The Civil War: The Final Year Told by Those Who Lived It*, ed. Aaron Sheehan Dean (New York: Library of America, 2014), 673.

52 **"capitalists ... incident"**: Beard and Beard, *Rise of American Civilization:* Vol. II, *The Industrial Era* 54. My reading of the historians of this period is indebted to T. Austin Graham, "Civil War Narrative History," in Coleman Hutchison, ed., *A History of American Civil War Literature* (Cambridge: Cambridge University Press, 2016).

52 **"the fighting"**: Beard and Beard, *Rise of American Civilization* 54.

54 **"the most vigorous"**: Blight, *Race and Reunion* 107.

54 **"as putty"**: I 731.

55 **"fed at"**: III 323.

55 **"Dem wuz"**: Thomas Nelson Page, *In Ole Virginia* (New York: Scribner's, 1887), 10.

THREE: THE FAMILY AND THE TOWN

59 **By 1850**: My account in this chapter of the novelist's Falkner ancestors relies on W Ch. 1–2 and B Ch. 3–8. Williamson offers the greater detail about the Old Colonel's career as a businessman and slaveholder.

59   Fannie Falkner . . . "shadow families": see W 65–69.

59   "though possibly": CS 727.

60   "Bowie Knife": W 21.

65   "small grassless plots": I 1101.

65   Mammy Callie: The most detailed account of Caroline Barr's life, and of Faulk-
      ner's relation to her, is in Judith L. Sensibar, *Faulkner and Love: The Women
      Who Shaped His Art* (New Haven: Yale University Press, 2009).

65   Nelse Patton: See W 157–61; B 113–15; D 323–26.

65   In 1935: SL 89.

66   "sixty two . . . Mayes": CS 169.

66   "damn . . . lying": Ibid. 170.

66   "No balanced . . . knew him": ESPL 338–43.

66   "in his personal": Neil R. McMillen and Noel Polk, "Faulkner on Lynching,"
      The Faulkner Journal 8, no. 1, 13.

67   "middleaged . . . black": ESPL 36–37.

68   "fought such": B 98.

68   Both of them: A survey of current students at the University of Mississippi in the
      spring of 2019 found that a majority support the removal of the monument.

69   "shabby grey . . . surrendered": *Faulkner in the University: Class Conferences at
      the University of Virginia, 1957–1958*, ed. Frederick L. Gwynn and Joseph L. Blot-
      ner (Charlottesville: University Press of Virginia, 1959), 249.

70   "no history": *Laws of the State of Mississippi for the Session Commencing January
      5, 1904*, 116. My understanding of the state's textbooks and educational system is
      indebted to conversations with two University of Mississippi historians, Charles
      Reagan Wilson and the late David Sansing.

71   "greatly agitated": Franklin L. Riley, *School History of Mississippi* (Richmond,
      VA: B. F. Johnson Publishing Company, 1900), 219.

71   "how the state": Ibid. 220.

71   "Our position": *The Civil War: The First* 183.

71   "gallant resistance": Riley 271.

71   "when the South": Ibid. 279.

72   "a number of": Ibid. 307.

72   "very burdensome": Ibid. 305

72   "greed of": Ibid. 311.

72   *The Clansman*: B 94.

73   "squadron": Thomas W. Dixon, *The Clansman* (New York: Doubleday, Page &
      Company, 1905), 369.

73   "black hordes": Ibid. 289.

73   "a man . . . race": Ibid. 93.

74   "into the mists": Ibid. 308.

74   "more prominent": Riley 293.

FOUR: POSTAGE STAMPS

75 **Elizabeth Prall:** Kim Townsend, *Sherwood Anderson* (Boston: Houghton Mifflin, 1987), contains a fuller account of both Prall and Faulkner's work for her than do any of the biographies of Faulkner himself. See also Faulkner's affectionate memoir of Anderson in ESPL 3 ff.

76 **"very small":** Sherwood Anderson, *Collected Stories* (New York: Library of America, 2012), 713.

77 **"Dr. Cammun":** *The Clansman* 271.

78 **"throwed":** IV 43.

78 **"kilt":** II 37.

78 **"mighty spindling":** II 40. The literature on the role of dialect in American fiction is a rich one. See, for starters, Gavin Jones, *Strange Talk: The Politics of Dialect Literature in Gilded Age America* (Berkeley: University of California Press, 1999); Stephen M. Ross, *Fiction's Inexhaustible Voice: Speech and Writing in Faulkner* (Athens: University of Georgia Press, 1989); and John N. Duvall, *Race and White Identity in Southern Fiction: From Faulkner to Morrison* (Palgrave Macmillan, 2008).

78 **"local color":** See especially Richard Brodhead, *Cultures of Letters: Scenes of Reading and Writing in Nineteenth-Century America* (Chicago: University of Chicago Press, 1993); and Judith Fetterley and Marjorie Pryse, *Writing Out of Place: Regionalism, Women, and American Literary Culture* (Champaign: University of Illinois Press, 2003). My argument in the following pages is indebted to Brodhead in particular.

81 **"No, dear . . . sea":** Sarah Orne Jewett, *Novels and Stories* (New York: Library of America, 1995), 402.

82 **Great American Novel:** The phrase was coined by John W. DeForest in an article for *The Nation*, January 9, 1868.

85 **"brisk . . . and think":** Anderson 25.

85 **"hungering":** Ibid. 166.

85 **"a background":** Ibid. 180.

86 **his biographer:** See B 210.

87 *A Vicarious Life*: Susan Snell, *Phil Stone of Oxford: A Vicarious Life* (Athens: University of Georgia Press, 1991).

87 **"singing . . . knees":** William Faulkner, "L'Après-Midi d'un Faune," *The New Republic*, August 6, 1919.

88 **"the Flauberts":** ESPL 295.

89 **"I won't ever":** B 365.

89 **"Anderson talked . . . write anything":** "A Note on Sherwood Anderson," in ESPL 3–10.

89 **"Sir Galwyn . . . gold":** William Faulkner, *Mayday* (written 1926; South Bend: University of Notre Dame Press, 1976).

90 **"terrific arrested motion"**: William Faulkner, *New Orleans Sketches*, ed. Carvel Collins (1958; rpt. Jackson: University Press of Mississippi, 2009), 48.

90 **"idiot . . . thought"**: Ibid. 55.

90 **"a courtesan"**: Ibid. 13.

91 **"Carry on"**: I 223.

92 **Cleanth Brooks**: See his *William Faulkner: Toward Yoknapatawpha and Beyond* (New Haven: Yale University Press, 1978), 99.

92 **"a hunch"**: *Letters of Sherwood Anderson*, ed. Howard Mumford Jones (New York: Kraus Reprint, 1969), 146.

92 **"bit like"**: Ibid. 155.

93 **"the father"**: LG 249.

93 **"one has . . . America too"**: ESPL 8.

94 **"I'm inclined"**: SL 185.

94 **"my own little"**: LG 255.

95 **"keystone"**: Ibid.

95 **"but he"**: SL 185.

95 **"Art is"**: ESPL 289.

95 **"we lack"**: Allen Tate, "The Profession of Letters in the South," in *Essays of Four Decades* (Chicago: The Swallow Press, 1968), 520.

96 **"estrangement . . . temper"**: George Washington Cable, "Literature in the Southern States," in *The Negro Question*, ed. Arlin Turner (New York: Doubleday, 1958), 40–50. This volume collects all of Cable's essays on racial issues.

97 **"two centuries . . . folk-lore."** From "The South as a Field for Fiction" in *Undaunted Radical: The Selected Writings and Speeches of Albion W. Tourgee*, ed. Mark Elliott and John David Smith (Baton Rouge: Louisiana State University Press, 2010), 203–210.

98 **"the most . . . new way"**: SL 185.

FIVE: INVENTING YOKNAPATAWPHA

99 **"He is"**: William Faulkner, *Father Abraham*, ed. James B. Meriwether (New York: Random House, 1983), 13.

100 **"the rise"**: Ibid. "Introduction."

100 **"where the light"**: Ibid. 14.

100 **"water runs"**: See *A William Faulkner Encyclopedia*, ed. Robert W. Hamblin and Charles A. Peek (Westport, CT: Greenwood Publishing Group, 1999), 446.

100 **"a soiled"**: "Father Abraham" 22.

100 **"wild as rabbits"**: Ibid. 24.

101 **"an armful"**: Ibid. 56.

102 **"the land and yet"**: Ibid. 19–20.

102 **"beneath the moth"**: Ibid. 17.

102 **"pine clad hills"**: Ibid. 16.

102 "my townspeople": SL 34.

102 "other things": SL 38.

103 "a legion . . . gesture": I 613–15.

103 "profane astonishment": I 678.

103 "act always . . . conflict": George Marion O'Donnell, "Faulkner's Mythology," in *Faulkner: A Collection of Critical Essays*, ed. Robert Penn Warren (Englewood Cliffs, NJ: Prentice Hall, 1977), 24.

104 "row after row": I 1131.

104 "Southern Negroes": LG 20.

104 "a native": ESPL 205.

104 "It'll taste": I 657.

105 Wright himself: See his review of Hurston's *Their Eyes Were Watching God* in *The New Masses* (October 5, 1937): 22–23.

105 "Him en Isom": I 611.

106 "man's felt hat . . . arm": I 1082.

107 "want nobody": 1087.

107 "like a . . . sistuhn": I 1103–4.

109 "Sartoris": See *William Faulkner Manuscripts*, vol. 5, part 1, ed. Joseph Blotner et al. (New York: Garland, 1986–87).

109 "old Colonel Sartoris": I 1012.

110 "we're frankly": B 560.

115 "Apotheosis": IV 627.

116 "One day": ESPL 292–93.

117 "still . . . try it": *Faulkner in the University* 84.

117 "forgotten what": SL 235.

117 "the damndest book": SL 41.

118 "you had": B 584.

118 "the faults": Mary Ellen Chase, "Some Intimations of Immortality," *Commonweal* 5 (June 1929).

119 "honor and sanity": Quoted in Sensibar, *Faulkner and Love* 253–54.

120 "lots of storming": Ibid. 12.

SIX: THE PRECIPICE

125 "hillsides worn . . . thought of": Frederick Law Olmsted, *The Cotton Kingdom* (1861; rpt. New York: Knopf, 1953), 410–11.

125 "expanding its waters": Quoted in Walter Johnson, *River of Dark Dreams: Slavery and Empire in the Cotton Kingdom* (Cambridge, MA: Harvard University Press, 2013), 318.

129 "beyond all price": Stark Young, *So Red the Rose* (New York: Scribner's, 1934), 86.

130 "You people . . . wane": Quoted in James Lee McDonough, *William Tecumseh Sherman* (New York: W. W. Norton, 2016), 234.

130   **L. Q. C. Lamar:** D Ch. 5 contains a detailed account of the debate about the coming war in Oxford and the surrounding Lafayette County.

131   "Two ... association": IV 627.

131   "pristine": IV 628.

132   "whirling into": IV 627.

132   "static in *quo*": IV 628.

133   "wild negroes": III 23.

133   "actually a little": III 60.

133   "summer of wistaria": III 25.

133   "last summer": III 86.

134   "a gutted house": III 89.

134   "the tale ... birthright": III 64–65.

134   "gallant mimic": III 101.

134   **University Greys:** See D 64; also Stephen Enzweiler, *Oxford in the Civil War* (Charleston: The History Press, 2010).

135   **Whitman:** See *Specimen Days* (1882); the book's concluding paragraphs are headed "The Real War Will Never Get in the Books."

136   "speeches and pamphlets": Edmund Wilson, *Patriotic Gore* (New York: Oxford University Press, 1962), ix.

136   "Fiction is so flat": Mary Chesnut, *Mary Chesnut's Civil War*, ed. C. Vann Woodward (New Haven: Yale University Press, 1981), 359.

137   "may hope": *The Children of Pride: A True Story of Georgia and the Civil War*, ed. Robert Manson Myers (New Haven: Yale University Press, 1972), 261.

137   "Why do they": Ibid. 526.

138   "intestine war": Ibid. 621.

138   "such an abundance": Ibid. 415

138   "hissing tongue": Ibid. 648.

138   "It means this": Ibid. 655.

138   "unmitigated rascality": Ibid. 655.

138   "finds no lodgement": Ibid. 667.

139   "cruel and": Erskine Clarke, *Dwelling Place: A Plantation Epic* (New Haven: Yale University Press, 2005), 444. This is a complement and corrective to *The Children of Pride*, paying due attention to the lives and fates of the enslaved on the Joneses' plantations.

140   "I wonder": Chesnut, *Mary Chesnut's Civil War* 29.

140   "thing we can't name": Ibid.

141   "how I saw ... hunted for one": Ibid. 116.

142   "green goose": Ibid. 45.

142   "And so we": Ibid. 41.

142   "sound and fury": Ibid. 47.

142   "ablaze": Ibid. 48.

142 "Not by one . . . their time?": Ibid.

143 "So we . . . people": Ibid. 51.

143 "We have risked": Ibid. 3.

143 "between crying": *The Letters of Henry Adams*, vol. 1, ed. Ernest Samuels and Jacob Levenson (Cambridge, MA: Harvard University Press, 1982), 208.

143 "her husband": Ibid. 231.

144 "in order": Ibid. 224.

144 "the attempt": *The Diary of George Templeton Strong: The Civil War 1860–1865*, ed. Allan Nevins and Milton Halsey Thomas (New York: Macmillan, 1952), 54.

144 "a regiment": Ibid. 94.

144 "but money": Ibid. 93.

145 "Extry . . . backbone": Ibid. 118–19.

145 "as rabbits": Ibid. 169.

145 "This is": Chesnut, *Mary Chesnut's Civil War* 115.

146 "cut and fitted": III 102.

146 official history: Steven H. Stubbs, *Duty, Honor, Valor: The Story of the Eleventh Mississippi Infantry Regiment* (Brandon, MS: Quail Ridge Press, 2000).

146 "fine figure": III 233. Both W (Ch. 2) and B (Ch. 4–5) offer detailed accounts of William Falkner's Civil War career.

147 Memphis *Appeal*: B 22.

149 "fool's paradise": Chesnut, *Mary Chesnut's Civil War* 111.

149 "old violent": III 67.

Seven: The Real War

151 "buried somewhere": III 732.

152 "sunimpacted . . . map": III 321.

153 "the cannon": III 329.

153 "There's your": III 322.

154 "even if": III 333.

154 "slept together": III 323.

155 "on a bright bay": III 335.

155 "bastud . . . smoke": III 336.

156 "her skirts": III 338.

156 "Broke . . . Sunday": III 338–39.

156 "We had heard . . . part in them": III 382.

157 war's very absence: See Wade Newhouse, "'Aghast and Uplifted': William Faulkner and the Absence of History," *The Faulkner Journal* 21, no. 1–2.

157 "You have heard . . . but didn't": Mark Twain, *Collected Tales, Sketches, Speeches & Essays, 1852–1890* (New York: Library of America, 1992), 863.

158 "the play . . . depression": Ibid. 867.

158 "and the enemy": Ibid. 877.

158   "my first impulse": Ibid. 879.

158   "I had never": Ibid. 880.

159   "frightened me": Ibid. 882. Bruce Catton, *Grant Moves South* (Boston: Little, Brown, 1960), remains a superb narrative of the general's career through the end of 1863, with a special focus on operations in Mississippi and Tennessee.

159   "told by a soldier": Ambrose Bierce, *The Devil's Dictionary, Tales, & Memoirs* (New York: Library of America, 2011), 660.

159   "long, deep": Ibid.

159   "deaf to duty": Ibid. 665.

160   "I thought not": Ibid. 671.

160   "unlovely looseness": Ibid. 674.

160   "necessarily group": Ibid. 672.

161   In April 1952: B 1412.

161   "the highest destiny": III 448.

162   "to get used to": III 223.

162   "was not one": Catton, *Grant Moves South* 226.

163   Foote: Shelby Foote, *The Civil War: A Narrative*, 3 vols. (New York: Random House, 1958–1963).

165   "elder-stalk": Abraham Lincoln, *Speeches and Writings, 1859–1865* (New York: Library of America, 1989), 346.

165   "their friends": Ulysses S. Grant, *Memoirs and Selected Letters* (New York: Library of America, 1990), 291.

166   "a verb": Ibid. 1120.

166   "and seeing": Ibid. 235

167   "Ulysses don't": These words are attributed to a soldier at Spotsylvania (1864) who saw the general calmly scribbling orders while under fire.

167   "never has": Wilson, *Patriotic Gore* 143.

168   "no feeling": SL 370.

169   "out-camp": Grant, *Memoirs* 357.

170   "the two armies . . . a feeling of sadness": Ibid. 383.

171   "Van Dorn's cavalry": II 751.

171   "traveled as fast": *Official Records of the War of the Rebellion*, XVII, 1 (Washington, DC: Government Printing Office) 477.

171   "The sky . . . doubt": II 757.

172   Jacob Thompson: see D 207–8 and Enzweiler, *Oxford in the Civil War* 81.

173   "born loony": III 368,

173   "I done . . . me free." III 369–70.

Eight: Freedom

174   "I belongs": III 369.

174   "Don't . . . him": III 370.

175 **"took everything"**: In George P. Rawick, ed., *The American Slave: A Composite Autobiography*, 12 vols. (Westport, CT: Greenwood, 1977), 2288.

175 **"went off"**: Ibid. 1068

175 **"You is"**: Image 215 of Federal Writers Project, Slave Narrative Project, Vol. 16, Texas, Part 1, Adams Duhon. https://www.loc.gov/resource/mesn .161/?sp=215&st=text.

176 **"Old Master"**: Rawick, *American Slave* 1155.

177 **governed under slavery**: See Edward E. Baptist, *The Half Has Never Been Told: Slavery and the Making of American Capitalism* (New York: Basic Books, 2014).

177 **biblical curse**: See Genesis: 9:22–27.

177 **"little of that"**: Ulrich B. Phillips, *American Negro Slavery* (1918; rpt. Baton Rouge: Louisiana State University Press, 1966), 307.

178 **"vigor of discipline"**: Ibid. 343.

178 **"curiously incomplete"**: W. E. B. Du Bois, *American Political Science Review*, 12, no. 4 (November 1918).

179 **"Fore God"**: III 370.

180 **"one of the enemy"**: *Official Records of the War of the Rebellion*, I, 2, 186.

180 **Lucindy Hall Shaw**: D 122.

180 **Hughes**: Louis Hughes, *Thirty Years a Slave* (1897; rpt. Montgomery, AL: New-South Books, 2002).

180 **land records**: Found through the 1850 census via Ancestry.com. My thanks to Pam Skinner of Smith's Neilson Library for help in tracking these details. There are no McGees listed as substantial landholders in the relevant counties; there are McGehees, bearing the first names that Hughes gives them.

181 **"eat or . . . sights"**: III 183.

182 **"difference between"**: III 187.

182 **"set aside"**: III 207.

182 **"subdued them"**: III 210.

183 **"In her youth"**: Chesnut, *Mary Chesnut's Civil War* 211.

183 **"the bare sight"**: Lincoln, *Speeches and Writings, 1859–1865* 440.

184 **"We ought"**: Chesnut, *Mary Chesnut's Civil War* 211.

184 **"thought of being afraid"**: Ibid. 199

184 **"why don't"**: Ibid. 113–14.

184 **"rise and burn"**: Ibid. 409.

185 **"What did . . . no sense"**: W. E. B. Du Bois, *Black Reconstruction in America* (1935; rpt. New York: Oxford University Press 2007), iv.

186 **"last Cent . . . from him"**: William Tecumseh Sherman, letter of August 24, 1862, in *The Civil War: The Second Year Told by Those Who Lived It*, ed. Stephen W. Sears (New York: Library of America, 2012), 374–76.

186 **"the rights"**: Crittenden-Johnson Resolutions, in *The Civil War: The First Year* 522–23.

186 **Adam Goodheart's**: Adam Goodheart, *1861: The Civil War Awakening* (New York: Knopf, 2011).

187 **"military necessity"**: *The Civil War: The First Year* 538–39.

187 **"we ought to take"**: Sherman, *The Civil War: The Second Year* 375.

187 **"in the course"**: Abraham Lincoln, "House Divided Speech," in *Speeches and Writings, 1832–1858* (New York: Library of America, 1989) 426.

187 **"war measure"**: *The Civil War: The Second Year* 743.

188 **"an outrage"**: Ibid. 567.

188 **"the negroes"**: Ibid. 573.

188 **"peculiar, cautious"**: Ibid. 561–62.

188 **"this is"**: Frederick Douglass, "Fighting Rebels with Only One Hand," *The Civil War: The First Year* 566.

189 **"believed . . . manhood"**: Edwin M. Stanton, Letter to Abraham Lincoln, December 5, 1863. Quoted in Paul S. Boyer, *Todd and Curti's The American Nation* (New York: Holt, Rinehart, & Winston, 1995), 385.

189 **"Enlist"**: Frederick Douglass, "Why Should a Colored Man Enlist?," in *The Civil War: The Third Year*, 119.

190 **"Always"**: John Q. Anderson, ed. *Brokenburn: The Journal of Kate Stone 1861–1868* (1955; rpt. Baton Rouge: Louisiana State University Press, 1995), 8

190 **"whipped by"**: Ibid. 218.

190 **"the officer"**: Ibid. 128.

190 **"pack of"**: Ibid. 182.

190 **"Mamma has"**: Ibid. 101.

190 **"must be"**: Ibid. 176.

191 **"Yankees and . . . owned"** : Ibid. 195–97.

192 **"after Kernel's place"**: III 232

192 **"God's own"**: III 369.

193 **"about fifty . . . daylight"**: III 375.

193 **"four chimneys"**: III 377.

194 **"couldn't count"**: III 380.

194 **"to hold them"**: III 381.

194 **"Negroes coming"**: Ulysses S. Grant to Henry Halleck, November 15, 1862. Quoted in John Eaton, *Grant, Lincoln and the Freedmen* (1907; rpt. New York: Negro Universities Press, 1969), 12.

194 **"in every . . . cities"**: Eaton, *Grant, Lincoln* 2.

195 **Chandra Manning**: My narrative in this section, my use of Eaton's memoir included, is greatly indebted to her *Troubled Refuge: Struggling for Freedom in the Civil War* (New York: Knopf, 2016). See especially Ch. 2.

195 **"the slaves"**: Eaton, *Grant, Lincoln* 2.

196 **"We never did . . . through them"**: III 388.

196 **"the horses' "**: III 390.

196 **"clap . . . faces"**: III 391.

197 **people who could not swim**: Foote, *Civil War*, vol. 3, contains a vivid account of this incident; see 649–50.

197 **Charles Kerr**: Kerr's letter is quoted in Anne Sarah Rubin, *Through the Heart of Dixie: Sherman's March and American Memory* (Chapel Hill: University of North Carolina Press, 2014), 89. My account of this incident relies on her scholarship.

198 **sublime**: See T. Austin Graham, "Reconstructions: Faulkner and Du Bois on the Civil War," in Jay Watson, ed., *Faulkner and the Black Literatures of the Americas* (Jackson: University Press of Mississippi, 2016).

198 **"captured loose"**: III 395.

199 **"straggling off"**: III 397.

199 **"I been"**: Leon Litwack, *Been in the Storm So Long: The Aftermath of Slavery* (New York: Knopf, 1979).

199 **"the law"**: Eaton, *Grant, Lincoln* 136.

199 **"some definite . . . Union cause"**: Ibid. 123.

200 **Du Bois's newly**: Ibid. 47.

200 **Douglas Egerton**: Douglas Egerton, *The Wars of Reconstruction* (New York: Bloomsbury, 2014).

NINE: THE STILLNESS

204 **"bombastic . . . undefeat"**: III 157.

204 **"about the very"**: III 55.

204 **"ode eulogy"**: III 8.

205 **"Long shall"**: See *"Words for the Hour": A New Anthology of Civil War Poetry*, ed. Faith Barrett and Cristanne Miller (Amherst: University of Massachusetts Press, 2005), 60.

205 **"Fold it up"**: Ibid. 124.

205 **Each side**: See Drew Gilpin Faust, *This Republic of Suffering: Death and the American Civil War* (New York: Knopf, 2008).

205 **"civil religion"**: Charles Reagan Wilson, *Baptized in Blood: The Religion of the Lost Cause, 1865–1920* (Athens: University of Georgia Press, 1980), 1.

206 **"marble man"**: Thomas Lawrence Connolly, *The Marble Man: Robert E. Lee and His Image in American Society* (New York: Random House, 1977).

206 **"walk out of"**: ESPL 15.

206 **"The other"**: Henry Timrod, "The Two Armies," in Barrett and Miller, *New Anthology* 323.

207 **"sign the"**: III 406.

207 **"back into the hills"**: III 411.

207 **"defeat with God"**: III 412.

207 **"they had received before"**: III 413.

207 **Stephanie McCurry**: See her *Confederate Reckoning: Power and Politics in the Civil War South* (Cambridge, MA: Harvard University Press, 2010), Ch. 4.

208 **"bride-widow"**: III 448.

208 **"astride like"**: III 379.

208 **"Uncle John"**: III 388.

208 **"a goodish-looking"**: Arthur Lyon Fremantle, *Three Months in the Southern States* (1864; rpt. Carlisle, MA: Applewood Books, 2008), 173.

208 **Current estimates**: McCurry, *Confederate Reckoning* Ch. 5.

209 **some Southern towns**: Drew Gilpin Faust, *Mothers of Invention: Women of the Slaveholding South in the Civil War* (Chapel Hill: University of North Carolina Press, 1996), 203.

209 **"like a man"**: III 379.

209 **"a lost woman"**: III 448

209 **"to hurt Yankees"**: III 449.

210 **"you lived"** III 387.

210 **"Generals as plenty"**: Chesnut, *Mary Chesnut's Civil War* 705.

210 **"look out"**: Ibid. 792.

211 **"the deep South dead"**: III 6.

211 **"narrow workless hands"**: IV 626.

211 **"the rush . . . undefeated"**: IV 629.

211 **"knell of"**: IV 630.

213 **"up Main street"**: IV 172.

213 *Bedford Forrest*: Andrew Nelson Lytle, *Bedford Forrest and His Critter Company* (1931; rpt. Nashville: J. S. Sanders, 1984).

214 **"Battles and Leaders"**: This series ran in the lavishly illustrated *Century* from 1883 to 1887 and in 1888 was collected into four large double-columned volumes, published in New York under the magazine's own imprint. It focused on military operations alone and excluded all political questions as a way of ensuring a supposedly national appeal: that is, an appeal to white Americans in the states of the former Confederacy as well as in those of the Union. That emphasis doubtless fostered the narrow interest in the minutiae of battlefield operations that still marks and at times mars much writing about the war; for all that, it remains a valuable source of testimony. The account of Fort Pillow appears on pp. 418–19 of Vol. IV, and a generous selection from the series appeared in 2011 under the title *Hearts Touched by Fire*, ed. Harold Holzer (New York: Modern Library).

214 **"butchery"**: *The Civil War: The Final Year* 44.

214 **"there was"**: Lytle, *Bedford Forrest* 279.

215 **"a big dusty . . . dragged"**: CS 691–92

216 **"cash money"**: III 402.

216 **"frightening white women"**: III 421.

216 "into the wet . . . sticks": III 423.

217 "tied hand and foot": III 435.

217 "thing hanging . . . quiet": III 439.

217 "two bright . . . rock": III 442–43.

218 "Countymaison": CS 755.

219 "nigra": CS 756.

219 "lost the privilege": CS 766.

219 "date or": III 107.

219 *"We have . . . to live"*: III 108–9.

220 *"to walk backward"*: III 286.

220 "red clay minuet": Foote, *Civil War*, Vol. 3, Ch. 3.

220 *"curiously . . . . We air"*: III 289–90.

221 *"at least have"*: III 285.

221 *"gutted mansion"*: III 107.

222 "seems to apprehend": *The Children of Pride*, 165.

222 "would be a great": Ibid. 1182.

223 "heavy losses": Ibid. 1175.

223 "we do not": Ibid. 1188.

223 "War is cruelty": *The Civil War: The Final Year* 384–86.

223 "forage liberally": W. T. Sherman, Special Field Orders No. 120, November 9, 1964. In Sherman, *Memoirs* (New York: Library of America, 1990), 652.

224 "Kentucky Irishman": *The Children of Pride* 1223.

224 "yelling . . . wives": Ibid. 1226–27.

224 "annals": Ibid. 1242.

224 "for this": Ibid. 1239.

224 "wild halloos . . . body": Ibid.

225 "effusion": Grant, *Memoirs* 727.

225 "proud of . . . actions": Edward Porter Alexander, *Fighting for the Confederacy* 531–32.

226 "brown-bearded": Bruce Catton, *A Stillness at Appomatox* (Garden City, NY: Doubleday, 1953), 380.

226 "depressed . . . fought": Grant, *Memoirs* 735.

226 "not . . . mule": Ibid. 739–40.

226 "as defeated . . . retribution": Elizabeth Varon, *Appomattox: Victory, Defeat, and Freedom at the End of the Civil War* (New York: Oxford University Press, 2014), 206.

227 chipped and battered: See Elizabeth Brown Pryor, *Reading the Man: A Portrait of Robert E. Lee Through His Private Letters* (New York: Viking Penguin, 2007).

227 "constancy . . . resources": Robert E. Lee, General Orders No. 9, *The Civil War: The Final Year* 673–74.

228 "we never": Quoted in Blight, *Race and Reunion* 93.

228 *"orderly came"*: III 288.

228   "*jutting nose...gray*": III 290–91.

229   "dodging Yankee": III 295.

Ten: The Shooting At The Gates

234   $6,000: B 653.

234   "I don't read": W 270.

235   "as someone": Elizabeth Spencer, *Landscapes of the Heart: A Memoir* (New York: Random House, 1988), 141.

237   "impotent and furious": CS 539–40.

237   "anecdote which...out": SL 78–79.

238   "mass...often": Ibid. 84.

238   "the best": B 927.

238   common enough question: See Natalie J. Ring, *The Problem South: Region, Empire, and the New Liberal State 1880–1930* (Athens: University of Georgia Press, 2012).

239   "the deep South": III 6.

239   "weary dead": III 5.

240   "thunderclap....Nothing": III 6.

240   "the son who": III 9.

241   "*maybe happen*": III 216.

241   "done shot": III 110.

242   Faulkner's critics: The classic reading remains Cleanth Brooks's in his *William Faulkner: The Yoknapatawpha Country* (New Haven: Yale University Press, 1963). But see also Peter Brooks (no relation), *Reading for the Plot: Design and Intention in Narrative* (New York: Knopf, 1984), Ch. 11.

242   "repudiated blood": III 74.

243   "the graceful": Olmsted, *Cotton Kingdom* 302. See also Emily Clark, *The Strange History of the American Quadroon* (Chapel Hill: University of North Carolina Press, 2013).

243   "culled and chosen": III 96–97.

244   "as a valid": III 76.

244   "drawing honor...missing": III 83.

245   "I never": III 124.

245   "alike as if": III 142–43.

246   "Sprung from": III 193.

246   "balloon face": III 194.

246   "incidentally of course": III 218

246   "adjunctive or incremental": III 199.

246   "*my brow*": III 258.

246   "*want to go*": III 269.

247   "He has known": III 244.

247 **"whatever it was"**: III 273.

248 **"both in Carolina"**: III 289.

248 ***"He cannot marry . . . negro"***: III 292.

248 ***"So it's . . . sister"***: III 293–94.

249 **John T. Matthews**: See his *William Faulkner: Seeing through the South* (Hoboken, NJ: Wiley-Blackwell, 2009), 191–93.

250 **latter word**: See Eric J. Sundquist, *Faulkner: The House Divided* (Baltimore: Johns Hopkins University Press, 1983), 108.

250 **"Who him"**: CS 537.

250 **servitude**: On the nineteenth-century history of the word, see Elizabeth Stordeur Pryor, "The Etymology of Nigger: Resistance, Language, and the Politics of Freedom in the Antebellum North," *Journal of the Early Republic* 36, no. 2 (2016).

251 **one-drop**: Allan Nevins, *The Ordeal of the Union* (New York: Scribner's, 1947), 509.

251 **"one-fourth . . . into society"**: See Charles W. Chesnutt, "What Is a White Man?," in Charles W. Chesnutt, *Stories, Novels, and Essays* (New York: Library of America, 2002), 839–41.

251 **"let flesh"**: III 115.

252 **"That Evening Sun"**: In CS 289 ff.

252 **"black man"**: W. E. B. Du Bois, "The Superior Race," *The Smart Set* 70 (April 1923), 60.

252 **"black or white"**: I 943.

253 **"a level dead"**: II 423.

253 **"saddle-colored"**: III 304.

254 **Sterling A. Brown**: "Negro Character as Seen by White Authors," *Journal of Negro Education* 2, no. 2 (April 1933). This essay is most readily available in *A Son's Return: Selected Essays of Sterling A. Brown*, ed. Mark A. Sanders (Boston: Northeastern University Press, 1996).

255 **"an old plantation"**: Olmsted, *Cotton Kingdom* 240.

255 **"folks sometimes"**: Chesnutt, *The Marrow of Tradition* 472.

256 **"send me"**: III 91.

256 **"a moral responsibility"**: George Washington Cable, "The Freedman's Case in Equity." Reprinted in *The Negro Question* 56.

257 **"vicious evasions"**: Ibid. 58.

257 **"in daily practice"**: Ibid. 67.

257 **"a disqualifying"**: Ibid. 62.

257 **"social intermingling"**: Ibid. 94.

257 **"national harmony . . . confusion"**: Cable, "The Silent South," in *The Negro Question* 130.

258 **"the dual threats"**: Barbara Ladd, *Nationalism and the Color Line in George W. Cable, Mark Twain, and William Faulkner* (Baton Rouge: Louisiana State University Press, 1997), 151.

258   **odd strain:** See Sundquist, *Faulkner: House Divided* 111.

258   **"Kilt him":** III 110.

259   **"mare . . . right":** III 236.

260   **"fusty":** III 297.

260   **"wasted hands . . . *Sutpen*":** III 306.

261   **palindrome:** See Peter Brooks, *Reading for the Plot* 306.

261   **"You cant . . . know":** III 297.

262   **"monstrous":** III 308.

263   **"just one . . . *it*":** III 211.

263   **"he not I":** SL 185.

ELEVEN: A LEGACY

264   **black middle class:** See Henry Louis Gates Jr., *Stony the Road: Reconstruction, White Supremacy, and the Rise of Jim Crow* (New York: Penguin Press, 2019), Ch 4.

264   **"to Pharaoh":** IV 278.

265   **"Mammy":** See Sensibar, *Faulkner and Love* 18.

266   **"two cross ties ahead":** III 469.

266   **"cyarpet baggers":** I 741.

266   **"they'll bleach out":** II 581.

267   **"waiting for":** III 446.

267   **"herding . . . men":** III 459.

268   **"We were":** III 453.

268   **"with what":** III 451.

268   **"organised the night riders":** III 470.

268   **"hot thick":** III 465.

269   **"same dang":** I 559.

269   **"carpet baggers":** III 470.

269   **"take this":** III 478.

269   **"the foreshortened":** III 488–89.

269   **"your boy . . . my boy":** III 464.

270   **"pet Negro":** Zora Neale Hurston, "The Pet Negro System," *The American Mercury*, May 1943.

270   **"Do you . . . nowhere else":** III 454.

270   **three-fifths:** Article 1, Section 2, Clause 3 of the Constitution held that for statistical purposes an enslaved individual counted as but three-fifths of a person.

270   **"They're free now":** IV 224–25.

271   **"turnt":** For this comparison, chosen at random, see William Faulkner, *Uncollected Stories* (New York: Random House, 1979), 237, and IV 94. My thanks to John T. Matthews for suggesting this line of inquiry.

271   **"This War":** III 454.

272   **Douglas Egerton:** Egerton, *Wars of Reconstruction* 447.

272 **"The proclamation"**: Hughes, *Thirty Years a Slave* 126

273 **"shoot the gizzards"**: Ibid. 129.

273 ***"as they always had done . . . compensation"***: James A. Hawley, in *Freedom: A Documentary History of Emancipation, 1861–1867*, ed. Steven Hahn et al. (Chapel Hill: University of North Carolina Press, 2008), 110–11.

273 **"amnesty oath . . . Slavery"**: Ibid 116.

274 **"An Act"**: In *Mississippi: Testimony as the Denial of Elective Franchise in Mississippi at the Elections of 1875 and 1876 Taken Under the Resolution of the Senate of December 5, 1876* (Washington, DC: Government Printing Office, 1877), 629–31.

274 **Lafayette County**: See D Ch. 8 for the details of Reconstruction in Faulkner's home county.

275 **"over a question"**: II 582.

275 **Colfax Massacre**: See Nicholas Lemann, *Redemption: The Last Battle of the Civil War* (New York: Farrar, Straus and Giroux, 2006), "Prologue"; and Tony Horwitz, *Spying on the South* (New York: Penguin Press, 2019), Ch 10.

276 **Mississippi Plan**: See C. Vann Woodward, *The Origins of the New South 1877–1913* (Baton Rouge: Louisiana State University Press, 1951), Ch 12; and Lemann, *Redemption* Ch 5.

276 **"the Negroes . . . incompetence"**: Du Bois, *Black Reconstruction* Ch 17.

277 **"dignified refusal"**: William Archibald Dunning, *Reconstruction: Political and Economic 1865–1877* (1907; rpt. New York: Harper Torchbook, 1962), 110.

277 **"well-established"**: Ibid. 58.

277 **"scientific poise"**: Du Bois, *Black Reconstruction* 590.

278 **"whipping or maiming"**: James Wilford Garner, *Reconstruction in Mississippi* (New York: Macmillan, 1901), 166.

278 **"much of . . . class"**: Ibid. 353.

278 **"the worst class"**: Riley, *School History* 286.

278 **"to aid the white people"**: Ibid. 318.

279 **"negro incapacity"**: Charles W. Ramsdell, *Reconstruction in Texas* (1910). Quoted in Eric Foner, *Reconstruction: America's Unfinished Revolution, 1863–1877* (New York: Harper, 1988), xviii.

279 **"Negro rule . . . manhood"**: Dunbar Rowland, "The Rise and Fall of Negro Rule in Mississippi," *Publications of the Mississippi Historical Society* (1898), 189.

280 **"the most dramatic"**: Du Bois, *Black Reconstruction* 1.

280 **He has figures**: Ibid. 367.

281 **"deep . . . laborers"**: Ibid 493.

282 **"You dont . . . upbringing"**: IV 203–4.

283 **"boundless folly"**: IV 206.

285 **"bondage has left"**: Tourgee, "The South as a Field for Fiction," 203.

285 **"laborers still . . . cotton"**: IV 188–89.

286 "injustice": IV 193.

286 *"Fibby . . . herself"*: IV 196–97.

286 "general . . . amortized": IV 196.

286 *"Tomasina"*: IV 198.

286 "before his father": IV 200.

287 "tremendously conceived": IV 193.

287 John Spencer Bassett: SL 120.

287 "the balance": John Spencer Bassett, *The Southern Plantation Overseer* (Northampton, MA: Smith College, 1925), 131.

288 "to relinquish": IV 188.

288 "as a commodity": Aldo Leopold, *Sand County Almanac* (1949; rpt. New York: Oxford University Press, 2001), 21.

289 "I'm trying": IV 213.

289 "lightless gutted": IV 214.

290 "rapine and pillage": IV 215.

291 "plowing and . . . land": IV 27–28.

291 "though he neither": IV 28.

291 "he approved": IV 33.

292 "A nation": Tourgee, "The South as a Field for Fiction," 204.

TWELVE: A NEW SOUTH

293 "slavery and secession": Henry W. Grady, *The Complete Orations of Henry W. Grady* (1910; rpt. Charleston, SC: Biblio Bazaar, 2008), 7.

293 "conscience and common sense": Ibid. 17

293 "on slavery . . . democracy": Ibid. 19.

293 "those among": Ibid. 18.

294 "bigger and older": IV 140.

294 "planing-mill": IV 236.

295 *"peace and dignity"*: CS 10.

295 "blond rug . . . smear": CS 12.

295 "urgent and quiring": CS 25.

296 "steady, curious": CS 22.

297 "universal conflict . . . world": George Marion O'Donnell, "Faulkner's Mythology," in *Faulkner: A Collection of Critical Essays*, ed. Robert Penn Warren (Englewood-Cliffs, NJ: Prentice-Hall, 1966), 24.

298 rich man's war: See Nancy Isenberg, *White Trash: The 400-Year Untold History of Class in America* (New York: Viking, 2016), Ch. 7.

298 "cane-and-cypress . . . farms": III 731.

299 "savage Arcadia": Cleanth Brooks, *William Faulkner* 167.

299 "farmer . . . at it": III 733.

299 "what it must": III 734.

299 "bad luck": III 733.

299 "old fat white horse": III 814.

300 run their own land: On land tenure and the changing economic system of the postwar South, see Gavin Wright, *Old South, New South: Revolutions in the Southern Economy Since the Civil War* (Baton Rouge: Louisiana State University Press, 1996); along with Edward L. Ayers, *The Promise of the New South: Life After Reconstruction* (New York: Oxford University Press, 1992), and Steven Hahn, *The Roots of Southern Populism: Yeoman Farmers and the Transformation of the Georgia Upcountry, 1850–1890* (New York: Oxford University Press, 2006).

300 "six-bit dollars": III 736. See David A. Davis, "Faulkner's Stores: Microfinance and Economic Power in the Postbellum South," in *Faulkner and Money*, ed. Jay Watson (Jackson: University Press of Mississippi, 2019).

301 "where she": II 405.

301 "slow and": II 406.

301 "pinewiney . . . forever": II 404.

301 "the sunny": II 419.

301 fixed it in place: On Faulknerian stasis see Edouard Glissant, *Faulkner, Mississippi* (1996), trans. Barbara Lewis and Thomas C. Spear (New York: Farrar, Straus and Giroux, 1999), 21.

303 "a feature": John Crowe Ransom, "Reconstructed but Unregenerate," in *I'll Take My Stand: The South and the Agrarian Tradition, by Twelve Southerners* (1930; rpt. Baton Rouge: Louisiana State University Press, 2006), 14.

303 "had hardly": Andrew Nelson Lytle, "The Hind Tit," ibid. 208.

303 "fancy tin-can": Ibid. 226.

304 "abolition alone": Ransom, "Reconstructed but Unregenerate" 14.

304 "for principles": Donald Davidson, "A Mirror for Artists," ibid. 52.

304 "positioned as white": Toni Morrison, *Playing in the Dark: Whiteness and the Literary Imagination* (New York: Random House, 1992), xii.

304 "not one": III 733.

305 "whitecaps": D 314.

306 "They came": II 136.

306 "mumbling his mouth": II 127.

306 "it aint": II 157.

307 "time: an irrevocable": II 96.

308 "words don't": II 115–17.

308 "rocketed": II 98.

Thirteen: The Saddest Words

309 "buttressed": From *The Bostonians* (1886), Ch. XXV. In *Henry James, Novels 1881–1886* (New York: Library of America, 1985), 1024.

309 "be indelicate": Ibid. 1023.

309   **"Well, so . . . tenderness"**: Ibid. 1024.

310   **"challenge . . . triumph"**: Ibid. 1024–25.

311   **"shared suffering"**: Faust, *This Republic of Suffering* xiii. See also her eloquent "Memory's Past and Future: Harvard's Memorial Hall," written from her perspective as that university's president, in Gary W. Gallagher and J. Matthew Gallman, eds., *Civil War Places* (Chapel Hill: University of North Carolina Press, 2019).

312   **emblem for their sections**: Ring, *The Problem South*, presents a cogent version of this argument.

312   **"Mississippi or"**: I 1011.

312   **"Ever tried"**: Samuel Beckett, *Worstword Ho* (New York: Grove Press, 1983), 7.

313   **"the only thing"**: ESPL 299.

313   **"Faulkner try it"**: *Faulkner in the University*, 84.

314   **"Now I can"**: ESPL 293.

314   **"the damndest"**: SL 41.

315   **Caddy is both**: See Minrose C. Gwin, "Hearing Caddy's Voice," in *The Feminine and Faulkner.*

315   **"To be traumatized"**: Cathy Caruth, "Trauma and Experience," in Cathy Caruth, ed., *Trauma: Explorations in Memory* (Baltimore: Johns Hopkins University Press, 1995), 4–5.

315   **"the unwitting"**: Ibid. 2

315   **"wound of the mind"**: Cathy Caruth, *Unclaimed Experience: Trauma, Narrative, and History* (Baltimore: Johns Hopkins University Press, 1996), 4. My thanks to my student Grace Hirt for calling my attention to Caruth's work, which is of course informed by that of Freud, *Beyond the Pleasure Principle* and *Moses and Monotheism* above all. See also Greg Forter, "Freud, Faulkner, Caruth: Trauma and the Politics of Literary Form," *Narrative* 15, no. 3 (2007).

316   **"her face tilted"**: I 992.

316   **hyperthymesia**: See Linda Rodriguez McRobbie, "Total Recall: The People Who Never Forget," *The Guardian*, February 8, 2017.

316   **"the day remembers"**: Phil Klay, *Redeployment* (New York: Penguin Books, 2015), 227.

316   **"then I can"**: I 993.

316   **"I was afraid"**: I 1013.

317   **"*amid the*"**: I 991.

317   **"too serious"**: I 1013.

317   **"heavy Chinese"**: I 947.

317   **"I say . . . said"**: I 999–1001.

318   **"he let me"**: I 1001.

318   **"surge of blood"**: I 1003.

318   **"temporary"**: I 1013–14.

320   **"Again"**: I 950.

320 "the inchoate": Sundquist, *Faulkner* 18.

321 "had already": II 752.

321 "a single instance": II 762.

321 "older at twenty than": III 309.

321 "struggling in the": John Irwin, *Doubling and Incest / Repetition and Revenge: A Speculative Reading of Faulkner* (Baltimore: Johns Hopkins University Press, 1975), 110.

321 "tragedy is": I 966.

322 "virgin space": Irwin, *Doubling* 112.

322 "in the moment": Warren, *The Legacy of the Civil War* 15.

322 "mystique of": Ibid 14.

322 center of time itself. See Caroline Janney, *Remembering the Civil War* (Chapel Hill: University of North Carolina Press, 2013), 272.

323 "the reality of war": Tolstoy, *The Raid and Other Stories*, trans. Louise and Aylmer Maude (New York: Oxford University Press, 1982), 1.

323 "Confederate soldier": I 1123.

323 Monuments remind us: This classic distinction belongs to Arthur Danto in his essay on the Vietnam Veterans Memorial in Washington, DC. *The Nation*, August 31, 1985.

325 "inability to mourn": Alexander and Margarete Mitscherlich, *The Inability to Mourn*, trans. by Beverley R. Placzek (1967; New York: Grove Press, 1975).

326 model to emulate: Susan Neiman's *Learning from the Germans: Race and the Memory of Evil* (New York: Farrar, Straus and Giroux, 2019) appeared after I had finished writing this chapter; I am happy to find another scholar thinking in these terms.

328 "almost all . . . experience": Warren, ed., *Faulkner: A Collection of Critical Essays* 1.

329 "abolished slavery": Warren, *The Legacy of the Civil War* 7.

329 "Great Alibi": Ibid. 54.

329 "equally corrosive": Ibid. 59.

329 "Treasury": Ibid. 64.

329 "bright surgical": Ibid. 98.

330 "The soldiers": *The Essential Holmes: Selections from the Letters, Speeches, Judicial Opinions, and Other Writings of Oliver Wendell Holmes, Jr.*, ed. Richard Posner (Chicago: University of Chicago Press, 2012), 80.

330 "touched with fire": Ibid. 86.

330 "far-away . . . gained": Henry James, *The American Scene*, in *Collected Travel Writings II* (New York: Library of America, 1993), 677–78.

331 "He could . . . improved": I 951.

333 "first Northern Negro regiment": In William James, *Essays in Religion and Morality* (Cambridge, MA: Harvard University Press, 1982). Neiman, *Learning from the Germans*, 261–63, offers an especially fine account of this speech.

Fourteen: The Human Heart Against Itself

335 "sickening, unhurried": I 810.

336 benighted land: See Fred Hobson, "Benighted South," in *The Encyclopedia of Southern Culture*, ed. William Ferris and Charles Reagan Wilson (Chapel Hill: University of North Carolina Press, 1989), 1100–1101.

336 "Once a bitch": I 1015.

336 "Get me": II 613.

337 James Silver: James W. Silver, *Mississippi: The Closed Society* (New York: Harcourt Brace, 1964).

337 "uncle to half": IV 5.

337 "the lap and": IV 263.

337 "almost like": IV 266.

338 "would that": IV 266.

338 "Get out . . . love": IV 267–68.

338 "the human heart": ESPL 119.

340 "literary stock exchange": Malcolm Cowley, *The Faulkner-Cowley File: Letters and Memories 1944–1962* (New York: Viking, 1966), 5.

341 "I should": SL 205.

342 "seems to reveal": Caroline Gordon, "Mr. Faulkner's Southern Saga," *The New York Times Book Review*, May 5, 1946.

342 Signet: See John N. Duvall, "An Error in Canonicity, or a Fuller Story of Faulkner's Return to Print Culture, 1944–1951," in *Faulkner and Print Culture*, ed. Jay Watson et al. (Jackson: University Press of Mississippi, 2015).

343 "*Pour les jeunes*": Cowley, *The Faulkner-Cowley File* 24.

343 "old universal truths": ESPL 120.

344 "behind the veil": II 424.

345 "Sold . . . antistrophe": IV 278–79.

346 "our politics . . . Tuesday": IV 400–401.

346 Gavin's argument: See Joel Williamson, *The Crucible of Race: Black-White Relations in the American South Since Emancipation* (New York: Oxford University Press, 1984), Ch. 14.

346 "We make": W. B. Yeats, "Anima Hominis," in *Essays* (New York: Macmillan, 1924), 492.

347 "even while hating": ESPL 36.

347 "despite . . . because": ESPL 43.

348 "deserve to": ESPL 223.

348 "had the courage": ESPL 101.

348 "neither of which": ESPL 93.

348 "white man's shame": ESPL 105.

348 "Northern radicals": ESPL 95.

348 "Weeping Willie Faulkner": ESPL 93.

349 "Go slow ... integration": ESPL 87.

349 "had given ... tragedy": LG 259–60.

349 "if it came to": LG 261.

349 "no sober": ESPL 225. See also B 1591.

350 "right morally": B 1603.

350 "the time ... now": Baldwin, "Faulkner and Desegregation," in *Collected Essays* 214.

352 "abolished and voided ... died": SL 285.

353 "Another nephew": See Kathleen W. Wickham, *We Believed We Were Immortal: Twelve Reporters Who Covered the 1962 Integration Crisis at Ole Miss* (Oxford, MS: Yoknapatawpha Press, 2017); and Dean Faulkner Wells, *Every Day by the Sun: A Memoir of the Faulkners of Mississippi* (New York: Crown, 2011).

353 "twice in": ESPL 98.

353 **1619**: See ESPL 101.

354 "the cloudy": IV 643.

354 *"Listen, stranger"*: IV 649.

354 "some perspective": SL 348.

354 "participated in": IV 5.

355 "Mr Hubert": IV 6.

355 "damn white": IV 7.

Index

Page numbers in *italics* refer to maps.

About the Author

MICHAEL GORRA IS THE Mary Augusta Jordan Professor of English at Smith College, where he has taught since 1985. His books include *The Bells in Their Silence: Travels through Germany* and *Portrait of a Novel: Henry James and the Making of an American Masterpiece*, a finalist for the Pulitzer Prize in Biography. A regular contributor to the *New York Review of Books* and other journals, he has received both a Public Scholar Award from the National Endowment for the Humanities and a Guggenheim Fellowship, along with the Balakian Citation from the National Book Critics Circle for his work as a reviewer. Born in New London, Connecticut, and educated at Amherst College and Stanford University, he now lives with his wife and daughter in Northampton, Massachusetts.